THE CULTURE OF CONTROL

The Culture of Control

Crime and Social Order in Contemporary Society

DAVID GARLAND

The University of Chicago Press

DAVID GARLAND is professor of law and sociology at New York University School of Law. He is author of *The Power to Punish* and *Punishment and Modern Society*. The latter received the Distinguished Scholar Award of the American Sociology Association and the Outstanding Scholarship Award of the Society for the Study of Social Problems

The University of Chicago Press, Chicago 60637
Oxford University Press, Great Clarendon Street, Oxford OX2 6DP

All rights reserved. Published in Great Britain by Oxford University Press in 2001
Published in the United States of America by The University of Chicago Press in 2001

Printed in the United States of America

10 09 08 07 06 05 04 03 02 01   2 3 4 5

Library of Congress Cataloging-in-Publication Data

Garland, David.
   The culture of control: crime and social order in contemporary society / David Garland.
     p. cm.
   Includes bibliographical references and index.
   1. Criminal justice, Administration of—United States.   2. Crime prevention—
United States   3. Criminal justice, Administration of —Great Britain.
   4. Crime prevention—   Great Britain.   I. Title.
   HV9950.G36   2001   364.973—dc21   00–051209
   ISBN: 0–226–28383–6 (alk. paper)

This book is printed on acid-free paper.

For Kasia and Amy
And for Anne
As always

Preface

This book is about the culture of crime control and criminal justice in Britain and America. Or, to be more precise, it is about the dramatic developments that have occurred in our social response to crime during the last thirty years and about the social, cultural, and political forces that gave rise to them. 'Crime control' and 'criminal justice' are shorthand terms that describe a complex set of practices and institutions, ranging from the conduct of householders locking their doors to the actions of authorities enacting criminal laws, from community policing to punishment in prison and all the processes in between. Since it might strike the reader as foolhardy to stretch an analysis across such a broad range of policies and practices, and across two such different societies, perhaps a word of explanation is in order right at the start.

In our attempts to make sense of social life, there is an unavoidable tension between broad generalization and the specification of empirical particulars. The standard response to any wide-ranging social or historical interpretation is to point to the specific facts that don't fit, the variation that has been missed, or the further details needed to complete the picture. 'Its more complicated than that!' or 'they do it differently in Minnesota!' (or for that matter, Manchester or Midlothian) are the inevitable critical complaints, and, in their own terms, these criticisms are often well taken. But the detailed case studies called for by this critical reaction suffer from exactly the opposite fate when they face up to their critical audience. Now the problem is not one of simplification but of significance. How does this study relate to the others that have been done, or might be done? Why should we be interested? What, in the end, does it tell us about the world in which we live?

For the individual author, there is no escaping from this dilemma. He or she must go back and forth between the general and the particular, the big picture and the local detail, until alighting upon a level of analysis that seems to offer the optimal vantage point—given the inevitable constraints of access, resources, skills, and stamina. For the scholarly community as a whole, however, the dilemma happily disappears. The division of academic labour ensures that whatever shortcomings are entailed in one style of analysis, these can usually be compensated and corrected by studies undertaken at the other end of the continuum. Sweeping accounts of the big picture can be adjusted and revised by more focused case studies that add empirical specificity and local detail. An accretion of small-scale analyses eventually prompts the desire for more general, theoretical accounts, while conveniently providing the latter with their inspiration and raw material. One kind of study provokes and facilitates the other, in a scholarly dialectic that requires them both.

In this study, I have chosen to focus on the whole range of our social responses to crime. I have made this choice because by analysing the problem at this level I believe I can identify some of the broad organizing principles that structure our contemporary ways of thinking and acting in crime control and criminal justice. There are obvious costs entailed in choosing to analyse things at this high level of abstraction—excessive simplification, false generalization, a neglect of variation, to name a few. But I hope to show that there are certain benefits as well: in particular, an ability to point to the structural properties of the field, and to identify the recurring social and cultural dynamics that produce them. Structural patterns of this kind simply do not become visible in localized case studies focused upon a single policy area or a particular institution. Only by observing the field as a whole can we hope to discover the strategies, rationalities, and cultures that give the field its distinctive structure and organization. Moreover, if such patterns do exist, and if I have helped to identify them, then subsequent case studies should be in a better position to confirm, disconfirm, or otherwise refine these findings.

The discovery of these organizing patterns in contemporary crime control, and my sense of their social and cultural underpinnings, prompted me to make my second, and perhaps even more foolhardy, choice of research focus—the decision to analyse crime control in both the UK *and* the USA. In order to avoid misunderstandings, I should explain right at the outset what I do and do not hope to achieve by giving my study this transatlantic scope.

My intention is certainly not to produce a comparative study, measuring American responses to crime against their British counterparts, comparing both nations on a point by point basis, or specifying their precise similarities and differences. Such a study would be impossibly large and well beyond my competence; and even if it were possible, it is not clear what its theoretical worth would be. Instead my concern is to point up what I take to be important similarities in the recent experience of these two countries and to suggest that these similarities stem not merely from political imitation and policy transfer—though there has been some of that—but from a process of social and cultural change that has recently been altering social relations in both societies. For want of a better term, I describe these social and cultural changes as the coming of late modernity, and I try to establish how this shared pattern of historical development has transformed the experience of crime, insecurity, and social order—first in America and subsequently in Britain as well. My argument will be that 'late modernity'—the distinctive pattern of social, economic and cultural relations that emerged in America, Britain and elsewhere in the developed world in the last third of the twentieth century—brings with it a cluster of risks, insecurities, and control problems that have played a crucial role in shaping our changing response to crime.

Of course the different social, institutional, and cultural characteristics of these two nations have influenced how these problems have been perceived, who has been held responsible, and which political responses have been preferred.

And it cannot be denied that the distinctive combination of racial division, economic inequality, and lethal violence that mark contemporary America have given its penal response a scale and intensity that often seems wholly exceptional. A Western liberal democracy that routinely executes offenders and incarcerates its citizens at a rate that is 6 to10 times higher than comparable nations can easily seem so divergent from international norms as to defy useful comparison. But if one attends to the *pattern* of these penal responses, and to the *recurring focal points* of public concern, political debate, and policy development, and if one is willing to suspend, for the moment, questions of size and degree, it becomes apparent that there are important similarities in the problems to which actors in both nations appear to be responding. The same kinds of risks and insecurities, the same perceived problems of ineffective social control, the same critiques of traditional criminal justice, and the same recurring anxieties about social change and social order—these now affect both nations. And recent crime control developments in the UK suggest that the USA is by no means unique in its response to crime or in the social processes that underlie it.

If this is indeed the case, one would expect that other societies experiencing late modern patterns of development will also have to grapple with problems and concerns of this kind. Scholars such as Thomas Mathiesen, Nils Christie, and Loic Wacquant have pointed recently to the growing tendency of European nations to emulate patterns of crime control first developed in the USA, even where these run counter to the historical traditions of the nations involved. If these scholars are correct in their observations, an explanation might lie in the fact that social, economic, and cultural developments in these countries increasingly expose them to the distinctive problems of social order that late modernity brings in its wake.

Any book-length examination of the USA and the UK—two large, more or less federated unions, with a multiplicity of distinct legal systems operating within their national territories—will involve an uncomfortable degree of simplification. My excuse for imposing errors of omission and overstatement upon the reader, or anyway the form of my special pleading, is that such an analysis allows me to get at structural patterns that are not otherwise available to inspection. But if that will not do, I would simply add, by way of mitigation, that this is an area of scholarship that stands in need of *more* generalizing studies, not fewer. As we know from the bracing impact of Michel Foucault's *Discipline and Punish*, attempts to delineate patterns of structural change will tend, whether or not their claims can be sustained, to have a productive effect in stimulating further empirical studies and an energetic critical response. It is in this spirit of provocation and productivity that the present study is offered to its readers.

Since the explanatory thesis I develop here is combined with an historical narrative and developed on a number of different levels, a preliminary sketch of the overall argument might serve as a useful guide. Here, and in what follows, I have tried to maintain a lightness of touch where theoretical matters are concerned, in order that the general reader will be able to follow my argument without undue effort. To the same end, I have placed most evidentiary sources and scholarly references in notes at the end of the book. While these Endnotes will be essential (and I hope, enlightening) reading for the professional scholar, those readers who simply want to follow the book's story and grasp its explanation need not be disturbed by their intrusion.

The study begins by contrasting our present-day policies and practices with those that existed up until the 1970s, and ends by presenting an analysis of how today's crime control arrangements reproduce a certain kind of social order in late modern society. Along the way, it outlines a history of the criminal justice state, a theory of social and penal change, and an account of how late modern social, economic and cultural forces have reshaped criminological thought, government crime policy, and the attitudes of popular culture. In these respects, the present study builds upon two of my previous books: *Punishment and Welfare,* which described the rise of a welfarist form of criminal justice at the start of the twentieth century, and *Punishment and Modern Society,* which developed a social theory of punishment that stressed the cultural as well as the political elements of penal institutions. *The Culture of Control* completes the trilogy by bringing *Punishment and Welfare*'s historical account up to the present, and by using the theory developed in *Punishment and Modern Society* to interpret and explain a concrete set of institutions and ideas.

As I have already suggested, my assumption is that the many transformations that have recently occurred in criminal law and its enforcement can best be understood by viewing the field as a whole rather than taking each element individually. Shifts in policing, sentencing, punishment, criminological theory, penal philosophy, penal politics, private security, crime prevention, the treatment of victims, and so on, can best be grasped by viewing them as interactive elements in a structured field of crime control and criminal justice. By comparing the field of present-day practices to the set of institutions and ideas that existed up until 1970, it is possible to identify a series of shared characteristics that help explain the dynamics of change and the strategic principles underpinning contemporary arrangements.

My argument will be that our contemporary crime control arrangements have been shaped by two underlying social forces—the distinctive social organization of late modernity, and the free market, socially conservative politics that came to dominate the USA and the UK in the 1980s—and the central chapters of the book describe these social forces in some detail. But instead of baldly asserting that crime control changes were a 'response' to broader social and political change, or were 'influenced' by them, I try to describe the actual processes through which the crime control field was affected by social change and the specific mechanisms by which crime policy was brought into line with contemporary culture and social relations.

To this end, the book provides a series of detailed analyses that show how political actors and government agencies—police forces, prosecution agencies, courts, prisons, government departments, elected officials—were confronted by a new set of practical problems in their daily operations. These problems chiefly flowed from the prevalence of high rates of crime and disorder in late modern society and the growing realization that modern criminal justice is limited in its capacity to control crime and deliver security. The book's central chapters analyse evidence showing how government actors and agencies understood the predicament that this situation posed for them, and how they invented specific strategies that allowed them to adapt to (or, in some cases, evade) the problem. These strategies took a variety of forms, and developed in contradictory directions. The ones that were most 'successful' (by which I mean, became most embedded, most indispensable) were the ones that resonated with the political, popular and professional cultures emerging in these years.

Having described these governmental adaptations and the politics of crime control to which they gave rise, I next explore the cultural conditions that account for their popular success. The odd fact that punitive 'law and order' politics have co-existed, in both countries, with an entirely different strategy—of preventative partnerships, community policing and generalized crime prevention—is explained by reference to the public's ambivalence about crime and crime control: an ambivalence that gives rise to quite divergent forms of action. The sensibilities that characterize this popular culture do not stem from media representations or political rhetoric, though these have a shaping effect. They originate in the collective experience of crime in everyday life and the practical adaptations to which it eventually gave rise.

During the same decades that criminal justice agencies struggled to come to terms with crime in late modern society, the population of citizens, communities, and corporations learned to adapt to a social world in which high rates of crime were a normal social fact. The private actors of civil society developed their own adaptations to the new pervasiveness of crime, their own routine precautions and social controls, and it is these adaptations (rather than crime rates themselves) that account for the political and cultural salience that crime has taken on in recent years. These practical everyday routines provide the social basis for many of the new crime policies of recent years, and shape the cultural formation—*the crime complex*—that has grown up around crime at the end of the twentieth century. They also contribute to the declining rates of crime that were a feature of the 1990s, and to the viability of policies such as community policing that depend upon the support of the public and the cultivation of widespread habits of prevention and control.

My analysis suggests that although the structures of criminal justice have changed in important ways in recent decades, the most important changes have been in the cultural assumptions that animate them. I describe how a new crime control culture has emerged that embodies a reworked conception of penal-welfarism, a new criminology of control, and an economic style of decision-making. I also indicate how this new culture of control meshes with the social and economic policies that have come to characterize contemporary Britain and America.

The roots of today's crime control arrangements lie in the character of contemporary social organization and the political and cultural choices that have been made in relation to it. And the new world of crime control provides, in its turn, important sources of legitimation for an anti-welfare politics and for a conception of the poor as an undeserving underclass. The mutually supportive character of today's penal and welfare policies—based on principles that are quite different than those described in *Punishment and Welfare*—is indicated by an analysis of the discursive tropes and administrative strategies that run through both of these institutional domains.

By way of a conclusion, I distinguish those historical developments that are structurally determined from those that are more contingent, indicating which aspects of present policy are liable to persist for the foreseeable future and which seem more amenable to political challenge. The study ends with a consideration of the social processes that will tend to lock us into an institutionalized culture of control, and of the countervailing forces that could yet allow us to escape that new iron cage. Stressing these possibilities for action should, I hope, ensure that my account of why things are as they are is not taken to suggest that our world currently is as it must be. As Raymond Aron once said, the point of social analysis is to make history intelligible—not to do away with it altogether.

More than my previous books, this one has grown directly out of the conversations and debates I have had with other scholars working on the same set of problems. In that sense, this book is the product of a collective effort, and any wisdom or insight it might contain is the fruit of that communal endeavour. The experience of taking part in ongoing sociological debates about contemporary crime and punishment has been a salutary one, and the works of Tony Bottoms, Stan Cohen, Adam Crawford, Malcolm Feeley, David Greenberg, James B. Jacobs, Pat O'Malley, Nikolas Rose, Stuart Scheingold, Clifford Shearing, Jonathan Simon, Richard Sparks, Philip Stenning, Michael Tonry, Loic Wacquant, and Frank Zimring have been especially important to me in this respect. And if my interlocutors and I have still not reached agreement about how to interpret our world, at least we can now disagree with rather greater precision than we did before. In this regard, I am also indebted to the editors and contributors of the journal *Punishment & Society* who have been constant sources of inspiration and ideas over the last few years, and an unwavering reminder of the rewards of collective work.

Beyond that diffuse collective debt, I owe specific thanks to a number of friends and colleagues who have helped me in the making of this book. The following individuals read entire drafts of the book and provided me with detailed criticisms and suggestions, many of which quickly found their way into the final text: Todd Clear, David Downes, Jeff Fagan, Barry Friedman, Doug Husak, James B. Jacobs, Ian Loader, Steven Morse, Kevin Reitz, Stuart Scheingold, Adina Schwartz, Jonathan Simon, Jerry Skolnick, Richard Sparks, and Michael

Tonry. I am hugely grateful to them all. I would also like to record my thanks to Vanessa Barker, Gretchen Feltes, Aaron Kupchik and Elana Dietz-Weinstein for excellent research assistance and bibliographical work, to Jim Jacobs and John Sexton for making NYU Law School a superb institution in which to work, to my colleagues in the NYU Department of Sociology, and to the Filomen D'Agostino and Max E. Greenberg Research Fund for its support of the research upon which this study is based. Substantially different versions of Chapters Five and Six first appeared in the *British Journal of Criminology* and I am grateful to the editors, referees, and readers of that journal for the comments and criticisms they provided. Finally, I would like to thank John Louth, Mick Belson, and John Tryneski for making the publishing of this book such an efficient and enjoyable process.

Anne Jowett has helped me in my work in ways too numerous to mention, and it is with love and gratitude that I dedicate this book to her, and to our daughters, Kasia and Amy.

Contents

1

A History of the Present

We quickly grow used to the way things are. Today more than ever, it is easy to live in the immediacy of the present and to lose all sense of the historical processes out of which our current arrangements emerged. In the USA the public now seems quite accustomed to living in a nation that holds two million of its citizens in confinement on any given day, and puts criminal offenders to death at a rate of two or more per week. In much the same way, the British public no longer seems surprised by the existence of private prisons that house an increasing proportion of Britain's prisoners, and citizens go about their business hardly noticing the surveillance cameras that stare down on the streets of every major city. On both sides of the Atlantic, mandatory sentences, victims' rights, community notification laws, private policing, 'law and order' politics, and an emphatic belief that 'prison works', have become commonplace points in the crime control landscape and cause no one any surprise, even if they still cause dismay and discomfort in certain circles.

To the moderately informed citizen who reads the papers or watches the television news, these are the taken-for-granted features of contemporary crime policy. They have the same familiarity and easy intelligibility as other common elements of our everyday world such as cable television, mobile phones, or suburban shopping malls. But the most striking fact about these crime policies, is that every one of them would surprise (and perhaps even shock) a historical observer viewing this landscape from the vantage point of the recent past. As recently as thirty years ago, each of these phenomena would have seemed highly improbable, even to the best-informed and most up-to-date observer. However obvious and common-sensical our present-day arrangements may appear to us now, they seem deeply puzzling and perplexing if considered from a historical viewpoint that is still very close to us in time. As I will argue in the pages that follow, the historical trajectory of British and American crime control over the last three decades has been almost exactly the contrary of that which was anticipated as recently as 1970. Rereading the government documents, research reports and expert commentaries of that period, one finds a set of assumptions and expectations that have been completely confounded by subsequent events.[1]

It is sometimes said that events become more easily predictable once they have actually occurred. But the historical processes that took us from the settled expectations of the early 1970s to the realized outcomes of the following decades continue to defy our understanding. We still do not really know how we got from there to here and why the crime control future—which is the present we now inhabit—turned out to be so different from the one that was widely expected a generation ago. As a counter to this social amnesia, this book sets out to develop a history of the present in the field of crime control and criminal justice. In the process of describing this history, it aims to solve a problem that has been perplexing commentators for much of the last twenty years—the problem of explaining how our contemporary responses to crime came to take the form that they did, with all their novel and contradictory aspects. Its task is to unravel the tangle of transformative forces that has, for decades now, been reconstituting those responses in surprising and unexpected ways and to understand the ensemble of practices and policies that has emerged out of these developments.

In describing this work as a 'history of the present' I hope to distance myself from the conventions of narrative history and above all from any expectation of a comprehensive history of the recent period. My primary concern is analytical rather than archival. That concern is to understand the historical conditions of existence upon which contemporary practices depend, particularly those that seem most puzzling and unsettling. Historical inquiry—together with sociological and penological analysis—is employed here as a means to discover how these phenomena came to acquire their current characteristics. The history that I propose is motivated not by a historical concern to understand the past but by a critical concern to come to terms with the present. It is a genealogical account that aims to trace the forces that gave birth to our present-day practices and to identify the historical and social conditions upon which they still depend. The point is not to think historically about the past but rather to use that history to rethink the present.[2]

If that genealogical account succeeds, it will provide a means to analyse the new practices of crime control that have been assembled during the past three decades, and to uncover the assumptions, discourses, and strategies that give form and structure to this social field.[3] It will also identify the political interests and cultural meanings that provide support for these new arrangements and the specific mechanisms that connect crime-control institutions to other social domains.

In the course of this analysis I pursue a series of questions that are both genealogical and sociological. The genealogical inquiry asks: 'What are the social and historical processes that gave rise to our present ways of controlling crime and doing justice?' and 'Upon what historical conditions do these institutions depend?' The sociological inquiry is more focused upon the field's contemporary structure and functioning. It asks: 'What are the rules of discourse and action that organize the diverse practices that make up this field?' 'How are these rules and these practices related to those of other social domains, such as welfare, politics, or the economy?' and 'What role do these practices play in the governance of late modern society?'

These questions are inspired, in large part, by the work of Michel Foucault, though my analyses are less philosophically ambitious and more sociologically oriented than much of the scholarship that has followed in his wake. They are primarily analytical questions, summoning up the resources of social and historical inquiry, but they also involve a normative aspect that ought to be made explicit. Whether he acknowledged it or not, Foucault's inquiries always carried within them a critical, normative dimension, urging us to identify the dangers and harms implicit in the contemporary scheme of things, and to indicate how our present social arrangements might have been—and might still be—differently arranged. The present book proceeds with the same critical intent, but I have chosen to subdue that normative voice until completing my analysis of how this field of practice is currently constituted in all its complexity and contradiction. One of the abiding lessons of Foucault's example is that if critical theory is to be taken seriously, it will have to first engage with things as they actually are.

The study thus tackles a problem that is at once historical, penological, and sociological:

Historical. As I will describe in more detail below, recent developments in crime control and criminal justice are puzzling because they appear to involve a sudden and startling reversal of the settled historical pattern. They display a sharp discontinuity that demands to be explained. The modernizing processes that, until recently, seemed so well established in this realm—above all the long-term tendencies towards 'rationalization' and 'civilization'—now look as if they have been thrown into reverse.[4] The re-appearance in official policy of punitive sentiments and expressive gestures that appear oddly archaic and downright antimodern tend to confound the standard social theories of punishment and its historical development. Not even the most inventive reading of Foucault, Marx, Durkheim, and Elias on punishment could have predicted these recent developments—and certainly no such predictions ever appeared.

The last three decades have seen an accelerating movement away from the assumptions that shaped crime control and criminal justice for most of the twentieth century. The central agencies of the modern criminal justice state have undergone quite radical shifts in their working practices and organizational missions. Today's practices of policing, prosecution, sentencing, and penal sanctioning pursue new objectives, embody new social interests and draw upon new forms of knowledge, all of which seem quite at odds with the orthodoxies that prevailed for most of the last century. What I will term 'penal welfarism'—the institutional arrangements that increasingly characterized the field from the 1890s to the 1970s, and which shaped the common sense of generations of policy-makers, academics, and practitioners—has recently been shaken to its roots. In the face of this disruption, a profusion of historical questions beg to be addressed. What is the nature of the change? What distinguishes today's reconfigured field from the penal-welfare one that existed for most of the twentieth century? What conjuncture of social and penal developments precipitated this turn of events? And how are these developments to be understood?

Penological. This rapid and far-reaching transformation has provoked dissension and not a little bewilderment among penal practitioners and commentators. In place of the expected progress along a predetermined line of development, or even the setbacks and temporary reversals that were familiar from the past, the new changes appeared as a fundamental attack upon the existing system. Practitioners who were trained before the 1980s have seen their cherished orthodoxies undergo major revisions; standing arrangements and codes of conduct rendered obsolete; the distribution of powers changed; and aims and objectives that had no place in the old system become increasingly prominent. Instead of 'change as usual' there has been the alarming sense of the unravelling of a conceptual fabric that, for the best part of a century, had bound together the institutions of criminal justice and given them meaning.

Within the brief time it takes to progress from basic training to mid-career, a whole generation of practitioners—probation officers, prison officials, prosecutors, judges, police officers, and criminological researchers—have looked on while their professional world was turned upside down. Hierarchies shifted precariously; settled routines were pulled apart; objectives and priorities were reformulated; standard working practices were altered; and professional expertise was subjected to challenge and viewed with increasing scepticism. The rapid emergence of new ways of thinking and acting on crime, and the concomitant discrediting of older assumptions and professional orientations, ensured that many penal practitioners and academics lived through the 1980s and 1990s with a chronic sense of crisis, and professional anomie.

As recently as 1970, those involved in the business of crime control shared a common set of assumptions about the frameworks that shaped criminal justice and penal practice. There was a relatively settled, self-conscious, institutional field and the debates and disagreements that occurred operated within well-established boundaries. Criminal justice textbooks and practitioner training manuals could articulate the premises that guided penal practice and confidently transmit this culture from one generation to the next. Today, for better or for worse, we lack any such agreement, any settled culture, or any clear sense of the big picture. Policy development appears highly volatile, with an unprecedented amount of legislative activity, much dissension in the ranks of practitioner groups, and a good deal of conflict between experts and politicians. The battle lines of debate seem blurred and rapidly changing. No one is quite sure what is radical and what is reactionary. Private prisons, victim impact statements, community notification laws, sentencing guidelines, electronic monitoring, punishments in the community, 'quality of life' policing, restorative justice—these and dozens of other developments lead us into unfamiliar territory where the ideological lines are far from clear and where the old assumptions are an unreliable guide.

The constant flux and febrile energy of this transition has left an older generation of criminal justice personnel exhausted and disillusioned, cast adrift from the landmark ideals and exemplars around which they were trained. Meanwhile, their younger colleagues lack any stable ideology or conceptual framework to guide their actions and shape their visions. Familiar folkways are now outmoded. Issues are hard to handle or even think about because there is no articulated and established ideology to govern our thinking and colour our judgement. What Pierre Bourdieu would call the *habitus* of many trained practitioners—their ingrained dispositions and working ideologies, the standard orientations that 'go without saying'—has been undermined and rendered ineffective. For at least two decades now, criminal law and penal policy have been working without clear route maps on a terrain that is largely unknown. If this field is to have any self-consciousness, and any possibility of self-criticism and self-correction, then our textbooks need to be rewritten and our sense of how things work needs to be thoroughly revised.

At the start of the twenty-first century, after several decades of flux and uncertainty, the new contours of the field appear to be taking shape with a solidity and a clarity that permit a little more confidence in our attempt to map its terrain. A regrouping has begun to occur, new principles are becoming established, new working assumptions are slowly coming into focus—though none of this is as yet clearly articulated, or fully self-conscious. As the landscape of crime control starts to settle, and its new regions become better known, we can begin to explore its character on a more comprehensive scale.

One aim of this book is to advance this process of self-consciousness and reflexivity and to identify the new frameworks that are now emerging. This aim is pursued not to smooth the system's functioning or to still the anxieties of penal functionaries. Instead its intent is to open up these arrangements to informed criticism and to help develop an understanding of the social effects and political significance of the system that is taking shape.

Sociological. Institutions of crime control and criminal justice have definite conditions of existence. They form part of a network of governance and social ordering that, in modern societies, includes the legal system, the labour market, and welfare state institutions. They refer to, and are supported by, other social institutions and social controls, and are grounded in specific configurations of cultural, political and economic action. So while the field of crime control has a certain autonomy, and a capacity for internally generated development and change, any major transformation in the field's configuration will tend to signal correlative transformations in the structure of the social fields and institutions that are contiguous to it.

This crime control field is characterized by two interlocking and mutually conditioning patterns of action: the formal controls exercised by the state's criminal justice agencies and the informal social controls that are embedded in the everyday activities and interactions of civil society. The formal institutions of crime control tend to be reactive and adaptive. They operate in ways that seek to supplement the social controls of ordinary life, though they sometimes interfere with these social controls and undermine their effectiveness. As the character of everyday life changes, its changing habits and routines often have consequences for the structure of informal controls, that can, in turn, cause problems for the functioning and effectiveness of the institutions of formal control. We have to bear in mind, therefore, that the field of crime control involves the social ordering activities of the authorities *and also* the activities of private actors and agencies as they go about their daily lives and ordinary routines. Too often our attention focuses on the state's institutions and neglects the informal social practices upon which state action depends.

A reconfigured field of crime control involves more than just a change in society's response to crime. It also entails new practices of controlling behaviour and doing justice, revised conceptions of social order and social control, and altered ways of maintaining social cohesion and managing group relations. The remodelling of an established institutional field, the emergence of different objectives and priorities, and the appearance of new ideas about the nature of crime and of criminals also suggests shifts in the cultural underpinning of these institutions. They suggest the possibility that, behind these new responses to crime, there lies a new pattern of mentalities, interests, and sensibilities that has altered how we think and feel about the underlying problem.

To investigate the new patterns of crime control is therefore, and at the same time, to investigate the remaking of society and its institutions for the production of order. It is to ask, 'what is the new problem of crime and social order to which the emerging system of crime control is a response?' 'What is the new strategy of governance of which it forms a part?' 'What are the new social conditions that helped bring these into being?' Such is the densely interwoven character of social relations, that an inquiry into the transformation of one institutional field inexorably leads to questions about contiguous fields and about the cultural, political and economic relations that underlie them. As I will argue in what follows, today's reconfigured field of crime control is the result of political choices and administrative decisions—but these choices and decisions are grounded in a new structure of social relations and coloured by a new pattern of cultural sensibilities.

Indices of change

So what are the changes to which I have been referring? What are the signs of movement and the visible landmarks of the emerging new terrain? Rather inconveniently, a simple statement of observed shifts and transformations brings with it some tricky theoretical problems and some delicate questions of historical and penological judgement. As the contentious literature on this subject attests, specifying *what* has happened is almost as controversial as explaining *why* it has happened. Nevertheless, it is possible to point to a set of developments that most informed commentators would recognize, if only as a starting point for discussion. At this stage I want merely to catalogue those signs of transformation that have been perceived by practitioners and academic commentators. I present them here as a first, under-theorized, approximation of what is going on, though as my analysis unfolds I will provide more detailed accounts of each one.

These 'observations' are, of course, already interpretations, insofar as they operationalize conceptual tools and analytical categories and make judgements about qualitative or quantitative change. But they are widely shared and regularly recurring interpretations that are not especially controversial, nor are they closely linked to any specific interpretation or theory. Beginning with this deliberately weak definition of the problem to be explained, the remainder of the book attempts to rethink this preliminary series of observations: to extend and elaborate them, to offer an account of how they came into being, and to explain their significance for crime control and social order in late modern society.

Here, and throughout the book, I draw upon evidence from the UK and the USA to make my case. My argument will be that the strong similarities that appear in the recent policies and practices of these two societies—with patterns repeated across the fifty states and the federal system of the USA, and across the three legal systems of the UK—are evidence of underlying patterns of structural transformation, and that these transformations are being brought about by a process of adaptation to the social conditions that now characterize these (and other) societies. I make no claim that the pattern of developments to be found in these two societies is universal: there are important national differences that distinguish the specific trajectory of these policy environments from one another and from those of other societies. Nor would I claim that the recent UK and US experiences are in all respects similar, and I will frequently point up differences of kind, of degree, and of emphasis that continue to distinguish them.[5] However, it is my claim that the institutional problems and policy responses that have taken shape in these two places are sufficiently alike to allow me to talk, some of the time, about structural tendencies that characterize them both. This also leads me to suppose that many of the underlying problems and insecurities are, or soon will be, familiar to other late modern societies, even if their cultural and political responses and social trajectories turn out to be quite different.[6] As I will suggest in the pages that follow, the pattern of risks, insecurities and control problems to which American and British governments, corporations and citizens have been responding are those typically generated by the social, economic and cultural arrangements of late modernity—even if the specific politics, institutions and cultural adaptations that shape their responses are not.

Abstracting from the extensive literature on crime control and criminal justice in America and Britain, it is possible to indicate the most important currents of change occurring over the last thirty years:

The decline of the rehabilitative ideal

If asked to describe the major changes in penal policy in the last thirty years, most insiders would undoubtedly mention 'the decline of the rehabilitative ideal'—a phrase that Francis Allen brought into common usage when he used it as the title of his 1981 book.[7] A more cautious description of what has occurred, written twenty years after Allen's book, might talk instead about the fading of correctionalist and welfarist rationales for criminal justice interventions; the reduced emphasis upon rehabilitation as the goal of penal institutions; and changes in sentencing law that uncouple participation in treatment programmes from the length of sentence served.

As we will see, 'rehabilitative' programmes do continue to operate in prisons and elsewhere, with treatment particularly targeted towards 'high risk individuals' such as sex offenders, drug addicts, and violent offenders. And the 1990s have seen a resurgence of interest in 'what works?' research that challenges some of the more pessimistic conclusions of the 1970s.[8] But today, rehabilitation programmes no longer claim to express the overarching ideology of the system, nor even to be the leading purpose of any penal measure. Sentencing law is no longer shaped by correctional concerns such as indeterminacy and early release. And the rehabilitative possibilities of criminal justice measures are routinely subordinated to other penal goals, particularly retribution, incapacitation, and the management of risk.

Nevertheless, Allen was right to observe that there was, from the late 1970s onwards, an astonishingly sudden draining away of support for the ideal of rehabilitation. This change of heart occurred first and most emphatically among academics, but eventually, and with more misgivings, it also affected the aspirations of practitioners, the practical reasoning of policy-makers and the expectations of the general public.[9] Within a very short time it became common to regard the core value of the whole penal-welfare framework not just as an impossible ideal, but, much more remarkably, as an unworthy, even dangerous policy objective that was counter-productive in its effects and misguided in its objectives.

This fall from grace of rehabilitation was hugely significant. Its decline was the first indication that the modernist framework—which had gone from strength to strength for nearly a century—was coming undone. Rehabilitation had been the field's central structural support, the keystone in an arch of mutually supportive practices and ideologies. When faith in this ideal collapsed, it began to unravel the whole fabric of assumptions, values and practices upon which modern penality had been built.

The re-emergence of punitive sanctions and expressive justice

For most of the twentieth century, penalties that appeared explicitly retributive or deliberately harsh were widely criticized as anachronisms that had no place within a 'modern' penal system. In the last twenty years, however, we have seen the reappearance of 'just deserts' retribution as a generalized policy goal in the US and the UK, initially prompted by the perceived unfairness of individualized sentencing.[10] This development has certainly promoted the concern for proportionality and fixed sentencing for which its liberal proponents had hoped. But it has also re-established the legitimacy of an explicitly retributive discourse, which, in turn, has made it easier for politicians and legislatures to openly express punitive sentiments and to enact more draconian laws. In a small but symbolically significant number of instances we have seen the re-emergence of decidedly 'punitive' measures such as the death penalty, chain gangs, and corporal punishment. And although British policy-makers have avoided the excesses of the southern states of America, one nevertheless sees echoes of this in the language adopted by government ministers in the UK when they urge that we should 'condemn more and understand less' and strive to ensure that prison conditions are suitably 'austere'. Forms of public shaming and humiliation that for decades have been regarded as obsolete and excessively demeaning are valued by their political proponents today precisely because of their unambiguously punitive character. Hence the new American laws on public notification of sex offenders' identities, the wearing of the convict striped uniform, or work on a chain gang, and also their milder British equivalents: the paedophile register and the requirement of uniforms and demeaning labour for those doing community service.[11]

For most of the twentieth century the openly avowed expression of vengeful sentiment was virtually taboo, at least on the part of state officials. In recent years explicit attempts to express public anger and resentment have become a recurring theme of the rhetoric that accompanies penal legislation and decision-making. The feelings of the victim, or the victim's family, or a fearful, outraged public are now routinely invoked in support of new laws and penal policies. There has been a noticeable change in the tone of official discourse. Punishment—in the sense of expressive punishment, conveying public sentiment—is once again a respectable, openly embraced, penal purpose and has come to affect not just high-end sentences for the most heinous offences but even juvenile justice and community penalties. The language of condemnation and punishment has re-entered official discourse and what purports to be the 'expression of public sentiment' has frequently taken priority over the professional judgement of penological experts.[12]

This open embrace of previously discredited purposes has also transformed the more formal, academic discourse of the philosophy of punishment. The latest wave of normative theory stresses the symbolic, expressive, and communicative aspects of penal sanctioning, as philosophers begin to create rationales for retributive measures that better express the cultural assumptions and political interests that now shape the practice of punishment.[13]

Changes in the emotional tone of crime policy

Official policies regulating crime and punishment always invoke and express a range of collective sentiments. Throughout the period when the penal-welfare framework prevailed, the dominant tone sounded by policy-makers was one of confident progress in combating crime and rationalizing criminal justice. The affect invoked to justify penal reforms was most often a progressive sense of justice, an evocation of what 'decency' and 'humanity' required, and a compassion for the needs and rights of the less fortunate. These sentiments were, no doubt, the aspirational values of political elites rather than the sensibilities of the general public, and there is a sense in which their evocation was a cover for professional interests and strategies of power. But the regular invocation of these sentiments served to deepen their hold upon the moral imagination and to justify many of the things that were done in their name. Today, such sentiments are still present, and still invoked—particularly by proponents of 'restorative justice' whose proposals are beginning to make some small inroads at the margins of criminal justice.[14] But they no longer set the emotional tone for public discourse about crime and punishment.

Since the 1970s fear of crime has come to have new salience. What was once regarded as a localized, situational anxiety, afflicting the worst-off individuals and neighbourhoods, has come to be regarded as a major social problem and a characteristic of contemporary culture.[15] Fear of crime has come to be regarded as a problem in and of itself, quite distinct from actual crime and victimization, and distinctive policies have been developed that aim to reduce fear levels, rather than to reduce crime. Government-sponsored research now regularly investigates the levels and character of this fear, categorizing and measuring the emotional reactions prompted by crime—concrete fears, inchoate fears, generalized insecurity, anger, resentment—and correlating these with actual patterns of risk and victimization.[16]

The emergence of fear of crime as a prominent cultural theme is confirmed by public opinion research that finds that there is a settled assumption on the part of a large majority of the public in the US and the UK that crime rates are getting worse, whatever the actual patterns, and that there is little public confidence in the ability of the criminal justice system to do anything about this.[17] This sense of a fearful, angry public has had a large impact upon the style and content of policy making in recent years. Crime has been re-dramatized. The stock welfarist image of the delinquent as a disadvantaged, deserving, subject of need has now all but disappeared. Instead, the images conjured up to accompany new legislation tend to be stereotypical depictions of unruly youth, dangerous predators, and incorrigible career criminals. Accompanying these projected images, and in rhetorical response to them, the new discourse of crime policy consistently invokes an angry public, tired of living in fear, demanding strong measures of punishment and protection. The background affect of policy is now more frequently a collective anger and a righteous demand for retribution rather than a commitment to a just, socially engineered solution. The emotional temperature of policy-making has shifted from cool to hot.

The return of the victim

Over the last three decades there has been a remarkable return of the victim to centre stage in criminal justice policy. In the penal-welfare framework, individual victims featured hardly at all, other than as members of the public whose complaints triggered state action. Their interests were subsumed under the general public interest, and certainly not counter-posed to the interests of the offender. All of this has now changed. The interests and feelings of victims—actual victims, victims' families, potential victims, the projected figure of 'the victim'—are now routinely invoked in support of measures of punitive segregation. In the USA politicians hold press conferences to announce mandatory sentencing laws and are accompanied at the podium by the family of crime victims. Laws are passed and named for victims: Megan's law; Jenna's law, the Brady bill. In the UK crime victims appear as featured speakers at political party conferences and a 'Victims' Charter' has been established with broad bipartisan support.

The new political imperative is that victims must be protected, their voices must be heard, their memory honoured, their anger expressed, their fears addressed. The rhetoric of penal debate routinely invokes the figure of the victim—typically a child or a woman or a grieving family member—as a righteous figure whose suffering must be expressed and whose security must henceforth be guaranteed. Any untoward attention to the rights or welfare of the offender is taken to detract from the appropriate measure of respect for victims. A zero-sum policy game is assumed wherein the offender's gain is the victim's loss, and being 'for' victims automatically means being tough on offenders.[18]

The symbolic figure of the victim has taken on a life of its own, and plays a role in political debate and policy argument that is often quite detached from the claims of the organized victims movement, or the aggregated opinions of surveyed victims.[19] This is a new and significant social fact. The victim is no longer an unfortunate citizen who has been on the receiving end of a criminal harm, and whose concerns are subsumed within the 'public interest' that guides the prosecution and penal decisions of the state. The victim is now, in a certain sense, a much more representative character, whose experience is taken to be common and collective, rather than individual and atypical. Whoever speaks on behalf of victims speaks on behalf of us all—or so declares the new political wisdom of high crime societies.[20] Publicized images of actual victims serve as the personalized, real-life, it-could-be-you metonym for a problem of security that has become a defining feature of contemporary culture.

Paradoxically, this vision of the victim as Everyman has undermined the older notion of the public, which has now been redefined and dis-aggregated. It is no longer sufficient to subsume the individual victim's experience in the notion of the public good: the public good must be individuated, broken down into individual component parts. Specific victims are to have a voice—making victim impact statements, being consulted about punishment and decisions about release, being notified about the offender's subsequent movements. There is, in short, a new cultural theme, a new collective meaning of victimhood, and a reworked relationship between the individual victim, the symbolic victim, and the public institutions of crime control and criminal justice.

Above all, the public must be protected

Protecting the public is a perennial concern of crime policy, and the correctionalist system was by no means casual about this. It was, after all, the penal-welfare reformers who invented preventive detention and the indeterminate sentence, and the system that operated for most of the twentieth century reserved to itself special powers to incarcerate 'incorrigible' and dangerous offenders for indeterminate periods. But in an age when crime rates were low and fear of crime was not yet a political motif, protecting the public was rarely the motivating theme of policy-making. Today, there is a new and urgent emphasis upon the need for security, the containment of danger, the identification and management of any kind of risk. Protecting the public has become the dominant theme of penal policy.

In the last few decades, the prison has been reinvented as a means of incapacitative restraint, supposedly targeted upon violent offenders and dangerous recidivists, but also affecting masses of more minor offenders. Probation and parole have de-emphasized their social work functions and give renewed weight to their control and risk-monitoring functions. Sentences that are higher than would be justified by retributive considerations are made available and even mandatory. Community notification laws publicly mark released offenders, highlighting their past misdeeds and possible future dangers. There is a relaxation of concern about the civil liberties of suspects, and the rights of prisoners, and a new emphasis upon effective enforcement and control. The call for protection *from* the state has been increasingly displaced by the demand for protection *by* the state. Procedural safeguards (such as the exclusionary rule in the USA and the defendant's right of silence in the UK) have been part-repealed, surveillance cameras have come to be a routine presence on city streets, and decisions about bail, parole or release from custody now come under intense scrutiny.[21] In these matters the public appears to be (or is represented as being) decidedly risk-averse, and intensely focused upon the risk of depredation by unrestrained criminals. The risk of unrestrained state authorities, of arbitrary power and the violation of civil liberties seem no longer to figure so prominently in public concern.

Politicization and the new populism

In another significant break with past practice, crime policy has ceased to be a bipartisan matter that can be devolved to professional experts and has become a prominent issue in electoral competition. A highly charged political discourse now surrounds all crime control issues, so that every decision is taken in the glare of publicity and political contention and every mistake becomes a scandal. The policy-making process has become profoundly *politicized* and *populist*. Policy measures are constructed in ways that appear to value political advantage and public opinion over the views of experts and the evidence of research. The professional groups who once dominated the policy-making process are increasingly disenfranchised as policy comes to be formulated by political action committees and political advisers. New initiatives are announced in political settings—the US party convention, the British party conference, the televised interview—and are encapsulated in sound-bite statements: 'Prison works', 'Three-strikes and you're out', 'Truth in sentencing', 'No frills prisons', 'Adult time for adult crime', 'Zero-tolerance', 'Tough on crime, tough on the causes of crime'.[22]

There is now a distinctly populist current in penal politics that denigrates expert and professional elites and claims the authority of 'the people', of common sense, of 'getting back to basics'. The dominant voice of crime policy is no longer the expert or even the practitioner but that of the long-suffering, ill-served people—especially of 'the victim' and the fearful, anxious members of the public. A few decades ago public opinion functioned as an occasional brake on policy initiatives: now it operates as a privileged source. The importance of research and criminological knowledge is downgraded and in its place is a new deference to the voice of 'experience', of 'common sense', of 'what everyone knows'.[23]

The politicization of crime control has transformed the structure of relationships that connects the political process and the institutions of criminal justice. Legislators are becoming more 'hands on', more directive, more concerned to subject penal decision-making to the discipline of party politics and short-term political calculation. This constitutes a sharp reversal of the historical process whereby the power to punish was largely delegated to professional experts and administrators. One sees this reverse transfer of power in a series of measures (fixed sentence law reforms, mandatory sentences, national standards, truth in sentencing, restrictions on early release, etc.) that have shifted detailed decision-making tasks back to the centre—first to the courts and later to the legislature itself.[24]

'Politicization' sometimes suggests a polarization of positions, but the populist form that penal politics has taken has had exactly the opposite effect. Far from there being a differentiation of policy positions, what has actually emerged, in the 1980s and 1990s, is narrowing of debate and a striking convergence of the policy proposals of all the major political parties. It is not just one party that has moved away from the old correctionalist orthodoxy: they all have. The centre of political gravity has moved, and a rigid new consensus has formed around penal measures that are perceived as tough, smart and popular with the public.

The reinvention of the prison

For most of the post-war period, imprisonment rates in America and Britain decreased in relation to the numbers of crimes recorded and offenders convicted. Within the post-war penal-welfare system, the prison was viewed as a problematic institution, necessary as a last resort, but counter-productive and poorly oriented to correctionalist goals. Much governmental effort was expended on the task of creating alternatives to incarceration and encouraging sentencers to use them, and for most of the twentieth century there appeared to be a secular shift away from incarceration and towards monetary penalties, probation, and various forms of community supervision. In the last twenty-five years this long-term tendency has been reversed, first and most decisively in the USA, but latterly in the UK as well.[25]

The reversal of this trend in the USA was followed by the steepest and most sustained increase in the rate of imprisonment that has been recorded since the birth of the modern prison in the nineteenth century. In the period from 1973 to 1997, the numbers of inmates incarcerated in the USA rose by more than 500 per cent. Equally remarkable, there was a rise in the relative frequency of custodial (as opposed to non-custodial) sentences, and in the average length of prison terms—a rise that continued long after official crime rates had trended downwards. After a century in which the secular trend was for crime rates to rise and imprisonment rates to fall, the recent period has seen the emergence, first in the USA and then in the UK, of precisely the opposite phenomenon—rising imprisonment rates and falling crime rates.[26]

In vivid contrast to the conventional wisdom of the previous period, the ruling assumption now is that 'prison works'—not as a mechanism of reform or rehabilitation, but as a means of incapacitation and punishment that satisfies popular political demands for public safety and harsh retribution. Recent years have witnessed a remarkable turnaround in the fortunes of the prison. An institution with a long history of utopian expectations and periodic attempts to reinvent itself—first as a penitentiary, then a reformatory, and most recently as a correctional facility—has finally seen its ambition reduced to the ground-zero of incapacitation and retributive punishment. But in the course of this fall from grace, the prison has once again transformed itself. In the course of a few decades it has gone from being a discredited and declining correctional institution into a massive and seemingly indispensable pillar of contemporary social order.[27]

The transformation of criminological thought

The criminological ideas that shaped policy during the post-war period were an eclectic mixture of abnormal psychology and sociological theories such as anomie, relative deprivation, subcultural theory, and labelling. Criminality was viewed as a problem of defective or poorly adapted individuals and families, or else as a symptom of need, social injustice and the inevitable clash of cultural norms in a pluralist and still hierarchical society. If there was a central explanatory theme, it was that of social deprivation, and later 'relative deprivation'. Individuals became delinquent because they were deprived of proper education, or family socialization, or job opportunities, or proper treatment for their abnormal psychological disposition. The solution for crime lay in individualized correctional treatment, the support and supervision of families, and in welfare-enhancing measures of social reform—particularly education and job creation.[28]

The intellectual repertoire of post-war criminology was capacious enough to contain many different emphases and theoretical disputes and it no doubt appeared open-ended and compendious to the criminologists and practitioners of the period. But in retrospect, it seems clear that this pattern of thought, this criminological *episteme*, was both historically distinctive and structured in a fashion that was well adapted to the individualizing processes of criminal justice and the social rationality of the welfare state.

In the period since the 1970s, a quite different set of criminological ideas has begun to emerge and to influence government policy. The theories that now shape official thinking and action are *control theories* of various kinds that deem crime and delinquency to be problems not of deprivation but of inadequate controls. Social controls, situational controls, self-controls—these are the now-dominant themes of contemporary criminology and of the crime control policies to which they give rise.[29]

The criminologies of the welfare state era tended to assume the perfectability of man, to see crime as a sign of an under-achieving socialization process, and to look to the state to assist those who had been deprived of the economic, social, and psychological provision necessary for proper social adjustment and law-abiding conduct. Control theories begin from a much darker vision of the human condition. They assume that individuals will be strongly attracted to self-serving, anti-social, and criminal conduct unless inhibited from doing so by robust and effective controls, and they look to the authority of the family, the community, and the state to uphold restrictions and inculcate restraint. Where the older criminology demanded more in the way of welfare and assistance, the new one insists upon tightening controls and enforcing discipline.

Contemporary criminology increasingly views crime as a normal, routine, commonplace aspect of modern society, committed by individuals who are, to all intents and purposes, perfectly normal. In the penal setting, this way of thinking has tended to reinforce retributive and deterrent policies insofar as it affirms that offenders are rational actors who are responsive to disincentives and fully responsible for their criminal acts. But in its more general implications for crime prevention, this new perception has had rather more novel consequences. One genre of control theories—which we might term *the criminologies of everyday life*—consists of theories such as rational choice, routine activity, crime as opportunity and situational crime prevention and has rapidly become a major resource for policy makers in the last two decades. The working assumption of these theories is that crime is an event—or rather a mass of events—that requires no special motivation or disposition, no pathology or abnormality, and which is written into the routines of contemporary social and economic life. In contrast to welfare state criminologies, which began from the premise that crime was a deviation from normal, civilized conduct, and was explicable in terms of individual pathology, faulty socialization or social dysfunction, these new criminologies see crime as continuous with normal social interaction and explicable by reference to standard motivational patterns.[30]

One important feature of this approach is that it urges official action to shift its focus away from criminality and the criminal individual towards *the criminal event*. The new focus is upon the supply of criminal opportunities and the existence of 'criminogenic situations'. The assumption is that criminal actions will routinely occur if controls are absent and attractive targets are available, whether or not the individuals have a 'criminal disposition' (which, where it does exist, is in any case difficult to change). Attention should centre not upon individuals but upon the routines of interaction, environmental design and the structure of controls and incentives that are brought to bear upon them. The new policy advice is to concentrate on substituting prevention for cure, reducing the supply of opportunities, increasing situational and social controls, and modifying everyday routines. The welfare of deprived social groups, or the needs of maladjusted individuals, are much less central to this way of thinking.

The expanding infrastructure of crime prevention and community safety

Over the past two decades, while national crime debates in Britain and America have focused upon punishment, prisons and criminal justice, a whole new infrastructure has been assembled at the local level that addresses crime and disorder in a quite different manner. Developed under the tutelage of the Home Office in Britain, and largely by private enterprise and local government in the USA, this network of partnership arrangements and inter-agency working agreements is designed to foster crime prevention and to enhance community safety, primarily through the cultivation of community involvement and the dissemination of crime prevention ideas and practices.

Community policing, crime prevention panels, Safer Cities programs, Crime Prevention through Environmental Design projects, Business Improvement

Districts, Neighbourhood Watch, city management authorities—all of these overlapping and interconnecting activities combine to produce the beginnings of a new crime control establishment that draws upon the new criminologies of everyday life to guide its actions and mould its techniques.[31] And while this new infrastructure has definite relations to the institutions of criminal justice—especially to the police and probation which sponsor or administer many of the major initiatives—it should not be regarded as merely an annex or extension of the traditional criminal justice system. On the contrary. The new infrastructure is strongly oriented towards a set of objectives and priorities—prevention, security, harm-reduction, loss-reduction, fear-reduction—that are quite different from the traditional goals of prosecution, punishment and 'criminal justice'. So while the most prominent measures of crime control policy are increasingly oriented towards punitive segregation and expressive justice, there is, at the same time, a new commitment, especially at the local level, to a quite different strategy that one might call *preventative partnerships*. Today's most visible crime control strategies may work by expulsion and exclusion, but they are accompanied by patient, ongoing, low-key efforts to build up the internal controls of neighbourhoods and to encourage communities to police themselves.

Civil society and the commercialization of crime control

One of the most interesting features of this new cluster of preventative practices and authorities is that it straddles the dividing line between public and private, and extends the contours of officially co-ordinated crime control well beyond the institutional boundaries of 'the state'. For most of the last two centuries the state's specialist institutions of criminal justice have dominated the field, and have treated crime as a problem to be governed through the policing, prosecution and punishment of individual law-breakers. Today we see a development that enlists the activity of citizens, communities and companies, that works with a more expansive conception of crime control, and that utilizes techniques and strategies that are quite different from those used by traditional criminal justice agencies.

This development is now increasingly being encouraged by government agencies as well by groups and organizations within civil society. On the one hand there has been a concerted attempt by central government (especially in the UK) to reach out beyond its own criminal justice organizations and to activate crime reduction activity on the part of individual citizens, communities, commercial concerns, and other elements of civil society. In a sharp reversal of the long-term tendency towards the monopolization of crime control by specialist government agencies, the state has begun to make efforts to 'de-differentiate' the social response—that is, to spread out the crime control effort beyond the specialist state organizations that previously sought to monopolize it.[32]

At the same time we have seen the remarkable expansion of a private security industry that originally grew up in the shadow of the state but which is increasingly recognized by government a partner in the production of security and crime control. Policing has become a mixed economy of public and private provision as more and more routine security functions are undertaken by private police and more and more businesses and households invest in the hardware and protective services offered by the commercial security industry. A similar mixture of public and private is beginning to appear in the penal sector with the startling growth of private prisons—this after more than a century during which the administration of penal institutions proceeded as a state function that largely excluded private or commercial interests.[33]

Until very recently, the settled assumption was that crime control and corrections were the state's responsibility, to be carried out by government employees in the public interest. These clear lines between the public and the private have now become blurred. Public sector agencies (prisons, probation, parole, the court system, etc.) are now being remodelled in ways that emulate the values and working practices of private industry. Commercial interests have come to play a role in the development and delivery of penal policy that would have been unthinkable twenty years ago. What we are witnessing is the redrawing of the established boundaries between the public and the private spheres, between the criminal justice state and the operative controls of civil society. The 'modern' field of crime control is being rapidly reconfigured, in ways that de-centre not only the state's specialist institutions, but also the political and criminological rationalities that sustained them.

New management styles and working practices

The last few decades have seen important changes in the objectives, priorities and working ideologies of the major criminal justice organizations. The police now hold themselves out less as a crime-fighting force than as a responsive public service, aiming to reduce fear, disorder and incivility and to take account of community feeling in setting enforcement priorities. Prison authorities see their primary task as being to protect the public by holding offenders securely in custody, and no longer pretend to be capable of bringing about rehabilitative effects in the majority of their inmates. Probation and parole agencies have de-emphasized the social work ethos that used to dominate their work and instead present themselves as providers of inexpensive, community-based punishments, oriented towards the monitoring of offenders and the management of risk. Sentencing has changed, particularly in the USA, from being a discretionary art of individualized dispositions to a much more rigid and mechanical application of penalty guidelines and mandatory sentences.

There is also a new and all-pervasive managerialism that affects every aspect of criminal justice. Within specific agencies and organizations, performance indicators and management measures have narrowed professional discretion and tightly regulated working practice. Across the system as a whole, new forms of system-monitoring, information technology and financial auditing have

extended centralized control over a process that was previously less well co-
ordinated and highly resistant to policy management.[34]

This emphasis upon the cost-effective management of risks and resources has
produced a system that is increasingly selective in its responses to crime and
offending. There is now a well-developed practice of targeting resources (on
crime 'hot-spots', career criminals, repeat victims, and high-risk offenders);
gate-keeping to exclude trivial or low-risk cases (except where these are deemed
to be linked to more serious public safety issues); and a generalized cost-
consciousness in the allocation of criminal justice resources, including investigative resources, court calendars, probation supervision and prison places.
Diversion, cautioning, statutory fines, fixed penalties, and *de facto* decriminalization of minor offences all embody this tendency to conserve expensive crime
control resources for the more serious offences and the more dangerous
individuals.

There are, of course, egregious instances where these cost-effectiveness principles and managerial strategies appear to have been disrupted or reversed. The
startling growth of the prison population first in the USA, and more recently in
Britain, is a stark example of fiscal restaint giving way before populist political
concerns. Mandatory sentencing laws have been legislated in forms that pay
scant regard to the need to preserve scarce penal resources or even to target high-
risk cases. 'Quality of life' and 'zero-tolerance' policing initiatives appear to
reverse the logic of selective enforcement, or at least define policing priorities in
radically new ways. Government-imposed restrictions on the availability of
bail, the use of repeat cautioning, or the early release of prisoners are other
instances where recent policies have undone the previous reliance upon low-
cost, low-impact penal measures, often in the name of public safety or in
response to scandals where these policies have been blamed for criminal out-
rages.[35] Such instances show quite clearly the extent to which the field continues to be marked by tensions and contradictions. Indeed, the combination of
cost-cutting in sectors of criminal justice that many experts regard as valuable
in the long term (drug treatment programmes, community-based prevention,
education in prisons, resettlement, half-way houses, etc.) together with profli-
gate spending on measures that are popular with the public but whose effectiveness is considered much more doubtful (mass imprisonment, 'the war on
drugs', mandatory sentencing laws, etc.) is a continuing source of tension
between sections of the practitioner community and political decision-makers.

A perpetual sense of crisis

For much of the last two decades an unmistakable malaise and demoralization
have beset the field. This is regularly expressed in talk of a 'crisis', though the
term is clearly inappropriate for a situation that has now endured for several
decades. Since the late 1970s, those who work in criminal justice have experienced a period of unrelenting upheaval and reform that shows no sign of letting

up. Throughout the 1990s, things moved faster than ever. There was a welter of new legislation, constant organizational reform, and an urgent, volatile pattern of policy development. Those working in criminal justice have been exposed to a sustained period of uncertainty and disruption, with all of the anxiety and unfocused effort that accompanies rapid institutional change. A reading of the professional journals and newsletters, or the programmes of practitioner conferences, makes this abundantly clear.[36]

But this is more than the psychological fall-out of a period of reform. There is now a growing sense that the 'modern' arrangements for crime control—organized through the specialist agencies of the criminal justice state—may no longer be adequate to the problem of crime and no longer coherent in themselves. The system's failings are now less easily viewed as a temporary problem, having to do with lack of resources or the under-implementation of correctionalist or deterrent programmes. Instead there is a developing realization that the modern strategy of crime-control-through-criminal justice has been tried and found wanting. Where high crime or recidivism rates would once have been attributed to *implementation-failure*, and prompted a demand to reinforce the existing system with more resources and greater professional powers, they are now interpreted as evidence of *theory-failure*: as signs that crime control is based upon an institutional model that is singularly inappropriate for its task.

One of the profound consequences of this situation—which I have elsewhere referred to as the 'crisis of penal modernism'—is that the expertise of the professional groups that staff the system has tended to become discredited, both by others and by members of the groups themselves. Part of the crisis, as experienced by these professionals, is that throughout this period the public has increasingly lost confidence in criminal justice and politicians have become more and more unwilling to entrust decision-making powers to criminological experts or criminal justice personnel. From a political point of view, the criminal justice system has come to be a danger zone—a constant generator of risks and scandals and escalating costs—whose officials can no longer be entrusted with autonomous powers and grants of discretion.

What everyone knows . . .

To list these twelve indices of change is to do no more than present a catalogue of developments that will be familiar to anyone informed about recent criminal and penal policy. But to collect them together like this, and to contrast them with the institutions and practices of the field that existed prior to the 1970s, points up more vividly than usual the surprising nature of the present state of affairs when viewed in a longer term perspective.

Grouping these changes together in this way prompts the observation that these criminological discourses, crime control practices and criminal justice institutions do, in fact, relate to each other as elements in a loosely bounded and differentiated structure that one might properly describe as a 'field'. This 'observation' (which is actually a theoretical premise) is basic to the investigation that I develop here, and, being a basic presupposition, is not subject to confirmation or disconfirmation by the study itself. However, if it helps elucidate phenomena that are not otherwise explicable, as I think it does, then it will have shown its pragmatic and heuristic value and served its immediate purpose.

In modern societies the field of crime control and criminal justice has its own organizational structure, its own working practices, and its own discourses and culture, all of which give it a certain degree of autonomy in relation to its environment. Of course the different elements of this field—agencies like the police, prisons, or parole; discourses like criminal law, criminology or penology; practices such as sentencing and crime prevention—are complex enough in themselves to warrant individual study, and the vast majority of scholarly analyses choose to focus on a specific topic of this kind. But a series of individual studies may miss some of the overarching principles that structure the relations between these elements, and so the present study looks at the field as a whole in an effort to identify shared trends and characteristics and to understand particular changes in the light of more general developments. The general analysis that I develop it is not a substitute for more detailed case-studies, without which the analysis could not have been written. It is instead a supplement to such studies that seeks to view individual elements in the context of their interaction, to understand the organization of the crime control field as a whole, and to examine that field's changing relation to its social environment.

Of course my description of the indices of change, set out in this way, collapses historical time and institutional space. Represented in the orderly sequence of a single list these different dimensions appear to co-exist on the same plane, in a unified categorical system, as so many aspects of the same thing, whereas, in truth, they summarize observations from many different settings, and stand for phenomena that occupy different levels of a complex, multi-dimensional field. Some of the developments I have described are connected and run in the same direction, forming part of the same causal sequence or institutional cluster. Others are contradictory, or else unconnected, operating on different discursive planes and levels of social action. In the course of my analysis, this complexity will have to be investigated before these relations can be untangled. But however misleading this initial approximation appears, however much it seems to simplify a reality that is always more complex and confusing, it at least gives us a place from which analysis can begin.

There is also the problem of judging significance. Some of the trends I have described may be straws in the wind or short-lived policy experiments, even though they strike today's commentators as the shape of things to come. It is difficult to be sure, and some developments may turn out to be more ephemeral than they currently seem. One must be careful not to exaggerate or extrapolate too readily, or to assume that the policy initiatives that have the highest visibility will also have the greatest empirical impact or practical significance. Nor should we confuse a proposal or initiative with an embedded policy. Any analysis of recent events and their structural significance must proceed with a degree of caution and bear in mind some basic methodological rules:

Do not mistake short-term movements for structural change. Short-term shifts in policy emphasis that are temporary and reversible must be distinguished from long-term structural transformations. In the same way, changes in rhetorical style and expression should be distinguished from more profound transformations in the underlying assumptions and styles of reasoning that structure criminological discourse and crime control policy.

Do not mistake talk for action. The rapid and sometimes radical changes that occur in official policy statements must not be mistaken for alterations in actual working practices and professional ideology. Nor should it be assumed that the discrediting of a particular vocabulary (such as 'rehabilitation' or 'welfare') means that the practices that it once described have altogether disappeared. At the same time, the social significance and practical efficacy of political rhetoric and official representations must not be ignored.

Do not assume talk is inconsequential. Political rhetoric and official representations of crime and criminals have a symbolic significance and a practical efficacy that have real social consequences. Sometimes 'talk' *is* 'action'.

Do not confuse means with ends. The relatively fixed infrastructure of penal institutions, apparatuses and techniques must be analysed separately from the more mobile strategies that determine aims and priorities and dictate how crime control resources are deployed.

Do not conflate separate issues. Developments in the USA and the UK; outlier cases and central tendencies; changes in the crime rate and changes in penal policy; political representations of public opinion and the actual beliefs and attitudes of the public; the penological effects of crime control practices and their political significance—one needs to resist the temptation to run together each term of these matched pairs. Each one involves analytically distinct questions that require quite different methodologies and data if they are to be properly addressed.

Do not lose sight of the long-term. Anyone undertaking a 'history of the present' must resist the temptation to see discontinuities everywhere, or to too readily assume that today is the beginning of an absolutely new era. As Michel Foucault once remarked,

One of the most harmful habits of contemporary thought is the analysis of the present as being precisely, in history, a present of rupture, of high point, of completion, or of a returning dawn . . . the time we live in is not *the* unique or fundamental irruptive point in history where everything is completed and begun again.'[37]

Nevertheless, and bearing in mind these cautionary rules of methodological good sense, *something* seems to be happening, and we do not quite know what it is. And, what is more, even the most cautious account of the present would have to acknowledge that the current reconfiguration of crime control appears to be intimately linked to the restructuring of other dimensions of social and economic life in late modern societies. This study tries to make sense of the current conjuncture by viewing it historically and sociologically. By tacking back and forth between specific developments and more general social patterns, I hope to increase the intelligibility not just of crime control but also of late modernity's distinctive forms of social ordering and social control.

Theoretical orientations

My aim in this book is to write a history of the present and to present a structural account of how crime control and criminal justice are presently organized. To do so requires a mapping of the social conditions of existence that underlie contemporary crime control, and an identification of the rules of thought and action that shape its policies and practices. One of the difficulties such a project entails is the question of how to discuss change in a complex field of practices, discourses and representations. Talk of 'structure' and 'structural change' is often too totalizing, too all or nothing. So too is the juxtaposition of one 'rationality' to another, as in the claim that a 'New Penology' is displacing the 'Old Penology' or that Modernity is being outmoded by Post-modernity.[38] A complex, multi-dimensional field that has undergone a process of transition will show signs of continuity and discontinuity. It will contain multiple structures, strategies, and rationalities, some of which will have changed, some of which will not. One needs a way of discussing change that will be attuned to this complexity and variation and will avoid the pull towards simplified dualisms and the false essentialism they imply.

My claim will be that one can identify at present the emergence of a reconfigured field of crime control and criminal justice. To claim this is not to assert a singular new logic, or a radically new set of institutions or structures. Nor does it suggest an epochal transformation, such as 'the death of the social' or the arrival of post-modernity. Instead I describe the emergence of a new configuration—a reconfigured complex of interlocking structures and strategies that are themselves composed of old and new elements, the old revised and reoriented by a new operational context, the newer elements modified by the continuing influence of working practices and modes of thought dating from the earlier period. My argument is thus couched in the terms of a weak structuralism that claims no more than the obvious truth that the introduction of new rationalities, practices, and purposes into an existing field will have consequences for the operation and meaning of the existing elements within that domain. It is these *structural* or *figurational* qualities of the field—its discursive rules, its logics of action, the systematic constraints upon what can credibly be said and done—that will form my primary object of study.

The changes described above have attracted much in the way of commentary and analysis. Everyone agrees that the field is changing, and in fundamental ways. There is, however, surprisingly little agreement about the precise character of this transformation, or about the causes that are bringing it about.

Scholars have drawn our attention to particular developments (the drift to a law and order society, the decline of rehabilitation, the shift to community corrections, the new penology, the bifurcation of penal policy, managerialism, and punitive populism) and offer theoretical resources for their analysis (economic and social crisis; postmodernism; governmentality; risk society; late modernity).[39] Each of them throws light on certain dimensions of the process, and their insights have done much to shape the analysis that I develop here. But none of these theories offers an analysis of the overall reconfiguration of the field, nor, in my view, do they provide a really compelling and comprehensive account of the social and historical forces that have brought it into existence.

The field of crime control and criminal justice is a relatively differentiated domain with its own dynamics and its own norms and expectations to which penal agents orient their conduct. The social and economic determinants of 'the outside world' certainly affect the conduct of penal agents (police officers, judges, prison officials, etc.), but they do so indirectly, through the gradual reshaping of the rules of thought and action within a field that has what sociologists call a 'relative autonomy'. Social trends—such as rising rates of crime and feelings of insecurity, economic crises, political shifts from welfarism to neo-liberalism, changing class, race or gender relations, and so on—have to be translated into the folkways of the field before they have an effect there. To assume that social and penal trends work closely in tandem, or that there is some kind of homological causation that always links one directly to the other, ignores a great deal of factual evidence that tends to undermine, or at least qualify, any such notion. It also neglects the need to specify the mechanisms whereby social forces in one domain come to be translated into outcomes in another.

Structures, and above all structural changes, are emergent properties that result from the recurring, re-iterative actions of the actors who occupy the social space in question. The consciousness of these actors—the categories and styles of reasoning with which they think and the values and sensibilities that guide their choices—is therefore a key element in the production of change and the reproduction of routine, and must be a major focus of a study of this kind. The actors and agencies who occupy the field of criminal justice—with their particular experience, training, ideologies, and interests—are the human subjects through whom and by whom historical processes are brought about. These actors' understanding of their own practice and of the system in which they work is crucial in shaping the operation of the institutions and the social meaning that they take on.[40] Discursive statements and rhetorics—and the knowledge-based or value-based rationales that they involve—will thus be as important as action and decisions in providing evidence about the character of the field. A new configuration does not finally and fully emerge until it is formed in the minds and habits of those who work the system. Until these personnel have formed a settled *habitus* appropriate to the field, enabling them to cope with its demands and reproduce it 'as a matter of course', the process of change remains partial and incomplete. So long as practitioners and policy-makers lack a focused sense of the system, the field will continue to display a high degree of volatility and its future direction will remain uncertain. For better or worse, a field in transition is a field that is more open than usual to external forces and political pressures. It is a historical moment that invites transformative action precisely because it has a greater than usual probability of having an impact.

This attention to actors' statements and their presuppositions is also important in respect of political actors and policy-makers, whose rhetorical statements and announced rationales are not merely a gloss on their actions but are actually a form of action in themselves. A major topic of this inquiry concerns the ways in which government officials and private actors experience and make sense of changing social circumstances and new predicaments, and the intellectual and technical means that they develop for dealing with them. It needs to be remembered that the emergence of structural phenomena such as rationalities, mentalities, and strategies is, in the first place, the outcome of problem-solving activity on the part of situated actors and agencies. There is no magical, automatic process of functional adjustment and system adaptation that exists apart from this. Analyses that rely upon such notions omit the real human stuff of disposition, choice and action—the stuff of which society and history are actually made.

An engagement with actors' categories and what they do with them is an engagement with ideas and with discourse, in this case primarily criminal law, criminology, and social policy discourse. Part of my concern therefore will be to trace and reconstruct the categories through which criminals and crime are apprehended and acted upon. This is not quite the same as a history of criminological ideas however, since many criminological theories and conceptions have had very little influence in practice, however much they are worth as intellectual achievements. My focus is upon 'official criminology' and upon the criminological conceptions that have shaped criminal law and crime control practice in its various forms. It is a study of working social categories and how these have changed over time—a matter of cultural and institutional history, rather than the history of ideas.[41] The criminological categories that interest me here are the ones that are sanctioned by social authorities and backed up by institutional power. Such categories actually constitute their criminal objects in the very act of comprehending them. They are regarded here not as 'true' or 'valid' or 'scientific' knowledge but rather as effective, truth-producing categories that provide the discursive conditions for real social practices. These categories are themselves a product (and a functioning aspect) of the same cultures and social structures that produce the criminal behaviours and individuals to which they refer.

My present account of penal and social change builds upon the theory I set out in *Punishment and Welfare*—a book that described the early twentieth-century formation of the penal-welfare field. In response to the erosion or breakdown of a previously established institutional configuration, all sorts of programmes and adaptations quickly appear to fill the vacuum. This proliferation of new proposals, this deluge of new ideas, is eclectic, diverse, and emerges from all sorts of places in the social field. There is no unified response, no developmental necessity, no progression from old to new. There is, however, a shared set of prior conditions, variously understood, and a history of prior failures and problems that form the background against which many of the new programmes are created. There is also, contiguous to the penal domain, a structured societal field (with its social, economic, and political domains) out of which fresh problems and initiatives constantly flow.

To the extent that these new developments become organized and coherent (and the configurations that emerge are only ever *loosely* organized and *relatively* coherent) this is produced by means of a process of political and cultural selection. There is, in effect, an evolutionary process of variation, environmental selection and adaptation, though of course the 'selection' mechanism is not at all 'natural'. It is, on the contrary, social and political and therefore a locus of calculation, contestation, and struggle. Moreover, the choices that cumulatively compose the selection process are made, more often than not, in a fashion that is blind to some of its consequences, and driven by value commitments rather than informed, instrumental calculation. Socially situated, imperfectly knowledgeable actors stumble upon ways of doing things that seem to work, and seem to fit with their other concerns. Authorities patch together workable solutions to problems that they see and can get to grips with. Agencies struggle to cope with their workload, please their political masters, and do the best job they can in the circumstances. There is no omnipotent strategist, no abstract system, no all-seeing actor with perfect knowledge and unlimited powers. Every 'solution' is based upon a situated perception of the problem it addresses, of the interests that are at stake and of the values that ought to guide action and distribute consequences.

The programmes and ideas that are thus selected are those that fit with field's dominant structures and the specific cultures that they support. They are the ones that mesh with the most powerful institutions, allocate blame in popular ways, and empower groups that currently command authority, esteem and resources. Crime control strategies and criminological ideas are not adopted because they are known to solve problems. The evidence runs out well before their effects can be known with any certainty. They are adopted and they succeed because they characterize problems and identify solutions in ways that fit with the dominant culture and the power structure upon which it rests.

This book is an account of change in a number of different social fields and on a number of different historical registers. In the foreground of the study is the problem of describing how our responses to crime and our sense of criminal justice came to be so dramatically reconfigured at the end of the twentieth century. But underlying this inquiry is a broader theoretical concern to understand our contemporary practices of crime and punishment in their relation to the structures of welfare and (in)security and in relation to the changing class, race, and gender relations that underpin these arrangements. In studying the problem of crime and crime control we can glimpse the more general problems of governing late modern society and of creating social order in a rapidly changing social world.

2

Modern Criminal Justice and the Penal-Welfare State

In the decades prior to the 1970s crime control in Britain and America had a settled institutional structure and an established intellectual framework. Its characteristic practices, and the organizations and assumptions that supported them, had emerged out of a long-term process of development during which the modern structures of criminal justice had first been assembled in their classic liberal form and then increasingly oriented towards a more correctionalist programme of action.

Like any structure that has been built and rebuilt over a long period of time, its various components dated from different periods and there was an historical eclecticism to its design rather than the purity of a singular style. The institutional foundations of the crime control field—the specialist institutions of police, prosecution, courts, and prisons—were more than 150 years old, as were the legal procedures and liberal penal principles that governed their activities and supplied their official ideologies. Overlaying this was a more recent modernist superstructure, created during the course of the twentieth century, with its distinctive correctionalist motifs (rehabilitation, individualized treatment, indeterminate sentences, criminological research) and the specialist arrangements that supported them (probation, parole, juvenile courts, treatment programmes, etc.). The result was a hybrid, 'penal-welfare' structure, combining the liberal legalism of due process and proportionate punishment with a correctionalist commitment to rehabilitation, welfare and criminological expertise. By 1970 the basic contours of this penal-welfare style were well established and there appeared to be a settled dynamic of progressive change moving in an increasingly correctionalist direction.[1]

This is not to deny that the field of criminal justice was internally contested and prone to disruption. There were episodic scandals and crises, day-to-day problems and recurring failures, oppositional groups and critical commentaries, and reformers regularly complained that progress was altogether too slow. But these problems occurred against the background of a broad professional consensus about the basic framework within which crime control should operate, and a widely shared sense of the goals and values that should shape criminal justice. The basic tensions that underlay the field—between penal aims and welfare aspirations, principles of law and criminological assumptions, the police function and the social work mission, the offenders' rights and the public interest—were tensions that had long since been knotted into the working arrangements and conceptual compromises that make up the fabric of any practical institution.

As late as the 1960s and 1970s, the literature of the political parties demonstrated the breadth of this consensus. So did the official reports and policy statements of the period, which talked of 'modern penal theory' in a way that assumed that such a thing existed, was known, and was largely uncontested. There was, quite unmistakably, an official philosophy in place: a structure of thought out of which policy emerged, within which serious debates took place, and to which practical action was necessarily oriented.[2]

It is true that the embedded, established nature of this system was disguised, for much of the post-war period, by the fact that the correctionalist programme was always in the process of becoming more fully realized. The central planks of its reform agenda—individualized sentencing, indeterminate sentences, classification, treatment programmes—were always less than fully implemented, and its proponents thought of themselves as modernist reformers pitted against the established structures of an outdated, legalistic, retributive system. But by the start of the 1970s these correctionalist reformers *were* the establishment, and most of the official policies and practices of crime control were oriented towards, or influenced by, their aims and expertise.

By the 1960s, in both the USA and the UK, penal-welfarism commanded the assent, or at least the compliance, of all the key groups involved in criminal justice—and the enthusiastic support of government department administrators, social work professionals, and liberal elites. The idea of 'progress in penal reform' was a conventional idea, and an intelligible one, because it captured the sense of the gradual implementation of a progressive programme that was widely shared and highly respected.[3] It is precisely because the field *was* well established and its culture and practices *were* deeply embedded that their transformations in the decades since have been experienced as so unsettling.

These penal-welfare arrangements were also part of the wider scheme of things. Their basic structure and functioning were rooted in the differentiated institutional arrangements of modern society, and their programmes and working ideologies were integral elements of the post-war welfare state and its social democratic politics. The very solidity and rootedness of this set of institutions at the start of the 1970s is what makes its subsequent transformation a problem for historical and sociological analysis. We would expect that an embedded structure of this kind would exert a forceful inertia against change—or anyway against radical, structural, change that was not part of the institutions' own programme of development. One would expect as well that the groups and agencies whose professional power and status derived from these penal-welfare arrangements would tend to protect their working practices and put up serious resistance to radical change. Finally, given the close linkages that tied crime control and criminal justice to contiguous social institutions (such as welfare agencies, the labour market, and the social controls of neighbourhoods and communities), one would expect that major change in this field would be possible only where accompanied by correlative changes in these other social arrangements.

To explain the process of change that came about in this field, we need to begin with a sufficiently detailed understanding of the arrangements that were being transformed. In an internally differentiated, multi-dimensional network of practices and institutions, change is never a matter of all or nothing. So while it is tempting to provide a single characterization of the process—'from rehabilitation to risk', 'penal regressions', 'the new penology' or 'the coming of postmodernism'—the real nature of the change is liable to be less singular and clear-cut. To better understand that process of change and resistance, and to better locate the dimensions and locales of transformation, we need to start with a more detailed account of modern criminal justice and crime control and their social conditions of existence. It is only by understanding the past that we can hope to discover what is genuinely new about the present.

Penal modernity: the emergence of a criminal justice state

The foundations of twentieth-century crime control were laid centuries before when our now-familiar criminal justice institutions first emerged as integral elements of the long-term process that produced the modern nation-state. At the start of that process, in the conditions of contested and unstable authority that characterized early-modern Europe, victorious sovereign lords held out the promise of *pax et justitia* to their subjects as their forces fought to pacify their newly won territory and impose 'the King's Peace'.[4] The guarantee of 'law and order' (which originally meant the suppression of alternative powers and competing sources of justice as well as the control of crime and disorderly conduct) was thus, from the beginning, a key feature of sovereign power. 'Law enforcement' was, in that setting, a matter of lordship and political rule. It was the process through which the King's sovereign will was imposed against that of his enemies and against rebellious or unruly subjects. Only later did law enforcement come to mean the state's system for the apprehension and punishment of criminals. Our modern tendency to think of 'law enforcement' as a synonym for 'crime control' reveals the extent to which we have become used to thinking about the state as the standard mechanism for dealing with crime.

In the course of the late eighteenth and nineteenth centuries, the policing, prosecution, and punishment of criminals came increasingly to be monopolized by the state, though important divisions between central and local government functions were preserved and survive to the present day in the UK and the USA. Private disputes and harms inflicted upon individuals come to be reconstituted as public matters to be tried in the criminal courts. Private vendettas and the claims of individuals who had been wronged or injured were gradually subsumed in the processes of state justice as state prosecution increasingly displaced private actions. Later, with the expansion of democracy in the nineteenth and twentieth centuries, this sovereign power was transformed into a 'public' power. Its law came to hold itself out as 'the will of the people' and their representatives, and although it continued to be enforced by state institutions, these were now to be directed by 'the public interest' rather by the wishes of political elites or powerful individuals.

As the nation state gradually wrested control of policing and the power to punish away from competing secular and spiritual authorities, and concentrated them in the new institutions of criminal justice, the institutions of police and punishment gradually took on their distinctive modern form. Policing ceased to be a widely dispersed activity entrusted to amateurs and private employees and became instead the task of trained, professional officers in a specialist organization that formed part of the state. The prosecution of offenders ceased to be a private cause of action and became instead a task of government, undertaken in the name of 'the people'. Punishments gradually lost their localized character and came to be more firmly and uniformly regulated by state authorities.

The modern system for apprehending, prosecuting, and punishing violators of the criminal law thus came to be a specialized, differentiated one, forming an integral part of the modern state apparatus. Over time it has come to be administered by professional bureaucracies, utilizing institutions, laws, and sanctions specially designed for that purpose. These historical processes of differentiation, statization, bureaucratization, and professionalization are the key characteristics of what we might term the 'modernization' of crime control and criminal justice.[5]

The problem of order and the path not taken

In the perspective of the long term, these were new forms of punishment and control, adapted to the distinctive conditions of modernity, and displacing traditional modes of control that had become either ineffective or intolerable. But behind this structure of criminal justice, and prompting its creation, there was a historically specific problem of order close to that described by Thomas Hobbes in his justification of law and state authority.[6] The story of early modern criminal justice—like the story of the state itself—is a story of a struggle between competing powers out of which there emerged a Leviathan-state that was capable of quelling violence and disorder. Over time, as this emergent power gained assurance and legitimacy, its sovereign will became both law and justice. The violent imposition of Leviathan's law, its forcible pacification of enemies and subjects alike, came in time to be the 'peaceable' (though still violent) maintenance of order and the provision of security to subjects.

In liberal democracies, the state's capacity to impose 'law and order' came to be viewed not as a hostile and threatening power but as a contractual obligation owed by a democratic government to its law-abiding citizens. The 'guarantee' of law and order, of security for the citizen against violence, crime and disorder, became one of the key public benefits conferred upon the people by the state and its agencies. In this process, the character of crime control slowly shifted from being a generalized responsibility of citizens and civil society to being a specialist undertaking largely monopolized by the state's law-enforcement system.

In establishing specialist state agencies whose chief method of controlling crime was the pursuit, prosecution, and punishment of individual offenders, modern societies turned away from an alternative model of regulation that had been practiced in the towns and cities of early modern Europe. The early modern idea of 'police' referred not to the specialist agency that emerged in the nineteenth century but to a much more general programme of detailed regulation, pursued by urban authorities in their efforts to create an orderly environment for trade and commerce. The aim of this kind of 'police' regulation was to promote public tranquillity and security, to ensure efficient trade and communications in the city, and to enhance the wealth, health, and prosperity of the population. To this end, city authorities promulgated detailed by-laws calling for the inspection of weights and measures, censuses of the population, programmes of street lighting, the regulation of roads and buildings, trade and foodstuffs, even going so far as to specify the appropriate manners and modes of dress of citizens. This body of police regulation was only incidentally concerned with crime, but in the late eighteenth century, Patrick Colquhoun drew upon its ideas to articulate a model of crime control that might cope with rising levels of crime occurring in London and other large cities.[7]

Colquhoun's proposals sought to conserve the existing policing practices of late eighteenth-century cities, but to strengthen and rationalize them, adapt them to the new challenges of commercial capitalism, and augment them by creating a centralized organization with full time officers. This alternative model entailed an emphatically *preventative* form of regulation—addressing itself to indigence as well as to crime—and a more generalized, undifferentiated conception of the agencies responsible for crime control and order-maintenance. In this vision, crime control was a diffuse, widely shared responsibility, involving strict regulation of social and economic activities, informal surveillance, and the avoidance of criminal opportunities. Colquhoun's model certainly involved the identification and pursuit of criminal offenders, and outlined the need for a specialist agency to organize this function. But rather than identify crime with the criminality of specific individuals, it assumed that crime was a normal response to temptation, widely distributed throughout the lower classes and closely related to idleness and indigence. The strategic response was not to pursue and punish individuals but to focus upon the prevention of criminal opportunities and the policing of vulnerable situations.[8]

Today, Colquhoun is remembered not for his vision of diversified regulation—a vision that was rooted in eighteenth-century styles of city governance—but as an early police reformer whose writings helped bring about the creation of the modern police force that began to appear in the 1820s. The irony of this false memory is that the development of the 'new police' actually marked the beginning of modern, differentiated crime control and the eclipse of the style of governance that Colquhoun was advocating.[9] This misunderstanding of Colquhoun's significance is testimony to the extent to which the modern criminal justice institutions have come to dominate our sense of what crime control is and must be. Of course it is not a matter of chance that Colquhoun's model was displaced by the emergence of a specialist state system. The historical development of criminal justice was part of a broad and powerful process of modernization that has seen the development of structural differentiation, bureaucratic organization, strong state agencies, and professionalization in most fields of modern social life. Moreover, the generalized policing advocated by Colquhoun was viewed with suspicion by liberals because of its associations with the absolutist regimes of continental Europe.[10] But the fact that an alternative model of crime control was available at the historical moment when our modern institutions emerged should teach us two lessons. It should remind us that our current arrangements were by no means inevitable, and it should alert us to the distinctive characteristics of the institutional field that did in fact develop. At a time when these 'modern' arrangements are once again being put in question, these lessons become particularly pertinent.

In nineteenth-century Britain and America, the new agencies of the criminal justice state worked in parallel with civil society's mechanisms of surveillance and crime control.[11] Over time, however, traditional forms of private justice gradually diminished in strength and importance. Private prosecutions diminished in number and societies for the prosecution of felons became obsolete. Private police forces dwindled as the public police extended their coverage and authority. Citizens increasingly oriented their complaints to the state and less frequently organized private responses or took steps on their own behalf. Meanwhile, the public police evolved from being a state instrument, protecting the interests of the state and a propertied elite, to being a more authentically public service, responding to individual citizen complaints, and, in theory at least, providing security and protection to the whole population.

By the middle decades of the twentieth century, the public police forces in both countries had come to occupy a dominant position in the field of security provision, and the public's standard response to victimization was increasingly to file a report with the police. As public provision expanded, the crime control activities of citizens and communities tended to atrophy. Of course people continued to buy locks for their doors, to cross the street to avoid troublemakers, and sometimes to dispense private justice to criminals caught in the act. But their willingness to actively intervene was gradually lessened over time. The presence of professionals tended to de-skill the people and to relieve them of the sense that crime control was their responsibility. Crime became something that 'the authorities' should do something about, a problem that professionals are paid to deal with.[12]

This crime control formula—which like most modern institutions, downplayed the role of informal action on the part of the public, and privileged the role of professionals and governmental officials—became increasingly entrenched in the course of the twentieth century.[13] Not the least reason for this was that it was widely perceived to have been effective. In spite of the dislocations brought about by urbanization, industrialization, and the coming of commercial society, and despite the political upheavals associated with democratization, the criminal justice state was able to claim a measure of success. In the first half of the twentieth century, with their new police, their reformed criminal law, their network of prisons and reformatories, and their new bureaucratic capacities to process case-records, collate information and provide regular statistical counts, the criminal justice institutions of Britain and America were able to claim victories in their war against crime. The phenomenon of falling rates of crime and violence—rates that continued at historically low levels until the 1950s—were credited as the achievements of the criminal justice system that had recently been put in place.[14]

In hindsight, however, it might be more accurate to credit much of this achievement to the resilience of social controls in working-class communities, to the impact of work discipline, to religious revivals, and to the moral campaigns of churches and reform organizations. The constraints on conscience and on conduct implicit in the institutions of civil society—the churches and temperance societies, the charities and settlements, friendly societies, trade unions, working men's associations, and boys clubs—provided a vigorous, organic underpinning to the more reactive, intermittent action of policeman state. So too did the more intimate and more binding controls of family, neighbourhood, and workplace. The social mores of the period, and the new apparatus of law enforcement tended to reinforce each other, however much hostility and suspicion there was between some working-class or immigrant communities and the state officers who policed them.[15]

From the 1890s until the 1960s, when steep rises in recorded crime and violence began to undermine this perception, the criminal justice state was widely believed to be capable of winning the war against crime, or at least turning back the tide of crime and disorder that industrialism had brought in its wake. However doubtful that perception has come to appear in retrospect, by the first decades of the twentieth century the credentials of modern criminal justice appeared to be well established and a confident programme of expansion, differentiation and reform began to be put in place. The correctionalist programme of penal reform, which would govern much of the change that occurred over the next sixty or seventy years, was thus launched in a context defined by low crime rates and widespread confidence in the credentials of the state's crime control institutions. It was out of this confident *fin de siècle* era that our modern penal-welfare institutions first emerged with their distinctive strategies and assumptions.[16]

Probably these were false credentials. It is more likely that the success of the police and prisons was a vicarious one, dependent upon quite other forces and social arrangements. More likely that the crime control achievements of the criminal justice state depended upon the informal controls of these private actors and agencies that the state would eventually drive out of the crime control business.[17] No matter. The achievement was perceived to be an institutional achievement, was accredited as such, and came to be embedded in official thinking for the best part of the century. As the late as 1970, the assumption was still, as a British election manifesto put it, that: 'Crime concerns us all, but only the government can take effective action.'[18]

The established formula of the modern criminal justice state—the credo of penal modernity—thus assumed that crime control must be a specialist, professional task of 'law enforcement', oriented to the *post hoc* pursuit and processing of individual offenders. No need for a policy to encourage private action. No need to involve the public or individual victims. No need for an emphasis upon social or situational prevention. All that was required was a framework of legal threats and a reactive response.[19] Perhaps we were historically and sociologically predisposed to think that way. After all, this credo is recognizably a criminological version of what James C. Scott has called *high modernism*: an ideology that believes social problems are best managed by specialist bureaucracies that are directed by the state, informed by experts, and rationally directed towards particular tasks. This modernist attitude thinks in terms of technologically refined, top-down mechanisms that minimize the involvement of ordinary people and spontaneous social processes, and maximize the role of professional expertise and 'government knowledge'. Whether or not we were predisposed to go this route, the distinctly modern arrangements that were set up at that time went largely unchallenged until recently.[20] And the penal-welfare institutions, ideologies and practices that developed in the second half of the twentieth century served only to reinforce these modernist characteristics. That crime was a problem to be dealt with by specialist state institutions was more and more taken for granted as criminal justice moved closer to the technicist, knowledge-based, social engineering of the correctionalist framework.

Penal welfarism and correctionalist crime control

With its roots in the 1890s and its most vigorous development in 1950s and 1960s, penal-welfarism was, by 1970, the established policy framework in both Britain and America. Its basic axiom—that penal measures ought, where possible, to be rehabilitative interventions rather than negative, retributive punishments—gave rise to a whole new network of interlocking principles and practices. These included sentencing laws that allowed indeterminate sentences linked to early release and parole supervision; the juvenile court with its child welfare philosophy; the use of social inquiry and psychiatric reports; the individualization of treatment based upon expert assessment and classification; criminological research focusing upon etiological issues and treatment effectiveness; social work with offenders and their families; and custodial regimes that stressed the re-educative purposes of imprisonment and the importance of re-integrative support upon release. Penal-welfare principles tended to work against the use of imprisonment, since the prison was widely regarded as counter-productive from the point of view of reform and individual correction. Specialist custodial regimes—youth reformatories, training prisons, correctional facilities, etc.—were preferred to the traditional prison, and the abatement of imprisonment in favour of community measures was a constant aim of correctionalist reformers. From the 1890s to the 1970s, fewer and fewer categories of offenders were deemed suitable for standard imprisonment.[21]

In the penal-welfare framework, the rehabilitative ideal was not just one element among others. Rather it was the hegemonic, organizing principle, the intellectual framework and value system that bound together the whole structure and made sense of it for practitioners. It provided an all-embracing conceptual net that could be cast over each and every activity in the penal field, allowing practitioners to render their world coherent and meaningful, and to give otherwise unpleasant, troublesome practices something of a benign, scientific gloss.[22]

Rehabilitation was not, however, the sole objective of the penal-welfare framework. Nor was it, in practice, the typical outcome. The individualizing, indeterminate and largely discretionary character of the correctionalist arrangements allowed the system's decision-makers extensive latitude in their treatment of convicted offenders or of juveniles in need of care. Offenders identified as dangerous, recidivistic or incorrigible could be detained for lengthy periods. Those with respectable backgrounds or strong connections to work and family could be let off more leniently. Penal measures could be adjusted to match the level of compliance or risk displayed by the offender; and offenders responsible for heinous crimes could be sentenced to punishments that accorded with their culpability and were in line with public expectations.[23]

In this system of indeterminate sentencing and early release, a sizeable gap opened up between publicly announced prison sentences and the actual time served by most inmates, so that the system's penal elements appeared more extensive than they actually were. This gap between 'bark' and 'bite' permitted the system to appear responsive to public demands for punishment while tailoring its real impact in a way that liberal professionals deemed more appropriate. So long as the system was not scrutinized too closely, and its internal workings were not fully understood by outsiders, it could simultaneously avoid public criticism and empower expert decision-making. The practicality and the durability of the penal-welfare framework lay precisely in the fact that it combined both penal and welfare aims, that it was flexible enough to emphasize one or the other according to circumstance, and that it was largely removed from close public scrutiny.[24]

In this structure, a central place was allocated to professional specialists and expert judgement. Criminological knowledge and empirical research findings were taken to be more reliable guides to action than custom and common sense, and post-war governments fostered the development of a criminological discipline in the universities and within government itself. As the British government declared in 1964, 'it is not enough to condemn crime, we need to understand its causes'—and this seemed especially important in the rapidly changing social and economic circumstances of the 1950s and 1960s in which crime rates were steadily rising.[25] Key decisions such as sentencing, classifying inmates, allocating them to different institutions and regimes, evaluating readiness for release and setting supervision license conditions, were increasingly placed in the hands of penal experts rather than judicial authorities. Where once the leading principle had been *nullem poena sine crimen* ('no punishment without a crime'), in the world of penal-welfarism it came instead to be *no treatment without diagnosis*, and *no penal sanction without expert advice*.

In the post-war decades criminal justice became the territory of probation officers, social workers, psychologists, psychiatrists, child-guidance experts, educationalists, and social reformers of all kinds. The development of the penal-welfare programme was not just the civilization and reform of criminal justice. It was also the colonization of a formerly legal terrain by 'social' authorities and professional groups. Its expansion was their expansion. 'Progress in penal reform', whatever else it involved, was a matter of increasing the numbers and the jurisdictions of social experts on delinquency.[26]

This grant of discretionary power to unaccountable professionals, whose decisions were typically issued without explanation and without being subject to judicial review, is an indication of the degree of trust that these professional groups then commanded, and also of the way in which their powers were perceived. In contrast to the judicial power to punish, which had long been subject to scrutiny and review, the powers of social workers and psychologists were regarded in a more benign, apolitical light. Their views on normal psychology, on the sources of anti-social behaviour, on how families should function and how individuals should behave, were assumed to be neutral, clinical judgements based upon scientific understanding and empirical research. Their normalizing practices and enforcement powers also tended to escape scrutiny, despite their implications for the privacy and liberty interests of the individuals with whom they dealt. Their mission was viewed as an uplifting, civilizing one that tried to distance itself and its objectives from the penal mechanisms in which it operated. Working in a setting that was coloured by the stigma of crime and punishment, they strove to be 'non-judgemental', their professed aim being the relief of individual suffering and the improvement of social functioning rather than doing justice or settling moral accounts. Social work knowledge and clinical judgement claimed a form of authority that viewed itself as quite different from claims of moral superiority, though, as critics would later point out, the distinction between them was no where near as great as its proponents imagined.[27]

This trust in professional experts extended into the policy-making process too. Adjustments of penal law, the creation of new sanctions, the reform of institutional regimes, the devising of early release mechanisms—all of these were largely the work of senior civil servants and expert advisers who were quite removed from public debate and media headlines. So long as scandals, escapes, and riots were avoided, political interference in the day-to-day running of the system was minimal, as was the involvement of the general public or their political representatives in most of the policy initiatives that characterized that period. The bipartisan approach that the major political parties adopted, and the sense that penal policy and crime control were largely technical matters best left to the professionals and practitioners, were further expressions of this trust and the credibility that professionals groups then enjoyed.[28]

Of course commitment to the *welfarist* aspects of penal-welfarism was quite variable—both across local jurisdictions and within the institutions, agencies and groups that made up the system. Probation officers, juvenile court personnel, reformatory supervisors, prison governors, criminological researchers, senior civil servants, and the system's psychologists, psychiatrists, and educationalists were usually much more enthusiastic than were rank and file prison guards, police officers, or public prosecutors. Nor was the system free of contention and conflict. In judges' chambers there were daily tussles between prosecutors and probation officers: the one arguing for a prison sentence, the other for non-custodial alternatives; one pressing the moral discourse of law with its stress on agency, individual responsibility and guilt, the other invoking the causal discourse of social work, with its concern for excusing circumstance, collective responsibility and positive outcomes. Sentencers had to balance offence-based considerations against offender-based ones, to set off the immediate appeal of an individualized measure against a background concern for the equality of sentencing and the protection of the public. This dilemma was somewhat softened however by the existence of post-sentencing procedures that, in effect, re-sentenced the individual on the basis of his or her behaviour in custody or prospects on release.

The positions that were marked out in these well-rehearsed debates invoked political ideologies as well as professional affiliations. Liberals stressed that crime was a symptom of inequality; that criminals needed to be understood before being judged; that the police could not be trusted to uphold suspects' rights; that punishments was less useful than treatment; that the prison was counter-productive and the death penalty unconscionable. Conservatives spoke of the deterrent powers of tough sentences and the need for lengthy imprisonment and capital punishment. They stressed the importance of individual responsibility; of upholding the law; of letting the police get on with their job and providing them with the legal powers and financial resources necessary to do it. But even they accepted that social and psychological circumstance should temper justice with mercy, and acknowledged the need for correctional treatment and welfare provision 'in appropriate cases'. The real disagreement was about 'the right balance', not about the range of considerations that were legitimately involved. Both sides spoke the language of penal welfarism, and put its principles into practice—a fact that is evidenced by the record of Conservative and Republican administrations, which did as much to establish this framework as did their Labour and Democrat opponents.[29]

Over time, these tensions were worked out in the course of daily interaction and institutional compromise. Delicate balances of power were engineered in law and in practice. Practical agreements and accommodations were developed that allowed institutions such as the reformatory prison, probation and the juvenile court to straddle the fault lines between these different interests and ideologies.

It was this practical penal-welfarism, rather than any specific theory or criminological conception, that shaped the thoughtways and habits of practitioners and policy makers. Their *habitus*, their working ideologies, their trained responses and decisions, were formed by and adapted to this overall pattern of ideas and institutions that made up the penal-welfare field. It was the field's overall character that shaped the debates that occurred and the policies that were invented. It gave rise to an institutionalized ontology that defined what the problem of crime was, and to an epistemology that dictated how it could be known, and what the appropriate means for understanding and addressing it were. It shaped the spectrum of penal politics, determining what was progressive and what was reactionary, and distributing the interest groups into their different positions. The criminology textbooks, the training courses for criminal justice staff, the structure of professional careers, the stories that practitioners told one another, all of these operated to reproduce the structures, the othodoxies and the standard narratives of the field, even as they bemoaned the failures of the system and the need for further reform.

The discourses and practices that made up the penal-welfare field were premised upon a few fundamental socio-political assumptions, a set of cultural commitments, and a determinate form of criminological knowledge. Together, they gave rise to an implicit set of rules, a kind of generative grammar that structured the standard language, the standard thinking, and the standard practices of the actors and agencies who operated within the field. In its detailed operation, this grammar was distinctive to, and a product of, the field of crime control and criminal justice. It took shape in this practical setting over an extended period of time and in response to a multitude of specific problems and interests. The grammar of penal-welfarism was thus, like all institutional phenomena, attuned to a specific set of practices and processes. But, as I will describe in a moment, it was also conditioned by social structures and cultural themes that were external to the field, and by a certain collective experience of crime that, in an important sense, was prior to it.

Right from its beginning in the late nineteenth century, penal-welfarism proceeded on the basis of two unquestioned axioms, both of which had been derived from the progressive political culture of the period. The first of these—born of the 'crime miracle' of the late nineteenth century and nourished by the liberal optimism of the twentieth—took it as self-evident that *social reform together with affluence would eventually reduce the frequency of crime.*

Generalized prosperity, in and of itself, was viewed as a natural means of crime prevention. The second axiom, equally a product of that specific historic moment, was that *the state is responsible for the care of offenders as well as their punishment and control.* Throughout the nineteenth century, the state had increasingly monopolized and rationalized the processing and punishment of offenders. But the working assumption was that if anyone was to care for offenders, aid them on release or provide for their social needs, it should be the churches and private philanthropy rather than the state. After the 1890s, this ceased to be the case, and the state was increasingly assumed to be responsible for the reform and welfare of offenders. *The state was to be an agent of reform as well as of repression, of care as well as control, of welfare as well as punishment.* Criminal justice in the emerging welfare state was no longer, or no longer exclusively, a relation between a Leviathan and an unruly subject. Instead, the criminal justice state became, in part, a welfare state, and the criminal subject, especially one who was young, or disadvantaged, or female, came to be seen as a subject of need as well as guilt, a 'client' as well as an offender. In the post-war decades, the standard response to problems of crime and delinquency—indeed the standard response to most social problems—came to be a combination of *social work and social reform, professional treatment and public provision.*[30]

Because the remit of criminal justice organizations was limited to dealing with individuals—or, at best, with individuals and their families—a crucial division of function quickly grew up. The standard institutional mechanism of crime control was the criminal justice response, triggered by a specific criminal act, and focused upon allocating penal-welfare sanctions to offending individuals. In the background was a much more diffuse and generalized policy of social reform and welfare provision, which, though it was rarely aimed specifically at crime or criminals, was expected to contribute towards crime reduction by improving the conditions of the poor and enhancing social justice. Although criminological theory pointed to the social roots of criminal conduct and implied the need for broad social measures of crime control, the more powerful logic of institutional differentiation and bureaucratic specialization dictated that the government's efforts to control crime would largely be channelled through the institutions of criminal justice. These were the government agencies specifically charged with responsibility with crime, the recipients of the state's crime control budget. However much a part other social measures ought to have played in the reduction of crime, bureaucratic demarcations ultimately shaped what was done. Government crime control thus continued to focus on the reactive sanctioning of criminal individuals, rather than the social prevention of crime.

This division of functions—which of course reflected the differentiated institutional structure of the modern state and its policy areas—was the underlying cause of a deep frustration regularly expressed by criminal justice personnel. It ensured that 'the rehabilitative ideal' that was put into practice was always narrowed and individualized and conducted in a penal setting. If crime is a social problem, the critics pointed out, then these individualized, correctionalist responses will inevitably fail to get at the root causes. They will intervene after the damage is done, addressing consequences rather than causes, focusing on already-formed (and often incorrigible) individuals rather than the social processes that are already producing the next generation. Penal-welfarism, located as it was within the criminal justice state, was structured in a self-limiting, self-defeating way.

The commitments of modernism

The correctionalist criminology that flourished in the middle decades of the twentieth century might properly be described as 'modernist' in its values and commitments. What made it modernist was its unquestioning commitment to social engineering; its confidence in the capacities of the state and the possibilities of science; and its unswerving belief that social conditions and individual offenders could be reformed by the interventions of government agencies. Whatever their political views or penological preferences, this brand of modernism formed the underlying belief system of the new class of criminological experts and knowledge-professionals who increasingly challenged the hold that lawyers and moralists had once had on this field.

With its implicit faith in scientific reason and the perfectability of man, this new correctionalist current was a legitimate child of Enlightenment thought—indeed in many ways it was the highest expression of that tradition's rationalist and utilitarian ambitions. But the new criminologists opposed the Enlightenment penology of Cesare Beccaria and Jeremy Bentham, and viewed their proposed reforms as an antidote to that programme rather than a development of it.[31] Punishment in general, and retributive punishments in particular, were viewed by the modernists as irrational and counter-productive, as remnants of pre-modern practices based upon emotion, instinct, and superstition. In their view, even the liberal principles of proportionality and uniformity were tainted by archaic thinking. The proper treatment of offenders required individualized, corrective measures carefully adapted to the specific case or the particular problem—not a uniform penalty tariff mechanically dispensed. One needed expert knowledge, scientific research, and flexible instruments of intervention, as well as a willingness to regulate aspects of life which classical liberalism had deemed beyond the proper reach of government. The normative system of law had to give way to the normalizing system of science, punishment had to be replaced by treatment.[32]

Of course the practical success of the modernist movement was always uneven and rarely satisfied its most enthusiastic proponents. There was resistance from liberals who insisted upon proportionality and just deserts, and also from exponents of an older, anti-modern tradition that saw punishment as a necessary end in itself and an important manifestation of law's sovereign power. As a result, the penal-welfare institutions that emerged were compromise-formations that balanced correctionalist and classical themes. But whatever the limitations of actual practice, by the early 1970s, the *discourse* of high modernism was established as the dominant form of expression among penal reformers, correctional experts and government officials.

As penal-welfarism developed in the post-war years, and as correctionalist language became more hegemonic, explicit expressions of punitiveness became increasingly rare. Sentiments and statements that had once been routinely called forth by the commission of grave crimes now came themselves to be the subject of condemnation. The urge to condemn crime in passionate terms; the desire to see wrongdoers suffer and victims avenged; the frank concern to register public outrage; the articulated claim that justice must be done, authority upheld and punishment endured as ends in themselves—all these expressions of traditional punitive justice came to be regarded as suspect and detrimental to a rational penology. Over time, the passionate, morally toned demand for punishment, which had always formed part of society's response to crime, became something of a taboo in the discourse of officials and policy elites. So much so, that critics who wished to assert an 'anti-modern' position were increasingly obliged to do so using the vocabulary of modernism itself. The word 'punishment' all but dropped out of the official vocabulary of modern penal policy, as did the expressions of passionate outrage that it traditionally entailed.[33]

Of course punitive sentiments did not disappear. They were instead repressed, forced underground, found to be embarrassing in polite company. Open displays of punitiveness were increasingly restricted to the inner life of institutions, to the untutored demands of the downmarket press and the *hoi polloi*, and to the outbursts of the occasional splenetic judge or unreconstructed politician. This subliminalization of such a forceful human and social response, this repression of such a powerful and primitive emotion, is a striking example of the civilizing process at work.[34] However, it was also a basis upon which a cultural rift grew up between criminal justice professionals and members of the general public. As we will see, the fact that the language and affect of punitiveness disappeared from official discourse while remaining strongly present in popular culture and common sense would re-emerge as an important source of tension in the 1980s and 1990s.

Correctionalist criminology and its central themes

As penal-welfare institutions developed, so too did the forms of knowledge upon which they depended and to which they gave rise: child-guidance, social case-work, forensic psychiatry, medico-legal science, and, above all, criminological discourse. The correctionalist criminology that developed alongside these institutions perceived crime as a social problem that manifested itself in the form of individual, criminal acts. These criminal acts, or at least those which appeared serious, repetitive, or irrational, were viewed as symptoms of 'criminality' and 'delinquency', that is to say, of underlying dispositions that were typically to be found in poorly socialized or maladjusted individuals. These underlying, individual dispositions—and the conditions that produce them—formed the proper object of criminological knowledge. They also formed the preferred target for correctional intervention, with penal treatment being focused upon the individual's disposition, and social policy being relied upon to deal with the wider causes.

A basic feature of the correctionalist framework was a routine differentiation between 'the normal' and 'the pathological' followed by a more or less exclusive focus upon the latter. Those individuals who offended, but who were judged to be essentially 'non-delinquent' or free of any real criminal disposition, became uninteresting for the purposes of criminological theory and penal practice. They could be dealt with minimally—by cautions or fines or, if their offence was serious, by deterrent penalties with no treatment component. The real focus of attention was upon *the delinquent, the criminal character*, or what the early twentieth-century criminologists termed the *'psychopathic offender'*. This is where scientific research was to be directed and institutional energies were to be targeted. These were the objects to which the system was to be geared. Correctional criminology and penal-welfare institutions jointly identified the maladjusted delinquent as the problem and correctional treatment as the solution. In consequence, the overwhelming mass of minor and occasional offenders were largely neglected by correctionalist practice, which rarely reached down into the local jails and prisons or the lower reaches of the system to deal with routine, petty offending. This helps explain the puzzling fact that one of the most frequently used sanctions of the post-war period—the fine—was completely devoid of rehabilitative pretensions, and commanded hardly any criminological attention.[35]

Within this criminological mind-set there was a recurring bias towards a form of causality that was long-term, dispositional, and operated through the formation of personality traits and attitudes. This notion of causality—popularized by Freudian depth psychology and widely adopted by the social work profession—focused upon deep underlying causes, unconscious conflicts, distant childhood experiences and psychological traumas. It tended to drive out all concern with proximate or immediate events (such as temptations and criminal opportunities) and to assume that surface meanings or conscious motivations are necessarily 'superficial' and of little explanatory value. To this way of thinking, occasional, opportunistic, rationally motivated offending was of little interest, however much it contributed to overall rates of crime, because the acts involved spoke to no particular pathology and offered no opportunity for expert treatment or correctional reform.

The primary concern of correctionalist criminological research was to identify the individual characteristics that differentiated 'delinquents' and 'criminal personalities' and to correlate these with other conditions that might provide clues to their aetiology and treatment. In its emphasis and conceptual interests, this criminology increasingly focused upon the individual, as did the penal-welfare institutions that it served. The *crime* problem came to be viewed as a *criminal* problem. Criminological knowledge was knowledge of individual delinquents and their differences. Even where the research was designed to address statistical distributions and patterns, or families and communities, the essential point was ultimately to understand the individual criminal, the correlates of criminality, and the ways in which social patterns and environment left their imprint upon individual offenders.[36]

A secondary concern of this criminology was to study and evaluate the impact of the various penal-welfare interventions: to ascertain 'what works' and why. This kind of research ensured that crime control institutions—most notably the police, the prisons, and probation—developed a built-in form of monitoring and reflexivity that provided feedback on the institutions' effects and data from which to measure their results. Not surprisingly, it tended to be this kind of criminological research, rather than the more ambitious investigations of aetiology, that attracted the greatest governmental funding and support.[37]

The theories developed within this framework slowly changed over time, even as the basic structures of correctionalist discourse remained intact. The criminology of the early twentieth century drew heavily upon psychiatric medicine and individual psychology, and focused upon the distinguishing traits of individual delinquents as revealed by the study of prisoners and reformatory inmates. In the 1920s and 1930s scholars using new statistical methods and multi-factorial analyses, began to think of criminality as an overdetermined effect of social deprivation. They found that those individuals with the most negative personality traits and criminal records were those who had most often experienced multiple forms of deprivation, including poor parenting and poverty. In the 1950s and 1960s when poverty and child neglect appeared to be declining in the more secure, more affluent circumstances of post-war Britain and the United States, this deprivation thesis began to be reworked as 'relative deprivation' or 'anomie' theory.[38]

The newer theories attributed criminal conduct not to absolute impoverishment but instead to the gap that had opened up between expectations and achievement. They thus entailed a modest critique of the welfare state and its achievements, pointing to the gap between rising expectations and actual opportunities, to the frustrations of those left behind in a prospering economy, and to the excesses of egoism associated with the new consumer society. Their call was for still greater social provision and in particular, the opening up of more accessible, legitimate routes to upward mobility. But for all their novelty and critical implications, these explanatory narratives remained true to the fundamental axioms of penal-welfarism: crime was still viewed a result of poverty and deprivation, and its cure still lay in the expansion of prosperity and the provision of social welfare.[39]

The correctional criminology that flourished in mid-century Britain and America was quite removed from the caricature versions that were later presented by its critics. Most correctional reformers and criminologists had no serious commitment to strict determinism, nor did they claim that the typical delinquent was 'sick' or deeply 'pathological'. The treatment programmes that were recommended and implemented were rarely intrusive, brain-washing measures, coercively imposed upon unwilling individuals, and the so-called 'medical model' of treatment was actually a less important point of reference than was the idea of educational development and social work support. And although correctionalist criminologists looked to the state to implement their programme and develop treatment regimes, their relationship to government was by no means uncritical. Correctionalists were typically outspoken critics of unreconstructed government policies, not the least of which was the death penalty.

What is most noticeable, in retrospect, in this criminological scheme and the theories it engendered, is not its scientific immaturity or its uncritical character. It is the particular pattern of attention that it established, and the blindspots this pattern entailed. It is the relative absence of any substantive interest in crime events, criminogenic situations, victim behaviour, or the social and economic routines that produce criminal opportunities. It thus differs considerably from what come later, and, if one recalls Colquhoun, from what went before. In effect, correctionalist criminology assumed the efficacy of criminal justice and the possibility of an individualized mode of crime reduction. It shared the institutional epistemology created by the criminal justice state which knew crime to be a problem of individual offenders with criminal dispositions. Again and again this way of thinking directed our attention to these individuals, and to the psychological processes that produced them, and thereby hid from view other ways of conceiving and acting upon the problem. At base, and despite its reformulations and internecine arguments, this was a criminology that shared in the progressive statist politics of the welfare state. It assumed without question the possibility and desirability of reintegrating delinquents and deviant individuals. And it looked to social work and social reform, professional treatment and public provision, to bring this about.

Social context and institutional supports

Like all social institutions, penal-welfarism was shaped by a specific historical context and rested upon a set of social structures and cultural experiences. Its ways of thinking and acting made sense to those who worked in the field, but they also resonated with the structures of the broader welfare state society, and with the ways of life that these reflected and reproduced. Penal-welfarism drew support from—and relayed support to—a particular form of state and a particular structure of class relations. It functioned within a specific environment of economic and social policies and it interacted with a set of contiguous institutions, the most of important of which were the labour market and the social institutions of the welfare state. In short, its characteristic ways of thinking and acting, particularly its modernism and its 'social' rationality, were embedded in the forms of life created by the political and cultural relations of the post-war years.

Like the modern welfare state of which it formed a part, penal-welfarism developed as a strategic solution to an historically specific problem of order and was underpinned by a particular kind of collective experience and collective memory. As we saw, penal-welfarism addressed itself to problems of individual maladjustment that were heavily concentrated among the poorer sections of the population, and which it attributed to poverty, poor socialization, and social deprivation. The problems it addressed were, in other words, the classic pathologies of industrialized, inegalitarian, class society.[40] It was precisely these problems of destitution and insecurity, and the political problems that they engendered (open class conflict, labour unrest, and fears of an unfit population, 'racial deterioration', declining national efficiency, etc.) that brought about the development of 'the social state' in the early years of the century. And it was similar fears—amplified by the collective memory of mass unemployment, economic collapse, and the descent into fascism and communism that could follow—that spurred the New Deal, the Beveridge plan, and the post-war expansion of welfare state programmes in the USA and the UK.[41] If it was a *Hobbesian* problem of order that first prompted the development of the criminal justice state in early modern Europe, one might say it was a *Marxist* problem of order—the social and political instability caused by class antagonism and unregulated economic exploitation—that first motivated penal-welfarism. To say this is not to claim that correctionalism was directly part of the politics of class struggle and compromise. No working-class movement in Britain or America (or anywhere else for that matter) ever demanded better treatment for criminals or social work for offenders. But the linkages were there nevertheless, since the state form, the social policy, and the class relations out of which penal-welfarism grew, were all strategic responses to precisely this socio-political problem.[42]

The British welfare state, and its American counterpart the New Deal regulatory state, institutionalized a series of strategic solutions to class conflict and economic disruption that were built around new forms of economic and social management. Regulatory law, state-directed social engineering, and Keynesian demand management came to be central tools of governance. Though the market and the private powers of wealth and capital continued to govern most aspects of life in Britain and America, these powers were increasingly subject to the restraining power of state regulation. Post-war governments in both countries increasingly tempered the risks of market capitalism and de-dramatized economic conflict by instituting social insurance and welfare measures that enhanced security and redistributed resources.[43] Over time, both nations established systems of progressive taxation, built schools and highways, regulated labour, subsidized housing, provided pensions and other forms of income support, and ensured minimal (or better) levels of education, health-care, and education for their citizens. They set up new mechanisms of economic management and public investment to alleviate the problem of booms and slumps. They extended state regulation into the workplace and the home to establish national standards of health and safety. By means of an interventionist state, pooled risk, and some degree of redistribution, new levels of economic and social security were made possible. The most immediate effects of this were experienced by those who fell out of the labour market due to ill health, injury, old age or forced unemployment. But at the same time, the population as a whole was being made more secure, and the national economies were being stabilized—processes that had major implications for politics and for social and economic policy in the post-war years.[44]

Within this new social structure, the prevailing politics was an inclusive, corporatist, social democratic one, and the characteristic form of social policy relied upon various forms of state intervention and social engineering. Its dominant ideology was a moderately solidaristic one that claimed to bring all individuals into full social citizenship with equal rights and equal opportunities. This new civic narrative of inclusion, usually associated with the European 'welfare state' was in fact just as much a characteristic of the USA, where it took the special form of the civil rights movement, and the vision of 'the Great Society'.[45] In its idealistic, altruistic aspects and its concern for social justice, this appeal to solidarity reflected the still vivid memories of the Depression and total war, the guilty consciences of upper class elites, the struggles of organized labour, and the aspirations of previously excluded groups. But it also embodied the actuarial concerns and enlightened self-interest of middle-class voters, who soon realized that they had much to gain from certain social policies and redistributions. Indeed it was precisely because the post-war welfare state provided cross-class benefits of economic security, improved health care, educational opportunities, and public sector jobs that it managed to sustain itself for decades to come.[46] For its supporters, the welfare state represented a new vision of social justice and equality, aptly expressed in John Rawls's influential argument that justice required a guaranteed minimum of provision before any competition for resources could begin.[47] For more conservative thinkers, the welfare state was the price that had to be paid for social peace, economic stability, and the proper education and training of the workforce. Whatever the various motivations, the result was a broad level of bipartisan support for welfare state provision—a pattern that was repeated in respect of penal-welfarism.

Penal-welfare and 'social' regulation

The development of these strategies of social and economic governance established a new style of exercising power, and a new type of social authority—that of social expertise. In this respect, the trajectory of penal-welfarism (in which penological experts increasingly displaced other authority figures) was precisely in keeping with that of the welfare state as a whole. During the first half of the twentieth century many key practices of government began to make use of a new way of reasoning about and acting upon the tasks that they faced. A whole series of problems—such as crime, or health, or education, or work, or poverty, or family functioning—came to be conceived of as *social* problems, with social causes, to be dealt with by means of social techniques and social work professionals. This new style of regulation empowered expert authorities to establish social norms and standards in areas of life (child-rearing, health care, moral education, etc.) that had not previously been formally regulated. In doing so, these agencies did not rely upon law or coercion, though these were used in the last resort. They relied instead upon the power of their expert authority, the persuasiveness of their normative claims, and the willingness of individuals and families to bring their conduct into line with that prescribed by the experts in the hope of achieving social promotion, economic security, or physical health and self-fulfilment.[48]

The welfare state thus accelerated the move towards a 'professional society' that was already well underway during the nineteenth century. It gave rise to new strata of professional workers who staffed the welfare state and the expanding public sector, ministering to the needs of citizens in an increasingly affluent, consumer economy. Further education expanded to train and certify these proliferating new groups. Social work became a growth industry, fed by the feedback loop of newly recognized problems in need of professional solutions.[49] In the 1960s there was a major growth in the personal social services, and the rise of new occupational groups such as 'social service professionals,' 'counsellors' and 'therapists' that had hardly existed before the Second World War. As the post-war trend towards greater income and status equality took hold, and the old hierarchies of class and rank began to fade, professionals and social experts came to enjoy an enhanced status and authority.[50]

The ideologies and interests of the new penal professionals thus articulated smoothly with the strategies of rule and forms of authority characteristic of the welfare state. 'Reform', 'rehabilitation', 'treatment and training', 'the best interests of the child'—all of these objectives meshed effectively with the new mechanisms of social regulation, with government through experts, and with ideological stress upon universal citizenship and social integration that characterized social politics in the post-war period.

The social basis of penal-welfarism

In her book *Risk and Blame*, Mary Douglas remarks that a 'no fault' approach to crime—which is what penal-welfarism implicitly tends towards—depends upon the existence of an extensive network of insurance and gift-giving. Where free market societies will tend to hold individuals responsible for loss and injury, and allow risk to lie where it falls, more solidaristic cultures (where individuals are tied into networks of trust and mutual reliance) can allow losses to be absorbed by the group, and can support norms of collective responsibility. Douglas's point is that a culture that relies upon restitutive processes rather than allocating blame and punishment is typically one where, in most people's experience, restitution can reasonably be expected and relied upon. Only against a material background of mutual trust and economic security can a 'no-fault' approach be sustained.

The welfare state and post-war prosperity enhanced economic security and social solidarity in Britain and America, and it seems reasonable to suppose that these social arrangements provided an important cultural underpinning for the 'no-fault' correctionalist institutions that flourished in the post-war years. The development of a more solidaristic culture was facilitated by the long boom of the 1950s and 1960s—a period of economic growth, full employment, narrowing inequalities and the expansion of the social service safety net. In this historical context, crime and delinquency could be viewed not as a threat to social order but as lingering relic of previous deprivations. And penal-welfare agencies could help alleviate this problem by extending help and treatment to the unfortunate individuals and problem families who had been left behind by the rising tide of prosperity and social progress.

There is also a more immediate sense in which the practices of penal-welfarism depended upon appropriate material conditions. Much of the effectiveness, and indeed the plausibility, of correctional practices such as custodial training, probation counselling, and parole supervision depended upon their ability to connect the offender with the world of work and domestic stability. In a period of full employment, expanding welfare services and relatively generous benefits, correctionalist practices of this kind came to be widely regarded as feasible and desirable. As subsequent experience has shown, the same attitudes do not tend to obtain in economic situations that are more recessionary and insecure.[51]

The expansion and elaboration of penal-welfare institutions paralleled that of the welfare state as a whole. Just as crime rates tended to increase most rapidly during times of economic growth, so too did the effort to develop a correctionalist strategy in response to them. Economic expansion and improved standards of living facilitated the growth of penal-welfarism. The more prosperous post-war environment relaxed the thresholds of 'less eligibility' and made available more public funds and social services for this purpose. Given that the most pressing problems of what used to be called 'the deserving poor' had been addressed (or so it was thought) by the development of the welfare state, it now became possible to focus more attention upon the undeserving, disreputable poor, and problem populations such as young delinquents, adult offenders and incarcerated criminals.

So what, in short, were the social and historical conditions that underpinned criminological modernism and the penal-welfare compromise?

A style of governance

Penal-welfare institutions were formed at a particular historical moment in response to a specific problem of order. In their developed form these institutions were associated with a social democratic form of politics and a civic narrative of inclusion, both of which drew their power from the class relations and collective memories that dominated the immediate post-war period in Britain and America. Penal-welfare practices embodied a style of 'social' governance that relied upon forms of social expertise and techniques of rule that were characteristic of welfare state societies. They also embodied the distinctive combination of humanitarian and utilitarian motivations that characterized the relations between ruling groups and the subordinate classes during the development of mass democracy.

A capacity for social control

Although it was not always apparent to their proponents, the effectiveness of penal-welfare agencies depended, in large part, upon the capacity of civil society to control individuals and channel their activities in law-abiding directions. The informal social controls exerted by families, neighbours, and communities, together with the disciplines imposed by schools, workplaces, and other institutions created an everyday environment of norms and sanctions that underpinned the law's demands and provided support for penal-welfare interventions. To the extent that the formal system succeeded in disciplining deviant individuals, or reintegrating them into mainstream society, it did so with the aid of these everyday controls.[52] The correctionalist programme that led to the creation of penal-welfare institutions was launched in a period of historically low crime rates and high levels of informal social control.

An economic context

Penal-welfare policies, like the welfare state itself, were developed against a background of economic conditions that were favourable to welfare provision, public spending, and a measure of redistribution. The sustained economic growth of the post-war decades, the improved standards of living enjoyed by the mass of working people, and the settled experience of full employment delivered by Keynesian demand management, had important, if indirect, consequences for correctionalist institutions and crime control policies. The sense of generalized and growing affluence permitted the relaxation of the 'less eligibility' concerns that typically depress penal conditions. The availability of work, even for unskilled and unreliable individuals, facilitated the resettlement work of probation and parole and gave purpose to the 'treatment and training' programmes of prisons. To the extent that penal-welfare policies required public legitimation, this was forthcoming in an expanding economy, where middle classes derived tangible benefits from public expenditure, and were broadly supportive of welfare policies.

The authority of social expertise

The power and collective influence of certain professional groups was another important condition facilitating the development of correctionalist criminal justice. In important respects, the development of penal-welfarism was the achievement of social and psychiatric professionals and their supporters. It was these groups with their distinctively social mode of regulation who succeeded in establishing a new set of correctional practices, objectives, and forms of expertise in a field that had previously been directed by legal principles and punitive ideals. It was these groups who staffed the key positions in penal-welfare institutions and it was upon their knowledge and expertise that the system increasingly depended for its functioning.

The support of social elites

The active support of political and social elites was crucial for the field's development. Government officials, especially those directly involved with the administration of justice, had to have confidence in the system. And to the extent that they have a role in formulating crime control policy, reforming organizations, academics, and the most influential sectors of the political classes had also to be supportive of such policies. What was important here was not so much support for particular policies—the details of which were usually worked out by administrators and experts without wider consultation—but rather a broad level of support for the *ethos* of penal-welfarism. The idea that there ought to be a rational, detached, 'civilized' approach to offenders, viewing them through categories of social need and citizenship, was an important background condition of the system. So too was its corollary: distaste for an emotive, hostile approach to crime that regarded the phenomenon as a fight against evil or the warding off of danger. From the late nineteenth century onwards, and particularly in the middle years of the twentieth century, these ideas and sensibilities were characteristic of liberal elites and the new middle-class professionals in both America and Britain.

Perceived validity and effectiveness

Like any government activity, penal-welfare institutions depended for their legitimacy upon the perceived integrity and effectiveness of their operations. For most of the twentieth century there was a high level of confidence within the academic and policy-making communities about the validity of correctionalist ideas and the likely effectiveness of properly implemented correctionalist practices. To the extent that the institutions appeared sometimes to be failing in their objectives—when crime rates continued to rise, or treatment resulted in recidivism rather than reform—a plausible narrative was available to explain away these failures. Problems of programme implementation and delivery, lack of trained staff and resources, the persistence of outdated attitudes, and the perennial need for more research and knowledge—all of these could be cited in defence of the system, so long as the basic credibility of the institution and its conceptual framework remained intact.

The absence of any active public or political opposition

Penal-welfare policies were the achievement of professionals and reforming politicians, not the result of any widespread popular movement. Nor did such policies command a great deal of active, popular support. Such evidence as there is suggests that public opinion, even as late as the 1960s, continued to be more punitive and 'traditionalist' than government policies.[53] Penal-welfarism was, for the most part, a policy imposed from above. Importantly, however, it was imposed with very little resistance from below, and no strong demand for any specific alternatives. If the general public was more punitive than its representatives and less convinced by correctionalism than were liberal elites, it was, nevertheless, not especially excited about the issue. Those developing penal-welfare policies could rely on a good deal of public apathy and ignorance. Aside from occasional outcries about outrageous crimes, lenient sentences or notable escapes, there was no very active popular involvement with the crime control politics and no very loud public criticism. As for the day-to-day running of the system, this was largely left to criminal justice personnel.

3

The Crisis of Penal Modernism

In the mid-1970s, support for penal-welfarism began to collapse under the weight of a sustained assault upon its premises and practices. In a matter of a few years, there was a rapid and remarkable shift in penal ideals and philoso-phy—a shift that marked the beginning of a turbulent period of change that has lasted until the present day. Over the following decades this would result in important changes in sentencing law, in the practice of prisons, probation and parole, and in the character of academic and political discourse about crime. This period of change was heralded by the critique of correctionalism and the concerted attack upon indeterminate sentencing and individualized treatment. But these developments soon led to a more fundamental disenchantment—not just with penal-welfare but with the whole criminal justice state in its modern form. The resulting transformation has reconfigured the field of crime control and criminal justice, and reoriented its policies and practices, often in ways that were quite at odds with the original critics' intentions. A movement that initially aimed to enhance prisoners' rights, minimize imprisonment, restrict state power, and end predictive restraint, ultimately ushered in policies that did quite the opposite. How is this strange turn of events to be explained?

These developments are made more puzzling by the fact that they were such a radical departure from the established trajectory of penal development. During the nineteenth and twentieth centuries, periodic bursts of penal reform activity occurred, but they were usually a long time in the making, and addressed problems and institutional shortcomings that were long recognized as such. Legislative action was typically the culmination of a prolonged process of agitation and persuasion, and was largely in keeping with well-established pro-grammes of reform. What is remarkable about the 1970s assault upon correc-tionalism is that far from being the culmination of existing reform programmes it was a sudden turning of progressive opinion against them.

No one could have predicted such an outcome, and no one did. The history of the previous one hundred years had seen the rehabilitative model gradually come to form the orthodox ideology of experts and policy makers and an ever-more important element of criminal justice practice. By the beginning of the 1970s, penal-welfarism and progressive penology were the central structuring elements of the field, and formed the programmatic basis for most policy pro-posals. The sudden critical onslaught, and the rapidity with which it changed the co-ordinates of criminal justice, were experienced by many criminal justice personnel as a bewildering, earth-shaking phenomenon.

If practitioners were caught unawares by the collapse of correctionalism, so too were criminologists and social theorists—though some of the latter provided intellectual and practical support for the turn against the old regime. If predictions had been forthcoming from them, the leading social theories of modernization and rationalization would most likely have predicted the opposite of what subsequently occurred. Writing in the mid-1970s, authors such as Michel Foucault and Michael Ignatieff argued that the correctionalist approach was rooted in the structures of modern Western society. The regulatory state, the structures of discipline and normalization, the ideology of welfarism, the growth of professionalism and research-based social policy, the inclusive politics of mass society—all of these provided supports for correctionalism and underpinned its institutions. If analyses such as these were to be believed, the rehabilitative tendencies of criminal justice appeared to be a part of the modern scheme of things. Correctionalism was an unfolding element of modernity itself, rather than just a fad that might come and go.[1]

And yet it did go. Or, to put it more precisely, it was suddenly dislodged from its central, axiomatic position and made to occupy a quite different and diminished role in subsequent policy and practice. In the course of a few years, the orthodoxies of rehabilitative faith collapsed in virtually all of the developed countries, as reformers and academics, politicians and policy-makers, and finally practitioners and institutional managers came to disassociate themselves from its tenets. With surprising speed, a liberal progressive ideal came to appear reactionary and dangerous to the very groups that had previously championed it. And nowhere was this about-turn more spectacular than in the USA which, until then, had been the nation most fully committed to correctionalist policies and practice.

This development leaves us with a profound problem for historical and sociological analysis: one that raises questions about penal institutions and their dynamics of change, but also about the social arrangements and cultural assumptions within which these penal institutions are grounded. This chapter will examine the details of this penological event and begin the work of historical and sociological explanation. In doing so, it is important to bear in mind that we are faced here with *two* historical problems. These two problems often get run together, but they are in fact quite distinct and they each require separate analysis and explanation. The first is the problem of the initial event: why did the penal-welfare approach suddenly lose its hold on the penological imagination and on institutional practice? This is the problem addressed in the present chapter. The other problem concerns the subsequent set of developments: why did subsequent policies and practices take the form they did? This rather different problem is addressed in the chapters that follow.

The transformation that began in the mid-1970s involved social forces and drew upon ideological resources that were an integral part of the welfare state and the progressive politics of social democracy. In important respects, these criticisms of the penal-welfare field were launched from *within* the basic structures and commitments of the field itself. But as the process of change unfolded in the late 1970s and 1980s, first in the USA, and then in Britain that process came to be dominated by other groups and social forces, and to be characterized by political and penological positions that spoke to quite different social structures, class relations, and cultural experiences. This chapter tells the story of the collapse of the intellectual foundations of the old field, and the immediate criminological causes that brought it about. Subsequent chapters will address the underlying social and cultural changes that made this transformation possible.

The American critiques of correctionalism

In the early 1970s there was a spate of American publications presenting damaging critiques of penal-welfarism and its 'individualized treatment model'. The first and most radical of these was the Report of the Working Party of the American Friends Service Committee—entitled *Struggle for Justice*—which was published in 1971. This Report roundly declared that 'the individualized treatment model, the ideal toward which reformers have been urging us for at least a century, is theoretically faulty, systematically discriminatory in administration, and inconsistent with some of our most basic concepts of justice'.[2] In developing their critique of correctionalism, the academics, activists and ex-prisoners who made up the Working Party explicitly allied themselves with the nascent prisoners rights movement and presented their work as a part of a wider struggle for social, economic, and racial justice. Their political objectives were, in this respect, much more explicit and much more radical than most of the subsequent voices in the debate, just as their proposals for reforming the criminal law were rather less precise. But the Report's powerful statement of its critical themes made a major international impact and set the agenda for the discussions and debates that followed.

The Report's fundamental target was the criminal justice system's discriminatory use of the power to punish, particularly its use of imprisonment, which the report viewed as a tool to repress blacks, the poor, the young and various cultural minorities. According to the Report's authors, this discriminatory use of state power was masked by the operation of the individualized treatment model, which legitimated and extended these abuses, while simultaneously glossing the harsh realities of punishment with a benign, paternalistic veneer. But if the public and practitioners could deceive themselves on this score, those who experienced the system—the prisoners themselves—were unimpressed. The Report talked of a 'low visibility revolution' taking place in the jails and penitentiaries, where strikes and upheavals had already begun, and it warned that 'prisoners will no longer submit to whatever is done to them in the name of "treatment" or "rehabilitation" '.[3]

The Report amounted to a root and branch critique of the criminal justice state and the correctionalist ideology that sustained it. 'Progressive penology' was criticized for its paternalism and hypocrisy, its naive faith that punishment can work useful results, and its willingness to impose 'treatment' in punitive settings, with or without the consent of offenders. The determinist theories and positivistic methods of correctionalist criminology were attacked. So too were its assumptions that violations of the criminal law are symptomatic of individual pathology and that the customs of the white middle classes are synonymous with the norms of social health. Above all, the Report mounted a critical assault on the discretionary penal power embodied in indeterminate, treatment-oriented sentencing and predictive restraint. This power—'awesome in scope and by its nature uncontrollable'—was systematically used in discriminatory, repressive ways that were dictated by the control needs of penal institutions or the political interests of the ruling class.

The programme of reform that the Report outlined was schematic and exhortatory rather than a well-drafted plan for legal change. Its penological demands were for restraints upon the state's power to punish—narrowing sentencing criteria to deal only with the criminal act, abolishing individualized sentencing in favour of uniform, proportionate penalties; minimizing punishments to the least costly, least harmful sanctions; and establishing a 'prisoners' bill of rights'. Its broader, political solutions emphasized 'social and economic change', the 'empowerment' of oppressed communities and abused groups, and 'getting the criminal justice system off our backs' through decriminalization and the use of voluntary, non-state methods for dealing with social problems. Finally, it proposed that 'a full range of therapy, counseling, and psychiatric and educational services be made available, free, on a voluntary basis, to the entire population, inside prisons and on the street'.[4]

The striking thing about this first major assault upon the penal-welfarism is the extent to which it was launched from *within* the framework of welfarist, social democracy, albeit a radicalized version thereof. As its prescriptions for action make clear, it continued to view crime as a product of social and economic deprivation, and looked to the state to provide the social reforms and welfare support needed to address this social problem. What radicalized the document, and differentiated it from the critical texts that preceded it, was a distinctive set of critical themes. A deep distrust of state power; a profound cynicism about professional motives; an insistence that treatment ought not to be bound up with punishment; a concern for the 'self-determination' and 'empowerment' of the poor and minority groups who formed the clientele of penal-welfare institutions—these were the hallmarks of this new critique.

In formulating its heretical claims, the Friends' Report drew upon criminological sources as well as upon the wider culture of 1960s civil rights radicalism and anti-war protest. Many of its theoretical points had already been made within academic criminology which, in an expanding higher education sector, had become less dependent upon the institutions of criminal justice and increasingly critical of conventional practice. By the end of the 1960s, a new style of sociological criminology had begun to distance itself from older theories that took crime to be the product of deprivation and pathology. These new 'sociologies of deviance' represented crime as a rational, meaningful form of action, the deviant status of which was negotiated rather than intrinsic. In their increasingly influential terms, the category of 'deviance' was a product of power relations rather than individual pathology. The *Struggle for Justice* Report effectively transformed this new theoretical perspective into a forceful critique of correctionalist practice.[5]

The authors' experience in the civil rights movement had brought home to them the pervasiveness of class and race discrimination in American society. This, together with experience of the harsh treatment of civil rights or anti-war protesters meted out by the police, highlighted the arbitrary, coercive potential of the criminal justice state and its uses as a tool of political oppression.[6] In effect, the new critique of rehabilitation was the extension of civil rights claims to the field of criminal justice, a process that had already begun with the Warren Court of the 1960s and its extension of due process protections to suspects and juveniles. It was also a forceful restatement of the values of legalism—a set of values that played a residual but continuing role in the penal-welfare field as the subordinate tradition in the compromise between social and legal modes of regulation. Many of the concerns expressed by the Report—about the abasement of the rehabilitative ideal in institutional practice, or the problem of unrestricted discretion—merely restated in more forceful terms points that had previously been made by writers such as Francis Allen and Kenneth Culp Davis. The difference was that Allen and Davis had been friendly critics of the system: the Report's authors were its outright opponents.[7]

The Report's argument against compulsory penal treatment embodied a concern for individual dignity and freedom of expression—a theme that played a prominent part of the youth culture in the 1960s. It was a protest against the politics of conformity, and against the tendency of big government and bureaucratic organizations to crush individuality, whether by coercive means or by expert persuasion. Concern for authenticity, for 'the little man' and his right to be different, and a fear of the authoritarian potential of government and of science, linked the Report with a powerful cultural current of its time. One sees these same motifs in popular novels and films of the period such as *A Clockwork Orange* or *One Flew Over the Cuckoos Nest*. One also sees it in the work of philosophers of punishment, some of whom reacted against the prevailing correctionalist brand of utilitarianism by reasserting the importance of individual moral integrity and the autonomy of the subject. The paradox, they argued, was that in the modern state, individualistic values were better protected by retributive punishment than by an invasive correctionalism that pressed everyone into conformity.[8]

To claim, in 1971, that the rehabilitative approach was ineffective when judged against its own criteria of recidivism reduction and crime prevention, was an act of criminological heresy. To state that the approach lacked any grounding in scientific knowledge, had no reliable diagnostic techniques, nor any generally effective treatment techniques was to argue, even more provocatively, that the established orthodoxy was based on a tissue of myths and falsehoods. But even this outrageous assertion did not come from nowhere. Rather, it drew upon a series of negative findings and evaluation studies, particularly about the impact of prison-based correctional programmes, that had been accumulating in the field for some time but which had been ignored because of their disturbing, paradigm-threatening character. The Report's outright rejection of the treatment model—a politically motivated position that was until then highly unusual in progressive circles—allowed it to re-interpret these results not as anomalies and soon-to-be-overcome limitations, but as empirical evidence of the model's fundamental deficiencies.

In the next few years, the themes of *The Struggle for Justice* were taken up and echoed in a more mainstream vein by a welter of publications voicing objections to existing arrangements. The empirical evidence of treatment failure was summarized in 1974 by Robert Martinson in a widely read and endlessly cited article in *The Public Interest* entitled 'What Works in Prison Reform?' On the basis of an analysis of 231 evaluation studies dating from the period 1945 to 1967, Martinson offered the devastating conclusion that '[w]ith few and isolated exceptions, the rehabilitative efforts that have been reported so far have had no appreciable effect on recidivism'. Before long, Martinson's findings were widely viewed as conclusive empirical evidence of the system's failure and became the basis for the claim that 'Nothing Works'. This overstated and somewhat nihilistic view was lent further credence by a series of research reports, including a number of UK government publications. Within a few years it was to become the new conventional wisdom.[9]

In 1973, Jessica Mitford published a wry account of the American prison system that brought the critique of prisons and rehabilitation to a wide public audience—an audience already primed for negative news by the publicity surrounding the 1971 Attica prison riot and its aftermath. The next year, Norval Morris, one of America's most prominent criminologists and a long-time supporter of the rehabilitative model, acknowledged the force of the emerging critique. His book, *The Future of Imprisonment* sought to temper the impact of criticism by limiting the discretionary powers of sentencers and uncoupling the processes of treatment from the decision to release.[10]

Perhaps unsurprisingly, in a society closely attuned to due process rights and problems of discrimination, the critical position that attracted the widest support was the attack upon indeterminate sentencing and the discretionary powers it conferred. In a series of widely read essays, and in his 1972 book *Criminal Sentences: Law Without Order*, Judge Marvin Frankel argued for legal controls on sentencing discretion—for an end to 'justice without law'. This demand for sentencing law reform was taken up and developed by Andrew von Hirsch in *Doing Justice: The Choice of Punishments—The Report of the Committee for the Study of Incarceration* and also by *Fair and Certain Punishment*, the report of the Twentieth-Century Fund Task Force, both of which were published in 1976. These reports argued for the repeal of indeterminate sentencing laws; restrictions on the use of parole; fixed-term, proportionate sanctions geared to the offence and not the offender; and 'presumptive sentencing' guidelines that would guide judicial decision-making and reduce sentencing disparity. The same kinds of criticisms and counter-proposals were to be found in Morris's book and in David Fogel, *We Are The Living Proof . . . the Justice Model of Corrections* (published in 1975) with the significant difference that Morris was prepared to leave some discretion to judges and parole boards, and both he and Fogel saw a role for the predictive restraint of 'dangerous' offenders. Such propositions were flatly rejected by the 'just deserts' retributivism advocated by Von Hirsch and the committee that produced *Doing Justice*.[11]

Unlike most other critical works, which continued to speak from within a utilitarian framework, albeit one which now emphasized doing less harm rather than doing more good, *Doing Justice* explicitly endorsed a *retributivist* philosophy of punishment. It stressed the moral superiority of proportional, backward-looking punishments—'just deserts'—and the immoral, authoritarian dangers of penal measures based upon predictions of future criminality, or upon evaluations of the individual's character and mode of life. For the first time in decades, and in stark contrast to the prevailing orthodoxy, a prominent work of penology argued a general case for retributive punishment as an end in itself.[12] The book's other novel feature—one that would quickly become a staple of sentencing law discourse and practice—was the appearance of a rudimentary sentencing grid: a two axis matrix that plotted a grid of presumptive sentences by reference to one axis measuring current offence scores and another measuring prior offending.[13] Over the next two decades, a major focus of penological discussion would be the elaboration of this revived retributivism and technical details of its application to sentencing law and practice.

James Q. Wilson echoed this new call for fixed and certain punishment in 1975 in his best-selling book *Thinking About Crime* but his work gave a very different meaning to the idea of determinate sentence reform.[14] In stark contrast to the American Friends, Wilson was scornful of attempts to reduce crime through social programs or economic redistribution, and a forceful proponent of the neo-conservative approach to social issues. He did express doubts about the fairness and utility of individualized treatments, and he heartily endorsed the idea of fixed-term punishments. But his concern was not to ensure 'just deserts' or 'minimize state power'. Instead he wanted to hold out deterrent penalties that would be rigorously enforced and tough enough to act as real disincentives to potential offenders. Better, more vigorous policing and harsher, more certain punishments were his preferred solution: more deterrence and control, not more welfare. Like Ernest Van Den Haag, whose book *Punishing Criminals* appeared the following year, Wilson insisted that American crime rates were high because the prospects of being caught, convicted and severely punished had become very low. He argued that deterrent considerations should fix the general level of sentencing and that dangerous or repetitive criminals should be subjected to extra-long, incapacitative sentences and, in some cases to death. These proposals were, of course, utterly anathema to the liberal authors who had begun the campaign for fixed-sentence reform.[15]

The impact on policy and practice in America and Britain

The movement for determinate sentencing reform created an unusually broad and influential alliance of forces. The campaign included not only radical supporters of the prisoners' movement, liberal lawyers and reforming judges, but also retributivist philosophers, disillusioned criminologists and hard-line conservatives. Moreover, its reach extended beyond the United States to influence thinking in the UK, where books and articles soon began to appear embracing the rehabilitative critique and endorsing the retributivist alternative.[16] Within a few years, the movement achieved a series of practical successes, most notably the passing of a 1976 determinate sentencing law in California—the state where indeterminate sentencing and individualized treatment regimes had been best established. In the next few years other states began to follow this pattern— most notably Minnesota which established a sentencing commission and closely adhered to the 'just deserts' proposals of *Doing Justice* report. Over the next two decades, fifteen states established sentencing guidelines, ten eliminated parole, and twenty-five enacted parole guidelines.[17] In 1970 all of the US states had indeterminate sentencing laws. In the thirty years since, nearly every state has in some way repudiated this, bringing about a major transformation in sentencing policy and practice. Other countries also adopted the 'just deserts' rationale, giving it a more explicit and more central place in official policy, as evidenced most notably by the British government's 1990 White Paper, *Crime, Justice and Protecting the Public* and the Criminal Justice Act of 1991.[18]

But sentencing was by no means the only area of practice affected. In Britain and America, prison officials from the late 1970s onwards began to de-emphasize the provision of treatment programs and the 'rehabilitative' aims of imprisonment and, for a time, were attracted to what came to be known as the 'justice model of corrections'. Funding for treatment programs and for treatment-oriented research was cut in the 1980s. Probation and parole staff began to rethink their mission in terms in non-treatment terms, at first stressing client support and provision, and later emphasizing the control and monitoring functions of probation. Legislation was passed that re-introduced due process considerations to juvenile courts, shifting the balance back towards a criminal process and away from the welfare and correctionalist ideologies that had dominated in the 1960s and 1970s.[19]

The legislative and practical changes that followed in the wake of this reform movement were often markedly inconsistent with the goals that had been set out by its initial proponents. In the last quarter of the twentieth century, the most popular American 'sentencing reform'—adopted in every state of the US as well as the Federal system—was the introduction of mandatory minimum sentences, a measure that played no part in the original 'just deserts' movement. And for every state such as Minnesota that took the liberal just deserts principles seriously, and endeavoured to increase fairness and uniformity without simultaneously increasing the use of imprisonment, there were many more that established sentencing structures that were more punitive and more incarcerative than before. The concern to replace indeterminate sentencing with more fixed and certain penalties gave rise to sentencing commissions and proportionate sentencing guidelines. But more frequently it resulted in mandatory minimum sentencing laws and sharply increased levels of imprisonment.[20] Over time, the liberal concern with just deserts, proportionality and minimizing penal coercion gave way to more hard-line policies of deterrence, predictive restraint and incapacitation, and eventually to expressive, exemplary sentencing and mass imprisonment—policies that were completely at odds with principles and intentions of the original liberal reformers. In much the same way, the critique of the prison and its correctional failures at first encouraged greater use of community corrections, and experiments with decarceration and decriminalization. But in later years, the disillusionment with prison's reformatory potential prepared the way for a rather different vision of imprisonment that stressed its effectiveness as a means of unalloyed punishment and long-term incapacitation.[21]

'Nothing works': The spread of the failure model

The collapse of faith in correctionalism began a wave of demoralization that undermined the credibility of key institutions of crime control, and, at least for a period, of the whole criminal justice system. During the late 1970s and 1980s the demoralizing influence of what David Rothman called 'the failure model' spread into most areas of criminal justice. Influenced by negative research reports and increasing crime rates, but also by a pervasive sense of disillusionment and pessimism, one institution after another began to be viewed as ineffective or counter-productive. First used in relation to prison-based treatment programmes, the notion that 'nothing works' came to be applied to other measures such as probation, intensive probation, community corrections, and, more generally, deterrent sentencing. From the late 1970s onwards, there was also a powerful body of opinion critical of the various social policies and job creation programmes that had been supposed to prevent crime as well as enhance welfare. The view came to be that 'treatment' simply did not work, whether it took the form of individual therapy or broader social programmes.[22]

Scepticism about the effectiveness of criminal justice soon affected policing as well. Widely cited research findings in the USA suggested that the police were much less good at preventing, deterring and apprehending criminals than was previously assumed. Studies such as the Kansas City preventive police experiment showed the limited impact of increasing police expenditures and patrols, and the limited impact of most routine policing. Heal and others reported similar findings in the UK and the Home Office published startling information about the rarity with which the police come across street crimes as they actually occur—on average, the report claimed, a police officer will do so only once every eight years.[23]

Before long, this sense of limited effectiveness and underachievement began to affect the whole criminal justice system, creating a demoralization that the new evidence from victim surveys did nothing to dispel. By the mid-1980s it was common to hear government officials point to the very limited extent to which criminal justice interventions made any impact at all upon crime. The Home Office frequently cited data to the effect that only 2 to 3 per cent of known offences actually resulted in a criminal sanction of any kind, and most of these were merely cautions or fines. This 'funnel effect' of the criminal justice system—first described by the Presidents Commission report in 1967—now became common knowledge as more and more experts came to view the system as largely a failure in the fight against crime.

Despite the fact that it was a thriving academic discipline, expanding its hold on the academy and producing more research and publications than ever before, criminology was also affected by this sense of having failed. Criminology's basic project—that of discovering the causes of crime and identifying means whereby it might be reduced—was increasingly viewed as having failed to produce anything worthwhile. This criticism was made most tellingly by the conservative writer James Q. Wilson who publicly despaired of criminology's inability to overcome its (left-liberal) ideological preoccupations and doubted its capacity to develop the kind of concrete, practical knowledge needed by policy-makers. But the same kind of view was also heard from other points on the ideological spectrum. Jock Young, a leading criminological radical, pointed to the 'aetiological crisis' of modern criminology—its failure to establish reliable causal accounts—and John Croft, the former head of the Home Office's criminological research unit, declared in 1981 that 'Criminological research . . . has been a failure.'[24]

As we will see in later chapters, this pervasive sense of failure, fuelled by the sharply increasing crime rates of the 1970s and 1980s, would eventually lead to a questioning of the state's ability to control crime and a rethinking of the role of criminal justice. It would prompt the emergence of new forms of criminology, a new crime control agenda, and a new understanding of the relation between state and non-state activities in the crime control field. But its most immediate effect was to create a kind of ideological vacuum in the criminal policy sphere. Rehabilitation and correctionalism did not disappear, but their stock was drastically depreciated. By the end of the 1970s no one could unabashedly support the old model: to do so was to appear out of touch, to endorse failure, to open oneself to attack from all sides. And yet there was no developed, alternative framework ready to take its place. The result was a tumultuous period of legislative activity in which a clashing multitude of new programmes and policy proposals developed to fill the void. Instead of being the highpoint of a century-long correctionalist project, the late 1970s became the ground zero for a newly contested field of crime control.

The assault on individualized treatment opened the floodgates for a period of change that has been with us ever since. It was the opening phase of a transformative process that has brought about major changes in institutions, ideas, and practices across the whole crime control field. Yet if we pause to consider what this means, we seem to be suggesting something rather unlikely. Is it really the case that a series of critical publications—most of them written by authors with no great standing in the criminological field, at a time when library shelves were laden with correctional literature—could so thoroughly destabilize the whole edifice of the penal-welfare state? Certainly that is now the standard account—the one the textbooks and general histories set out to explain the historical reorientation of crime policy.[25] But can critical assessments really have been so effective here when they seem to have so little effect elsewhere? One thinks, for example, of the critical literature on imprisonment, where devastating criticism and negative findings have for centuries accompanied the practice to no very great effect. To put matters in this way strongly suggests that the standard historical account is decidedly out of balance. How did these critical interventions come to have such major consequences? How could it be that a series of critiques could set off such a serious chain reaction? How could a few academics prompt an institutional structure to collapse like a house of cards?

The limits of the standard account

Raymond Aron once observed that major historical events are always 'born of general causes [and] completed as it were, by accidents.' Only the most superficial analysis would therefore seek to explain such an event in the currency of contingent actions without reference to more fundamental historical processes.[26] And yet the standard account of recent penal change attributes this major event to the impact of a series of published criticisms. The received wisdom today focuses upon criticisms that were directed at the correctionalist model and assumes that these attacks were sufficient to undermine the model's viability. The assumption is that such was the power of the critical arguments suddenly arrayed against the penal-welfare regime that it simply collapsed in the face of overwhelmingly negative assessment. If one takes a closer look, however, there is reason to doubt that the field's sudden and continued disruption can be adequately explained in this way.

For one thing, there were professional interests at stake, and an extensive infrastructure of practice and belief that would not normally be overturned by the force of academic criticism or contrary ideas. For another, the theoretical, philosophical and political criticisms levelled at rehabilitation in the 1960s and 1970s were not newly discovered objections: these arguments had formed a constant refrain accompanying correctionalist proposals ever since the nineteenth century. It was precisely because correctionalist proponents had succeeded in persuading policy-makers that such criticisms were groundless, or could be put aside in exchange for other benefits, that penal-welfarism had been established in the first place.[27]

The notion that rehabilitation was abandoned because critics woke up one day and realized that it had dangerous possibilities and was prone to being abused is a modern version of the fairy story of Enlightenment reform. In his history of torture and the law of proof, John Langbein describes as a 'fairy story' the account offered by historians when they claim that the abolition of torture came about as a result of the moral critiques developed by Enlightenment thinkers. Against this standard account, Langbein argues that torture was abandoned in the late eighteenth century not because of the *philosophes*' critical writings, but because of institutional and cultural circumstances that gave these writings a contextual power that had not been present when previous writers had made the same criticisms. This is an explanatory lesson that should be borne in mind when thinking about the collapse of correctionalism.[28]

It might be objected that although criticisms of a theoretical or political kind may not have been new, the negative empirical findings were, and that these were sufficient to rob rehabilitation of its appeal and tilt the balance of opinion against it. This is more persuasive, and certainly these empirical findings weighed heavily with officials and policy makers. But there are reasons to be sceptical about this interpretation too:

First, negative research findings have been produced by evaluative research ever since the 1930s. Such findings had previously been used to adjust and refine treatment regimes—for example, by improving selection and classification procedures—rather than to throw doubt on the idea of treatment itself.[29]

Secondly, the findings that were available in the mid-1970s were by no means unequivocal. Even Martinson's tendentious summary of the literature identified some successes here and there and subsequent re-analyses of his data produced more sanguine interpretations. In fact, Martinson soon retracted and reformulated many of his original claims, though this retraction received little publicity and was largely ignored. In the circumstances, it would certainly have been possible to mount a strong counter-critique of Martinson's methods of meta-analysis and of the unrealistic evaluation standards that he applied. Some such criticisms were made at the time, but they did not command attention until much later.[30]

Thirdly, as we saw in the previous chapter, there was a whole stock of responses available to defenders of the status quo that could have been used to fend off criticism. Rehabilitation was under-funded; its impact was undermined by custodial and punitive contexts; there was a need for more staff training, better inmate selection, more individualization, more follow-up, and so on and so forth. It could have been claimed that rehabilitative institutions were victims of their own success: that they had beeen unwarrantably generalized, applied to all kinds of offenders whether they were suitable for treatment or not. In other words, it would have been quite possible to define the problem as one of implementation failure—a view for which there was boundless evidence and much professional support, and one that had previously allowed officials successfully to finesse their failures. As for problems of fairness or civil liberties, it would have a simple matter to develop safeguards and limited reforms without abandoning the overall framework—which is precisely what was proposed by leading figures such as Norval Morris in America and Nigel Walker in Britain.[31]

Of course rises in the recorded rates of crime and violence and new evidence (from self-report and victim surveys) about the generality of deviance made it harder to argue that the status quo was working well. But criminologists could point to the effect of demographic factors, or to changes in reporting and recording practices, or to the need for still greater efforts in respect of social prevention and therapeutic intervention. And in any case, if the penal-welfare system was fairing badly in this respect there was no evidence that alternative approaches would do a better job. Had these defences been fully mobilized, one might have expected them to prevail, at least to the extent of warding off radical change. It is, after all, notoriously difficult to overcome the inertia of an institutional system once it has become established. But these defences were not widely adopted, and where they were adopted, they were not widely successful. How can we account for this? Why were the penal-welfare defences so weak? What internal and external developments undermined that framework and empowered the forces that attacked it?

The changing character of academic criminology

When the critique of penal-welfarism crystallized in the middle years of the 1970s there already existed a series of currents in academic criminology that resonated powerfully with the new movement. These criminological developments had intellectual and institutional roots of their own that were quite distinct from those of the reform movement, but they meshed together smoothly, and in time, came to seem part of the same critical reaction to the penal-welfare system.

In the late 1960s, in both the US and the UK, 'positivist' criminology faced an onslaught of academic criticism, drawing upon sources as disparate as labelling theory and ethnomethodology, Marxism and the philosophy of science. In the relative freedom of expanding academic departments, and in a cultural milieu becoming critical of the ideas of expert authority and value consensus upon which positivist criminology relied, criminologists began to reconnect their subject-matter with the larger and more critical traditions of sociological theorizing. They also began to re-evaluate and redescribe the problem of crime in ways that were quite different from traditional criminology—less a problem of individual or social pathology, more a matter of labelling and media-generated moral panics, or else of power relations and insufficient tolerance for healthy diversity. The generality of deviance was, in the 1960s, an increasingly acknowledged social fact, made visible by self-report studies, the experience of the juvenile court, and by new patterns of youth culture that were regarded as deviant by older generations.[32] This, together with the experience of the civil rights and anti-war movement, prompted younger sociologists to identify more closely with deviants and misfits and to adopt a more 'appreciative' stance towards them. The actions of offenders were to be regarded as meaningful, worthy of analysis and perhaps even respect, just as in radical welfare politics, the voices of the poor and the claimant were beginning, for the first time, to be heard. American writers such as David Matza, Howard Becker, and Edwin Lemert and their counterparts in the National Deviancy Conference in Britain problematized the status of deviance and crime and the official processes of reaction and control. They focused attention upon offence behaviour which was ambiguous in its meaning and morality—crimes without victims, lifestyle and sexual offences, soft drugs, minor delinquency—and argued that these problems were constructed by the very control processes that were designed to deal with them. From the viewpoint of this new sociology of deviance much criminal conduct was in fact normal, healthy, and widely enjoyed—expressive of human diversity, not dangerous pathology. The real problem lay in overzealous control, not in the deviance itself.

This radical criminology, so influential in academic circles in the late 1960s and 1970s, has a cultural and historical significance that is worth remarking on. Although its appearance coincides with some of the fastest rising crime rates recorded in the twentieth century, many of its themes appear quite disconnected from that phenomenon in several respects. That it could, in spite of this, be so influential in academic circles suggests that fear of crime was much less widespread then than it subsequently became, and that it had little salience for the young, educated middle classes who formed its primary audience. In the late 1960s and early 1970s, it was still possible to regard popular crime anxieties as largely a media-engendered phenomenon—as 'moral panics'. It was also possible, for this criminological literature largely to disregard hard core crime—robbery, burglary, assault, rape, homicide—and to focus instead upon those forms of deviance that were most contested in meaning and least clear in the social harm they produced.

In retrospect, the radical labelling theories look like a first acknowledgement that crime is normal, that deviance is endemic, that 'everyone does it'. And what is most interesting about this, and most characteristic, is that it is an *unworried* reaction. Its message was that deviance and illegality were widespread but that one could live with them. The best reaction was to be tolerant, to play it down, to refuse to overreact. 'Crime' so it was implied, was not the problem. 'Control'—state repression, but also well-intended, paternalistic, welfare-style control—was the problem to which we should attend. Like the counter-cultural movement of the 1960s whose concerns it closely echoed, the new criminology's central theme was expressive freedom and the liberation of individuals from arbitrary authority. Thoughts of security and public safety, of fear of crime and concern for its victims, had little prominence in this literature.[33]

The new criminologists—and their allies in the radical social work and radical psychiatry movement—engaged in a critique of their own academic discipline and challenged the expert credentials that had been the basis of the criminologist's authority. To most occupational groups, in most periods, this would look like professional suicide. In the context of new-found academic freedom, political idealism and cultural radicalism, such considerations were largely disregarded. At that historical moment, few radical writers worried too much about hostages to fortune, or the reactionary uses of radical arguments. Instead, they mounted an attack on the institutional epistemology of the criminological mainstream, showing the limits of its social vision and the patronizing cast of its reformist politics. Out of this audacious critical move came some of the most insightful and powerful writing ever produced on crime and punishment, and an intellectual tradition that lives on to this day. But the political consequences of this move, at least in the medium term, were the reverse of what its proponents had intended.

These radical criticisms turned out to be a transition point in the history of crime policy. They marked, despite themselves, the highpoint of a certain long-term development. Like their American counterparts, the Friends Service Committee, the British radicals were mostly committed to the goals as penal-welfarism, to the same social values, only more so. They pushed the welfare aspect to its limits, and were impatient with the failures of the welfare state to deliver its promise of equal opportunity social justice, individual, freedom, and citizenship rights for all. This younger generation of writers and academics—many of them the product of the welfare state's extended access to further education, all of them heirs to decades of post-war prosperity and rising expectations—was characterized by a strong idealism and radicalism. They embraced a critical, democratic culture that questioned all restrictions on freedom and individual expression, and assumed the mantle of critical intellectuals deploring the system of which they formed a part. When they studied criminal justice they measured it in terms of their radical social ideals, not in terms of its distance from the more punitive reality of the recent past. In the face of the system's rather shabby reality, and the shakiness of its rehabilitative claims, they mostly dismissed correctionalism as a dangerous sham.

For the most part, radical criminology was an intellectual development with no large constituency outside of the academy, but its critical themes chimed perfectly with the political critiques of criminal justice that came into being in the USA (and later in the UK) at the start of the 1970s.[34] This elective affinity between critical theory and practical critique made it possible for young criminologists to take up positions that would have been anathema to most members of their discipline only a decade before. In a remarkably brief period of time, 'progressive' academics went from being a natural constituency of support for penal-welfarism to being devastating critics of it. At precisely the point when defenders of correctionalism were forced back to first principles, these principles were being decisively undermined by their erstwhile academic proponents.[35]

This is especially important when we recall that the penal-welfare program was primarily supported by the knowledge class professionals who ran it. Its main constituency was a set of occupational groups of recent origin and uncertain social standing, supported by a liberal establishment. Such groups were particularly vulnerable to changes in knowledge, or to the discrediting of their specific claims to expertise. Unlike other aspects of welfare state policy, such as pensions, or social security, or health care, or educational provision, the mass of the public derived no immediate benefit from penal-welfare institutions. On the contrary, the public might feel itself to be ill served by a system that was too lenient or ineffective. For the most part, the middle classes and the working classes had no stake in the system. Correctional policies had been passively tolerated by these sections of the public, not demanded or enthusiastically supported by them. What had been tolerable in a period of progressive growth and liberal optimism, with low crime rates and confidence in penal reform, was vulnerable, in a different climate, to being viewed as an indulgent and counterproductive waste of public money. In this context, the disaffection of the professional groups who served the system could have very significant consequences.

Reflexivity

If the shifting allegiances of progressive criminologists were a challenge to the status quo, they became more destabilizing still when taken together with the negative research findings that their fellow criminologists were producing. A distinctive feature of late twentieth-century crime control, when compared with earlier eras, is its high level of reflexivity. Over time, criminal justice agencies developed mechanisms designed to monitor their own practices, and subject them to controlled evaluation. Indeed it is one of the ironies of penal-welfarism, with its stress on the use of social scientific knowledge, that this commitment has generated a large body of evidence pointing to the system's failures. Much of the criminological research that has been undertaken in the twentieth century, and most of that which is directly funded by government, is devoted to this form of reflexive monitoring. The irony is that the empirical findings of these inquiries often tended to undermine the premises upon which they (and the penal-welfare institutions) were based. In the late nineteenth century and for much of the twentieth, correctionalist reformers could be bullish in their attitudes and promise positive results. By the 1970s the system was sufficiently longstanding and sufficiently reflexive to be judged in terms of its actual results, not the hopes and expectations of its supporters.

At the same time there was an accumulating experience of the system's potential for abuse. Correctional practices that looked attractive in theory turned out to have unexpected problems in practice. Those who were supposed to benefit from the system turned out to be far from grateful. Liberal reformers in particular were surprised to find that their progressive system was often despised by its supposed 'beneficiaries'. By the late 1960s then, all the ingredients existed to produce a major review of the correctionalist model and its implications, But a critical reassessment is one thing, a full-scale rejection is another. We still have to explain why these various elements were interpreted, as they were, as *theory-failure* rather than something less profound. What made wholesale rejection more practical than piecemeal reform?

The form of the reaction

Perhaps we should be literal in these matters. Perhaps we should see the 'collapse of faith' in rehabilitation as being literally that: not a reasoned criticism, not an adjustment to negative findings, but something akin to a stockmarket crash. That confidence in the system could so suddenly collapse in this way suggests that the structural underpinnings of the system were already seriously eroded. The over-emphatic character of the reaction also suggests that this dramatic change of heart was overdetermined, that it was motivated by conscious or unconscious considerations that lay beyond the immediate issues. There was, in the turn against correctionalism, something of a hysterical disproportion between the problem and the response, an overreaction that seems almost symptomatic in its vehemence. Such a reaction ought perhaps to be diagnosed rather than merely explained.

One piece of evidence for this view is the character of the 'Nothing Works!' sentiment that became so commonplace in the late 1970s and 1980s. This aggressively disappointed reaction, with its emphatic overstatement of negative data and its suppression of all contrary evidence, was less an informed view of the system than a cathartic reaction to the problems and conflicts the system entailed. That such an emotive overreaction could so quickly become conventional wisdom suggests there were other interests and emotions involved in shaping this response—forces that had little time for criminological details or the careful interpretation of empirical research.

Perhaps some of the extremity of the reaction can be understood as the righteous anger of the disillusioned. Just as revolutions occur on the back of rising expectations that are suddenly thwarted, reactions of a major kind occur when a programme with high expectations produces disappointing results. There is a dialectic of hubris and nemesis, of unrealistic optimism, and downcast despair. Glowing expectations and vaulting ambition are followed close behind by overstated criticism and nihilistic despondency. But in this instance, the dialectic of rehabilitation's rise and fall seems to be linked into a wider history. As we will see, it carries with it the force of a reaction not just against professional society and the welfare state, but against more general ideals such as the utopias of social engineering, the perfectability of man, and the rationalist faith of the Enlightenment.

A second indication of the disproportionate nature of the reaction is the way that it tended to spread indiscriminately, influencing areas where it seemed far from practically relevant. Academics and practitioners in the UK were deeply influenced by the American movement, and before long monographs and text-books repeated word for word the critiques borrowed from the USA—despite the fact that correctionalism was much less well developed in UK law and prac-tice, and the abuses that could be laid at its door were consequently fewer. In the British setting, with its less frequent use of indeterminate sentencing, its more muted problems of race and discrimination, and with most of its prisoners serv-ing their time in local prisons that lacked any rehabilitative character or intent, the critique was for the most part a caricature. But still it resonated none the less. And before long it found its way into government documents and the com-mon-sense of prison governors and probation workers.[36] A reason for this, no doubt, is academic fashion and the law of imitation. But somehow the force of the critique was sustained—even if critics had to rely upon worst case scenarios, look at the most sinister potential of a programme rather than its actual effects, omit variation and local detail, and altogether ignore the existence of counter-vailing forces and safeguards.[37] This strongly suggests that the reaction against penal-welfarism was not based solely upon penological considerations and that it had some further source of resonance and appeal.

The third symptom to notice is the specific language of opposition and the formal rhetorical qualities of the critical arguments. On close inspection, it becomes apparent that the anti-correctional arguments are a classic instance of what Albert Hirschman has called 'the rhetoric of reaction'. According to Hirschman, the history of political reaction against the French Revolution, against universal suffrage, and against the welfare state, reveals the existence of a recurring rhetoric that organizes the form typically adopted by the 'reac-tionary' opponents of an established set of 'progressive' reforms. Typically, the rhetoric of reaction attacks the existing system in its fundamentals. It assumes a total opposition rather than a reforming or a refining critique, intended not to repair the system but to discredit and reject it. Hirschman shows that three key theses recur again and again in reactionary discourse—the claims of perversity, futility, and jeopardy.[38] Each of these theses was prominent in the oppositional movement that grew around the penal-welfare system:

A *perversity thesis*. Correctionalism produces perverse and unintended out-comes. It makes offenders worse not better. Rehabilitative policies bring about a rise in crime not a reduction. *'Everything backfires.'*

A *futility thesis*. Correctionalism will always fail. It isn't possible to reform people or to bring about correctional change. Rehabilitative efforts are futile and wasteful. *'Nothing works.'*

A *jeopardy thesis*. Correctionalist practices undermine fundamental values such as moral autonomy, the rights of the individual, due process and the rule of law. Rehabilitative policies jeopardize cherished liberal democratic values. *'Justice is in jeopardy.'*

Taken together, this is a set of indictments that strikes at the foundations of the field. It is literally, *reactionary*. If we are to understand the shift in crime control we must explain the character of this reaction and the vehemence it entailed.

The fourth and final indication of this 'motivated hostility' and of underlying, displaced conflicts has to do with the substance rather than the form of the various critiques that formed against correctionalism. These were not coherent, singular rebuttals of the logic of rehabilitation that together formed an unanswerable case. Rather, they were miscellaneous clusters of quite different criticisms, some of which were well founded, others of which were not. They added up to a mutually inconsistent ragbag of direct negatives, rather than a reasoned counter-argument. In normal circumstances, and in the absence of other social forces, this incoherence would have made it easier to resist the critical challenge. Defenders of the status quo could have prised apart the contradictory claims, the incompatible premises and the implied policy prescriptions and shown that they lead nowhere positive. They could have argued that the negative vectors cancel each other out. A rehabilitative measure cannot be too lenient *and* too oppressive. Penal-welfarism cannot be ineffectual *and* authoritarian. Professional power cannot be tamed merely by shifting it from one professional group to another. Sentencing guidelines can satisfy their liberal or their conservative proponents but not both. And so on and so forth. But these were not normal circumstances, and as we will see in subsequent chapters, other social forces were not absent.

What gave this complex of critical discourses its strength was not its intellectual power as a criminological position but rather its knotted together strength as a reactionary movement. The (negative) fact of objecting to rehabilitation united left, right and centre, liberal, radical, and conservative.[39] The power of the opposition lay not in its ability to refute the orthodox theory but in its ability to create a momentary alliance of the accumulated enemies of the now established penal-welfare approach. It was a kind of catharsis—a pouring forth of the discontents of the penal-welfare state—directed against a new establishment that had been a long time in the making and which had been erected in the face of deep misgivings and contrary interests.

This critical movement obviously derived strength from its political echoes. It resonated with, and borrowed from, the wider rhetoric of reaction against the welfare state. But the form of the reaction—its intemperate tone, its overreaction, its refusal to reason and compromise, to seek to reform and repair the rehabilitative practices—suggest that something more was at stake. It suggests deeper forces at work: changing cultural commitments, changing social structures, changing political alliances and viewpoints. In these circumstances, basic presuppositions came to be questioned. What was placed in doubt was not just the effectiveness of particular policies, but the basic capacity of the state to control crime and to promote welfare.

Finally, there is a fundamental question. Why was it that the changes that followed the destabilization of the old framework did not embody the critics' own preferences and values, but turned out to be so different? As I noted earlier, some of the new measures were precisely the opposite of those originally proposed by rehabilitation's critics. The principled opposition to predictive restraint did not envisage the emergence of 'incapacitation' as the central goal of sentencing. The claim that rehabilitation was overly coercive did not imagine the shift towards mass imprisonment and a revived death penalty. The proponents of fixed sentencing reform did not intend to spark off a political competition to set the highest mandatory sentences. The argument that rehabilitation was not good for offenders was not meant to mean that it was 'too good for them'. Other measures that were soon to dominate the penal landscape—expressive punishments, victims, public protection, punitiveness—simply did not figure at all in the original reform literature. Somehow, the anti-correctionalist movement opened the way for a set of changes that it did not envisage and could not control.

How is it that the reconfigured field of crime control that emerged in the 1980s and 1990s bears so little relation to the proposals of the reform movement that initiated this reconfiguration? As it happens, the structure of this historical problem is precisely the same as that described by Michel Foucault in *Discipline and Punish*. Foucault argues that the emergence of generalized imprisonment in the nineteenth century was a reflection not of the ideas of reformers but of the emerging structure of social institutions and governmental power in the modern period. In the following chapters I will develop the same kind of answer to the question posed here. The new field of crime control and criminal justice was shaped not by the programmes of reformers or by criminological ideas but by the character of late twentieth-century society, its problems, its culture and its technologies of power. My argument will be that the new institutional arrangements originated as problem-solving devices growing out of the practical experience of government agencies and their constituencies rather than the ideological programmes of reformers. The crime control field is an institutionalized response to a particular problem of order, growing out a particular collective experience. My account of crime control change looks at the way in which the field was affected by the emergence of new security problems, new perceptions of social order, and new conceptions of justice, all of which were prompted by the social and economic changes of late twentieth-century modernity. The reconfigured field of crime control and criminal justice are the products of that history and attempts by various actors to adapt to the opportunities and problems that it posed.

The next chapter asks what developments led to the erosion of penal-welfarism's social and institutional support? What were the new problems posed by the new social arrangements and everyday routines that developed in the second half of the century? How did fundamental perceptions and presumptions come to change so markedly? My claim will be that the structures and ideologies of modern crime control collapsed (where they did indeed collapse) not just because of intellectual critique, nor even because of a penological failure, but because they lost their grounding in supportive ways of life and consonant forms of belief. The social structures and cultural sensibilities that supported the field were themselves transformed. The critique of correctional-ism occurred precisely at the cusp of a social transition that involved convergent processes of economic, political, and cultural change. As we have seen, it was launched at the end of a period dominated by welfare state policies and social democratic politics, and its criticisms were originally anchored within that underlying framework. But the programmes and policies that were ushered in by this critique emerged in a different political and cultural context, and brought quite different feelings and attitudes to bear upon the issues.

The processes that undermined the credibility of the penal-welfarism were not the same as the ones that subsequently unravelled it. The original damage to the structure came about in the early 1970s as a result of radical and reactionary forces working in tandem, but with the former in the dominant position. The critique of rehabilitation was originally a progressive critique. The further assault on the system in the 1980s and 1990s occurred in the context of a more regressive public mood and temper, against the background of a changed per-ception of the motivating problem and as part of the creation of a new and less inclusive civic narrative. As we will see, the new crime control programmes and strategies responded to the supposed failure of the criminal justice state in its penal-welfare mode, and moved into the institutional space created by the assault on correctionalism. But they also adapted to the new social, political, and cultural conditions of late modern society, and to the new class and race relations to which they gave rise.

4

Social Change and Social Order in Late Modernity

The crime control changes of the last twenty years were driven not just by crim-inological considerations but also by historical forces that transformed social and economic life in the second half of the twentieth century. For our purposes it is useful to distinguish two sets of transformative forces:

First, the social, economic, and cultural changes characteristic of late moder-nity: changes that were experienced to a greater or lesser extent by all Western industrialized democracies after the Second World War and which became most pronounced from the 1960s onwards.

Secondly, the political realignments and policy initiatives that developed in response to these changes, and in reaction to the perceived crisis of the welfare state, in the USA and the UK from the late 1970s onwards. These changes in social and economic policy—a combination of free-market 'neo-liberalism' and social conservatism—had echoes in other states such as New Zealand, Canada, and Australia. But they were developed in their most thoroughgoing form in America under the Reagan and Bush administrations (1981–92) and in Britain under Prime Minister Thatcher (1979–92) and they have continued in more muted forms in the New Democrat administrations of Bill Clinton (1993–2000) and, in Britain, under the Conservative government of John Major (1992–7) and the New Labour government of Tony Blair from 1997 onwards.[1]

Leaving aside for a moment the national differences that distinguished the American experience from that of Britain, one can summarize the impact of these developments as follows: The first set of forces—the coming of late modernity—transformed some of the social and political conditions upon which the modern crime control field relied. It also posed new problems of crime and insecurity, challenged the legitimacy and effectiveness of welfare institu-tions, and placed new limits on the powers of the nation-state. The second set of forces—the politics of post-welfarism—produced a new set of class and race relations and a dominant political block that defined itself in opposition to old style 'welfarism' and the social and cultural ideals upon which it was based.

Without this political realignment, the most likely response to the critique of correctionalism would have been incremental reform, improved safeguards, enhanced resources, the refinement of procedures. Instead, what occurred was a sharp reversal of policy and opinion and a remaking of the whole crime control field. This chapter will argue that the turn against penal-welfarism took a 'reactionary', all-encompassing form because underlying the debate about crime and punishment was a fundamental shift of interests and sensibilities. This historical shift, which had both political and cultural dimensions, gave rise to new group relations and social attitudes—attitudes that were most sharply defined in relation to the problems of crime, welfare, and social order. These new group relations—often experienced and expressed as highly charged emotions of fear, resentment and hostility—formed the social terrain upon which crime control policies were built in the 1980s and 1990s.

The causes of this historical shift had little to do with criminal justice, but that did not prevent it from being massively consequential in its criminological effects. Broad social classes that had once supported welfare state policies (out of self-interest as well as cross-class solidarity) came to think and feel about the issues quite differently. Changes in demography, in stratification and in political allegiance led important sections of the working and middle classes to change their attitudes towards many of these policies—to see them as being at odds with their actuarial interests and as benefiting groups that were undeserving and increasingly dangerous. In this new political context, welfare policies for the poor were increasingly represented as expensive luxuries that hard working tax-payers could no longer afford. The corollary was that penal-welfare measures for offenders were depicted as absurdly indulgent and self-defeating.

If the searing experience of Depression and war had been the social surface on which the welfare state and penal-welfarism were built in the 1930s and 1940s, by the early 1980s that matrix of politics and culture was a dim historical memory. The politics of the later period addressed a different set of problems—many of which were perceived as being caused by welfarism rather than solved by it. I will argue that the gradual formation of new class interests and sensibilities came about in response to the crisis of the welfare state and the transforming dynamics of late modern social life, but I will also insist that this response was the result of political and cultural choices that were by no means inevitable. In the following pages I give an account of this social and political realignment. This account looks at the social and historical processes that have reconfigured the way that we live in the last third of the twentieth century and the ways in which we have come to think and act in relation to crime. It is the story of the development of late modernity, our political and cultural reactions to it, and the implications that these have had for crime, crime-control, and criminal justice.

My account is not intended as a history of the period, but rather as an exploration of social changes that influenced, or posed problems for, the crime control field. Much of what follows will be familiar to the reader—part of 'what everyone knows' about the late twentieth century. But it is important to recall it nevertheless. By calling to mind some of the great social facts of our recent history, I hope to unseat the 'presentist' mindset that so often dominates our discussions and diagnoses. All too often we tend to see contemporary events as having only contemporary causes, when in fact we are caught up in long-term processes of historical change and affected by the continuing effects of now-forgotten events. Our present-day choices are heavily path dependent, reflecting the patterns of earlier decisions and institutional arrangements, just as our habits of thought reflect the circumstances and problems of the periods in which they were first developed.

The theory of historical change I bring to bear in what follows is an action-centred, problem-solving one in which socially situated actors reproduce (or else transform) the structures that enable and constrain their actions. My substantive claim is that the political, economic and cultural supports that had previously underpinned modern crime control were increasingly eroded by late modern social trends and the intellectual and political shifts that accompanied them. These trends, in turn, posed novel problems, gave rise to new perceptions, and shaped a variety of practical adaptations, out of which gradually emerged the crime control and criminal justice practices of the present period. The theory assumes that the emergence of these practices is typically the outcome of practical problem-solving and of political and cultural selection. In consequence, it is a complex process in which competing accounts of problems and solutions are always in play, different interests and sensibilities are always at issue, and the capacity to select solutions on the basis of hard information is only ever partial at best.

The dynamics of change in late twentieth-century modernity

The large-scale social changes of the second half of the twentieth century have been the subject of much sociological reflection and debate. For some analysts these changes herald the coming of post-modernity and a form of social organization and consciousness that is quite distinct from modernity. Others, wishing to mark the distinctiveness of the world these changes have brought into being, but also to recognize its continuity with what went before, talk of 'late modernity', 'high modernity', or 'reflexive modernity'. Terms such 'New Times', 'post-Fordism', 'post-welfare', and 'neo-liberalism' also identify the peculiarities of the present, but the first of these is rather too vague and the others are rather too specific. My own preferred term is 'late twentieth-century modernity'—which indicates an historical phase of the modernization process without assuming that we are coming to the end, or even to the high point, of a centuries-old dynamic that shows no signs of letting up. Unfortunately such a phrase is even more cumbersome than the others and is of limited use for theoretical generalization. So I will use the term 'late modernity' for convenience, though readers should bear in mind the sense of my usage.

The major transformations that swept society in the second half of the twentieth century were at once economic, social, cultural, and political. To the extent that these can be disentangled, they can be summarized under the following headings: (i) the dynamic of capitalist production and market exchange and the corresponding advances in technology, transport and communications; (ii) the restructuring of the family and the household; (iii) changes in the social ecology of cities and suburbs; (iv) the rise of the electronic mass media; and (v) the democratization of social and cultural life.

These great forces of historical change transformed the texture of the developed world in the second half of the twentieth century—all the way up to global economic markets and the nation-state system, all the way down to the daily lives and psychological dynamics of families and individuals. While the contours of capitalist, democratic modernity still frame our social existence, the second half of the twentieth century has ushered in profound changes in the way that life is lived—changes that have had important implications for issues of crime and its control. To begin a discussion of any one of these interwoven threads of social change inevitably leads on to all the others. Here I begin and end with what I take to be the most basic transformative forces of modern times: the economic force of capitalist competition and the political struggle for social and political equality.

The modernizing dynamic of capitalist production and market exchange

The most powerful and fateful of these historical forces—as vigorous today as it was in the time of Karl Marx—was the unfolding dynamic of capitalist production and exchange. Directly or indirectly, all of the major transformations of the second half of the twentieth century can be traced back to the process of capital accumulation and the unceasing drive for new markets, enhanced profits, and competitive advantage. Military undertakings such as the arms race and the Cold War no doubt played a part, but it was the profit-motive above all else that drove the ultra-rapid transformation of technology, transportation and communications that has characterized the last forty years. Automobiles and aeroplanes, electronic valves and microchips, telephones and fax machines, personal computers and the Internet—each of these has had dramatic consequences for social relations and the texture of daily life. They gave rise to the 'information society' that we now inhabit; made possible the cities and suburbs in which we dwell; linked the four corners of the globe into a single accessible world; and created new social divisions between those who have access to the high-tech world and those who do not.

It was the mass production and mass marketing of goods that gave rise to the world of supermarkets and shopping malls, labour-saving devices and electronic gadgetry, hire purchase and extended credit, the fashion industry and built-in-obsolescence—in short to a whole ethos of 'consumption' and 'consumerism' and the cultural attitudes that go with it.[2] It was the iconoclasm of economic rationality that helped diminish age-old social divisions that had for centuries allocated men and women, blacks and whites, to different social roles. Contrariwise, it was these same 'bottom-line' considerations that allowed rampant inequalities and the social exclusion of groups who could not easily be turned to profitable use. It was the unending search for new markets, for higher returns, and for a more efficient division of labour that created international markets, non-stop flows of information and money around the planet, and a globalized economy in which nation-states are less and less able to control the economic and social destinies of their subjects.

The events of the late 1980s may have consigned Marx and Engels to the scapheap of failed ideologies, but their description of capitalist modernity in the *Communist Manifesto* remains as true today as it ever was:

Constant revolutionizing of production, uninterrupted disturbance of all social conditions, everlasting uncertainty and agitation distinguish the bourgeois epoch from all earlier ones. All fixed, fast-frozen relations, with their train of ancient and venerable prejudices and opinions are swept away, all new-formed ones become antiquated before they can ossify. All that is solid melts into air, all that is holy is profaned, and man is at last compelled to face with sober senses, his real conditions of life, and his relations with his kind.[3]

'The Golden Years': 1950 to 1973

For a quarter century after 1950 the economies of Britain and America—like most of the developed industrial world—experienced a remarkable and continuous process of growth and rising living standards. Thanks to the spread of mass production techniques, the expansion of consumer markets at home and abroad, the low cost of energy, and the success of Keynsian demand management, they succeeded in warding off the cyclical booms and slumps of previous eras and enjoyed almost three decades of uninterrupted expansion and prosperity. For the mass of working people 'full employment' and the new welfare safety net lent an unprecedented level of economic security to their lives, and the growth of trade unions, rising wage levels and progressive taxation had the effect of reducing the gap between the rich and the poor.[4]

In the USA the spread of consumerism and middle-class affluence that had begun before Second World War resumed and accelerated in the years after, and the American suburban family quickly became a universal symbol of a comfortable and desirable 'lifestyle' equipped with all 'modern conveniences'. Once the period of post-war rationing and reconstruction was at an end, Britain embarked on the same trajectory, catching up with the new consumption patterns established across the Atlantic. By the 1950s the mass production of affordable consumer durables such as cars, washing machines, refrigerators, radios, and television sets, allowed large sections of the working population routine access to goods that had previously been available only to the very rich. By the 1960s, this *embourgoisement* had reached a level where many of the skilled working class took for granted luxuries—new cars, foreign holidays, homes of their own, fashionable clothes—that their parents had only dreamed of possessing.[5]

The technological revolution in manufacturing brought portable electronic devices—televisions, radios, stereos, and later computers—into virtually every home and opened up huge new markets in home entertainment and advertising. Shopping—in the new malls, supermarkets, boutiques, and tourist resorts—ceased to be a mere necessity and became something of a pleasurable pastime, as more and more people found themselves with disposable income to spend and greater leisure time in which to spend it. And if sections of the work-force were not sufficiently well paid to acquire those commodities that increasingly defined individuals' identities, then the wide availability of credit and hire-purchase agreements ensured that they were not entirely left out.

For the first time, the masses were able to imitate the rich in passing on some of their wealth to their offspring—not in the form of inheritances and landed estates, but by paying them allowances and spending money. This, together with wages from part-time employment, opened up an important new market sector that expanded rapidly in the 1960s. Within a few years the 'youth culture' and 'teenagers' became a major market sector to which advertising executives in the clothes, music, and entertainment industries directed their attention. With the extension of compulsory schooling, the expansion of higher education, and, thanks to improved diet, the earlier onset of puberty, this age cohort occupied a newly extended period between childhood and full-time work and family commitments. With its numbers swelled in the 1960s by the large post-war birth cohort then reaching its teenage years, this newly defined social stratum took on a distinctive identity and became a leading force in cultural change, at least at the level of lifestyle and consumer preferences.

It was during this post-war period that monopoly capitalism re-invented itself as consumer capitalism. This consumption-oriented system was sustained by the purchasing power of a mass of active consumers, marketing techniques that helped generate a constant flow of unfulfilled desires, and corporatist agreements between government, employers and unions that stabilized the system and gave an economic basis to its inflationary dynamic. New occupational groups emerged (management, public service professionals, knowledge workers, finance and banking, marketing, media, and service industry) and the institutions of higher education grew in order to equip a workforce with the skills and technical training that these new occupations required.[6]

Whichever political party was in power, the politics of expansion was always the dominant theme—its critics would come to call it 'tax and spend' politics—as governments responded to the tide of rising expectations and the demand for what T. H. Marshall called 'social rights'. In these decades a massive new public sector grew up—providing social work and social services, health care, child support, education, and housing, as well as income support for those who fell out of the workforce. This was funded, of course, by tax revenues and therefore depended on the continued capacity of the private sector to generate wealth and employment. Whether or not their politicians welcomed the name, the America and British states became 'welfare states', 'regulatory states', 'big governments'—

increasingly responsible for managing economic life, increasingly expected to guarantee the wellbeing and prosperity of its population, increasingly the insurer and social problem-solver of last resort.[7]

Economic prosperity provided the motor for civil rights, for a 'politics of solidarity', and for progressive policies like correctionalism and rehabilitation. It also provided the basis for the expansion of democracy, for increased egalitarianism, and for the widespread cultural changes that followed in their wake. The long economic boom underpinned the political optimism and progressivism that marked these decades, especially the late 1960s. Two decades of sustained post-war growth, in a world that looked very different from its pre-war predecessor, markedly raised expectations, gave a sense of 'post-scarcity' possibilities, and helped erase the memories of depression and insecurity that had made the welfare state so essential and its ethos so widespread. But the very success of this post-war settlement gave rise to contradictory currents and new forms of opposition. For instance, it was precisely this economic buoyancy and the pervasive sense that much more was possible that funded the youth radicalism of the late 1960s and the newly critical stance that these radicals took up towards the wefare state.[8]

The Crisis Decades: 1970s and 1980s

What capitalist markets give, so also do they take away. With a sudden and unexpected jolt, the oil crisis of the early 1970s ushered in a period of economic recession and political instability throughout the Western industrialized nations. The re-appearance of 'negative growth', now complicated by a built-in inflation and the politically underwritten expectations of unionized workers, exposed the underlying problems of the UK and US economies and opened them up to harsh competition from newly developing economies abroad. In this recessionary context, the tools of Keynsian demand management failed to bring supply and demand into line; wage and price inflation continued; production and trade fell precipitously; balance of payments crises appeared as public expenditures outran income; and bitter strife began to mar the relations between the erstwhile 'social partners' of government, employers and unions. Within a decade, mass unemployment re-appeared, industrial production collapsed, trade union membership massively declined, and the labour market restructured itself in ways that were to have dramatic social significance in the years to come.[9]

This restructuring of the labour market—which had begun some time before but which now accelerated in response to the downturn—saw the collapse of industrial production, and with it the shedding of millions of jobs that were previously occupied by unskilled male workers. Where it continued, industrial manufacturing became more capital-intensive and technologically sophisticated, resulting in fewer jobs and demanding more skilled workforces. And as international investment markets grew, making capital more mobile and less closely linked to nations and regions, the pressure to increase productivity or decrease wages exposed the inefficiencies of the older industries and undermined the capacity of trade unions to protect their low-skilled members. When economic recovery came—as it did after the recessions of 1973–5 and 1981–3— it was slower and more modest than before, and it was concentrated in service sectors and high technology. The result was a different kind of employment pattern: one that leaned towards low-paid, part-time, usually female workers, or else highly skilled, highly trained graduate employees.[10]

From the late 1970s onwards, the labour markets of the USA and the UK became increasingly precarious and 'dualized'. The life-time job security that industries and the public sector had offered in the post-war years became a thing of the past as workers were forced to become more mobile, more willing to develop transferable skills, more used to retraining and relocating. The male wage-earner bringing home a family wage was increasingly displaced by female, part-time labour with little job-security and few benefits.[11] And while the best-qualified strata of the work-force could command high salaries and lucrative benefits packages, at the bottom end of the market were masses of low-skilled, poorly educated, jobless people—a large percentage of them young, urban, and minority—for whom continuous unemployment was a long-term prospect. These new wage patterns, which in the 1980s were reinforced by increasingly regressive tax structures and declining welfare benefits, reversed the gains of the last half century, as income inequalities increased, and large sectors of the population (especially those with children) fell below the poverty line.[12]

Nor were these changes temporary. Even in the 1990s, when a strong stock-market and low-wage costs led to a sustained period of growth and high levels of employment, whole sectors of the population—particularly inner-city youths in poor or minority communities—were systematically excluded from the labour market just as many of their parents had been before them. The consequence was a more sharply stratified labour market, with growing inequalities separating the top and bottom tiers; a diminished sense of shared interests as the power and membership of mass unions declined; greater contrasts in working conditions, lifestyle and residence; and ultimately, fewer ties of solidarity between these groups.[13]

Changes in the structure of the family and the household

One of the central social changes of post-war Britain and America was the mass entry of married women and mothers into the paid workforce. In 1941 married women who lived with their husband and worked for pay formed less than 14 per cent of the total female population in the USA. By 1980 they formed more than half. In the UK, the pattern was the same, with women forming 29 per cent of the active workforce in 1951 and 43 per cent by 1991.[14]

Over the same period, the structure of the family was substantially transformed. There was a marked decline (and concentration in time) of fertility, with women marrying later, having fewer children, and re-entering the paid workforce sooner after giving birth.[15] There was also a sudden and remarkable rise in the frequency of divorce, particularly in England, where the ratio of divorces to weddings went from 1 to 58.0 in 1938 to 1 to 2.2 by the mid-1980s. This new pattern of divorce and separation sharply increased the numbers of children living in single-parent households, bringing in its wake new problems of child and female poverty. The occurrence in the same period of a steep rise in the numbers of children born to single mothers strongly reinforced this trend, particularly in the USA, where by the early 1990s, more than 30 per cent of all children were born to unmarried women, a figure that rose to nearly 70 per cent in African American communities, where 58 per cent of all families were headed by a single woman. In the space of only forty years, the traditional image of the nuclear family—a married couple living together with children—had come to bear little relation to the real domestic lives of most of the population in America and Britain.[16]

The post-1960s expansion of college education and professional opportunities for middle-class women, and the growth of jobs (especially part-time jobs) in the new service industries and in light manufacturing for their working-class sisters gradually transformed the post-marriage career paths of the average woman. So did the greater effectiveness of birth control and the new, more tolerant norms surrounding its use. Over time, many families came to be 'two-income' families, with consequences for everything from expenditure patterns, child-care needs, and time spent in the home to the average price of family houses, the numbers of cars per household, and the levels of stress reported by males and females.[17]

A related change occurring over the same period concerned the changing characteristics of households. Since 1950 there has been a steady decline in the average household size, with more and more people living alone or in small family units. During the first third of the century, only about 6 per cent of households in the UK were people living alone. By 1991 the proportion had reached 25 per cent, and as high as 50 per cent in many big cities. Average household size decreased over the same period from 3.4 persons to 2.7. These changes were a result of the patterns of child-birth and family-formation mentioned already, but they were also caused by a larger number of teenagers going to college and by more older people living on their own.[18]

Social forces operating outside as well as inside the family brought about these changes. Higher income levels, better healthcare, and increased welfare benefits allowed the elderly to live longer and more independently; enabled single parents to survive on benefits or with part-time jobs; provided teenagers with state funds to go to college; relieved families of some of their traditional caring tasks and gradually changed the norms and expectation that surrounded these. Changes in the labour market allowed more women to enter the workforce, and brought about the decline of the family wage. Movements in cultural and legal norms—particularly the rise of feminist ideals in the 1970s, the growing tolerance for 'alternative' family forms, and the diminishing stigma of divorce, illegitimacy and homosexuality—also contributed. And of course the relationship was reciprocal. As we will see, these changes in family structure brought about important practical consequences in every aspect of daily life.

As a result of these changes, households and families today look quite different, and operate quite differently from those that were typical of the 1950s or early 1960s. The question of what functional effects follow from these structural changes is, of course, one of the most contentious issues of our time. But what is not in doubt is that the question of the changing family and its social meaning has formed a central theme of political and cultural debate throughout the last quarter century. And these debates have repeatedly highlighted issues of crime and welfare.

Changes in social ecology and demography

The post-war decades saw two major developments in social ecology: the spread of the private automobile and the development of new dwelling patterns, the most important of which were suburban private housing tracts and public housing estates on the peripheries of large cities. The advent of the motor-car and the network of roads and highways that was built to accommodate it, were well established in the USA before the war, and developed rapidly in the 1950s and 1960s in the UK. Between 1950 and 1994 the total number of registered automobiles, trucks, and buses in the USA quadrupled, rising from 49.2 to 198 million. In the UK, car-ownership was slower to develop, and never so extensive, but the basic pattern was much the same.[19]

One consequence of car-ownership and the spread of mass transport was a relaxation of the need for close proximity between home and work. In the post-war decades there was a large-scale migration of people from the cities to the commuter suburbs, and the average distance travelled between home and work, home and shops or leisure, and home and school all increased markedly.[20] In both the USA and the UK this shift was prompted, in part, by the growing demand for new family housing and the desire of young families to escape the decaying inner cities and their social problems. The urban renewal projects of the 1960s continued this process by demolishing many of the inner city neighbourhoods that got in the way of the new highways and traffic systems, and rehousing the council tenants in new, high density housing projects. The effect was often to concentrate the poor and minority families in areas quite far removed from the city and lacking in basic amenities such as shops, jobs and good public transport.[21]

These two ecological developments have together transformed the way in which the elements of everyday life are bound together in time and space, with major consequences for how daily life is lived. Between them, they account for a multiplicity of social changes—the out of town shopping mall; the lengthy commute to work and school; the depopulation of the inner cities; the mobility of the labour force; the suburbanization of employment; the declining importance of local loyalties and face-to-face interaction settings; and the increased privatization of individual and family life.

These ecological shifts interacted with other demographic factors to bring about new forms of segregation and social division. In the USA one of the dynamics of suburbanization was 'white flight', as the mass migration of southern blacks to the Northern and Mid-Western cities from the 1940s onwards prompted many white city residents to move away. By the 1960s the combination of white suburbanization and extensive black in-migration had led to an unprecedented increase in the size of the ghetto in cities such as Chicago, Los Angeles, Newark, and Detroit.[22] In the UK a similar, if less visible, segregation was effected as the housing policies of local authorities combined with the market choices of more affluent householders to produce a concentration of the worst-off residents in 'sink estates' and decaying inner city areas. In the 1980s the contrasts between the middle-class white suburbs and the poor, often black, urban neighbourhoods, were exacerbated by the cut-back of government support associated with the 'New Federalism' of Reagan and Bush and the local government spending caps imposed by Mrs Thatcher's government.[23]

The social impact of electronic mass media

If the automobile and the suburb transformed social space in physical terms, the coming of television and the broadcast media did so in a psychological sense that was equally profound and consequential. Mass circulation newspapers had established a national news community as early as the nineteenth century, and already by the First World War the industry had begun to consolidate in the form of national press conglomerates. But it was not until the development of broadcast radio in the 1920s and 1930s and the spread of television a decade or two later, that the 'mass media' established itself as a central institution of modern life. In the UK and the US, the television viewing audience grew from nothing to virtually universal coverage in less than a generation. In 1950 9 per cent of American homes and 10 per cent of British ones had television sets. By 1963 fewer than 10 per cent of homes were without them.[24]

The television revolution transformed the rest of the media. As its viewing figures increased, television's impact upon popular tastes and its increased share of advertising revenues forced newspapers to compete more and more on television's terms. The consequence was a further consolidation of the newspaper industry, the advent of the tabloid newspaper, and a growing tendency towards an imperceptible merging of news and entertainment.

The TV revolution also changed social relations and cultural sensibilities. The emergence of a single nation-wide information system to which everyone has constant access had major consequences for group identities and relations, particularly somewhere as large and diverse as the USA, or as class divided as the UK. National and cosmopolitan perspectives became available to groups whose experience was previously shaped by the more inward cultures of local-ism, social class, and ethnic group. Members of groups that were previously iso-lated were better able to recognize their disadvantage and to demand equal rights and treatment. The electronic media thus rendered the experience of being excluded or relatively disadvantaged much more readily apparent and therefore, much less acceptable. It was hardly surprising, then, that 'tensions over racial and other forms of integration peaked as television completed its invasion of the American home'.[25]

Consumption patterns and lifestyles that were once confined to the rich and famous were now held out to everyone, with disturbing consequences for the expectations of masses of would-be consumers. As Joshua Meyrowitz pointed out in 1985, 'through television, today's ghetto children have more points of ref-erence and higher standards for comparison. They see what they are deprived of in every program and commercial'.[26] At the same time, risks and problems that were previously localized and limited in significance, or else were associated with specific groups of victims, increasingly came to be perceived as everyone's problem, as the images of the behaviours in question (racism, sexism, crime, violence, child abuse, wars, famines . . .) began to appear in the living rooms of the whole population. The visibility of events and individuals ceased to depend on a shared locale and direct experience, and came instead to depend upon the media and its decisions about what and how to broadcast.

Television also changed other aspects of cultural life. Unlike the other news media, television was capable of conveying intimate, 'expressive' information—impressions of the speaking subject that were previously available only in direct encounters. Television news conveyed a sense of immediacy and intimacy, bringing the viewer 'face to face' with the subject of the interview or presenta-tion. This led to a new emphasis upon the emotive and intimate aspects of events, and a tendency to reveal more and more of the 'personalities' involved.[27] It also led to a greater exposure of what Erving Goffman called 'backstage behaviour'. Authority figures, celebrities and members of the public were shown in more revealing ways, as interviewers sought to provoke unrehearsed reac-tions and reveal the feelings that lay behind prepared statements and public per-sonas. Institutions too, were subjected to closer scrutiny, as the prying eye of the camera sought to get behind the outward appearances and show the viewer 'how it really is'. In this way, television has tended to undermine propriety. The media, in the name of realism and candid reporting, no longer respect the tradi-tional demands of privacy and intimacy. More back-stage behaviour is routinely revealed, as are the failings and foibles of public figures and institutions. Its self-serving and much abused—but none the less democratic—shibboleth is that 'the public has a right to know'.[28]

These changes in the media have helped create a greater level of transparency and accountability in our social and governmental institutions. Bad decisions and shoddy practices are now much more visible that ever before and there is a closer scrutiny of what is going on behind the scenes. Official secrecy and government privilege are increasingly challenged by an emboldened and popular press. As Meyrowitz observes:

As the confines of the prison, the convent, the family house, the neighbourhood, the executive suite, the university campus and the oval office are all invaded through electronics, we must expect a fundamental shift in our perceptions of society, our authorities and ourselves.[29]

The democratization of social life and culture

The 1950s, 1960s, and 1970s were decades in which democratic institutions in Britain and America were broadened and made more all-encompassing. The civil rights of groups such as blacks, women, gays, prisoners, and mental patients, were increasingly affirmed and extended in this period, and important shifts occurred in the balance of power between government and governed, employers and employees, organizations and consumers. These changes were the result of prolonged struggles by members of the disadvantaged groups and are testimony to the power of egalitarian ideals, the liberal mood of political elites, and the activism of reforming governments and, in the USA, of the Supreme Court. But they also had roots in the structural conditions of late modern society. Welfare state institutions, corporatist politics, the mass media, and the new culture of consumerism all contributed to this end. So did the functional democratization that grew out of the ever-lengthening chains of interdependency that characterized the division of labour, giving specialized workers, managers, and technicians a greater measure of power in the workplace, particularly where they were scarce or else well organized.

In this period the discourse of equality and the politics of equal rights came to play a major role in political culture, however often their claims were breached in practice. In principle, there was no reason why any individual should be treated unequally or denied the full benefits of citizenship.[30] There was a cultural expectation of fair treatment for the individual in the face of authority or large organizations, and new mechanisms (employment tribunals, rent reviews, sex discrimination laws, TV consumer shows) were developed to enforce these claims. A similar expectation of equal rights and social inclusion transformed the expectations (if not always the life chances) of minority groups who had previously been assigned low rank and status. And while these new expectations did not always lead to the diminution of social distinctions and class barriers, they did produce a cultural effect that Ralph Miliband termed 'desubordination'—a decline in the levels of deference and respect for social superiors that previously reinforced the stratification system. In the 1960s and 1970s this push for democracy and egalitarianism extended beyond the political sphere into private domains of the family, the workplace, the universities, the schools—with major consequences for authority and control in these settings.[31]

In many organizations, and especially in larger, well-run corporations and public institutions, this shift brought about a change in management styles and balances of power. 'Management by command', where a superior orders an inferior to behave in particular ways, was increasingly displaced by 'management by negotiation'.[32] Workers, particularly skilled, organized workers, were no longer prepared to act like the servants of their employers. The clients of government bureaucracies began to act like customers. Women demanded more power in the home. Pupils and students and children and prisoners wanted some say in running the institutions that housed them. Experts and expert knowledge were subject to popular scepticism, even as the public became more and more reliant upon them.[33] And although the result was often a change in form, rather than a real shift in status and power, these changing forms did make a difference—not least to people's expectations and their sense of entitlement. From the 1960s onwards, and in more and more social settings, absolute authority and top-down decision making became much more difficult to sustain.[34]

In the post-war period, moral absolutes and unquestionable prohibitions lost their force and credibility, as the rigid and long-standing social hierarchies on which they relied began to be dismantled. This, in turn, weakened the moral powers of the church and the state, and encouraged the spread of a more relativistic, more 'situational' moral sensibility.[35] In the course of a few years, quite radical changes occurred in the norms governing such matters as divorce, sexual conduct, illegitimacy, and drug taking. With the development of new social movements, and more and more groups asserting the legitimacy of their particular values and lifestyles, a much more pluralistic politics began to take shape. The result was an identity politics that disrupted the old political party system and a more diversified public opinion that questioned the possibility of moral consensus and the power of a singular dominant culture that it implied.[36]

The 1960s assault on established social hierarchies and moral authorities also encouraged the development of a different intellectual culture and worldview—one that would become increasingly pervasive in the decades that followed. The characteristic thinking of this period tended to be more sceptical, more pragmatic, and more perspectival than before. The ending of absolutes and the development of a more pluralistic culture had consequences for intellectual life as well. 'Positivist' thinking became increasingly untenable—not just in criminology but in every sphere of social thought. The positivist notion that there were widely shared observations, a universally experienced reality, a given realm of real facts, the possibility of a theory-free science—none of this seemed very plausible once pluralism and relativism became part of the cultural atmosphere. Even 'rationality' was subject to challenge, as post-modern intellectuals and excluded groups rejected the idea of single shared standard. In cultural life, as in world of social institutions, the Enlightenment's legacy of scientific reason was increasingly put in question and its social engineering ambitions were no longer viewed as an unquestioned human good.[37]

One of the most profound consequences of these social and cultural changes was the emergence of a more pronounced and widespread moral individualism. In one setting after another, individuals were made less subject to the constraining influence of group demands and absolutist moral codes. More and more of the population were encouraged to pursue the goals of individual expression, self-fashioning, and gratification that the consumer society held out to everyone. The grip of tradition, community, church and family upon the individual grew more relaxed and less compelling in a culture that stressed individual rights and freedoms and which dismantled the legal, economic, and moral barriers that had previously kept men, women, and young people 'in their place'. The result was a shift in the balance of power between the individual and group, a relaxation of traditional social controls, and a new emphasis upon the freedom and importance of the individual. Some aspects of this new culture had an egoistic, hedonistic quality, linked to the non-stop consumption ethos of the new capitalism. But to the extent that it did entail a morality it was that of liberal individualism—a morality in which mutual toleration, prudent self-restraint, and respect for other individuals take the place of group commands and moral imperatives. In this moral universe, the worst sin was cruelty to individuals or the restriction of their freedom; obligations to the group or even to families were much more conditional.[38]

It is true that as 'communities of fate' declined, and loosened their social grip upon individuals, new 'communities of choice' emerged—subcultures, consumer and lifestyle identities, professional associations, internet chat rooms—bringing people together in new ways, and subjecting them to new social norms. But these new forms of solidarity did not press so close in the controls that they exerted. They were not face-to-face, not local, not grounded in a shared sense of place or in the tight bonds of kinship. They did not affect people in the same intimate ways as the old family and neighbourhood ties had done. Instead individuals checked in and out of multiple networks, relating to them in a segmental fashion, rather than as 'whole persons' who derive most of their identity from belonging to that particular group. Moreover, these new modes of association were not all encompassing. They excluded as well as included. Typically they operated to the exclusion of the poor, and minorities, many of whom were set apart from the community and controls of the workplace, the new social movements, and the legitimate sources of consumer identity. The declining hold of the family and the local community thus affected the poor more adversely than others.

The impact of late modern social change upon crime and welfare

The broad changes just described left their mark across the whole terrain of late modern social organization, and in every case, their impact was mediated by the ways in which policy makers and social actors understood and responded to the new developments. But before going on to outline the differing responses and adaptations that these changes provoked, I want to pause to consider some of the ways in which they impacted upon the two domains that are at the heart of this study: (i) crime and social control and (ii) the institutions of the welfare state.

Crime and social control

The transformative dynamics of late modernity had their most pronounced and dramatic effects in the two decades after 1960. That period coincided, more or less exactly, with a rapid and sustained increase in recorded crime rates—not just in the USA and the UK, but in every Western industrialized nation.[39] The growth of crime in this period is a massive and incontestable social fact, notwithstanding the evidentiary problems inherent in criminal statistics and the possibility that these statistics were affected by changes in reporting and recording patterns. Between 1955 and 1964 the number of crimes recorded by the police in England and Wales doubled—from half a million a year to a million. It doubled again by 1975 and yet again by 1990. Recorded offences thus rose from about one per 100 people in 1950 to five per 100 in the 1970s to ten per hundred in 1994.[40] In the USA, crime rates rose sharply from 1960 onwards, reaching a peak in the early 1980s when the rate was three times that of twenty years before, the years between 1965 and 1973 recording the biggest rise on record. Moreover, the increases occurred in all the main offence categories, including property crime, crimes of violence and drug offending.[41]

This correlation between late modern social change and increased crime rates was no mere coincidence. The most likely explanation for a cross-national pattern of rapid and sustained increase is a social structural one that points to common patterns of social development. Despite considerable variation from place to place and in respect of the various offence categories, and despite the impact of different regimes of social and legal control, the evidence strongly suggests a causal link between the coming of late modernity and society's increased susceptibility to crime.[42] Furthermore, one can give a plausible account of the mechanisms that link the specific social, economic and cultural changes of the late twentieth century with an increased susceptibility to crime. This increased susceptibility is by no means an inevitable, inexorable feature of late modern life. Some societies, most notably Japan and Switzerland, maintained a high and effective level of (largely informal) crime control, while most others eventually found methods of stemming the rising tide of crime. But the initial impact of late modernity was to make high rates of crime much more probable as a direct consequence of the new social and economic arrangements that it put in place.

Late modernity's impact upon crime rates was a multi-dimensional one that involved: (i) increased opportunities for crime, (ii) reduced situational controls, (iii) an increase in the population 'at risk', and (iv) a reduction in the efficacy of social and self controls as a consequence of shifts in social ecology and changing cultural norms.[43] The consumer boom of the post-war decades put into circulation a mass of portable, high-value goods that presented attractive new targets for theft. This exponential increase in the number of circulating commodities created, as a matter of course, a corresponding increase in criminal opportunities. At the same, there was a reduction in situational controls as shops increasingly became 'self-service', densely populated neighbourhoods were replaced by sprawling suburban tracts or anonymous tower blocks, down-town areas became entertainment centres with no residents, and more and more well-stocked houses were left empty during the day while both wives and hus-bands went out to work. The coming of the motor car—which helped bring about this more spread-out, more mobile society—was itself a prime instance of its criminogenic properties. Within a few years, the spread of the automobile brought into existence a new and highly attractive target for crime, available on every city street at all times of the day and night, often completely unattended. Thefts of and from motor vehicles quickly became one of the largest categories of property crime.

Another ingredient for the 1960s rise in crime was the arrival of a large cohort of teenage males—the age group most prone to criminal behaviour. As a result of the changes described earlier, this generation of teenagers enjoyed greater affluence and mobility than earlier generations, as well as longer periods outside the disciplines of family life and full-time work. Teenagers were able to spend more time outside the home, had greater access to leisure activities, and were subject to less adult supervision, and more liable to spend time in subcultural settings such as clubs, cafes, discos, and street corners. This baby-boom gener-ation, which grew up in a universalistic commercial culture and experienced a whole new level of desires, expectations, and demands for instant gratification, supplied most of the recruits for the crime-boom that followed in its wake.[44]

Finally, one should add that this period also saw a relaxation of informal social controls—in families, in neighbourhoods, in schools, on the streets—partly as a result of the new social ecology, partly as a consequence of cultural change. Social space became more stretched out, more anonymous and less well supervised, at the very time that it was becoming more heavily laden with crim-inal temptations and opportunities.[45] At more or less the same time, there was a questioning of traditional authorities, a relaxation of the norms governing conduct in the realm of sexuality and drug-use, and the spread of a more 'per-missive', 'expressive' style of child-rearing. For some sections of the population, especially the emerging voices of the new youth culture, 'deviance' came to be a badge of freedom, and 'conformity' a sign of dull, normalized repression. The old categories of 'crime' and 'delinquency' became less obvious in their behav-ioural reference and less absolute in their moral force.

Taken together these social trends had a definite and pronounced effect upon crime. The high crime rates of the 1960s and 1970s were a precipitate of these social changes—an unplanned but altogether predictable product of the inter-action of these elements.[46] Put more sociologically, the sharply increased crime rates were an emergent property of the converging social and psychological changes of the post-war period. The new social and cultural arrangements made late-modern society a more crime-prone society, at least until such time as new crime-control practices could be put in place to counter these structural tenden-cies.

The coming of late modernity also had immediate practical consequences for the institutions of crime control and criminal justice, quite aside from the impact that higher crime rates would eventually have. The automobile, the tele-phone and the stretching out of social space prompted the 1960s shift to what Americans call '911 policing'—a reactive policing style that took police officers off the streets and out of communities, placed them in patrol cars, and concen-trated on providing a rapid response to emergency calls.[47] The rise of the mass media, the universalizing of democratic claims, and what Edward Shils called the politics of 'mass society' put in place new laws and forms of accountability with regard to criminal justice authorities. The balance of power between the police and criminal suspects or between prison officials and prison inmates was altered slightly in favour of the latter and these institutions were subjected to greater levels of legal scrutiny and media exposure. Finally, the social deference and taken-for-granted moral authority that underpinned the idea of doing reha-bilitative work with juveniles, in prisons and on probation ceased to be so read-ily available. As the ethics of work and duty lost their appeal and the idea of a moral consensus was progressively undermined, the idea that state employees could 'correct' deviants came to seem authoritarian and inappropriate rather than self-evidently humane. In the late modern context, the sullen, deep-seated resistance that working-class offenders and minority communities had often shown to the agents of the penal state, now took on an explicit, ideological aspect that made policing and punishing that much more difficult. The declin-ing availability of work for ex-offenders after 1970 added further to the implau-sibility of the whole correctional project.[48]

Welfare institutions

To talk about the impact of late modernity upon the welfare state is to isolate one side of an inextricably interactive historical process. It was, after all, Britain's welfare state and America's New Deal equivalent that provided the basic institutional environment in which post-war capitalism flourished and social democracy established itself. It was the Keynesian state that regulated economic life, secured labour's living standards, fine-tuned the money supply, built highways, undertook capital investment, and generally managed prosper-ity. It was this same state that funded education, health, and housing, passed laws permitting divorce, and provided benefits to individuals who did not have a job or a family to support them. The welfare state was thus one of the engines that helped shape late modernity, leaving behind the boom—slump insecurities of the inter-war years and opening up the new culture of liberal individualism and social democracy.

But the historical irony of this process is that the very economic and social changes that the welfare state ushered in, would, in their turn, undermine the effectiveness and legitimacy of welfarist forms of government. By the late 1970s the welfare state was being attacked on the basis of the late modern conditions that it had brought into being. Before discussing the anti-welfare politics of the 1980s and 1990s, I want to briefly describe the sources of this negative dynamic.[49]

The first element of this self-negating process was the feedback effect that followed the creation of welfare and social service agencies. It turned out that the institutions designed to meet the population's need for housing, or health care, or education, or social work or income support had a tendency to discover more and more unmet need, so that the problems appeared to become larger rather than smaller. So although budgets were regularly increased, they continually appeared inadequate. From the Second World War until the present, public expenditure on social services in the USA and the UK has had a built-in tendency to increase, both in absolute terms and as a proportion of gross domestic product.[50] But welfare problems did not get 'solved': instead they became an object of policy and administration and, in the process, became more visible, more complex, and more demanding of state funds. Even where welfare solutions were effective—e.g. in combating destitution, or malnutrition, or poor health and housing—this still tended to produce more rather than fewer cases.[51] People came to rely upon the state and its social services rather than on parents, husbands, moneylenders, or low-paying jobs. This development is usually described by its critics as 'dependency creating' but a better term might be *dependency shifting*, as individuals chose to become the claimants and clients of state agencies rather than accept more traditional and more personalistic forms of dependency.

The second self-negating dynamic was the tendency for expectations to rise. Three decades of post-war prosperity had provided the tax base for an expanding schedule of welfare services, but this prosperity also created problems for welfare state provision. For one thing, it continually raised the base line against which living standards were judged, particularly since 'relative deprivation' became the most common measure of social and psychological poverty. The consequence was that benefit levels in the 1960s and early 1970s reached levels that were far in excess of anything that Beveridge or Roosevelt had envisioned. Eventually expectations were raised to a point where it was all but impossible for state provision to meet them. Sustained prosperity and full employment gave working people a sense of affluence and security, and allowed them to enjoy a standard of living that was well above that supplied by state benefits. Over time, this led large sections of the middle class and skilled workers to regard state provision as unacceptably meagre in comparison to private housing, private health, private education, and private pensions. As one of its critics put it in 1981:

The welfare state is withering away because it is being undermined by market forces in changing conditions of supply and demand. Consumers are increasingly able to pay for, and will therefore demand, better education, medicine, housing and pensions than the state supplies, and suppliers are increasingly able to provide alternatives in the market.[52]

In this way, the groups who had formed the central constituency and tax-base for the welfare state gradually began to dissociate themselves from it, to view it as a drain on their taxes, and to regard its institutions as being for the benefit of others rather than themselves.[53]

The third self-negating dynamic had to do with problems of big government and the unresponsive bureaucratic machinery that administered welfare benefits. The more the state did, the more unwieldy it appeared to become, both at the level of the individual client and in respect of the economy as a whole. The new consumer capitalism had given rise to a revolution of individuated tastes and a commercial service culture that by contrast made welfare agencies appear rigidly bureaucratic and unresponsive to client needs and preferences. Instead of empowering individuals and enhancing the social rights of citizenship, the system was prone to formalism, and to upholding the prerogatives of agency administrators and managers.[54] And at the level of the economy, the larger the share of economic behaviour that was directed by the state, the more the economy was subjected to political constraints that reduced the effects of 'market disciplines' and diminished the capacity of the economy to respond to exogenous forces such as shifts in global trade or the appearance of new technologies.

Finally, and most ironically, the institutionalization of the welfare state, together with the prolonged period of prosperity that it brought in its wake, had the effect of concealing the economic and political problems that welfarism had been designed to address and highlighting instead a whole series of problems that it appeared to create. The welfare state's success tended to undermine its credibility. As collective memories of depression, mass unemployment and destitution began to fade, the state appeared to many to be the problem rather than the solution.[55]

Political discourse and the meaning of late modernity

The changes brought about by the forces of late modernity in respect of crime, welfare, and every other aspect of social life appear in retrospect to have a material reality that is indisputable. But for those living through these changes their precise meaning and political implications were far from obvious. People in the post-war decades were very conscious that they were living through a period of rapid social change and there was an extensive, often anxious, literature reflecting on modernization and its discontents. There were, of course, many ways to 'read' and respond to these social developments, and different currents of thought emerged in relation to them. As we will see, from the 1970s onwards, British and American political culture was characterized by a predominantly reactionary attitude towards late modernity and the social changes it ushered in: that is to say, by an attitude that generally regretted the changes and aspired to reverse them where possible. But it is worth pausing to recall that up until that point, the leading current of political thought was a social democratic one that largely embraced late modernity as an embodiment of economic progress and democratic social change.

The progressive reading

At least until the early 1970s the UK and US governments tended to view the direction in which social change was headed as an achievement rather than a problem. The governing parties of this period aimed not only to deliver continuing prosperity and full employment through a highly regulated economy but also to push ahead with a social agenda of extended welfare, expanded civil rights, and enhanced personal freedoms. There was, of course, deep-seated opposition to this agenda, particularly from traditionally conservative constituencies such as the Tory shires in England and the southern states in the USA, and from those sectors of capital and commerce that resisted regulation. But this opposition had less influence at the national level and was not formulated as an organized political ideology. The politics of expansion were in office. *Economic control* and *social liberation* were the watchwords of the day.

To the extent that the welfare state was problematized in these years, it was not in the name of a free market alternative, but in the cause of expanding its services and provision, allowing more community control and participation and taming the big government bureaucracies.[56] The standard critique of the welfare state was that it was not doing enough, that its benefits were too meagre, its procedures too demeaning, its decision-making too inflexible, its experts insufficiently accountable. The preferred, progressive solutions involved transforming claims into social rights and entitlements, making benefits universal rather than means-tested, reforming the bureaucracy to make it more responsive, and rendering the whole process less patronizing and more empowering for clients and for poor communities. By the late 1960s this critical framework was a well-established and increasingly influential position in social policy circles. A few years later, radical critics of criminal justice would, as we have seen, launch a critique of correctionalism in essentially the same terms.

Even the problem of rising crime rates failed to evoke much doubt or hesitation in the social democratic worldview. Although British and American crime rates increased every year from the mid-1950s onwards, and attracted much anxious commentary, the problem was often played down by government officials and treated with scepticism by criminological experts. Government reports attributed the rising rates to the dislocations of wartime, or the continuing problems of poverty and relative deprivation. Criminologists pointed to the pitfalls of official statistics, the effects of labelling and enforcement, or the media's over-reporting and moral panics. Many policy-makers and experts remained committed to the belief that the beneficial effects of welfare and prosperity would eventually reach into the inner cities and the poorest communities and remedy the crime problem. The penal-welfare paradigm and its criminological analysis thus continued to shape practical reasoning until the early 1970s, despite the emergence of facts that tended to contradict its claims.[57]

The same penal-welfare paradigm shaped the predominant ways in which criminal justice institutions were regarded. Right up until the mid-1970s the most vocal reform proposals were for the improvement of rehabilitative services, the reduction of oppressive controls, and the recognition of the rights of suspects and prisoners. The demand was to criminalize less, to minimize the use of custody, to humanize the prison, and where possible to deal with offenders in the community. Radical proposals such as 'non-interventionism' and even 'abolitionism' emerged in these years—at the very height of the crime wave—and were influential in shaping the practice of juvenile justice, police cautioning, and prosecutorial diversion. This situation in which crime rates were rising and penal levels were being decreased would strike many subsequent commentators as absurd and self-defeating. But it made perfect sense within the prevailing penal-welfare framework which assumed that crime was primarily responsive to welfare interventions rather than to punitive ones.[58] To the extent that the penal-welfare framework was seriously challenged during these years, it was a challenge from the left, pointing to the system's inadequate provision of treatment programmes and the limits of its individualistic, correctionalist approach.

The political discourse of social democracy thus embraced late modernity, downplayed the problems of crime and the limits of the welfare state, and offered a vision of the future that stayed faithful to the fundamental values and assumptions of welfarism. It was precisely because of this constancy in the face of change that social democracy would come to appear so completely out of touch once political attitudes took a reactionary turn in the 1980s and 1990s.

The political watershed of the 1970s

Social democratic politicians may have refused to rethink their commitments in the light of late modern developments, but by the early 1970s, many voters were reconsidering their own allegiances. Even prior to the recession of 1973, sections of the working population in Britain and America had experienced a change in their economic position that had made them think differently about the welfare state and their relation to it. Voters who had previously been strong supporters of social democratic parties increasingly took the view that the welfare state no longer worked to their benefit. There was a sense of shifting actuarial interests as people became conscious that, in all probability, they would not have need of many of the state benefits that their ever-increasing tax contributions were paying for. For these recently arrived middle classes, there was also a growing anxiety that their hard-won success could be undermined by a dynamic of change that appeared to be running out of control. Social issues such as growing crime, worsening race relations, family breakdown, growing welfare rolls, and the decline of 'traditional values'—together with concerns about high taxes, inflation, and declining economic performance—created a growing anxiety about the effects of change that conservative politicians began to pick up on and artic-ulate.[59] One sees this from the mid-1960s onwards in the speeches of presiden-tial candidates Goldwater and Nixon, even though the Republican party would remain Keynesian in its basic economic policies until Ronald Reagan took office in 1981. In the UK, the post-war social democratic consensus remained intact until the election of Margaret Thatcher in 1979, but as early as the late 1960s Conservative politicians such Enoch Powell began to articulate a reactionary (and sometimes racist) social vision that drew a great deal of popular attention.

These gradual shifts of interest and sentiment, which took place from the mid-1960s onwards, formed the background for the major political realignment that was eventually to follow. But it was not until the tumultuous events and economic collapse of the following decade, and the rapid shifts of public opin-ion that followed, that these underlying conditions were given clear political expression. Televised images of urban race riots, violent civil rights struggles, anti-war demonstrations, political assassinations, and worsening street crime reshaped the attitudes of the middle-American public in the late 1960s, just as stories of 'mugging' and increased street crime, militant trade unionism, chronic industrial disputes, and long lines of unemployed workers eventually convinced many British voters that the politics of social democratic centrism had had its day. Together with the devastating economic impact of the mid-1970s recession, these factors triggered the collapse of the post-war political settlement.[60] As social democratic governments around the world tried in vain to steer a Keynesian course out of the recession, the parties of the right grasped their opportunity. At the end of the decade, Republican and Conservative govern-ments swept into office on platforms that were explicitly hostile to welfarism and 'big government', to the 'permissive culture' of 1960s, and to the 'consensus politics' of social democracy that had governed for a quarter of a century.

What is striking about both the Reagan and the Thatcher election victories is that they owed less to the appeal of their economic policies—which at that stage were conspicuously underdeveloped—than to their ability to articulate popular discontent. Hostility towards 'tax and spend' government, undeserving welfare recipients, 'soft on crime' polices, unelected trade unions who were running the country, the break-up of the family, the breakdown of law and order—these were focal points for a populist politics that commanded widespread support. Appealing to the social conservatism of 'hard-working', 'respectable' (and largely white) middle classes, 'New Right' politicians blamed the shiftless poor for victimizing 'decent' society—for crime on the streets, welfare expenditure, high taxes, industrial militancy—and blamed the liberal elites for licensing a permissive culture and the anti-social behaviour it encouraged.[61]

Whereas post-war governments had taken it as their responsibility to deliver full employment and generalized prosperity, these New Right governments quickly abandoned both of these undertakings. Claiming that unemployment, like prosperity, was a market-generated phenomenon that reflected the under-lying health of the economy—rather than a policy outcome in the grasp of the

nation-state—these governments stood back and allowed market forces to operate largely unchecked, while simultaneously imposing severe public expenditure
cuts.[62] The predicable result was the rapid collapse of industrial production and
the re-emergence of structural unemployment on a massive scale not seen since
the 1930s. Both of these phenomena were turned to political effect as the Reagan
and Thatcher governments took steps to weaken the trade unions, shift power
back towards managers and capital, deregulate economic life, reverse the 'rights
revolution', and 'roll back' the welfare state. Within a few short years, the progressive politics of the post-war decades had been displaced by political regimes
that defined themselves in reaction to the welfare state and the social and cultural currents of late modernity.[63]

The reactionary reading of late modernity

The political projects of the Thatcher and Reagan governments differed over
time and from each other. However coherent they appear in retrospect, they
were in fact more opportunistic, more contradictory, and less fully implemented
than either their supporters or their critics supposed. Nevertheless, the policies
and political ideologies of these governments had a thematic unity that allows
us to characterize them, in a way that is abstract but not altogether inaccurate,
as *reactionary* in a quite specific sense.[64]

They were reactionary in that their policies were marked by a profound
antipathy to the economic and social revolution that had transformed Britain
and America in the post-war decades: that is to say, to the politics of the welfare
state and to the culture of late modernity. Both governments were absolutely
committed to undoing many of the social arrangements that had been established
in these years, and to attacking the economic and political orthodoxies that
underpinned them. The often contradictory combination of what came to be
known as 'neo-liberalism' (the re-assertion of market disciplines) and 'neo-conservatism' (the re-assertion of moral disciplines), the commitment to 'rolling
back the state' while simultaneously building a state apparatus that is stronger
and more authoritarian than before—these were the contradictory positions that
lay at the heart of the Thatcher and Reagan regimes.[65] They made ideological
sense, and commanded extensive popular support—in spite of their incoherence—because together they represented a reversal of the progressive revolution
of the post-war decades and a promise that the market would re-establish the
economic prosperity that the interventionist state had failed to maintain. The
framework of Keynesian social democracy ceased to be a catch-all solution and
became, instead, the key problem to be attacked by government policy. Its faulty
economic assumptions and permissive styles of thought lay at the root of all the
new social and economic ills—low productivity, high taxes and inflation, the culture of dependency, declining respect for authority, the crisis of the family.[66] The
achievements of the welfare state were systematically discredited or forgotten,
and instead its limitations and failures came to stand centre-stage.

Throughout the 1980s and much of the 1990s, these New Right politics dominated social and economic policy in the USA and the UK. Reversing the solidaristic solutions of the welfare state, with its concern for social equality, social security, and social justice, the new neo-liberal politics insisted on market fundamentalism and an unquestioning faith in the value of competition, enterprise, and incentives, as well as in the salutary effects of inequality and exposure to risk.[67] To this end, governments in both countries passed laws to tame the trade unions, reduce labour costs, deregulate finance, privatize the public sector, extend market competition and reduce welfare benefits. Tax rates for the rich were greatly reduced, and the resulting state deficits brought about further cuts in social spending. The result was a widening of inequalities and a skewed structure of incentives that encouraged the rich to work by making them richer and compelled the poor to work by making them poorer.[68]

Neo-conservatism introduced into political culture a strikingly *anti-modern* concern for the themes of tradition, order, hierarchy, and authority. These themes were most clearly articulated by the American religious right, which developed as a political force from the mid-1970s onwards. But they were also argued with great force and influence by 'neo-con' intellectuals such as Irving Kristol, Gertrude Himmelfarb, Charles Murray, and James Q. Wilson, and by their British equivalents Roger Scruton, Digby Anderson, Norman Dennis, and Sir Keith Joseph. This brand of moral conservatism was implacably opposed to the liberal culture of the 1960s, and to the democratizing, liberating themes of the 'permissive era', which were blamed for all of the social and economic ills of the subsequent decades. By the 1980s, the demand to get 'back to basics', to restore 'family values' and to re-impose 'individual responsibility' had become familiar themes on both sides of the Atlantic. So too were calls for more discipline in schools and families, an end to 'libertarian license' in art and culture, condemnation of the new sexual morality, and a generalized return to a more orderly, more disciplined, more tightly controlled society.[69]

These conservative calls for tighter order and control ought to have clashed head on with the policies of deregulation and market freedom that were, at precisely the same time, releasing individuals and companies from the grip of social regulation and moral restraint. That they did not is testimony to the success of their supporters in representing the problem of immoral behaviour as, in effect, a problem of poor people's conduct. Despite the all-encompassing rhetoric, the actual policy proposals that emerged made it clear that the need for more social control was not a generalized one, undoing the culture of late modernity, but instead a much more focused, much more specific demand, targeted on particular groups and particular behaviours. The well-to-do could continue to enjoy the personal freedoms and moral individualism delivered by post-war social change—indeed they could enjoy even more freedoms and choices as society became more marketized. But the poor must become more disciplined. Thus the new conservatism proclaimed a moral message exhorting everyone to return to the values of family, work, abstinence, and self-control, but in practice its real moral disciplines fastened onto the behaviour of unemployed workers, welfare mothers, immigrants, offenders, and drug users.

If the watchwords of post-war social democracy had been *economic control and social liberation*, the new politics of the 1980s put in place a quite different framework of *economic freedom and social control*.[70] And though this reactionary movement claimed to be undoing the political and cultural regime that had been developing since the war, in reality its assault upon late modernity took a very particularized form and left the major social arrangements largely untouched.

The conservative call for a return to moral discipline and traditional values did result in a renewed discipline and a tightening of controls, but these were directed mainly at poor individuals and marginalized communities and did nothing to constrain the great majority of citizens. The neo-liberal call for an extension of market freedoms and the dismantling of the 'nanny state' certainly produced more freedom for those with the resources to benefit from a deregulated market, but it also resulted in chronic unemployment for the weakest sectors of the workforce and a growing sense of insecurity for the rest. The irony here was that even with meaner, more restrictive benefits, the fact of massive unemployment ensured that social spending was higher at the end of Reagan and Thatcher's terms than at the beginning. Moreover, the welfare programmes that most benefited the middle classes—cheap mortgages, social security, tax breaks, and education subsidies—remained firmly and expensively in place.[71]

The politics of the 1980s and 1990s were heavily class-based in their impacts, even as they claimed to be generalized in their intent. And although the rich and the employed middle classes derived huge economic benefits from these new arrangements, the ending of solidaristic politics and the opening of class and race divisions had definite social costs that affected them too. Not the least of these was that the new politics produced a cultural mood that was defensive, ambivalent, and insecure, in stark contrast to the confident, emancipatory culture of a few decades before. Introduced in the name of freedom, the politics of reaction gave rise to widespread insecurities, and would eventually produce a renewed obsession with control. One reason for this was that even those who were well placed to take economic risks and reap their rewards were less comfortable with other kinds of risks—such as the threat of crime and violence—that were inherent in the deregulated society. There was a dim but widespread awareness that the costs of the new market freedoms were largely being born by the poorest most vulnerable groups. And even if some could justify this by notions of desert and economic utility, it was hard to forget the implicit dangers involved in amassing a sizeable population of dispossessed youths and disaffected minorities.[72]

In this situation, insecurity, group hostility, and some measure of bad conscience flourished and played a role in focusing discontent. Perhaps the pluralism of late modernity meant that living with 'difference' was everyone's irreversible fate and reactionary politics could do little to change this. As Émile

Durkheim long ago pointed out, social arrangements of this kind pose acute problems of social order and call for the creation of governmental institutions and civic associations that can build social solidarity and ensure moral regulation.[73] Complex societies need more organization, not less, and while markets can organize economic efficiencies, they do little to bring about moral restraint, social integration, or a sense of group belonging. In the absence of such initiatives, the new culture of diversity remained a source of frustration to many, and a constant source of grumbling cultural commentary. Among polite society at least, lipservice to multiculturalism and individual rights meant that objections to other people's lifestyles tended to be muted and displaced. But there were some behaviours and some people that did not have to be tolerated, and new and more coercive policies of social and penal control increasingly targeted these.[74]

A central outcome of the politics of the 1980s was thus a hardening of social divisions.[75] As neo-liberal policies reinforced rather than resisted the stratification produced by the global economy and a dualized labour market, stark new divisions emerged in the populations of the USA and the UK. The social and economic distance between the jobless and those in work, blacks and whites, affluent suburbs and strife-torn inner cities, consumers in a booming private sector and claimants left behind in collapsing public institutions grew ever greater in these years, until it became a commonplace of political and social commentary. In place of the solidaristic ideals of the Great Society or the Welfare State there emerged a deeply divided society—variously described as 'the dualized society', the 'thirty, thirty, forty society', the 'seduced and the repressed', or, in the USA where social divisions were overlayed by racial ones, 'American Apartheid'— with one sector being deregulated in the name of market enterprise, the other being disciplined in the name of traditional morality.[76] These new divisions worked to further undermine the old solidarities and collective identities upon which the welfare state had depended. The possibilities of inter-class identification, of mutual sympathy across income divides, of a shared citizenship and mutual regard—these became increasingly unlikely as the lives and adaptive cultures of the poor began to look altogether alien in the eyes of the well-to-do.[77]

In this new social context, it was hardly surprising to find that social problems such as violence, street crime, and drug abuse worsened, particularly in those areas where economic and social disadvantage were concentrated. So although property crimes in the USA began to decline after their peak in 1982, homicides and violent crime rose sharply in the second half of the 1980s, particularly among young people, and often in association with the growing market in hard drugs. In Britain under Mrs. Thatcher's law and order administration, the crime rate doubled in a decade.[78]

But more important for our purposes is the way in which crime came to take on a new and strategic significance in the political culture of this period. Crime—together with associated 'underclass' behaviours such as drugs abuse, teenage pregnancy, single parenthood, and welfare dependency—came to function as a rhetorical legitimation for social and economic policies that effectively punished the poor and as a justification for the development of strong disciplinary state. In the political discourse of this period, social accounts of the crime problem come to be completely discredited.[79] Such accounts, so it was said, denied individual responsibility, excused moral fault, watered down punishment, encouraged bad behaviour and in that respect were emblematic of all that was wrong with welfarism. Crime came to be seen instead as a problem of indiscipline, a lack of self-control or social control, a matter of wicked individuals who needed to be deterred and who deserved to be punished. Instead of indicating need or deprivation, crime was a matter of anti-social cultures or personalities, and of rational individual choice in the face of lax law enforcement and lenient punishment regimes.

In this watershed period, effective crime control came to be viewed as a matter of imposing more controls, increasing disincentives, and, if necessary, segregating the dangerous sector of the population. The recurrent image of the offender ceased to be that of the needy delinquent or the feckless misfit and became much more threatening—a matter of career criminals, crackheads, thugs, and predators—and at the same time much more racialized.[80] And the compassionate sensibility that used to temper punishment now increasingly enhanced it, as the sympathy invoked by political rhetoric centred exclusively on the victim and the fearful public, rather than the offender. Instead of idealism and humanity, penal policy discussions increasingly evoked cynicism about rehabilitative treatment, a distrust of penological experts, and a new righteousness about the importance and efficacy of punishment. If 'radical non-interventionism' epitomized the progressive ideal of the 1960s, the term that best captures the new right's ideal is that of 'zero tolerance'. In the political reaction against the welfare state and late modernity, crime acted as a lens through which to view the poor—as undeserving, deviant, dangerous, different—and as a barrier to lingering sentiments of fellow feeling and compassion. In this reactionary vision, the underlying problem of order was viewed not as a Durkheimian problem of solidarity but as a Hobbesian problem of order, to which the solution was to be a focused, disciplinary version of the Leviathan State.

5

Policy Predicament: Adaptation, Denial, and Acting Out

So how did the social changes of late modernity come to impress themselves upon the field of crime control and criminal justice? Not directly to be sure, but through a series of accommodations and adjustments undertaken by various agencies in response to the specific pressures, problems or opportunities that these agencies encountered. Sometimes these stimuli were experienced as coming from the outside the system; at other times they were generated from within the criminal justice agencies themselves. But as the new social relations and sensibilities of late modernity worked their way in and through these crime control institutions the distinction between 'inside' and 'outside' became increasingly obscure. Late modernity and the new politics to which it gave rise changed how organizations thought about crime and punishment, justice and control, just as it changed the terrain on which these organizations operated.

The present chapter seeks to describe and explain the recurring forms of calculation and decision-making that gave rise to the practices of the contemporary period. It is not a narrative account of policy developments although it does describe the key policies and how they took shape.[1] It aims instead to describe the kinds of considerations that drove decision-making in this period, and the sorts of policies that emerged in consequence.

The last quarter of the twentieth century saw the emergence of non-correctionalist rationales for crime control—new criminologies, new philosophies of punishment, new penological aims, and objectives. Over the same period there was also an attempt on the part of politicians and others to improve the fit between crime policy and the new political and cultural context in which it operates—to invent new and more effective mechanisms of crime control as well as new ways of representing crime and justice. This ongoing attempt to reorient crime control institutions and revise their relation to a changing social environment was very much a matter of patchwork repairs and interim solutions rather than well thought-out reconstruction.

Any substantial challenge to a society's institutional arrangements creates practical problems and uncertainties—for the publics served by the institutions, as well as for the institutions' leadership and staff. In this chapter and the next I examine the problems posed by the challenge to penal modernism. My assumption is that whenever societal change displays a distinctive structural pattern, with one field of social action (in this case crime control) appearing to align itself with structures and sensibilities that have developed in other fields, the explanation should be couched in terms that respect the motivations and actions of the actors and agencies involved. Instead of talking in the abstract about 'structural alignment', or assuming that 'underlying forces' are capable of automatically working their effects across different social fields, we should instead attend to specific actors and agencies. We should ask how they perceive their situations and how they address the problems that these situations pose for them. And we should attend to the perceptions and reactions of civil society's actors as well as state actors, particularly where the institutions involved have such a central significance for the public at large.

This problem-solving account of institutional change finds support in the fact that historical periods in which institutional arrangements are undermined also tend to be ones in which there is an outpouring of reform proposals and policy-making inventiveness. Whatever the problems and dysfunctions it brings in its wake, the process of institutional collapse tends also to act as a spur to action. Its immediate effect is to release energies and to foster new ideas, new programmes and new reform initiatives. As the old institutions relax their grip, new ways of thinking and acting are brought into existence. Novel ways of framing problems become more thinkable and more urgently relevant. New forms of action can be tried out. No wonder then, that the field of crime control in the 1980s and 1990s saw such constant ferment and reform.

It would be going too far to say that criminal justice suffered a 'collapse' or a 'breakdown' in the period after the mid-1970s, but there is no doubt that the institutional arrangements of penal-welfarism and, more generally, of modern criminal justice, were undermined and unsettled in these years. The field was disrupted, and so was the criminological framework that it had anchored. In the years that followed, a deluge of new programmes and policy initiatives flooded forth, proposing new institutional aims and objectives, new policing and penal regimes, and new conceptions of the crime problem and its solution.

Some of these, such as the radical projects of abolitionism, decriminalization, and de-institutionalization that appeared in the 1970s, captured the imagination of academics and radicals but had little sustained impact upon government thinking and institutional policy. Some, such as the movement for fixed sentencing reform, have come to form central ingredients of contemporary policy and practice, though not in the form that their proponents intended. Others schemes, such as the proposals for mediation and restorative justice, have been allowed to operate on the margins of criminal justice, offsetting the central tendencies without much changing the overall balance of the system. Yet others, like the reintroduction of chain gangs and corporal punishments in some of the southern states of America have left their emblematic mark on the culture of punishment, even when their impact upon actual penal practice has been much more slight.

Many of the reforms that now constitute important elements in the crime control field—such as the victims' movement, privatized corrections, or community-based policing and crime prevention—began as low-key, local initiatives that at first attracted comparatively little public attention. Others measures which have had great public visibility and wide public and support—such as mandatory sentencing of repeat offenders and 'sexual predators', or community notification of released sex-offenders—have been rapidly implemented with immediate repercussions, though these have often been less significant than either their supporters or critics claimed.[2] Finally, there have been developments of the first importance—above all the emergence of very high rates of imprisonment in the USA—that were not originally articulated as reform programmes, nor implemented as explicit policies. Instead, they emerged over time as the overdetermined outcome of various converging processes. And though they subsequently became *de facto* strategies attracting widespread support and multiple *ex post facto* rationales, the plan followed the practice rather than the other way around.[3]

This confusing maelstrom of developments makes it difficult to sort out why some proposals are taken up and legislated while others fail to produce practical results, particularly when outcomes often have little to do with proven credentials, research evidence, or even professional support. To render the process intelligible we need to examine more than just the details of the proposals themselves. We must also inspect the motivations and thought-processes of the authorities who select and implement them, and the cultural and political contexts in which their choices are validated. This chapter will focus on the problem of crime control as it was perceived and managed by the agencies and authorities of the criminal justice state, and the considerations and contexts that shaped their decisions. The chapter after this will look more closely at the issue of cultural context, examining the new collective experience of crime and the structures of feeling to which it gave rise, and the behaviour of various non-governmental actors who have become actively involved in the effort to govern crime.

The new predicament

During the last thirty years, the criminal justice authorities of the UK and the USA have had to formulate policy within a changing set of pressures and constraints. They have had to reorient their practices in the wake of internal developments, such as the critique of correctionalism; adjust to changes in adjacent fields, such as the decline of work and welfare; and accommodate to the newly dominant political currents of neo-liberalism and neo-conservatism, however much these currents pulled in different directions or went against the grain of their own beliefs. Above all, however, they have had to face a new criminological *predicament*—a new and problematic set of structural constraints that formed the policy horizon within which all decisions must be made.[4] This predicament has its origins in two major social facts of the last third of the twentieth century: *the normality of high crime rates* and *the acknowledged limitations of the criminal justice state*.

Over time, this predicament has appeared more or less pressing. In the 1970s and early 1980s it became starkly apparent to many administrators, although elected officials were often slower and more reluctant to recognize its force. In the late 1990s, with the falling off in crime rates, it has temporarily eased its effect, and it has become easier for politicians (and maverick police chiefs) to publicly deny it. But however much it shifts in and out of consciousness, the limits imposed by high crime rates and low criminal justice effectiveness remain a fundamental constraint upon contemporary policy and practice.

High crime rates as a normal social fact

In the post-war period, high rates of crime became a fact of life in the USA and the UK, just as they did in most Western societies. From the mid-1960s onwards, rates of property and violent crime that were double and treble those of pre-war rates increasingly became an acknowledged and commonplace feature of social experience. By the early 1990s, despite some levelling off, the recorded rates were as much as ten times those of forty years before.[5] Between the 1960s and the 1990s, a whole complex of related phenomena had grown up around the fact of crime—most notably a widespread fear of crime, routine avoidance behaviours, pervasive media and cultural representations, and a generalized 'crime consciousness'. In that sense, high crime—and the responses to it—had become an organizing principle of everyday life, an integral part of social organization. If commentators in the immediate post-war period could regard increased rates as a temporary aberration, by the 1970s society's vulnerability to high rates of crime came to be viewed for what it was—a normal social fact. At the end of the 1990s, despite much publicized decreases, American and British rates of crime and violence remain at an historically high level, and are widely perceived as such, particularly by older people who recall the very different circumstances of the 1950s and early 1960s. Whatever successes police and politicians may claim, crime avoidance remains a prominent organizing principle of everyday life, and fear of crime persists at unprecedented levels.

Despite the fact that crime has a very uneven social distribution, and high risks of victimization are disproportionately concentrated in the poorest urban districts, crime is now widely experienced as a prominent fact of modern life. For most people, and especially for those living in cities and suburbs, crime is no longer an aberration or an unexpected, abnormal event.[6] Instead, the threat of crime has become a routine part of modern consciousness, a standing possibility that is constantly to be 'kept in mind'. Crime has come to be regarded as an everyday risk that must be routinely assessed and managed in much the same way that we have come to deal with road traffic—another mortal danger that has become a normal feature of the modern landscape. High rates of crime have, over the period of a single generation, become a standard, background feature of our lives—a taken-for-granted element of late modernity. The now ubiquitous security advertisements telling us that 'a car theft occurs every minute', or 'a credit card is lost or stolen every second' express the experience quite well: crime forms a part of our daily environment, as constant and unremitting as time itself.[7]

High crime rates have become patterned regularities—normal and more or less intelligible features our social and economic routines that are widely regarded as an inevitable accompaniment of modernization. Until recently, and with a consistency rarely seen in other social data, recorded crime statistics showed an annual increase, in most crime categories, in virtually every year for more than thirty years. This secular pattern established a set of cultural assumptions and collective representations that are now hard to dislodge. Public opinion polls since the 1970s show that the majority of people believe that the crime problem is bad and getting worse and that crime rates will continue to rise in the future: a belief that persists even in periods where both recorded and actual rates are stable or declining.[8] We will see in the next chapter how the normality of high crime rates came to form the focal point for a whole cluster of other beliefs and behaviours—a new cultural complex that shapes and expresses the contemporary experience of crime. But for now the point I wish to make is that the emergence of this new social fact has had major implications for government and particularly for the agencies responsible for crime control and criminal justice.

The limits of the criminal justice state

The second social fact shaping the new predicament is closely related to the first, and concerns the way in which the criminal justice system has come to be regarded by the public, by the political authorities, and by its own personnel. If the 1970s is the period in which the normality of high crime rates began to be recognized as a fact, even by those with reason to resist this interpretation, it is also the period in which the criminal justice system came to be viewed primarily in terms of its limitations and propensity for failure rather than its prospects for future success.

It is not that rising crime rates had never before perturbed criminal justice, or presented the system with problems. Rises in recorded crime had been a nagging problem for the authorities ever since the Second World War. But as late as the 1960s criminal justice institutions were quite capable of absorbing challenges of this kind and turning them to their own advantage. In 1964 the UK government White Paper *The War Against Crime* acknowledged that there had been an 'upsurge in crime and delinquency' that had continued unabated since the mid-1950s, but saw no need to question the penal-welfare framework to which it remained fully committed. Like its forerunner of 1959, *Penal Practice in a Changing Society*, the 1964 White Paper expressed confidence that the

penal-welfare strategy was the right approach, and asserted that vigorous policing and correctional measures, guided by research into the causes of crime and
the effectiveness of penal treatments, would begin to stem the rising tide of
crime. To the extent that these measures seemed to be failing, this was seen as a
problem of resources and knowledge, or of methods and implementation, and
plans were laid for further research, increased funding and the expansion of
child welfare services. If there was any doubt about the state's capacity to deal
with the problem it did not surface in these government statements. On the contrary, the thrust of the announcements was that the state would win the war
against crime, just as the warfare state had vanquished its enemies and the welfare state was now tackling the social and economic problems of peacetime.

The reaffirmation of the existing paradigm in the face of growing evidence of
its ineffectiveness was also a feature of the US President's Crime Commission
Report of 1967. That Report responded to rapidly rising crime rates by asserting that with more federal resources, improved research and information management, and the crime-preventing effects of the government's War on Poverty,
contemporary crime would be brought under control. Whatever problems 'the
challenge of crime in a free society' might entail—and this in the midst of major
urban riots and an all-time record rate of increase in UCR crime rates—these
did not dispel confidence in the correctional, case-processing assumptions that
framed the criminal justice state and its monopoly of crime control.[9]

In the period since the late 1960s official discourse has moved away from the
confident position set out in these documents. There is no longer a commitment
to the penal-welfare framework, and the correctionalist assumptions that it
entailed. But nor is there any settled confidence in the capacity of the criminal
justice state to control crime and provide law and order, no matter what framework it adopts. The state's claims have become more modest and more hesitant,
at least in certain contexts and addressing certain audiences. Particularly in the
1980s and early 1990s there was clear sense of the failure of criminal justice
agencies, a new focus upon their limitations, and a much more restricted sense
of the state's power to regulate conduct and prevent crime.[10] This official view,
usually expressed *sotto voce*, is more loudly echoed in public opinion, which has
become highly critical of the system (particularly of courts and sentencers) viewing the standard penalties as much too lenient and the penal system as too little
concerned with public safety.[11] This sense of the state's impotence in the face of
crime has become so well established in recent decades that developments which
challenge it—such as the claimed success of certain American police methods in
America or the British government's claim that 'prison works'—have generated
huge amount of media and professional attention.

The first signs of this challenge to penal modernism took quite specific and
localized forms. From the late 1960s onwards an influential body of literature
questioned the efficacy and legitimacy of rehabilitative measures and the individualized sentencing model. This opened the way to a more sweeping critique
of criminal justice, as the sense of failure became widespread and iconoclastic

evaluative research became more common. One by one, the limitations of prisons and young offenders institutions, probation and parole, conventional policing, and deterrent sentencing structures were carefully documented, each study contributing to the sense that the credibility of the whole criminal justice state was very much in doubt.[12] The 'Nothing Works' slogan, which became pervasive in the late 1970s, may have been an hysterical overreaction, but it had the effect of establishing a new, more pessimistic mood that that would persist long after the data upon which it was based had been discredited.

Since that time, a more sober and abiding sense of the limits of criminal justice has become a central feature of policy discourse and criminological common sense. From the mid-1980s onwards, it has become increasingly common for government policy documents, Chief Constable and Police Commissioners' reports, even political party manifestos, to emphasize that government agencies cannot, by themselves, succeed in controlling crime.[13] Modest improvements at the margin, the better management of risks and resources, reduction of the fear of crime, reduction of criminal justice expenditure, greater support for crime's victims, more expressive penal measures—these have become the new policy objectives, as policy analysts deem it more realistic to deal with the *effects* of crime rather than address the thing itself. For the first time since it was fully established in the late nineteenth century, confidence in the criminal justice state's capacity to control crime and provide security was seriously undermined. Even in the mid-1990s, when crime rates in the USA and the UK declined, few experts were willing to attribute this change to the effective actions of criminal justice agencies.

The myth of the sovereign state and its monopoly of crime control

This state of affairs was quite new and carried significant implications for government authorities and for criminal justice agencies. The perception of high crime rates as a normal social fact, together with the widely acknowledged limitations of the criminal justice system, had the effect of eroding one of the foundational myths of modern society: the myth that the sovereign state is capable of delivering 'law and order' and controlling crime within its territorial boundaries. This challenge to the state's law and order mythology was all the more persuasive and all the more troublesome because it occurred at a time when the wider notion of state sovereignty was already under attack on a number of different fronts.[14]

Like all historically developed political concepts, sovereignty is a complex and much contested notion. Strictly defined, it refers to the competence of a state legislature to make or unmake laws without challenge by other law-making authorities. But the term has also a wider meaning that relates to the sovereign state's claimed capacity to rule a territory in the face of competition and resistance from external and internal enemies. Over time, the effective control of crime and the routine protection of citizens from criminal depredations had come to form elements of the promise that the state holds out to its citizens.[15]

For all its importance in guiding state formation and strategies of rule, this notion of state sovereignty has proved unsustainable. In crime control, as in other spheres, the limitations of the state's capacity to govern social life in all its details have become ever more apparent, particularly in the late modern era. So, having arrogated to itself control functions and responsibilities that once belonged to the institutions of civil society, the late modern state is now faced with its own inability to deliver the expected levels of control over crime and criminal conduct. Like all myths, the myth of the penal sovereign and its 'law and order' powers is too deeply inscribed, too long-standing, and too politically potent to be easily dismantled by rational critique and administrative reform. No doubt it will continue to be invoked, and will, for some time to come, retain some of its power to persuade. But what has changed in the last decade or so, is that the myth has itself become problematic—a source of ambivalence rather than reassurance. In consequence, it no longer forms the taken-for-granted frame for policy and practice in the field of crime control.

The *predicament* for government authorities today, then, is that they see the need to withdraw their claim to be the primary and effective provider of security and crime control, but they also see, just as clearly, that the political costs of such a withdrawal are liable to be disastrous. The consequence is that in recent years we have witnessed a remarkably volatile and ambivalent pattern of policy development—one that has become increasingly febrile in the urgency with which each policy initiative succeeds the one before.

The emergent outcome is a series of policies that appear deeply conflicted, even schizoid, in their relation to one another. On the one hand, there has been an attempt to face up to the predicament and develop pragmatic new strategies that are adapted to it: through institutional reforms aimed at overcoming the limits of the criminal justice state, or else through accommodations that recognize these limitations and work within them. But alongside these difficult *adaptations* to the reality principle, there is a recurring attempt to evade its terms altogether, particularly on the part of elected officials who play an increasingly prominent role in criminal justice policy-making. This politicized reaction takes two recurring forms. Either it wilfully *denies* the predicament and reasserts the old myth of the sovereign state and its plenary power to punish. Or else it abandons reasoned, instrumental action and retreats into an *expressive* mode that we might, continuing the psychoanalytic metaphor, describe as *acting out*—a mode that is concerned not so much with controlling crime as with expressing the anger and outrage that crime provokes. It is this predicament and the authorities' deeply ambivalent reactions to it—rather than any coherent programme or singular strategy—that have shaped crime control and criminal justice in the late modern period.[16]

The structured ambivalence of the state's response

The predicament I have described has different implications for different kinds of authorities. For *political actors*, acting in the context of electoral competition, policy choices are heavily determined by the need to find popular and effective measures that will not be viewed as signs of weakness or an abandonment of the state's responsibility to the public. Measures with which elected officials are identified must be penologically credible but, above all, must maintain political credibility and popular support. In the choice of policy responses, those that can most easily be represented as strong, smart, and either effective or expressive are most attractive. Those that are most easily represented (by opponents or by the public) as a retreat, or an acknowledgement of failure, or as out of touch with public sentiment, are the ones that present the greatest difficulties. The problem is one of political rhetoric and appearance as much as practical effectiveness.

For *administrative actors* charged with the running of organizations, problems of political spin and public relations are also important, and act as an external constraint upon decisions. But on a day to day basis these are not the primary considerations that govern administrative decision-making. Rather, administrators are driven by the need to maintain the integrity of internal processes, to adjust their organization to keep pace with changes in its external environment, to repair perceived deficiencies and to address organizational failures. Their reference groups are other administrators as well as experts, researchers, and reform organizations. And though they must obey the laws and directives issued by politicians, the latter are regarded as a troublesome, external force, with different interests and agendas, rather than an integral part of the permanent organization.

The relation between the organization and its political masters routinely involves conflict over budgets and resources, especially in the context of neoliberal public expenditure cuts. It can also entail more substantive conflicts, particularly when measures are proposed that clash with the organization's view of its mission and the most effective methods of pursuing it. (This kind of conflict has been increasingly pronounced in recent years, as the neoconservative political agenda generates populist measures that few experts support.) Administrative decisions are thus shaped by two agendas, one internal, the other imposed from the outside, and it is the administrators' job to pursue their organizational tasks in ways that at least appear to accord with the concerns of their political masters.[17]

The politician typically views policy initiatives in terms of their political appeal and in relation to other political positions; acts within the time horizon set by electoral competition and in the full glare of media publicity; and relies primarily upon 'political' knowledge—about public opinion, focus group preferences, opposition tactics, political values—rather than organizational experience or detailed research findings. Political initiatives are often reactive, triggered by specific events, and deliberately partisan. As a consequence they tend to be urgent and impassioned, built around shocking but atypical cases, and more concerned to accord with political ideology and popular perception than with expert knowledge or the proven capacities of institutions.

In contrast, *the administrator* can and must focus upon the interests of a single organization, is oriented towards a longer time frame, and operates at a greater distance from press and public scrutiny. Statistical reasoning, resource management, and cost–benefit analysis are the stock-in-trade of organizational management. The administrator has a more realistic understanding of the organization's processes and impacts, and more ready access to hard information about their costs and consequences. His or her primary concern is for the organization's core business: the flow of activity, the modal decisions, the standard cases. Public opinion, partisan politics, and impassioned concern with atypical cases are disruptive distractions from the central organizational mission.

The politician and the administrator. Political discourse and administrative discourse. The scope and conditions for action in each case are quite different, as are their guiding rationalities, values, and interests. As we will see, these positional differences have shaped the different ways in which the predicament of crime control has been handled, and produced serious tensions in the process of policy formation.

As for government ministers and secretaries of state, caught in a contradictory location between the administrative and political domains—they run a department and are responsible for its actions; they are elected officials who must represent policy to the public and their party and contest future elections—theirs is a structurally generated ambivalence. Their position requires that they simultaneously attend to quite different interests, represent policy to different audiences, and continuously trade off administrative rationality and political advantage. They need to look both ways. To facilitate administrative efficiency but also to please the public. To put in place viable policies but also to minimize the political risks entailed in doing so. To pursue the goals of criminal justice but also to avoid the scandals and injustices that inevitably result. To be an effective administrator but also a popular politician.

This ambivalence is worsened by the quite unrealistic assumptions about criminal justice that are embodied in public opinion. Common sense attitudes are often characterized by an 'absolutist' conception based on front-stage appearances and ideological shibboleths—a conception that demands justice, punishment and protection, whatever the cost. In this way of thinking, criminals should be prosecuted to the full extent of the law, the guilty should always be punished, dangerous individuals should never be released, prisoners should serve their full terms, and an offender's sentence should precisely reflect his offence. And somehow, at the same time, the innocent should always be acquitted, the rule of law upheld, and expenditure held within reasonable levels. The fact that there are serious incompatibilities between these 'absolute' imperatives, and that each shining public principle is routinely undermined by the backstage realities—of resource rationing, evidentiary limits, plea negotiations, and sentencing compromises—means that the public is easily scandalized by many of the decisions that are routinely made.

These problems of public perception are exacerbated by the fact that the criminal justice system is, in any case, a minefield. It routinely deals with emotionally laden, high visibility cases that strain the meaning of justice and provoke hostile reaction on one side or the other. It manages risks and dangerous individuals, frequently releasing offenders back into the community when their legal sentence comes to an end, or worse, because of misguided parole decisions or scandalous escapes. In the context of a high crime society, both politicians and the public regard such a system with scepticism and distrust. A constant source of danger, injustice and insecurity, it becomes a part of the crime problem rather than a solution to it.

Major policy decisions will often depend upon how government ministers respond to these very different considerations and constituencies. And of course the dynamics of this process change when crime control issues are politicized and subject to fierce electoral competition and intense public scrutiny. As the system became more politicized in the 1980s and 1990s, the balance of forces often shifted away from the logic of administration and expert decision-making towards a more political and populist style. The following pages describe the contradictory ways in which ambivalent state authorities and their various agencies have responded to the predicament over time, sometimes adapting to it in a creative, realistic manner, sometimes evading it by means of forceful denials and expressive acting out.

Adaptive responses

Over the last three decades, and still today, these contradictory responses to the predicament of crime control have co-existed, with the authorities sponsoring quite different kinds of policy at different times and at different points in the crime control field. Over time, however, there has been a perceptible shift in emphasis, with adaptive solutions being increasingly eclipsed by more politicized, more expressive, alternatives. In the USA this shift can be dated to the mid-1980s and President Reagan's declaration of a 'War on Drugs' while in the UK, the most pronounced shift occurred in 1993 when Mr Major's government abandoned the 'punishment in the community' approach in favour of a tougher, more populist policy based around the slogan that 'prison works'. But prior to these shifts of emphasis, the authorities' response to the problem was more often characterized by adaptive measures, usually developed by means of cumulative, low-visibility administrative decisions, rather than as announced policies subject to political or public debate. I will describe in turn the six main types of adaptation—the rationalization of justice; the commercialization of justice; defining deviance down; redefining success; concentrating upon consequences; and redistributing responsibility—and then outline the new style of criminological reasoning that accompanied and facilitated them.

Professionalization and the rationalization of justice

For the administrators in charge of criminal justice agencies, high rates of crime brought with them immediate problems of increased caseloads and strained resources as well as growing anxieties about a loss of public confidence. From the 1960s onwards, in both the USA and the UK, the rising levels of recorded crime increased the 'throughput' of the criminal justice system, with steep increases in the numbers of crimes reported to the police, prosecutions brought, cases tried, and offenders sanctioned. This fact alone meant that criminal justice agencies had to expand their capacities and transform their practices in order to keep pace with its new workload. But the increase in crime was also experienced as the failure of crime control, and above all, of the police, the courts and the prisons. This has led, in the last two decades, to frequent and sometimes quite radical reformulations of the objectives and priorities of these organizations.

The police have been on the frontline of this losing battle. This was particularly so in the USA in the 1960s and 1970s, where increased crime complaints, allegations of widespread corruption, and a series of urban riots and political demonstrations combined to reduce the legitimacy of the police and draw them deeper into the social conflicts that troubled the cities.[18] Police departments across the USA responded to this crisis by seeking to professionalize themselves, by investing in the hardware and information systems made available by the Law Enforcement Administration Authority (LEAA), and by embracing the new, more reactive styles of '911 policing' made possible by the telephone and the automobile. The outcome—which was quickly copied by British forces—was a motorized police force, withdrawn from close community involvement (to avoid charges of corruption), and intent on providing a 'rapid response' in answer to emergency call-outs from the public. The unintended consequence was that relations between the police and the public became more distant and more strained, particularly in poor or minority neighbourhoods. Without co-operation from the public, the ability of the police to clear-up crimes decreased. Without the presence of police officers on foot patrolling the streets, fear of crime get worse. Without informal relations with residents and community leaders, police became less sensitive to the nuances of the neighbourhood, less responsive to the wishes of its law-abiding members, and less capable of keeping order and preventing crime. By the 1980s the folly of this hands-off style of policing approach was perfectly apparent and today a return to 'community policing' has come to be viewed as a universal panacea.

If the police initially responded to the predicament by seeking to professionalize themselves, a more general response was the attempt to rationalize the practice of criminal justice. As early as 1967 the US President's Commission Report had emphasized this solution, and had encouraged the criminal justice agencies to take a more informed, systematic approach to their work. A widespread demand for the curtailment of discretion and for a more formalized, more accountable, decision-making process—a demand that was endorsed by a series of Supreme Court decisions—lent further impetus to this development. From the 1970s onwards there was a major effort, led by the LEAA, to improve the efficiency of the criminal justice process by introducing more systematic information gathering, better caseload management, and new strategies of system integration and monitoring.[19]

From this time onwards, the costs of criminal justice became an explicit feature of policy debate, thereby bringing into focus awkward questions about resources and the rationing of justice more candidly than ever before. The comparative costs of penal measures came to be a significant consideration in deciding between them, particularly when none of them appeared especially effective, and the 1970s and 1980s saw a series of government initiatives designed to shift sentencing away from expensive forms of custody towards cheaper sanctions such as intensive probation, half-way houses, and boot camps.[20] These cost considerations were also applied to the other criminal justice functions. Prosecution became more selective; court expenses were reduced by shifts towards summary justice (the introduction of summary fines, the reduction of jury trials; more diversion, etc.) and probation offices developed 'gate-keeping' formulae designed to ensure that their case-loads included only those who were otherwise at risk of going to custody.[21]

At one level, this was an obvious organizational response, and emulated reform patterns to be found in other areas of public administration.[22] But it also registered, and for the first time, an official perception of the criminal justice system that saw the system not primarily as an embodiment of justice, or a solution to the crime problem, but instead as a problem in and of itself. From this point onwards, one can trace a settled perception that the criminal justice process is characterized by arbitrariness and injustice, with a tendency to generate uncontrolled costs and unplanned outcomes, and to create risks and dangers for the public it should be protecting. 'Taming the system'—its costs, its discretionary powers, its liability to expose the public to dangers—came to be part of the project of government in this field.[23]

This systematization of criminal justice—using information technology, operational models, and computerized data processing as well as new mechanisms for promoting inter-agency co-ordination—has been an important feature of the 1980s and 1990s. It has been enthusiastically sponsored by central government in the UK and by both state and federal government in the USA, often in the face of opposition from the organizations themselves, who have been concerned to preserve the decision-making autonomy and institutional integrity that they previously enjoyed. To the extent that it has been achieved—and it varies greatly from place to place—this systematization has allowed a greater measure of central planning and control to occur, and has enhanced government's capacity to pursue system-wide policy objectives.

Once these information technologies and management practices were put in place, reflexivity and self-monitoring became standard parts of the system's operations. Martinson's question—'what works?'—has come to haunt the practices of criminal justice, not as a critique of rehabilitative treatment, but as a routine feature of every aspect of criminal justice practice. Throughout the 1980s its most important impact was upon the control of criminal justice staff, who were subject to increased levels of monitoring, assessment, and accountability. And by the 1990s the new infrastructure of computers, information technology, and detailed data gathering had given rise to a new generation of 'smart' crime control, as the police, sentencers and prison authorities began to use computers and geo-coded data to focus decision-making and target interventions.

The commercialization of justice

This drive towards formalization and managerial accountability was furthered by the sweeping public service reforms of the 1980s. For most of that decade criminal justice was sheltered from the public expenditure cuts that were being imposed in other areas, but the spreading ethos of business management, monetary measurement and value-for-money government was inescapable. By the mid-1980s criminal justice agencies in the USA and the UK had developed a managerialist, business-like ethos that emphasized economy, efficiency and effectiveness in the use of resources. The continuing effort to 're-invent government' led to the development of clearly specified 'performance indicators' against which an organization's activities might be measured, as well as an emphasis upon strategic planning, line management, devolved budgets and financial responsibility within the agencies.[24] In time, these new practices affected not just the management of the organizations, but also their mission. Probation officers, prison governors and police chiefs found that their new budgetary responsibilities and financial reporting duties made a difference to how they responded to their staffs, the public and their clients. The reforms gave rise to new patterns of accountability, set formulae for decision-making, and brought about a gradual lessening of discretion and autonomy for rank and file staff.

The most publicized aspect of this new business ethos has been the rapid process of privatization and commercialization that has taken place in criminal justice, first in the USA and then from the mid-1980s onwards, in Britain. Specific criminal justice functions, ranging from court escort duties, routine parole supervision, and specialist prison services to the building and management of penal institutions, have increasingly been contracted out to commercial companies such as Securicor, Group 4, Wackenhut and the Corrections Corporation of America. What were once state-monopolized powers have increasingly been devolved to private, 'for-profit' contractors, who are allowed to pursue their commercial interests so long as they remain within the constraints established by their contract with the government authorities and submit to various forms of monitoring and regulation.[25] These privatization measures, which correspond precisely to the fiscal and ideological principles of neo-liberal government, were imposed by central government and state legislatures in the face of strong opposition from penal professionals; especially from staff unions who feared that their conditions of work would deteriorate as a result of cheap competition and cost-trimming. But as prison populations expanded in the 1980s and 1990s, government reliance upon the private sector has increased, not least because of the comparative speed and low cost with which commercial companies could provide new prison places.

More recently, and for similar reasons, this willingness to blend public and private provision has begun to affect policing, as the public police have been encouraged to recognize and co-operate with their counterparts in the rapidly growing private sector police.[26] This embrace of the private sector is liable to have fateful consequences, as it begins to transform the character of the crime control field, setting up new interests and incentives, creating new inequalities of access and provision, and facilitating a process of penal and security expansion that might otherwise have been more constrained.

If business management techniques have provided criminal justice with ways of responding to problems of cost and overload, the private sector model has also shaped the system's response to problems of legitimacy and public confidence. The ethos of 'customer relations' that is so pervasive in the commercial sector, and so central to business management, has begun to influence the practice of government agencies as well. Organizations such as the police and the courts that used to view their task as being to uphold 'the public interest'—in ways that were largely defined by the organization itself—have sought to become more responsive to the voices and preferences of the specific publics they serve, and to take steps to elicit these preferences. They have redefined their mission as being to serve particular 'consumers' such as local communities and businesses; victims and victims' families; occasionally even inmates and their families. Like other public sector organizations, the bureaucracies of the criminal justice system have had to become more responsive, more attuned to the interests of individual consumers and stakeholders, and less assured in their definition of what constitutes the public interest.[27]

Defining deviance down

In the face of high crime rates and high caseloads criminal justice agencies began to limit the demands placed upon them by means of a variety of devices that effectively 'define deviance down'.[28] This reduction effect was achieved either by filtering complaints and cases out of the system, or else by lowering the degree to which certain behaviours are criminalized and penalized. This process occurs at the 'shallow' and hence less visible end of criminal justice and typically takes place over a period of time and by administrative fiat, well away from the gaze of the mass media and politicians.[29] This strategic adaptation (which began in earnest in the USA in the 1960s and about a decade later in the UK) was made possible by the coincidence of cost-saving concerns with a criminological perception that viewed the criminalization of minor violations as unnecessarily stigmatizing and counter-productive. (As we will see, some twenty years later this convenient merging of fiscal and policy interests would be disrupted by a very different criminology that viewed the relaxation of low-level enforcement not as good sense but as an unmitigated disaster.)

The defining down process emerged in a number of contexts, ranging from the on-the-street decisions of individual police officers to the standardized procedures that managers developed to guide decisions about prosecution, probation, and parole. These patterns of decision-making were typically developed informally and 'in-house', though occasionally they were the result of legislative action, as with the juvenile court reforms that embraced deformalization and de-institutionalization.[30] Often the changes were incremental, making them hard to detect from the outside except by retrospective comparison or focused research.

Police cautioning and diversion from prosecution; fixed penalties and summary hearings for offences that were previously prosecuted at more serious levels; the decriminalization of behaviours that were once routinely prosecuted; monetary penalties for offences that would once have attracted probation; community sentences for offenders who would previously have gone to custody—all of these had the effect of defining deviance down.[31] So too did the emergent police policy that refused to expend investigative resources on offences that had a low likelihood of detection and a low priority for the public.[32] This downwards shift in the threshold of enforcement continued for many years before it became publicly visible and a topic of some controversy. But, despite criticism from victims and the emergence of 'zero-tolerance' ideas, the practice of setting priorities and rationing the police response continues today.[33]

Despite these attempts to define deviance down, the numbers processed through the criminal justice system continued to expand for much of the period under discussion. During the 1970s this was because of the marked increase in crime complaints that had, of course, prompted the process in the first place. In the UK, these increases continued into the 1980s and 1990s, although reductions in police clear-up rates and diversion from formal prosecution resulted in a drop in the number of persons sentenced for indictable offences after 1982.[34] In the USA the situation was rather different. Here the increased caseload was produced not by property crime rates—which actually declined after the early 1980s, or by violent crimes, which fluctuated around a (high) mean, but instead because of the War on Drugs that produced increasing numbers of arrests and prosecutions throughout the 1980s and 1990s. This 'war', as we will see, was the outcome of a quite different dynamic within crime control policy.

For much of the last twenty years we have been experiencing a situation that is rather more complex, and rather more contradictory than is suggested by conventional analyses of 'net-widening' that voice concern about an ever-expanding criminal justice state. During this period, the state agencies of criminal justice have been steadily increasing in size, in 'productivity', and in the numbers of cases processed. At the same time, until quite recently, they have been reducing the extent to which they actually process and penalize minor offence behaviour. The recent focus on misdemeanour arrests and the 'broken windows', 'zero-tolerance' approach in New York is a very public exception to this, but even there it has become apparent that many arrestees are not subsequently prosecuted and punished. To do so would be to incur expenses that are too great, even for the law and order politics of New York City under Mayor Giuliani.[35]

Redefining success

State agencies have also reacted to criticism by scaling down expectations, publicly redefining their aims, and seeking to change the criteria by which failure and success are judged. Rather than contest the charges of ineffectiveness, the agencies of criminal justice have increasingly adopted a self-conscious realism in the way that they represent themselves. Over the last two decades they have begun to admit their failings, emphasize the constraints that affect the system, and point to the limits of their capacity to control crime.

The police still claim success in solving serious crimes and in bringing the worst offenders to justice, and recently some American police departments have made much of their ability to make streets safer by vigorous action against low level crime and disorder. But they generally hold out low expectations for the control of what they now refer to as 'random' and 'opportunistic' offending, which, in fact, constitutes the great majority of criminal behaviour.[36] Similarly, the prison authorities focus more and more upon their ability to hold offenders securely in custody (and thus 'incapacitate' and punish them) and are much more circumspect in claiming the capacity to produce rehabilitative effects.[37] Probation and community service agencies do much the same, highlighting their ability to deliver inexpensive forms of monitoring and community-based control, and placing their traditional rehabilitative function more and more in the background of their public rhetoric.[38]

At the same time, the discourse of these agencies seeks to shift responsibility for outcomes onto the 'customers' with whom they deal, thereby offsetting the organization's liability. The prison inmate is now said to be responsible for making use of any reformative opportunities that the prison might offer; the offender on probation or community service must sign a contract accepting responsibility for adhering to a prescribed course of conduct; the police emphasize that it is the victim's responsibility to protect property, remain alert and avoid dangerous situations.[39]

Increasingly these organizations seek to be evaluated by reference to internal goals, over which they have near total control, rather than by reference to social goals such as reducing crime rates, catching criminals, or reforming inmates, which involve too many contingencies and uncertainties. The new performance indicators are designed to measure 'outputs' rather than 'outcomes', what the organization does, rather than what, if anything, it achieves. Prison regimes are assessed in terms of the number of hours that inmates spend in 'purposeful' activity, not in terms of whether these programmes reduce subsequent offending.[40] Police forces ask to be judged by the number of officers on the beat, the number of emergency calls processed, the speed of response following a call, or other measures of 'economy and efficiency', not by the effect these actions have had upon rates of crime or criminal convictions.[41]

In much the same way, the shift of sentencing policy towards mandatory penalties, sentencing guidelines, and 'just deserts'—whatever other dynamics may have contributed to its development—has the effect of focusing attention firmly upon process and away from outcome. When sentencing becomes merely the application of pre-existing penalty tariffs it loses much of its former social purpose. It shifts away from the older framework in which sentencers aimed to bring about a social outcome—the reduction of crime through individualized sentencing—to one where the key objective (fitting the punishment to the offence) is well within the capacity of the courts, and much less likely to 'fail'.[42] The same lowered ambition and retreat from positive social purpose reinforces the new meaning of imprisonment and probation, both of which are increasingly represented as modalities of punishment and incapacitative control, rather than as transformative measures.

Criminal justice organizations have sought over the last two decades to become more self-contained, more inwardly directed, and less committed to externally defined social purposes, and to some extent they succeeded in establishing this more defensive posture. But while the central government has often encouraged and colluded in developing these reduced and more realistic mission statements, part of the price of failure is that these agencies are no longer permitted the professional autonomy and discretion with which they were once entrusted. Agencies like the police, probation and prisons that were once given statutory powers and responsibilities, an annual budget and a degree of freedom to get on with it, are now increasingly subject to state-imposed standards and guidelines, and are closely monitored and inspected to ensure that they comply. The long-term trend towards professional autonomy and the delegation of penal powers has been abruptly reversed, and the state has begun to tighten its grip upon criminal justice agencies and employees.[43]

By these various means, the crime control agencies have begun to represent themselves in ways that suggest a more modest and more self-contained remit. The promise to deliver 'law and order' and security for all citizens is now increasingly replaced by a promise to process complaints or apply punishments in a just, efficient and cost-effective way. There is an emerging distinction between the *punishment of criminals* which remains the business of the state (and becomes once again a significant symbol of state power) and the *control of crime*, which is increasingly deemed to be 'beyond the state' in significant respects. And as its control capacity comes to be viewed as limited and contingent, the state's power to punish takes on a renewed political salience and priority.

Concentrate upon consequences

Another emergent pattern of adjustment is the tendency of state agencies to give more priority to dealing with the *consequences* of crime rather than its *causes*. In government crime policy and in the priorities of police chiefs, there has emerged a new emphasis on tackling the harmful effects of criminal conduct— by supporting victims, mitigating crime costs, addressing public fear and reducing insecurity—rather than intervening in ways that address crime itself.[44] This is, to some extent, a predictable result of the worsening of crime as a social problem. As its effects become more widespread, so too do the demands for relief from those most affected. But it also represents a strategic shift on the part of criminal justice agencies, whose former claim to be addressing the problem at its roots now appears increasingly empty.

Victims

One can see this very clearly in the emergent field of 'victim policy'. Ever since the nineteenth century there had been repeated calls for government and its agencies to do more to relieve the plight of crime victims. As critics pointed out, the victim's role in criminal justice was routinely reduced to that of complainant and witness, rather than a party to the proceedings, and the injuries victims suffered typically went unacknowledged and uncompensated. While the system, so it was said, lavished care and attention upon individual offenders, seeking to understand their needs and bring about their rehabilitation, it had little to offer to individual victims, who were neither consulted nor informed about the way in which 'their' case was handled. Until recently, the system's standard response to this criticism was that the victim's interests were subsumed within the public interest, and that, in the long run, the state's correctionalist policies would work to the interest of both the public and the offender.

Since the 1970s this response has come to seem aloof and unresponsive, as well as of doubtful credibility. With the forceful encouragement of elected officials, criminal justice agencies have developed an entirely different relationship to individual victims, and also to the organized victims' movement which became a growing presence on the policy scene in the 1980s and 1990s. In stark contrast to previous policy, victims have become a favoured constituency and the aim of serving victims has become part of the redefined mission of all criminal justice agencies.

As we will see, politicians came to develop their own, rather punitive, conception of how to act in the victim's interests, but the approach of the criminal justice agencies has typically focused upon more modest, more responsive goals. Ever since the 1980s police, prosecution, and courts agencies have increasingly made it their policy to ensure that victims are kept informed, treated with more sensitivity, offered access to support, and given compensation for their injuries. New forms of restitutive justice grew up in the form of court-mandated compensation orders, victim–offender mediation, and treatment programmes for offenders that highlighted the impact of crime upon victims. Victims came to be accorded a series of rights, and a voice in criminal proceedings. These ranged from uncontroversial innovations such as separate waiting rooms in courthouses to much-disputed developments such as 'victim-impact statements' and 'victim opinions' offered to the judge about sentencing, and to parole boards about release. In these various ways, the criminal justice system strove to reinvent itself as a service organization for individual victims rather than merely a public law enforcement agency.[45]

Fear of crime

Like victims and their injuries, the fear of crime has always been a concomitant of crime. Until recently it was assumed, without much discussion, that measures to combat crime were also the best means of reducing the fear and insecurity associated with it. No doubt this way of thinking about policy would have continued, had efforts to reduce crime been shown to have any likelihood of success. However, in the late 1970s and early 1980s, when crime-reduction efforts appeared conspicuously unsuccessful, a number of studies suggested that public fear of crime is a measurable phenomenon that is to some degree independent of crime and victimization rates. When a series of police research studies suggested that some measures might fail to reduce actual crime rates but nevertheless succeed in reducing the reported levels of fear and insecurity, the way was opened for a new policy aim. From the 1980s onwards, police departments and government authorities in the USA and the UK began to develop mission-statements and practices that took the reduction of fear as a distinct, self-standing policy goal.[46]

Early discussions of the problem tried to suggest that much fear was irrational, and could be dispelled by a dose of reliable information. Thus in the mid-1980s the Home Office embarked on a publicity campaign that used British Crime Survey data to show that public fear was often misplaced or overstated when measured against the actual risk of victimization.[47] This debunking approach soon came to be viewed as a mistake, and subsequent efforts were more respectful of the strength and significance of public fears, however great the gap between these fears and the statistical risks involved. So the police reintroduced street patrols and enthusiastically sponsored neighbourhood watch schemes, all the time aware of research showing such measures to be much more effective at reassuring the public than actually reducing crime rates. In the 1990s, 'quality of life' policing was widely adopted, not because of a belief in its proven success—that came later—but because it was perceived as being popular with the public and liable to change public perception in a positive direction.

Relocating and redefining responsibilities

Over the course of the 1970s and 1980s, government authorities became increasingly aware that crime control is 'beyond the state' in two important and distinct respects. Crime control is 'beyond the state' inasmuch as the institutions of the criminal justice state are severely limited in their crime control capacities and cannot by themselves succeed in the maintenance of 'law and order'.[48] But it is also 'beyond the state' inasmuch as there are crime control mechanisms operating outside the state's boundaries, and relatively independently of its policies. The effort to address these limits, first by reforming the state institutions, and subsequently by mobilizing and harnessing non-state mechanisms, has been the basis of the most innovative policies of the recent period.

The community as the solution

A constantly recurring solution to the problem of the limitations of the criminal justice state has been the effort to relocate the work of crime-control 'in the community'. Since at least the 1960s criminal justice administrators, echoing the calls of academics and reformers, have urged that their tasks could be more effectively undertaken outside of state institutions in what they call 'community' settings. Drawing on critiques of total institutions, arguments about the dangers of stigma and exclusion, and a belief in the healing powers of community relations, there has been a whole series of reform initiatives that identify the community as the proper locale for crime control and criminal justice. Since the 1960s we have seen the development of one community programme after another—community corrections, community policing, punishment in the community, community crime prevention, community prosecution, community justice.[49] 'The community' has become the all-purpose solution to every criminal justice problem.

Many of these developments, for instance, community corrections and 'punishment in the community', consisted of state employees, carrying out state policies, under the auspices of state organizations. 'Community' in these instances meant merely 'non-custodial' or 'occurring outside of prisons and reformatories'. They might be less costly than institutionalization, less stigmatizing, and less liable to deprive the offender of the supports of family and work, but they were actually state sanctions with little or no involvement of non-state actors. Others measures engaged with 'community' in a more innovative and radical manner, seeking to respond to the concerns and enlist the help of neighbourhood residents and organizations. Community policing and community crime prevention in particular sought to enlist the support of voluntary agencies, businesses and residents groups, harnessing the social control efforts of these bodies and aligning them with the efforts of the official crime control agencies.

Community policing initiatives began to develop from the late 1960s onwards, in large part as a corrective to the reactive, remote policing styles that had been adopted earlier that decade. Often prompted by urban riots or the breakdown of police–public relations in minority neighbourhoods, community policing attempted to improve the police image by working more closely and responsively with local community organizations and leaders. Beat policing, schools liaison, public consultation, even a degree of local accountability—all of these were seen as important methods of ensuring an adequate level of public co-operation, and avoiding an image of the police as a hostile army of occupation.

By the 1980s community policing had become an all-pervasive rhetoric, and was being used to describe any and every policing practice, however conventional.[50] Beneath this rhetorical gloss, however, there were in fact some significant new developments in contemporary policing. The most important of these was the effort increasingly being made to reach out and enlist the activities of non-state actors, linking up their informal crime-control practices to the more formal activities of the police themselves. This out-reach policy, enhanced and encouraged by community crime prevention schemes using the same principles, gave rise to a self-conscious strategy that has become a prominent aspect of government policy in the 1980s and 1990s in both the UK and the USA.

The responsibilization strategy

The attempt to extend the reach of state agencies by linking them up with the practices of actors in the 'private sector' and 'the community' might be described as a *responsibilization strategy*.[51] It involves a way of thinking and a variety of techniques designed to change the manner in which governments act upon crime. Instead of addressing crime in a direct fashion by means of the police, the courts and the prisons, this approach promotes a new kind of indirect action, in which state agencies activate action by non-state organizations and actors. The intended result is an enhanced network of more or less directed, more or less informal crime control, complementing and extending the formal controls of the criminal justice state. Instead of imagining they can monopolize crime control, or exercising their sovereign powers in complete disregard of the powers of other actors, state agencies now adopt a strategic relation to other forces of social control. They seek to build broader alliances, enlisting the 'governmental' powers of private actors, and shaping them to the ends of crime control.[52]

This is the essence of the new crime prevention approach that has been developed by the governments of the USA and (especially) the UK over the last two decades. It is also a crucial element in the community policing policies, properly so-called. The key phrases of the new strategy are terms such as 'partnership', 'public/private alliance', 'inter-agency co-operation', 'the multi-agency approach', 'activating communities', creating 'active citizens', 'help for self-help' and the 'co-production of security'. The primary objective is to spread responsibility for crime control onto agencies, organizations and individuals that operate outside the criminal justice state and to persuade them to act appropriately.[53]

This 'responsibilizing' task is made much more difficult by the prior division of labour in the field, and by the long-established assumption that the state is always and exclusively the authority responsible for crime control. As Engstad and Evans point out, it is difficult to persuade private organizations to take responsibility for what they continue to see as public functions.

It is most unlikely that the group or corporate body to whom responsibility is being shifted will immediately acknowledge that their property or operations are generating a substantial strain in police resources, accept that they have a duty, up to their competence, for the control of crime, and take appropriate action. In our view, the failure of many . . . crime control efforts can be attributed to the absence of some means of ensuring that members of the community accept and effectively discharge their responsibilities.[54]

Redistributing the task of crime control, rendering others responsible, multiplying the number of effective authorities, forming alliances, arranging things so that crime control duties follow crime-generating behaviours—these are the new and institutionally radical goals that are now being pursued. The criminal justice state is, in this area at least, shedding its 'sovereign' style of governing by top-down command and developing a form of rule close to that described by Michel Foucault as 'governmentality'—a modality that involves the enlistment of others, the shaping of incentives, and the creation of new forms of co-operative action.[55] How does the state go about this new task of bringing about action on the part of others? How does it succeed in 'stimulating new forms of behaviour', 'stopping established habits' and arranging 'the right distribution of things'?[56]

The first step is 'to identify people or organizations which have the competence to reduce criminal opportunities effectively, and . . . to assess both those who have a responsibility to do so and whether this responsibility can be enforced'.[57] A number of targets and techniques of persuasion are identified by such analyses. The simplest, but also the most wide-ranging, is the publicity campaign, targeted at the public as a whole. These campaigns, conducted through television advertising and the mass leafleting of households and businesses, aim to raise public consciousness, interpolate the citizen as a potential victim, create a sense of duty, connect the population to crime control agencies, and help change the thinking and practices of those involved.[58] Similar goals are pursued by the police, who offer expert support and encouragement to residents and citizen self-help groups, helping them to form crime-prevention projects such as 'block watch' or 'neighbourhood watch', raising their awareness of crime, and linking them more closely to the public authorities.

The UK and US governments have established a whole series of quasi-governmental organizations such as the National Crime Prevention Council, Crime Concern UK, and the Safer Cities schemes. Their remit is to set up crime prevention and 'community safety' projects, and, more generally, to establish local structures that will help govern crime problems by means of inter-agency co-operation and the activation of private initiatives. Within the state agencies themselves, organizational changes have been introduced to further these ends, including the promotion of strategic planning, inter-agency co-operation, and shared decision-making between departments that were previously quite separate.

The recurring message of this approach is that the state alone is not, and cannot be, responsible for preventing and controlling crime.[59] For the first time since the formation of the modern criminal justice state, governments have begun to acknowledge a basic sociological truth: that the most important processes producing order and conformity are mainstream social processes, located within the institutions of civil society, not the uncertain threat of legal sanctions. The project of establishing a sovereign state monopoly has begun to give way to a clear recognition of the dispersed, pluralistic nature of effective social control. In this new vision, the state's task is to augment and support these multiple actors and informal processes, rather than arrogate the crime control task to a single specialist agency. [60]

The state's new strategy is not to command and control but rather to persuade and align, to organize, to ensure that other actors play their part. Property owners, residents, retailers, manufacturers, town planners, school authorities, transport managers, employers, parents, individual citizens . . . the list is endless . . . must all be made to recognize that they have a responsibility in this regard. They must be persuaded to exert their informal powers of social control, and if necessary, to modify their usual practices, in order to help reduce criminal opportunities and enhance crime control. Government authorities are, in this field of policy as in several others, operating across and upon the boundaries that used to separate the private from the public realm, seeking to renegotiate the question of what is properly a state function and what is not. In doing so, they are also beginning to challenge the central assumption of penal modernism, which took it for granted that crime control was a specialist task, best concentrated within a differentiated state institution.

Sometimes the desired effects are achieved simply by exhortation, as where automobile manufacturers are persuaded to build in greater security in their products, or insurance companies are encouraged to give discounts wherever Neighbourhood Watch schemes operate. Sometimes persuasion can take the form of an analysis of interests, for instance where retailers and city-centre firms are presented with data on fear of crime and how this affects their trade, in order to encourage them to adopt improved security practices and co-operate in joint initiatives. To this end, every local authority in the UK was required to conduct a 'crime audit' in the late 1990s. Increasingly preventative action takes the form of establishing co-operative, inter-agency structures that bring together public and private organizations in order to initiate local projects, or else works through Business Improvement Districts that see neighbourhood tranquillity and security as a means of advancing commercial interests.[61]

Sometimes more forceful methods are proposed. It has been repeatedly suggested, for example, that the government should apply the 'polluter pays' principle to criminogenic activities. Thus it might make retail firms do more to reduce shoplifting and retail crime by threatening to shift the costs of theft prosecutions to the retailers themselves. Or it might treat the manufacturers of 'hot products' as being partly responsible for bearing the costs of the crimes to which they regularly give rise.[62] These tougher schemes—which aim to spread the costs as well as the responsibility for crime control—would mesh neatly with neo-liberal policies of privatization and public expenditure reduction, but so far they have mostly been suggestions and implied threats rather than enacted policy. There is a real reluctance to penalize the 'suppliers' of crime opportunities that contrasts markedly with the enthusiasm with which their 'consumers' are punished.

The motivation behind these 'responsibilizing' developments is not merely the off-loading of troublesome state functions, though the sharing of responsibility is clearly an attractive strategy for criminal justice executives hoping to avoid being blamed for the shortcomings of their organizations. Nor is it simply the 'hiving off' or the 'privatization' of crime control, although the desire to reduce state costs is certainly a factor, and one of the effects of the strategy has been to further stimulate the already growing market for private security. Rather, it is a new conception of how to exercise power in the crime control field, a new form of 'governing-at-a-distance' that introduces principles and techniques of government that are by now quite well established in other areas of social and economic policy.[63]

The new criminologies of everyday life

One of the most significant developments of the last two decades has been the emergence of a new style of criminological thinking that has succeeded in attracting the interest of government officials. With the fading of correctionalist rationales for criminal justice, and in the face of the crime-control predicament, officials have increasingly discovered an elective affinity between their own practical concerns and this new genre of criminological discourse. This new genre—which might be termed the *new criminologies of everyday life*—has barely impinged upon public attention, but it has functioned as a crucial support for much recent policy. One can trace its influence not just in the responsibilization strategy and in the new crime prevention apparatus, but also in recent policies of penal deterrence and incapacitation. This new way of thinking has, quite rapidly, become one of the key strands of official criminology, shaping government policies and organizational practice in both the USA and the UK. Despite its thoroughly practical and atheoretical character, this new way of thinking expresses very well some of the key ways in which the crime control field is currently being reconfigured.

The new criminologies of everyday life are a set of cognate theoretical frameworks that includes routine activity theory, crime as opportunity, lifestyle analysis, situational crime prevention, and some versions of rational choice theory.[64] The striking thing about these various criminologies is that they each begin from the premise that crime is a normal, commonplace, aspect of modern society. Crime is regarded as a generalized form of behaviour, routinely produced by the normal patterns of social and economic life in contemporary society. To commit an offence thus requires no special motivation or disposition, no abnormality or pathology. In contrast to earlier criminologies, which began from the premise that crime was a deviation from normal civilized conduct and was explicable in terms of individual pathology or faulty socialization, the new criminologies see crime as *continuous* with normal social interaction and explicable by reference to *standard* motivational patterns. Crime comes to be viewed as a routine risk to be calculated or an accident to be avoided, rather than a moral aberration that needs to be specially explained.

In the past, official criminology has usually viewed crime *retrospectively* and *individually*, in order to itemise individual wrongdoing and allocate punishment or treatment. The new criminologies tend to view crime *prospectively* and in *aggregate* terms, for the purpose of calculating risks and shaping preventative measures. This shift of perspectives is significant in its intellectual and practical consequences, since it opens up a whole series of new ways of understanding and acting upon crime. But it is also significant in institutional terms, as a sign of a changing field, because it entails a view of the crime problem that is no longer that of the criminal justice state. Up until this point, and in spite of intellectual arguments to the contrary, official criminology (and much academic criminology) viewed the problem of crime from the perspective of the criminal justice system, insisted on seeing crime as a problem of individual offenders, and tended to see offenders as typified by those in captivity. The new criminologies reject this institutional point of view, seeing crime in a social and economic perspective that owes nothing to process of law enforcement. The official endorsement of the new criminologies of everyday life thus represents a significant shift of perspective on the part of criminal justice administrators, and suggests the diminishing power of the institutional epistemology that previously shaped thinking and action in this field.

This new criminological approach emerges in a context where high crime rates are taken as a given, and where the data of self-report and victim studies testify to the normality of crime. Its emergence is testimony to the declining credibility of the criminal justice state, or at least of the myth of its sovereign capacity to control crime by itself. Many of the practical prescriptions that flow from these theories are addressed not to state agencies such as the police, the courts and the prisons, but *beyond* the state apparatus, to the organizations, institutions, and individuals of civil society. The theories simply take it for granted that the criminal justice state has a limited capacity, and they look to the everyday life world as the appropriate locus for action.

As well as empowering different agencies, these new theories identify different targets and new means of addressing them. Their programmes of action are directed not towards any and every individual offender, but instead towards the conduct of potential victims, to criminogenic situations, and to those routines of everyday life that create criminal opportunities as an unintended by-product. Where an older criminology concerned itself with disciplining delinquent individuals or punishing legal subjects, the new approach identifies recurring criminal opportunities and seeks to govern them by developing situational controls that will make them less tempting or less vulnerable. Criminogenic situations, 'hot products', 'hot spots'—these are the new objects of control. The assumption is that 'opportunity creates the thief' rather than the other way around. Such an approach promises to maximize the return for effort, since it focuses upon those elements of the criminal encounter that are most identifiable, fixed and predictable. As Nigel Walker puts it, 'potential offenders are numerous and by no means always recognisable. By contrast, we do at least know what property to protect, and where it is'.[65]

This is, in effect, 'supply side criminology', shifting risks, redistributing costs, and creating disincentives. It aims to embed controls in the fabric of normal interaction, rather than suspend them above it in the form of a sovereign command. Rather than rely upon the uncertain threat of deterrent sentences, or the dubious ability of the police to catch villains, it sets in place a more mundane set of reforms, designed not to change people but to redesign things and reshape situations. A thousand small adjustments are required. Replace cash with credit cards. Build locks into the steering columns of automobiles. Employ attendants in parking lots and use close circuit TV cameras to monitor city centre streets. Co-ordinate the closing times of rival clubs and discos. Lay on late night buses and special routes to and from football games. Advise retailers about security. Encourage local authorities to co-ordinate the various agencies that deal with crime. Remind citizens of the need to safeguard their property and supervise their neighbourhoods.

In contrast to correctionalist criminology, this approach no longer takes the state and its agencies to be the primary or proximate actors in the business of crime control. And to the extent that it depicts a criminal subject, this figure is no longer the poorly socialized misfit in need of assistance, but instead the opportunistic consumer, whose attitudes cannot be changed but whose access to social goods could be barred. This criminal figure—sometimes described as 'situational man'—lacks a strong moral compass or any effective internal controls, aside from a capacity for rational calculation and a healthy will to pleasure. [66] In the hands of other writers, this might be intended as a form of cultural critique or a commentary on contemporary consumerist mores. But there is no hint of irony in the flat, deadpan prose of the new criminological texts.

If the main effect of these criminologies has been to encourage new forms of action that go 'beyond the state', they have also helped revive some more traditional modes of action. Criminological discourses are always polyvalent in their relation to practical action, so it should not surprise us that the new criminologies of everyday life have influenced policy in more than one direction. As well as being put to use in strategies of prevention attuned to the new conditions of late modernity, these discourses have also played a part in the revival of older strategies that tend to ignore these conditions and rely upon the traditional penal powers of the sovereign state. The stripped down, skeletonized depiction of human motivation developed by rational choice theory has helped advocates of situational crime prevention to shift the focus of crime control away from individual disposition towards situational opportunity. But this rational choice conception also carries implications about the efficacy of penal threats that have made it useful in a quite different and much less innovative strategy: the renewed use of harsh penal sentences as a means to deter criminal conduct.[67]

Rational choice theories revive a simple utilitarian account of criminal conduct that had long since been displaced by positivist and sociological theories. Where correctional criminology took criminal conduct to be a product of social influences and psychological conflicts, and regarded the criminal as a deep subject, not altogether in control of his or her behaviour, the rational choice model regards criminal acts as calculated, utility-maximizing conduct, resulting from a straightforward process of individual choice. This model represents the problem of crime as a matter of supply and demand, with punishment operating as a price mechanism.[68] It sees offenders as rational opportunists or career criminals whose conduct is variously deterred or dis-inhibited by the manipulation of incentives—an approach that makes deterrent penalties a self-evident means for reducing offending. Where correctionalist criminology treated crime as a problem with social, temporal and psychological dimensions, the rational choice model treats it as a function of price.

The penological corollary of this is that the concern with 'root causes', 'social problems' and 'individual needs' is displaced by a more singular focus upon 'pricing', and the effort to ensure that the penal consequences of criminal offending are sufficiently swift, certain, and severe to operate as an effective disincentive. After more than a century of social scientific research that complicated and refined the understanding of criminal offending; after a mass of evidence has been accumulated to show that criminal acts are typically embedded in, and produced by, definite social and psychological relations; rational choice analyses have, abruptly and without ceremony, swept aside all such complexity and empirical findings. With the certainty of armchair philosophers and economic modellers they insist that crime is, after all, simply a matter of individual choice—or anyway can be treated as if it were.[69] It would be wrong to say that the rational choice criminology had caused the shift towards harsher sentencing laws and a greater use of deterrent threats. But it is certainly plausible to argue that this kind of reasoning has functioned to legitimate these tougher policies and give them a gloss of respectability. Penal policy, like welfare assistance to the poor, has rediscovered market discipline and purity of coercive disincentives.

In the reactionary political context of the 1980s and 1990s, with its scepticism about welfare programmes and its emphasis upon individual responsibility, the simplicity of an account that blames the offender, silences excuses, ignores root causes, and sees the punishment of wrongdoers as the proper response, has a popular and a political appeal that runs well beyond its criminological merit. It is as if bestowing so much criminological attention upon the offender, and developing such exquisite analyses of criminal aetiology were suddenly deemed to be morally degenerate, as well as politically unacceptable. This cultural backlash against what Ronald Reagan called 'soft social theories' and 'pseudo-intellectual apologies for crime' is memorably encapsulated in James Q. Wilson's casual, reactionary insistence that 'Wicked people exist. Nothing avails except to set them apart from innocent people'—a claim that simultaneously re-asserts the most simplistic common sense, gives up on social and rehabilitative programmes, and dismisses the whole project of a social scientific criminology.[70] That such a position could be asserted by a prominent Harvard-based policy analyst, and repeatedly taken up as if it were an insight of great merit, attests to the political and cultural climate that formed around crime control policy in the 1980s.

Non-adaptive responses: denial and acting out

These deterrent policies and the utilitarian theories that rationalized them were part of a second line of policy development, this time a more politicized, populist, regressive one. Up until this point I have been describing a series of adaptive responses to what I termed the 'new predicament' of crime control in late modern society. Whatever one thinks of them, and however many problems they raise, these strategies are characterized by a high level of administrative rationality and creativity. The agencies involved have, over time, recognized the predicament they face (or at least a version of it), and responded to its challenges by revising their practices, renegotiating their external relationships, and building new institutions. But these developments form only one aspect of a deeply contradictory response. As the administrative machine of the state has gone about its business of devising strategies, adapting to its limitations and coming to terms with its changing environment, the state's political machine has repeatedly indulged in a form of evasion and denial that is almost hysterical in the clinical sense of that term.[71]

This political reaction has become more pronounced as the conditions of political speech have changed over time. In the course of the 1980s and 1990s, policy-making in this area became more intensely politicized, more fraught with political danger, and more subject to press and public scrutiny. As crime and punishment came to be highly charged election issues, government and opposition parties competed to establish their credentials as being tough on crime, concerned for public safety, and capable of restoring morality, order and discipline in the face of the corrosive social changes of late modernity. And while the neo-liberal agenda of privatization, market competition and spending restraints shaped much of the administrative reform that government imposed on criminal justice agencies behind the scenes, it was the very different neo-conservative agenda that dictated the public face of penal policy. Instead of acknowledging the limits of the sovereign state and adapting to them, the political agenda governing high profile policies was to 'restore public confidence' in criminal justice while asserting the values of moral discipline, individual responsibility, and respect for authority. In penal policy as in welfare policy, the imperative was the re-imposition of control, usually by punitive means. In both cases the population singled out as being most in need of control was composed of the welfare poor, urban blacks, and marginalized working-class youth.

Disregarding evidence that crime does not readily respond to severe sentences, or new police powers, or a greater use of imprisonment, legislatures have repeatedly adopted a punitive 'law and order' stance. In doing so, they routinely deny limitations that are acknowledged by their own administrations. Far from adapting to the limits of state power in this domain, they seek to expand and reassert these powers by force of sovereign command. Of the many examples of this pattern, the most clear-cut is British Home Secretary Michael Howard's *volte face* of 1993, which introduced new mandatory sentence laws with the declaration that 'prison works!'—only months after his own government had publicly declared that 'imprisonment is an expensive way of making bad people worse'.[72] The result of this official endorsement of the power to punish and denial of its limitations has been a sharp and sustained rise in the UK prison population from 1993 to the present day. But this example pales in comparison with the massive denial involved in the American government's 'War on Drugs' which has utterly transformed law enforcement in the USA, as well as filling a hugely expanded prison system with disproportionate numbers of poor blacks. This massively expensive and largely futile attempt to change a widespread and deeply entrenched pattern of behaviour by means of criminal punishments has all the hallmarks of a sovereign state dealing with its limitations by denying they exist. Motivated by the politically urgent need to 'do something' decisive about crime, in a context where the federal government mostly lacks jurisdiction (other areas of crime control being the prerogative of the states and local authorities) the war on drugs was the American state's attempt to 'just say no'. Disregarding evidence that the levels of drug use were already in decline, that drug use is not responsive to criminal penalties, that criminalization brings its own pathologies (notably street violence and disrespect for the authorities), and that declaring a war against drugs is, in effect, to declare a war against minorities, the US government proceeded to declare such a war and to persist in pursuing it, despite every indication of its failure.[73] Why? Because the groups most adversely affected lack political power and are widely regarded as dangerous and undeserving; because the groups least affected could be assured that something is being done and lawlessness is not tolerated; and because few politicians are willing to oppose a policy when there is so little political advantage to be gained by doing so.

Other legislative measures might be described as a form of *acting out*—which is to say that they engage in a form of impulsive and unreflective action, avoiding realistic recognition of underlying problems, the very fact of acting providing its own form of relief and gratification. Many of the laws passed in the 1990s—Megan's law, Three Strikes, sexual predator statutes, the reintroduction of children's prisons, paedophile registers, and mandatory sentences—take this form and might best be understood in these terms. Such measures are designed to be expressive, cathartic actions, undertaken to denounce the crime and reassure the public. Their capacity to control future crime, though always loudly asserted, is often doubtful and in any case is less important than their immediate ability to enact public sentiment, to provide an instant response, to function as a retaliatory measure that can stand as an achievement in itself. Typically these measures are passed amidst great public outrage in the wake of sensational crimes of violence, often involving a disturbingly archetypal confrontation between a poorly controlled dangerous criminal and an innocent, defenceless middle-class victim.[74] And because legislatures—particularly in the USA—are on now a 'war footing' with respect to crime, and exercise direct control over sentencing levels, the system is set up to produce an instant response.

From the point of view of the political actors, the finer points of penological realism become secondary considerations easily subordinated to political ends.[75] Their most pressing concern is to do something decisive, to respond with immediate effect to public outrage, to demonstrate that the state is in control and is willing to use its powers to uphold 'law and order' and to protect the law-abiding public. Some of these laws—such as the reintroduction of the chain gang, boot camps, shaming punishments, and attempts to revive corporal punishment—have a 'made for television' quality that betrays their main purpose.[76] Some—such as mandatory sentences, 'truth in sentencing' laws and the expedited death penalty—have an absolutist quality designed to reassure a distrustful public that the system will not betray them once the case goes out of view. Others—such as community notification, sexual predator laws, supermax prisons, electronic monitoring and the recriminalization of juvenile justice—involve public safety considerations of doubtful efficacy and a barely sublimated punitiveness that suggests a complete disregard for the rights or humanity of those being sanctioned.[77] Such policies become particularly salient where a more general insecurity—deriving from the precariousness of social and economic relations in late modern society—is widely experienced and where the state is deemed to have failed in its efforts to deliver physical and economic security to key social groups. The politics of crime control provide these emotions with a ready-made, deeply unpopular, target population against whom they could be directed.

Michel Foucault, in his description of the execution of Robert Damiens in 1757 showed in graphic detail how harsh punishments have long been used to reaffirm the force of law and to reactivate the myth of sovereign power.[78] And though today's democratic regimes do not much resemble that of Louis XV, whenever state authorities 'wage war on crime', flourishing penal powers to send law-breakers to their death, or to impose life-cancelling terms of imprisonment, they are deliberately employing the same archaic tactics. Whether one views this as a cynical manipulation of collective emotions for political gain, or as a good faith attempt to give democratic expression to public feeling, the outcome is the same. Policymaking becomes a form of acting out that downplays the complexities and long-term character of *effective* crime control in favour of the immediate gratifications of a more *expressive* alternative.[79] Law making becomes a matter of retaliatory gestures intended to reassure a worried public and to accord with common sense, however poorly these gestures are adapted to dealing with the underlying problem. A show of punitive force against individuals is used to repress any acknowledgement of the state's inability to control crime to acceptable levels. A willingness to deliver harsh punishments to convicted offenders magically compensates a failure to deliver security to the population at large.

It will come as no surprise to observe that administrators and criminal justice professionals are often implacably opposed to legislation of this kind, and tend to dilute its effects in the process of implementation.[80] 'Populist', 'punitive' measures (such as 'Three Strikes' laws with their mandatory sentences) that aim to abolish all administrative discretion and are passed with little expert support are particularly unpopular and have prompted a variety of subterfuges and evasive procedures that allow prosecutors and judges to circumvent the statute.[81] But of course the conflict between political and administrative actors works in both directions, and elected officials often have a very difficult relation to the 'adaptive' administrative measures I described above. During the 1980s and 1990s, governments have frequently been embarrassed by incidents or press reports that reveal under-enforcement by the police, lenient sentences or bail decisions by the courts, lax security in prisons, or the release of convicted offenders who subsequently re-offend—the Willie Horton case being the paradigm instance. Strategies such as 'defining deviance down' or 'redefining success', however reasonable they appear to professionals, can strike the press and the public as scandalous, and it is usually elected officials rather than administrators who are held responsible. Some of the key developments of the 1980s and 1990s—such as 'truth in sentencing', 'prison works' and 'zero tolerance'—have been political attempts to recover public confidence following the discrediting of adaptive strategies that became a source of political embarrassment.[82] And many of the 'get tough' measures of the 1990s have been concerned to reverse adaptive cost-cutting policies that had been quietly adopted in earlier decades.[83]

It is here that we see most clearly the myth of the sovereign state and its resilience in the face of all contrary evidence. For political actors, faced with the immediate pressures of public outrage, media criticism and electoral challenges over the subject of crime, it is extremely difficult to shrug off full responsibility for crime control and point to the state's limits. Few governments have done this publicly, or for a sustained period. Faced with these pressures, the essential and abiding attractiveness of the 'sovereign' response to crime (and above all of retaliatory laws that create stronger penal sanctions or police powers) is that it can be represented as an immediate, authoritative intervention. Such action gives the impression that *something is being done*—here, now, swiftly and decisively. Like the decision to wage war, the decision to inflict harsh punishment or extend police powers exemplifies the sovereign mode of state action.[84] No need for co-operation, no negotiation, no question of whether or not it might 'work'. Such measures are sovereign acts that can expect to command widespread popular support and to excite little in the way of organized political opposition. The cumulative outcome of such sovereign acts in Britain in the 1990s has been an unprecedented rise in sentencing levels and rates of imprisonment. In the USA it has been the emergence of mass incarceration on a scale never before witnessed in a modern democracy and the revival of a 'killing state' committed to the speeded-up execution of an increasing number of offenders.[85]

Criminology and the collective unconscious

Accompanying these more politicized policies is a criminological discourse that looks quite different from the criminologies of everyday life that we encountered earlier. Whereas the latter 'normalize' offenders, depicting them as rational opportunists, little different from their victims, the criminology invoked by the sovereign state strategy is instead one of essentialized difference. Frequently appearing in the wake of sensational high-profile crimes (which is to say, highly unusual cases that are made to appear 'all-too-typical') this is a criminology that trades in images, archetypes, and anxieties, rather than in careful analyses and research findings. In its deliberate echoing of public concerns and media biases, and its focus on the most worrisome threats, it is, in effect, a politicized discourse of the collective unconscious, though it claims to be altogether realist and 'common-sensical' in contrast to 'academic theories'. In its standard tropes and rhetorical invocations, this political discourse relies upon an archaic criminology of the criminal type, the alien other. Sometimes explicitly, more often in coded references, the problem is traced to the wanton, amoral behaviour of dangerous offenders, who typically belong to racial and cultural groups bearing little resemblance to 'us'.

With these ideas in the background, crime-control policies can invoke images of 'the criminal' that depict him (less often her) as profoundly anti-social. Individual offenders come to be seen as 'career criminals', 'drug-addicts', 'thugs' and 'yobs' with few redeeming features and little social value. Some—particularly 'paedophiles', 'sexual predators', or juvenile 'superpredators'—are evoked in ways that are barely human, their conduct being essentialized as 'evil' or 'wicked' and beyond all human understanding.[86] Whole communities are anathematized by talk of an undeserving 'underclass', locked into a culture and mode of life that is both alien and threatening.

These are not real people or even criminological categories. They are imaginary figures that operate as tokens in a political process that exploits what Mary Douglas calls the 'political uses of danger'. The risks they are perceived as posing, the anxieties they call forth, the sense of powerlessness that they engender, all work to reinforce the felt need for the imposition of order and the importance of a strong state response. Nor are these figures representative of the real dangers that crime undoubtedly involves, since its inventory of risks focuses almost exclusively on street crime and forgets the serious harms caused by criminal corporations, white-collar criminals or even drunk drivers. Each figure is, instead, selected for its usefulness as a 'suitable enemy'—usefulness not just for the criminal justice state in its sovereign mode but also for a conservative social politics that stresses the need for authority, family values, and the resurrection of traditional morality.[87]

In this inflammatory rhetoric, and in the real policies that flow from it, offenders are treated as a different species of threatening, violent individuals for whom we can have no sympathy and for whom there is no effective help. Biological and genetic explanations of crime and violence have always been part of the criminological repertoire, even at the height of penal-welfarism, but in the 1980s and 1990s these became more prominent in public discourse and in sectors of the academy—Wilson and Herrnstein's best-selling *Crime and Human Nature* being the most prominent example. These reductionist accounts certainly provided support for a criminology of the other, and also fuelled public debates about the supposed links between race and crime. But more important were what one might term 'culturalist' accounts of the alien other—accounts that assumed offenders had been born into the 'dependency culture' of the 'underclass', that they lacked all work skills and moral values, and that they were tied into habits of drug abuse, crime, and welfare fraud.[88] In these accounts, the reality and humanity of individual offenders is replaced by an imagery that comes from horror films, as when President Reagan invoked the 'stark, staring face—a face that belongs to a frightening reality of our time: the face of a human predator . . . nothing in nature is more cruel or more dangerous'.[89] The public knows, without having to be told, that these 'superpredators' and high-rate offenders are young minority males, caught up in the underclass world of crime, drugs, broken families, and welfare dependency. The only practical and rational response to such types, as soon as they offend if not before, is to have them 'taken out of circulation' for the protection of the public. Many of the most politicized policies of recent years—mandatory sentences, incapacitation, the revived death penalty—are designed to do precisely this and little else.

This criminology's characterization of the 'paedophile' or child sex offender is revealing in a different way. In Britain and America today, these offenders are now an obsessive focus of media and political discussion, quite out of proportion to the frequency of such offending, or to the amount of harm it does when compared to more structural forms of injury and neglect, such as child poverty, poor health care, or parental child abuse. The paedophile is typically represented as dangerous, driven, unreachable—an unreformable creature who poses a grave risk to our most innocent, vulnerable victims: our children. Like most of the modern world's dangers, the paedophile lurks unseen in our daily environment, his 'otherness' concealed beneath his apparent normality. Once identified, he has to be marked out, and either set apart or else continuously monitored. Forget that such heavily stigmatized marking contributes to the problem, or that predictions of future dangerousness are notoriously unreliable: these are the hesitations of a more innocent time. Given our cultural commitments—our heightened sensitivity to criminal risks, our obsessive urge to manage them, our diminishing concern for the liberties of anyone deemed dangerous—the concealed nature of the criminal's other-ness makes us all the more determined to act on whatever evidence we have. The chimeral obscurity of criminal difference, together with the assumption that such people are, indeed, different, is what drives the concern to mark those who have 'revealed themselves'. It is what makes people and lawmakers all too ready to take up any signs that might be of service—whether it be a criminal record, a style of deportment and demeanour, or merely the colour of a person's skin.

The contradictions of official criminology

If one considers the whole range of government discourse on crime—not just the statements of elected officials but also those of the administrative agencies—it becomes apparent that official discourse is structured by a barely suppressed set of conflicts and tensions. Increasingly in the 1980s and 1990s, governments have relied upon criminological assumptions that are, taken as a whole, quite schizoid in character. At the level of individual agencies and government departments these contradictions are experienced as struggles between different actors, different levels of the organization, and different ways of framing problems. But at the level of the state as a whole, and its impact upon the crime-control field, the result is a set of policies that are increasingly dualistic, increasingly polarized, and increasingly schizophrenic.

Behind these contradictory policies and practices stand criminological frameworks that are diametrically opposed in crucial respects. There is a *criminology of the self*, that characterizes offenders as normal, rational consumers, just like us: and there is a *criminology of the other,* of the threatening outcast, the fearsome stranger, the excluded and the embittered. One is invoked to routinize crime, to allay disproportionate fears and to promote preventative action. The other functions to demonize the criminal, to act out popular fears and resentments, and to promote support for state punishment. The excluded middle ground between these two poles is, precisely, the once-dominant welfarist criminology that depicted the offender as disadvantaged or poorly socialized and made it the state's responsibility, in social as well as penal policy, to take positive steps of a remedial kind. This older social democratic criminology has not disappeared or been scientifically discredited. But it has become increasingly irrelevant to policy-makers as they struggle to come to terms with the new predicament of crime control, and the politics of reaction that followed in the wake of the welfare state.

Over the last two decades, populist, punitive, state-centered policies have accompanied and contradicted the strategies of normalizing crime, responsibilizing others, and defining deviance down. While agency administrators, government departments, and local authorities have been busy de-escalating the criminal justice response to crime, or building a new infrastructure of 'preventative partnerships', elected officials and legislatures have been escalating the penal response and promoting what amounts to a strategy of punitive segregation. Within one set of government calculations, influenced by neo-liberalism, high rates of imprisonment represent an ineffective waste of scarce resources. Within another, shaped by a neo-conservative agenda, they represent a positive symbol of the state's willingness to use force against its enemies, to express popular sentiment, and to protect the public by whatever means necessary. State sovereignty over crime is simultaneously denied and symbolically reasserted. The limits of police and punishment are recognized in one policy only to be ignored in another. One strategy seeks to build institutions better suited to the conditions of late modernity, another cranks up the old powers of the state in an attempt to overcome these same conditions. And although this contradiction is sometimes rationalized as a policy of 'bifurcation', its real roots lie in the political ambivalence that results from a complex state machine confronted by its own limitations.[90]

Adaptation, denial and acting out. If these ambivalent responses to the crime control predicament have produced policies that, however incoherent in their own terms, fit remarkably well into the broader framework of contemporary social and economic policy, it is not by some miracle of system alignment. It is because neo-liberalism and neo-conservatism shaped the ideological environment in which criminal justice decisions were made, and because these wider political currents are characterized by the same deep ambivalence in their relation to the realities and predicaments of the late modern world.

6

Crime Complex: The Culture of High Crime Societies

The previous chapter set out an argument that sought to explain recent developments in crime control from the point of view of the governmental agencies and political actors directly responsible for policy formation. Here I develop that argument by describing the ways in which certain shifts in social structure and cultural sensibilities have made policies of this kind more likely. The claim I will make is that the policies that have emerged over the last few decades have their roots in a new collective experience of crime and insecurity, an experience that is itself structured by the distinctive social, economic and cultural arrangements of late modernity.

The perceptual and emotional strands of this collective experience have been taken up, reworked, and inflected towards particular outcomes by politicians, policy-makers and opinion-formers: the political process is, in that sense, determinative. But it would be a mistake to focus all of our attention upon these processes of political transformation and representation. The newly emerging policies of crime control also depend for their possibility and their popular resonance upon the pre-existence of certain widespread social routines and cultural sensibilities. These routines and sensibilities are the extra-political conditions that now make policies of this kind possible (in the technical sense) and desirable (to key sectors of the electorate) in the UK and the USA.[1]

Since it is in the political realm that crime-control strategies are developed, argued for, and legislated, it is not surprising that most commentary has focused upon this political process and the interests and ideologies involved. I will argue, however, that the new politics of crime-control are socially and culturally conditioned; and that the content, timing, and popular appeal of these policies cannot be understood except by reference to shifts in social practice and cultural sensibility. This is not, I repeat, to imply that political decisions and policies are determined, or made inevitable, by events and circumstances occurring elsewhere. Politics and policy always involve choice and decision-making and the possibility of acting otherwise. My argument is that policies of the kind discussed here have certain conditions of possibility and that the presence of these background conditions substantially increases the probability that these policies will occur.

Let me begin by restating, in summary form, the analysis of the last chapter. In the UK and the USA at the present time, the field of crime control exhibits two new and distinct patterns of action: an *adaptive strategy* stressing prevention and partnership and a *sovereign state strategy* stressing enhanced control and expressive punishment. These strategies—which are quite different from the penal-welfare policies that preceded them—were formed in response to a new predicament faced by government in late-modern societies. This predicament arose because at a certain historical moment high rates of crime became a normal social fact; penal-welfare solutions fell into disrepute; and the modern, differentiated, criminal justice state was perceived as having failed to deliver adequate levels of security.

The state's need to acknowledge these realities without appearing to retreat in the face of them constitutes an acute and recurring political problem. Political actors and state officials increasingly recognize this predicament and adapt to it, for example, by focusing upon the effects of crime (victims, fear, costs, etc.) rather than its causes. One important response has been to withdraw the state's claim to be the chief provider of security and to attempt to remodel crime-control on a more dispersed, partnership basis. In this arrangement the state works *through* civil society and not *upon* it, and emphasizes proactive prevention rather than the prosecution and punishment of individuals. Adaptive solutions of this kind are politically difficult and institutionally radical. They involve the formation of hybrid organizations that traverse the old public/private boundaries; the activation of preventative action on the part of communities, commercial firms, and citizens; and the redefining of the organizational mission of agencies such as the police, probation, and the prisons. Governments in both Britain and America have begun to develop adaptive responses, to reach out to the private sector for partnership support, and to put in place a new infrastructure of crime prevention and community policing.

But government authorities—and especially elected officials—are deeply ambivalent about these strategies, and they frequently retreat from their implications. Under certain circumstances, or with respect to certain kinds of offences and offenders, they respond to the predicament by denying it and reactivating the old myth of the sovereign state. The result is the emergence of expressive and intensive modes of policing and punishment that purport to convey public sentiment and the full force of state authority.

I want to continue that analysis now by asking a series of questions about these two strategies. For convenience, I will term these the strategies of *preventative partnership*—by which I refer to the effort to share responsibility for crime control and build a crime prevention infrastructure beyond the state—and the strategy of *punitive segregation*, which refers to the new reliance upon measures, above all incapacitative imprisonment, designed to punish and exclude.[2] I want to ask, where do these strategies come from? What are their historical conditions of existence? From what sources do they derive their social support and cultural resonance?

An analysis of the conditions of existence of these two strategies actually leads in two different directions and tackles two quite different problems, even though the two strategies emerged out of the same historical conjuncture. The key question in respect of punitive segregation relates to its cultural and social support. This, after all, is a highly visible, highly politicized policy that could not operate in the absence of broad public commitment. In regard to preventive partnerships, the problem of preconditions is rather different. Preventive partnerships, like most of the administrative adaptations, are not high profile policies, nor do they require much in the way of popular electoral support. But they do involve the invention of new ways of thinking and acting, and the appearance of new habits and routines on the part of private actors and organizations. If we are to understand how this strategy became feasible as and when it did, we will have to explain where these ideas and forms of action came from.

Preventive partnerships involve a whole new infrastructure of arrangements whereby state and non-state agencies co-ordinate their practices in order to prevent crime and enhance community safety through the reduction of opportunities and the extension of crime-consciousness. On both sides of the Atlantic we have seen the growth of community policing in its various forms. We have seen the co-ordination of local government agencies such as housing, transport, planning, education, and social work in an effort to increase their crime control responsibilities. We have seen the creation of public–private partnerships such as Business Improvement Districts, crime prevention panels, and neighbourhood watch schemes that seek to harness the energies and interests of private citizens and commercial associations and turn them to crime-prevention purposes.[3] This strategy, which is constantly invoked by criminal justice officials on both sides of the Atlantic, entails a set of criminological assumptions (the new criminologies of everyday life); a style of governance (responsibilization; governing-at-a-distance); and a repertoire of techniques and knowledges, all of which are quite novel and at variance from the previously established ways of thinking and acting.

Where did these new knowledges come from? Who invented them and how did they come to influence public policy? And how was it possible for state agencies to find support for these policies in the habits and routines of private sector actors? These are questions I will address a little later in this chapter but first I want to focus on the sovereign state strategy of punitive segregation. The actual measures that make up this strategy—mandatory sentences, mass imprisonment, penal marking—required little in the way of inventiveness or originality. But they did require a level of public and political support that needs to be explained. In my analysis up to now, I have characterized punitive segregation as a form of denial and acting out on the part of political actors involved. But even policies that react to the contemporary predicament by denying its existence have certain conditions of existence that shape their form and content. It is to these conditions that I now turn.

The strategy of punitive segregation

Harsher sentencing and the increased use of imprisonment; 'three strikes' and mandatory minimum sentencing laws, 'truth in sentencing' and parole release restrictions; no frills prisons laws and 'austere prisons'; retribution in juvenile court and the imprisonment of children; the revival of chain gangs and corporal punishment; boot camps and supermax prisons; the multiplication of capital offences and executions; community notification laws and paedophile registers; zero tolerance policies and Anti-Social Behaviour Orders.[4] There is now a long list of measures that appear to signify a punitive turn in contemporary penality.[5] My analysis to this point has represented these measures primarily in political terms—as forms of acting out, or retaliatory legislation, or symbolic gestures of sovereign might, or politically orchestrated rituals of mechanical solidarity. Harsh punishments—and the old rhetoric of 'law and order'—are deployed by the state as a commanding gesture of lordship and popular reassurance. They are supported by a public audience, for whom this process of condemnation and punishment serves as an expressive release of tension and a gratifying moment of unity in the face of crime and insecurity. It is the standard gesture of 'expressive justice' and it is all too familiar in the pages of history. But, if we develop the analysis further, it becomes apparent that today's punitive policies are distinctive in a number of respects, and that these distinctive features can be shown to be shaped by the late modern social context out of which they emerge. In particular, today's version of the 'sovereign state strategy' depends for its social support upon the pre-existence of certain widespread social routines and cultural sensibilities that came into existence only in the latter decades of the twentieth century.

The first point to make about the new 'tough on crime' measures is that however much they engage in an expressive mode of action—punishing for its own sake, conveying public sentiment, emphasizing punitive or denunciatory objectives—they simultaneously evince a more instrumental logic. Typically each measure operates upon two different registers: an expressive, punitive scale that uses the symbols of condemnation and suffering to communicate its message; and an instrumental register, attuned to public protection and risk management. The favoured modes of punitive expression are also, and importantly, modes of penal segregation and penal marking. The policy concern today is neither purely punitive nor solely oriented towards public protection. The new penal ideal is that the public be protected and its sentiments be expressed. Punitive segregation—lengthy sentence terms in no frills prisons, and a marked, monitored existence for those who are eventually released—is increasingly the penal strategy of choice.

The second distinctive feature of these measures is that they are *populist* and *politicized*.[6] Policy measures are constructed in ways that privilege public opinion over the views of criminal justice experts and professional elites. The professional groups who once dominated the policy-making community are now increasingly disenfranchised. Policy is formulated by political action committees and political advisers—not by researchers and civil servants.[7] Policy initiatives are announced in political settings—the party convention, the party conference, the televised interview. They are encapsulated in sound-bite statements: 'Prison works', 'Three-strikes and you're out', 'Truth in sentencing', 'No frills prisons', 'Tough on crime, tough on the causes of crime'. Often these initiatives are under-researched and lack the elaborate costings and statistical projections that are a standard feature in other areas of policy.[8]

The third feature of this strategy is that it purports to give a privileged place to victims, though in fact that place is occupied by a projected, politicized, image of 'the victim' rather than by the interests and opinions of victims themselves. When introducing new measures of punitive segregation, elected officials now routinely invoke the feelings of 'the victim' as a source of support and legitimacy. The need to reduce the present or future suffering of victims functions today as an all-purpose justification for measures of penal repression, and the political imperative of being responsive to victims' feelings now serves to reinforce the retributive sentiments that increasingly inform penal legislation.

If victims were once the forgotten, hidden casualties of criminal behaviour, they have now returned with a vengeance, brought back into full public view by politicians and media executives who routinely exploit the victim's experience for their own purposes. The sanctified persona of the suffering victim has become a valued commodity in the circuits of political and media exchange, and real individuals are now placed in front of the cameras and invited to play this role—often becoming media celebrities or victims movement activists in the process. We have become used to seeing crime victims or their families accompany American politicians as they announce new mandatory sentencing laws, or declare measures that will alert communities to the dangers that released offenders represent. British party political conferences have also been a stage on which crime victims have been displayed or, as they say, 'given a voice'—though the voice they are given is not necessarily theirs, having been carefully stage-managed to ensure that it fits the political message of which it now forms a part.

As I noted above, the new political imperative is that victims must be protected; their voices must be heard, their memory honoured, their anger expressed, their fears addressed. The naming of criminal laws and penal measures for crime victims (Megan's law, Jenna's law, Stephanie's law, and most recently the British press campaign for 'Sarah's law') purports to honour them in this way, though there is undoubtedly an element of exploitation here too, as the individual's name is used to fend off objections to measures that are often nothing more than retaliatory legislation passed for public display and political advantage. This sanctification of victims also tends to nullify concern for offenders. The zero sum relationship that is now assumed to hold between the one and the other ensures that any show of compassion for offenders, any invocation of their rights, any effort to humanize their punishments, can easily be represented as an insult to victims and their families.[9]

As a consequence of these usages, the symbolic figure of the victim has taken on a life of its own, and plays a key role in political debate and policy argument. The crime victim is no longer represented as an unfortunate citizen who has been on the receiving end of a criminal harm. His or her concerns are no longer subsumed within the 'public interest' that guides prosecution and penal decisions. Instead, the crime victim is now, in a certain sense, a *representative character* whose experience is assumed to be common and collective, rather than individual and atypical.[10] His (or more often her) suffering is represented in the immediate and personalized idiom of the mass media, and speaks directly to the fears and angers of the viewing public, producing effects of identification and reinforcement that are then turned to political and commercial use.

The British Labour Party—at least while in opposition—warned that 'Everyone's a Victim' and promised a policy that accords with this new reality. President Reagan's Victims Task Force Report insists that its readers must engage the issue not via the intellect but instead through the emotions, and the immediacy of empathy and identification: 'You cannot appreciate the victim problem if you approach it solely with your intellect. The intellect rebels. The important proposals contained here will not be clear unless you first confront the human reality of victimization.' This statement is followed by a harrowing account 'based on the testimony of these and other victims we have drawn a composite of a victim of crime. The victim is every victim, she could be you or related to you.'[11] This personalizing trope, repeated endlessly on television news and documentaries, represents the crime victim as the real-life, 'it-could-be-you' metonym for the problem of personal security. And in so doing, it shifts the debate away from the instrumental reasoning of crime control analysis towards the visceral emotions of identification and righteous indignation. Once this shift has been effected, the terms of the debate are transformed and 'facts' become 'less persuasive than the moral authority of grief'.[12] If the centre-piece of penal-welfarism was the (expert projection of) the individual offender and his or her needs, the centre of contemporary penal discourse is (a political projection of) the individual victim and his or her feelings.

To understand the expressive, punitive aspects of this strategy *and* its concern with security and segregation, we have to explore the new collective meaning of victimhood.[13] We have to examine the new experience of crime and insecurity that it implies, and the reworked relationship between the individual victim, the symbolic victim, and the public institutions that represent their interests and administer their complaints. How did 'the public' come to reconstituted as so many individual crime victims? How did each of us come to take on that identity? These questions require us to look beyond the domain of political action and add a cultural and social psychological dimension to our analysis.

Today's policies of punitive segregation should not be dismissed as merely another outbreak of some eternally present punitive instinct or primitive emotion. Collective emotions are certainly a calculated component of such policies, as is made clear by the inflammatory political rhetoric that typically frames legislation of this kind. But there is something about contemporary culture that invites this emotivism and the emphatic expression of feeling, and pushes political discourse about crime in that direction. Outrage and anger are the culture's antidotes to fear and anxiety, and the open expression of these emotions is part of the consolation and therapy it offers.[14] The sentiments we now see expressed are quite specific ones, grounded in definite features of our social organization rather than in some timeless punitive instinct. They are conditioned, evoked and channelled by the social routines and cultural practices of contemporary society, and they are they taken up and articulated by the strategy of punitive segregation in particular ways as a result of specific political and cultural processes.

The problem of historical explanation

The emergence of this strategy demands an analysis that can explain its distinctive elements, its timing, and the extent of its popular and political appeal. Penal control policies are not always phrased in terms of the needs of victims or the imperative of public protection. They are not always and everywhere a recipe for political success. Nor has crime control always appeared well suited to populist phrasing and discussion. For most of the twentieth century, punishment and crime control have hardly featured in electoral competition, particularly at the national level.[15] It was not until the 1960s in the USA and the mid-1970s in the UK that the Republican and Conservative political parties began to give prominence to crime in their election manifestos. Several elections passed before their Democratic and Labour Party opponents began to respond in kind, a response that raised the stakes rather than changed the game. The old conventional wisdom was that elected officials ought best to avoid contentious pronouncements in an area where policy failure was highly probable.[16] Until recently, the details of corrections and crime control were frequently left to criminal justice professionals and 'public opinion' was viewed as an occasional brake upon penal policy rather than a privileged source of policy-making initiatives. Somehow, the relation between politicians, the public and professionals has been transformed, with major consequences for policy and practice.

The capacity of professional groups to secure control over the formulation of penal policy and effectively to de-politicize crime control issues was a concomitant of the penal-welfare framework that dominated policy-making in the decades following the Second World War. Social welfare professionals succeeded in characterizing crime control issues as essentially technical issues, best governed by expert knowledge and empirical research. They also succeeded in characterizing retributive or expressive concerns as irrational and inappropriate—unworthy emotions that ought best to be repressed—to the point where explicitly punitive sentiments came to be more or less absent from official discourse about crime and its control. If the re-emergence of punitiveness in penal policy represents the return of the repressed, then this suggests a shift in the balance between populism and professionalism in policy-making. We need to ask how did public opinion come to be so exercised about crime and why did criminal justice professionals lose their capacity to limit the public's impact on policy?

It is sometimes claimed that public support for punitive measures is a shallow, media-generated phenomenon. The claim tends to be that tough-on-crime policies do not originate in any real groundswell of public demand; that the public are not truly committed to these policies; and that such commitment as does exist has been artificially aroused and excited by media images and campaigns that misrepresent both crime and public sentiment. Public support for enhanced 'law and order' is, on this account, the fabricated result of manipulative political rhetoric and a rabble-rousing popular press. There can be no doubt that tabloid news and television fiction are important definers of popular knowledge concerning crime and that this results in a great deal of misinformation and mythologizing. It is also true that public attitudes about crime and punishment are conditioned by information, and may sometimes be changed by educative means.[17] But it is a mistake to infer from this that the voting public is easily led and infinitely malleable, that mass support for 'law and order' policies can be conjured up from nothing,[18] or that newspapers and television can create and sustain a mass audience for crime stories without certain social and psychological conditions being already in place.[19]

Tough crime policies are not without costs. The policies currently being pursued in the USA and Britain entail unprecedented levels of correctional expenditure.[20] Public spending on 'law and order' either increases the tax burden or else reduces other heads of public expenditure, such as education, health-care or job-creation programs.[21] New powers for police, higher sentencing levels, restrictions on the freedom of ex-offenders—each of these carries a price in terms of the erosion of civil liberties and the reduced power of the citizen *vis-à-vis* the state. Popular support for such policies—like the well-documented fascination of large sections of the population with crime news and crime fiction—are phenomena that have certain preconditions.[22] They are not summoned up out of nowhere by the magical powers of ideology, nor by the ineluctable force of political rhetoric. If masses of people are now emotionally invested in crime control issues and supportive of tougher legislation, casting their votes and spending their taxes in support of these laws, then this is a phenomenon that requires explanation. The evidence of ideological manipulation and political misrepresentation is relevant here, but it does not seem weighty enough to carry the full burden of explanation.

Finally, there is the question of timing. The widespread expression of punitive sentiments by legislators and the emergence of penal laws and policies that express these sentiments, do not correlate directly with increasing crime rates. The peaks of penal reaction, which in both the USA and the UK have tended to occur in the mid- to late 1990s, lag well behind the peaks of criminal victimization. In the case of the USA, this 'lag' is one not of months or years but of decades.[23]

A new experience of crime

My argument will be that the strategies of preventative partnership and punitive segregation are conditioned by, and adaptive to, an historically distinctive experience of crime that began to take shape in the 1960s and 1970s. The co-ordinates of that experience were established earlier, and more intensively in the USA than in the UK, and each country has its distinctive characteristics and emphases. But it is their similarities that I want to highlight here.

I argued earlier that high rates of crime have become a normal social fact in the USA and the UK, and that this new social fact, together with a number of related phenomena, created a new crime control predicament for governmental agencies and political decision-makers. We have seen how governmental and political actors responded to this predicament, and how the contemporary strategies of crime control were constructed in this process of reaction, adaptation and problem solving. But if high rates of crime have become a normal social fact—a routine part of modern consciousness, an everyday risk to be assessed and managed—then it is a fact that is initially encountered and negotiated by the population at large, by people going about their normal business, leading their daily lives. And it is the active engagement of the population (or rather the individuals, households, communities, and organizations that compose it) with that new social fact that has gradually produced a new collective experience of crime, and a new set of possibilities for crime control.

By 'experience' here I do not have in mind that impossible empiricist conception, a direct, unmediated encounter with the real. Individuals may be directly on the receiving end of criminal acts, but none of us experiences 'crime' in an unmediated, untutored, unscripted way. The historically situated experience of crime to which I refer is that which is constituted for, and lived by, socially situated individuals who inhabit the complex of practices, knowledges, norms, and subjectivities that make up a culture. It is a collective cultural experience, one that weaves its threads of meaning into every individual encounter, and is, in turn, inflected and revised by the thousands of such encounters that take place every day. To talk about an 'experience of crime' in this way is to talk about the meaning that crime takes on for a particular culture at a particular time.[24] It is to talk about a densely interwoven fabric of collective mentalities and sensibilities and a set of terms through which these are publicly represented—a cultural web that is tied into specific forms of life, and for that very reason, is slow to change and resistant to deliberate alteration.

Such a concept is, of course, too broad, too abstract, and too general to be of much use for most purposes. But it does, I think, permit us to mark out some broad historical contrasts, such as the contrast between the experience of crime that previously underpinned penal-welfarism[25] and the new experience that underpins the reconfigured field that is currently taking shape. It also enables us to identify the basic elements of perception and concern with which government policies engage and to which they claim to respond.

The collective experience of crime is, of course, highly differentiated and stratified, particularly in modern societies. Social groups and individuals are differentially placed in respect of crime—differentially vulnerable to victimization, differentially fearful about its risks, differentially oriented by values, beliefs and education in their attitude to its causes and remedies. Mapping out these differences is, not, however, necessary to the argument I wish to make here.[26] What I am seeking to isolate and explain is not the distribution of punitive sentiments, but a specific shift that has occurred over the last two or three decades—a shift that has had the effect of making crime much more salient as a social and cultural fact.[27]

We have already seen how, in the 1970s and 1980s, shifts in the economic and social position of large sections of the middle and working classes facilitated the political formation of new class alliances and race relations and the rise to dominance of a more conservative political regime. For reasons already discussed, this political block was opposed to policies that appeared to benefit the 'undeserving poor', cynical about 'welfare', and supportive of more aggressive controls for an 'underclass' that was perceived to be disorderly, drug-prone, and dangerous. Opinion polls provide evidence of a corresponding shift of public opinion in a more punitive direction in both the UK and the USA over the last twenty years.[28] But before assuming that these broad shifts in public opinion explain the subsequent shifts in crime policy, we should recall that, for most of the twentieth century, policy was not at all dictated by 'the public', which acted as a brake upon penal reform rather than its chief sponsor. Penal modernism was, instead, the creation of government departments encouraged by the influential voices of experts, professional practitioners, and reformers, and broadly supported by the best educated sections of the middle classes and what are often termed the 'liberal elites'. These high-status groups were the key supporters of the penal-welfare framework, the firmest opponents of punitive measures and the most enthusiastic proponents of a research-based policy process. Any serious analysis of recent law and order policies must explain how these groups came to exert less influence or else to change their attitudes to crime and the policy preferences that flowed from them. The strategic focus for analysis is not public opinion as a whole, but rather the changing experience and political position of this specific group. While public opinion has indeed shifted in a more punitive direction I will suggest that it is this group whose attitudes and dispositions have been most thoroughly transformed over the last three decades. And it is their adaptations to the experience of high rates of crime that have had the most significant impact upon penal politics and crime-control.[29]

The professional middle classes and penal-welfarism

Liberal elites, the educated middle classes and public sector professionals (sometimes collectively referred to by sociologists as 'the new classes') were the groups that did most to support the welfarist and correctionalist objectives of post-war penal policy, and to insist upon a professionalized, technical, expert approach to dispensing criminal justice.[30] They did this as a political constituency, providing bedrock support for welfare-state and Great Society programmes, and also in their capacity as a new set of occupational groups (social workers, educationalists, psychologists, psychiatrists, probation and parole officers, state administrators, etc.) who staff the large public sector of the welfare state. Penal policy-making was, until recently, somewhat removed from critical public scrutiny and from the full force of popular opinion and so the professional and administrators who ran the system were able to exert a disproportionate influence over its direction.[31]

Three conditions linked the professional middle classes with correctionalist crime control policies. First, there were political and economic interests that tied the middle classes into welfare state politics and institutions. It was these groups—rather than the poor or the commercial and business classes—who had most to gain from the redistributive effects of compulsory national insurance, social security, national health-care, mortgage subsidies, and state-funded education.[32] It was their sons and daughters who took advantage of the new opportunities for upward mobility offered by the opening up of further education on a mass scale. And it was these groups who went on to fill the new occupational positions offered by the expansion of the state, particularly its new social work and child-care sectors.[33]

Secondly, for the educated middle classes, a 'civilized' attitude towards crime—stressing social circumstances rather than individual responsibility, remedial treatment rather than punishment—has been a sign of cultural distinction, marking off urbane, educated, cultured opinion from the more vulgar, more reactionary views of those groups immediately above and below in the stratification hierarchy. The contrast with the 'small minded' petty bourgeoisie, with 'red-neck' and 'blue collar' attitudes, was particularly important to a certain middle-class self-image, but so too was the critique of their social superiors who appeared to put property values above humanism and compassion.[34]

The third consideration has to do with the social distance that, until quite recently, separated the professional middle classes from crime and insecurity. Unlike the poor, or even the lower middle classes, the professional middle classes in the 1950s and 1960s typically lived at a distance from criminal events.[35] They occupied low-crime parts of the city and the suburbs. Their children attended schools that were well disciplined and largely free of crime, drugs, and violence. Their daily routines did not often expose them to the threat of crime, nor did fear of crime occupy a prominent place in their consciousness. As a result, their thinking about crime was largely shaped by stereotypes and ideology—in this case the stereotypes of modern criminology and a progressive, social democratic ideology—and was largely unencumbered by concrete facts or first-hand encounters. Their preferred image of the criminal was that of the under-socialized, undereducated, undernourished adolescent—the juvenile delinquent, for whom social reform and correctional treatment were the appropriate response. This class's experience of crime, which was highly influential in shaping penal policy, was thus shaped by its social distance from the problem, its low levels of victimization, and the expert knowledge and welfare-state ideologies through which it made sense of this 'poor people's problem'.[36]

The professional middle classes were, moreover, an economically prosperous social group, enjoying the security and status afforded by educational certification and professional credentials in the increasingly professional society of the post-war decades. From this vantage point the group was able to adopt a civilized attitude towards crime and criminals. They viewed crime as a social problem linked to, and explicable by, poor social conditions, and susceptible to the professional, expert, social engineering solutions in which they, as a group, now specialized. For this group to adopt a correctionalist, non-punitive attitude was, at once, to disdain the vulgarities of the under-educated, to express compassion for the poor masses, and to further their own professional interests. The de-politicization of penal policy, the suppression of punitive themes, the professionalization of criminal justice, and the dominance of correctional objectives—all the key elements that characterized crime-control in the post-war period—were in large part the achievements of this social group and their political representatives, acting in a structural context that was highly amenable to outcomes of this kind.

The declining influence of social expertise

What has happened in the last few decades to undermine this arrangement? Why has the tight connection between the middle classes and penal-welfarism come undone? Two explanations offer themselves, each of which appears plausible on the available evidence. One possibility is that professional elites have become less successful in resisting the impact of popular opinion in the realm of policy-making—either because the character of policy-making has become more politicized, or else because these professional groups have lost some of their status and credibility. Another is that the professional middle classes have themselves become less supportive of penal-welfarism and more supportive of punitive responses to crime. I will suggest that there is reason to suppose that both of these processes are at work.

Welfare professionals have, since the 1970s, experienced a sharp decline in status and political clout—a decline that is part of a more general reaction against the welfare state and the types of social expertise that formed its mainstay.[37] Market solutions, individual responsibility and self-help have increasingly displaced welfare state collectivism and social policy has come to place more emphasis upon accounting and managerial expertise than upon professional social workers and clinicians. A key support for penal-welfare policies has thus declined in significance.

Criminal justice professionals, whose policies and ideologies had come to be associated with decades of rising crime and institutional failure, did not escape this downward trajectory.[38] These groups experienced a process of demoralization and self-doubt as a consequence of the critique of professional authority that took hold in the late 1960s. When, in the early 1970s, faith in the rehabilitative ideal began to collapse, important sections of the penal-welfare professions joined academic criminologists and radical reformers in embracing this critique and making public their misgivings about the correctional project.[39] When the whole penal-welfare ethos later began to be challenged by more reactionary, retributive currents, the groups most closely associated with that ethos were internally divided and incapable of mounting effective opposition to change.

Since the mid-1970s, legislatures have increasingly reclaimed the power to punish that they had previously delegated to experts, thus reversing the historic pattern that had accompanied the rise of the penal-welfare framework. This undoing of what Foucault called 'the Declaration of Carceral Independence' began with the American prisoners rights litigation and the gradual spread of due process considerations into the prison system.[40] Since that time, a variety of devices—mandatory minimum sentences, sentencing guidelines, national guidelines on probation and community service, decreased scope for early release, more intense political scrutiny of institutional regimes—have further reduced the authority of the experts and professionals who previously administered the system.

The standing of social professionals within the criminal justice system has thus been challenged from the late 1970s onwards and this was exacerbated in the 1980s by organizational reforms that shifted decision-making power away from clinicians and practitioners towards accountants and managers.[41] This reduction in the credibility and political influence of criminal justice experts and social professionals has had major consequences for criminal justice policy. Up until recently, these professionals functioned as a kind of buffer, shielding the processes of policymaking and day-to-day administration from the full impact of public opinion. The declining influence of these groups, together with the politicization of crime policy, has altered the dynamics of policymaking in this area, making it much more open to populist pressure from the outside.

But the changing fortunes of professional groups provide only a partial explanation for a quite radical shift in the direction of policy. Had they occurred by themselves, these internal developments might have been expected to bring about a modification of penal-welfarism—a curtailment of discretion, more juridification of decision-making, perhaps a shift towards more penal objectives. But it is hard to believe that the reconfiguration of penality would have gone so far if liberal elite opinion outside the system had stayed firmly behind the penal-welfare orthodoxy.

In fact it did not. The liberal optimism and correctionalist ideologies of these groups underwent a serious decline starting in the 1970s and by the 1980s many of their members were supporting parties committed to tougher crime policies.[42] This shift of opinion occurred in two stages. The first of these—the shift from correctionalist ideologies to concern for 'just deserts' and due process—has already been much discussed and is relatively easy to explain as an outcome of the processes described in Chapter Three.[43] What is much more difficult to explain is why this 1970s scepticism about correctionalism eventually issued, in the 1980s and 1990s, in the particular strategies that actually emerged—strategies that bore little resemblance to the original reform programmes. The conventional explanation for this is an emphatically political one. The liberal movement towards just deserts and measured retribution was quickly hijacked by elected officials and hard-line legislatures who—in a new context of high crime and moral panic—raised the punitive stakes and escalated sentencing levels far above anything that had been contemplated by rehabilitation's liberal critics.[44] This is no doubt true as far as it goes. But this explanation fails to account for the dog that did not bark. It fails to mention the professional middle classes, an otherwise powerful and articulate group, who have done little to oppose the drift towards punitive policies. It is true, of course, that liberal voices have not been altogether silent, and they are still are still to be heard opposing the punitive and the inhumane. But they now sound like voices in the wilderness, echoing the sentiments of an earlier era, lacking real support in the political domain. And they increasingly appear as isolated voices, lacking strong support even within their own social class. What has shifted middle-class opinion away from its traditional civilized approach to penal issues and brought it closer to the new politics of punishment and protection?

The increased salience of crime

The social and spatial changes that gave rise to the high crime rates of the 1960s and subsequent decades also, and independently, transformed the middle-class experience of crime. From being a problem that mostly affected the poor, crime and incivility (and particularly vandalism, theft, burglary, and robbery) increasingly became a daily consideration for anyone who owned a car, used the subway, left their house unguarded during the day, or walked the city streets at night. Victimization continued to be unevenly distributed, with the poor and minorities bearing the brunt of the increase, but, within a single generation, crime became a prominent fact of life not only for the urban middle classes, but for many middle-class suburbanites as well.[45] The groups that had been the prime beneficiaries of the post-war consumer boom, now found themselves much more vulnerable than before in the face of the increased levels of crime and violence that this boom brought in its wake. And as the tell-tale signs of crime and disorder became more visible on the streets—in the form of vandalism and graffiti, the incivility of unsupervised teeenagers, or the erratic behaviour of the newly deinstitutionalized mentally ill—fear of crime became an established part of daily existence.[46] What were once, for much of the middle-class population, fleeting, occasional fears, linked to particular situations and unusual circumstances, now became much more routine, much more a part of the *habitus* of everyday life, particularly in large cities.[47] The social distance between the middle classes and crime was greatly diminished, with consequences for point of view and perspective.

No doubt the distribution of fears was a very inexact match for the actual patterns of victimization and risk, but increasing levels of concern about crime were certainly triggered by the steep increases in reported crime (especially violent offending) that occurred in the decades after 1960. As more and more of the population were themselves burgled or robbed or assaulted, or else had a close friend or relative who had been; as theft of and from cars became a normal concomitant of car ownership in many cities; as the visible evidence of vandalism and drug abuse began to manifest itself on city streets and schools; and as US statistics showed an increasing percentage of homicides committed by unknown assailants, rising crime rates ceased to be a statistical abstraction and took on a vivid personal meaning in popular consciousness and individual psychology. [48] These anxieties about crime, on top of the more inchoate insecurities prompted by rapid social change and economic recession, paved the way for a politics of reaction in the late 1970s. This politics, in its turn, helped shape these diffuse middle-class anxieties into a more focused set of attitudes and understandings, identifying the culprits, naming the problem, setting up scapegoats. As the middle classes found themselves becoming regular victims of crime, they were simultaneously encouraged to view themselves as victims of big government, of tax and spend policies, of irresponsible welfare programmes, of union-led inflation, and in the USA, of affirmative action programmes. All of these were said to work against the interests of 'decent, hard-working middle-class people' and to benefit the undeserving and increasingly disorderly urban poor. If the middle classes were now the new victims, their victimizers were an undeserving underclass, fostered by wrongheaded welfare policies, social service professionals with vested interests, and out-of-touch liberal elites who did not live in the real world.

Major, high-visibility events—such as the urban riots that occurred in the USA in the 1960s and in the UK in the early 1980s, or the massive publicity given to heroin or crack cocaine use and its attendant pathologies, or atrocious crimes such as the killings of James Bulger or Polly Klaas[49]—dramatized this for many, transforming crime and violence into national issues and fixing them as channels for the expression of more inchoate fears. Media images of rioting youths, violent 'crack-heads', and an alienated, angry, self-destructive 'underclass' were especially potent in deepening the alarm felt by the middle-class public and linking crime to questions of class and race.[50]

Fear of crime is closely related to fear of strangers and the social class dynamics of the 1980s and 1990s (which concentrated the poverty and worklessness of inner city youth and especially black males, intensifying their social and cultural exclusion, and building a perception of them as a newly dangerous, alien class) tended to exacerbate such fears.[51] The neo-liberal social policies that increased the exclusion and hardship of specific social groups thus produced new problems of order and new fears about its maintenance. Fears were also increased by the transformation in the crime mix that occurred in the 1980s in the USA and a little later in the UK: the relative increase in crimes of violence, and particularly of drug-related crimes (such as robbery, burglary, and homicide) was especially worrisome, not least because those involved in such crime were often portrayed as desperate, driven, and capable of mindless violence.

Social change and middle-class attitudes towards crime and control

These new middle-class concerns about crime were significantly affected by three social developments that unfolded over the same time period.

Crime and the middle-class household

The first of these had to do with some basic changes that occurred in the characteristic organization and 'life-style' of many middle-class families.[52] The comparative solidity of the middle-class household in the 1950s has given way to a more complex and more fragile organization that requires much more in the way of management, scheduling and co-ordination than was previously the case. The major social trends of the post-war years—the spread of the automobile; the mass migration to the suburbs; the lengthening commute to work; the movement of women into the labor market; the rise of two-career families; increased rates of divorce; the outsourcing of household tasks and child-care—all of these have had a major impact upon middle-class households in both the UK and the USA. Most of these developments have substantially increased the freedom, opportunities and affluence of the members of these households (and particularly of women) and these are gains that few would be prepared to give up. But the cost of these historic achievements has often been a deep sense of vulnerability, of insecurity, of precariousness. In today's 'work-rich' middle-class households, there is a constant need to manage time; to co-ordinate people and events; to schedule school, work, shopping, and leisure.[53] Heads of household, which in practice usually means wives and mothers, must continuously struggle to impose some semblance of control upon a hectic round of activities and involvements. The tendencies towards 'the separation of time and space', and the 'disembedding of social systems' that sociologists point to as characteristic of late modernity are experienced and managed on a daily basis by individuals as they strive to transport the children across town to school or child-care, commute to work, organize the household chores, keep in touch with distant friends and family, get the car repaired, while keeping tabs upon expenditures, investments, retirement plans, as well as work on their relationships and worry about their health. [54]

The problem of *managing*, of exerting control over events, of staving off impending domestic chaos, is altogether more intense than when a more rigidly gendered division of labour ensured that the woman was at home to take care of these tasks herself, and the man earned a 'family wage' sufficient for the whole household's needs.[55] The sense of precariousness, of the strung-out nature of existence, is an important new element in people's lives, even as these lives grow more varied and mobile and exciting. This sense of ontological insecurity is magnified by recent changes in the nature of work and by the changing character of the professional career. It is also exacerbated by the shift from state-provided social security polices to the responsibilized autonomy of private retirement plans and market-based welfare provision, and by widespread inchoate anxieties about the collapse of social institutions and the break-up of the family.[56] But my point is that this new element of precariousness and insecurity is built into the fabric of everyday life, and will tend to persist even as economies go though their periodic cycles or are chilled by globalization and its effects. Little surprise then, that the felt need to establish control over risks and uncertainties, and the desire to stave off insecurity, become ever-more urgent aspects of middle-class psychology and culture.[57] Little surprise too that people increasingly demand to know about the risks to which that are exposed by the criminal justice system and are increasingly impatient when that system fails to control 'dangerous' individuals who are within its reach.

These economic and ecological developments made households and their individual members more vulnerable to crime than previously. The absence of a stay-at-home guardian; the accumulation of high-value, portable goods; the possession of motor cars; the spaced-out, detached homes of suburbia, stripped of the natural controls of close neighbours or passers-by—all of these increased the likelihood of victimization.[58] So too did the retreat of 'respectable' adults and families from the public spaces of the towns and cities into their homes and other privatized leisure settings—a development that made public parks, squares and streets appear increasingly disorderly and unsafe particularly to those groups who had deserted them.[59]

Over the post-war years, the structure of everyday life became more porous, more open-textured, more generative of opportunities for criminal victimization. What came to be seen as a failure of the criminal justice state might better be seen as a stretching of the social fabric as late modern processes of 'time-space distanciation' relaxed organic controls and produced a more porous, more vulnerable, civil society.[60] Both Britain and America were transformed in ways that increased crime opportunities, weakened traditional situational controls, and relaxed some of the constraints that tied individuals into group conformity. High rates of crime and disorder were a precipitate of the changing social structure. Crime has become one of the threats that the contemporary middle-class household must take seriously—another problem to manage, another possibility that must be anticipated and controlled.

The psychological reactions of individuals to this new situation do, of course, vary greatly. For some, the crime problem has become a source of anxiety and frustration; an urgent daily reminder of the need to impose control, to take care, to secure oneself and one's family against the dangers of the modern world. Anxieties of this kind are often mixed with anger and resentment and, when experienced *en masse*, can supply the emotional basis for retaliatory laws and expressive punishments. At the opposite end of the spectrum, other individuals react with measured stoicism, inuring themselves to crime's irritations and risks, adapting to this 'fact of life' in the same humdrum way that they adapt to the daily grind of commuting, or the tendency of the cost of living to rise. The presence of crime in daily life creates a psychological and cultural response, but this response is neither singular nor unambivalent.[61]

Crime and the control deficit

The second development shaping the middle classes experience of crime was, in part, the unplanned result of the policy changes that I described in the previous chapter. From the 1960s onwards, one of the major responses of the criminal justice state to increasing levels of crime was to define deviance down, to raise the threshold of law enforcement, in effect to tolerate low-level crime and misdemeanours, or else respond to them with minimal penalties. This pattern of under-enforcement, for all its bureaucratic rationality, produced the unintended consequence of markedly increasing public anxiety—particularly on city streets, public transport, and the poorer housing schemes where incivilities and minor disorder were most prominent. While the police and the courts concentrated their resources upon serious crime, minor offending often went unchecked and the signs of disorder became more and more apparent, spreading into the public sphere occupied by the middle classes going to and from work or school or leisure. This quite rapid change in the urban landscape, at a time when crime and the fear of crime were anyway rising, led many to believe that, in minor but highly significant ways, the state was retreating in the face of the problem. The resulting sense of a control deficit—of a law enforcement effort that was being relaxed at the very moment when community controls were also weakening—was deeply disturbing to many.[62] That this occurred in a period of social and political upheaval in which traditional institutions and forms of authority appeared to many to be close to collapse, only served to exacerbate the felt need to take a tougher line with the control of crime and disorder.[63]

These middle-class fears were, no doubt, overlaid by an element of guilt and bad conscience. This was, after all, the society that these classes had chosen; the one they voted for again and again in the 1980s and 1990s. To elect neoliberal governments was deliberately to reduce state provision and 'liberate' market forces. Low tax and low welfare regimes meant that every citizen has became more dependent upon his or her market position and less able to rely upon the state. By opting for the market, getting the state 'off their backs', and freeing up individuals and investments many voters had made themselves very wealthy. But in so doing they had also undone the delicate webs of solidarity and community that are so important in providing individuals with a sense of security for themselves and their children. The decline of public institutions through underfunding, the reduction of state benefits, the disinvestment in the inner cities, the social and economic marginalization of the poor—these are policies that engender insecurity, and not just for those most disadvantaged by them.

The neo-liberal choice has been a fateful one in emotional as well as economic terms. Every individual is more and more obliged to adopt the economic attitude of the responsibilized, competitive entrepreneur. The corresponding psychic posture is that of tensed-up, restless individuals, regarding one another with mutual suspicion and no great deal of trust. The pursuit of freedom—moral freedom, market freedom, individual freedom—brings with it the risk of insecurity and the temptation to respond with repression. In this cultural setting, it is no wonder that the undeserving poor are feared and resented. 'Choosing freedom' comes at a cost, and all too often it is the poor and the powerless who are made to pay.[64]

Crime and the mass media

The third development I want to highlight is the impact of mass media, and particularly of television, upon popular perceptions of crime. Television viewing emerged as a mass phenomenon at much the same time that high crime rates began to become a normal social fact, i.e. between about 1950 and 1970. TV's focus upon national rather than local news; its affinity for crime as a theme; its sympathetic portrayal of individual victims who have suffered at the hands of criminals and been let down by an uncaring, ineffectual system—all of these have transformed perceptions of crime and further reduced the sense of distance from the problem that the middle classes once enjoyed.

The dynamics of the televised press conference or interview have also made it more difficult for administrators and professionals to avoid the emotional force of popular opinion. Unlike the Congressional hearing or the commission of inquiry, the televised interview regularly pits the rationality of 'the system' directly up against the anguish of individuals injured by the system's policies.[65] In effect, TV has changed the rules of political speech. The TV encounter—with its soundbite rapidity, its emotional intensity, and its mass audience—has tended to push politicians to be more populist, more emotive, more evidently in tune with public feeling. The spectre of the defeated Michael Dukkakis, with his supposedly 'soft on crime' liberalism and his too-rational technocratic idiom, has cast a long shadow over political debate in the USA and beyond.

The increased prominence and popularity of TV crime shows since the 1960s has itself been a cultural concomitant of the normality of high crime rates in contemporary society. The partly subconscious fears and resentments that are such a feature of life in high crime societies find a cultural outlet and expression on the TV screen. They are played out there in the form of revenge dramas and morality tales, narratives of crime and punishment, stories of criminals brought to justice, and news of atrocities that ignite outrage and demand catharsis.[66] These media representations undoubtedly give shape and emotional inflection to our experience of crime, and do so in a way that is largely dictated by the structure and values of the media rather than the phenomena it depicts. Television's selective coverage of factual crime stories and its unrealistic crime dramas tend to distort public perceptions of the problem.[67] So too does its privileging of what might be called 'victim discourse' over 'system discourse'—its rhetorical preference for the personal accounts of those let down by the criminal justice system rather than policy analyses of those who represent it. This emphasis pushes us to respond to crime as an emotional, human drama and prompts us to think of criminals as more numerous, more threatening, and more dangerous than they typically are.

This is not to say that the media has *produced* our interest in crime, or that it has *produced* the popular punitiveness that appears as such a strong political current today. Without a grounded, routine, collective experience of crime, it is unlikely that crime news and drama would attract such large audiences or sell so much advertising space. My point is rather that the mass media has tapped into, then dramatized and reinforced, a new public experience—an experience with profound psychological resonance—and in doing so it has *institutionalized* that experience. It has surrounded us with images of crime, pursuit, and punishment, and it has provided us with regular, everyday occasions in which to play out the emotions of fear, anger, resentment, and fascination that our experience of crime provokes.

This institutionalization increases the salience of crime in everyday life. It also attunes the public's response not to crime itself, or even to the officially recorded rates, but to the media through which crime is typically represented and the collective representations that these media establish over time.[68] Public knowledge and opinion about criminal justice are based upon collective representations rather than accurate information; upon a culturally given experience of crime, rather than the thing itself. So while ecological changes may have reduced the social distance separating the middle classes from crime, the simultaneous spread of these cultural practices has reduced psychological and emotional distance even more.

Cultural adaptations

Changes in the frequency and distribution of crime, in patterns of law enforcement, or even in the quality of middle-class life, are not, in themselves, sufficient to explain changes in social attitudes to crime. There is no automatic adjustment in perception that follows changes in the 'objective' co-ordinates of a phenomenon such as crime.[69] Social developments do not determine the political and cultural responses to which they give rise. They do, however, pose definite problems that demand adjustments, adaptations or solutions of some kind. For the purpose of explaining the social support for contemporary penal politics, these political and cultural responses to high crime rates are more important than the crime rates themselves.

So what were the responses? How did these groups adapt to their new situation, to their new relation to crime and insecurity? Part of their response was to demand better provision by the state and greater effectiveness on the part of its criminal justice agencies. But middle-class groups were not so dependent upon state provision, or so lacking in resources that they could not develop private responses of their own.

One major development that grew up in these years was the victims' movement. Initially this took the form of a multitude of self-starting local initiatives, run largely by volunteers and former victims, offering support and counselling to crime victims. Over time, these support groups built up referral relationships with local police departments and probation offices, and operated quietly on the margins of the system, providing support to individuals who lacked the solace of family or neighbours and were largely ignored by the criminal justice system. Eventually, in the 1980s, the victims movement was discovered by the media and by politicians, whereupon the issue of victims and victim's rights began to take on a very different political significance. What began as a grass roots movement became a government-subsidized function. Meanwhile, the (supposed) interests of victims came to be a central reference point in party politics, and featured in debates about punishment that had formed no part of the movement's original concerns.

Another important story of the last two decades concerns the invention, typically by private actors, of social and situational controls, and their retrofitting to a context in which the state's criminal justice agencies were increasingly perceived as ineffective. In the face of high crime rates, and in the absence of adequate levels of state-provided security, the energies and inventiveness of civil society were stimulated to provide new lines of defence and new measures of control. In recent years we have seen a shift in the character and organization of what is often termed 'informal social control'. As we saw, the development of late modernity reduced the extent and effectiveness of 'spontaneous' social controls—which is to say, the learned, unreflexive, habitual practices of mutual supervision, scolding, sanctioning, and shaming carried out, as a matter of course, by community members. The current wave of crime prevention behaviour tries to revive these dying habits, and, more importantly, to supplement them with new crime control practices that are more deliberate, more focused, and more reflexive.

What were these adaptations and inventions? A proper answer to this question would document a multitude of tiny, mundane actions and techniques, spreading across the social field in a process of imitation, re-invention and recurrence rather like the emergence and spread of disciplinary techniques that Foucault describes in early modern Europe.[70] All I can do here is provide a sketch of the most prominent sources and types of action.

The commercial sector

The reaction of the commercial sector has been to develop a repertoire of private security arrangements. The re-emergence of private policing; the development of segregated spatial enclosures; managerial routines that make security an integral part of the organization's functioning; the development of cost–benefit crime-control analyses; security audits; the blocking of opportunities for crime; harm reduction; supply-side approaches to crime and its prevention—all of these responses first took shape in the private sector.[71] Many of them were developed within the private security industry which has expanded very rapidly over the last three decades, selling its services to organizations that required greater levels of security than the public police could provide, and tailoring their crime management procedures to suit their own commercial ends.[72]

Commercial organizations have come to regard public law enforcement as sub-optimal—precisely because the system subordinated the firm's interests to the public interest—and have developed more autonomous processes of 'managing' crime. These privatized, managerial approaches emphasize prevention and reduction strategies and devalue prosecution and punishment. They focus upon the flow of offending behaviour, and target its most persistent or most costly forms rather than seeking to enforce the law in an even-handed or comprehensive way. They opt for integrated technological solutions, embedding the crime control mechanisms in the practices of the firm in ways that are non-intrusive and do not interfere with the core business of the enterprise—promoting sales, creating confidence, making a profit.[73]

These adaptations on the part of the business community—to the heightened crime threat, to the ineffectiveness or inconvenience of the criminal justice response, to the new conditions of commercial life—have led, over time, to the development of 'private justice' enclaves, in which potential and actual offenders receive quite different treatment from that meted out by the public justice system. In these private settings (many of which are mass public spaces such as shopping malls that happen to be privately owned and administered) individuals may be required to submit to searches, or be monitored and filmed, and they may be subject to exclusion without cause shown. There is here a rough justice of *exclusion* and *full-force surveillance* that has become more and more routine in our experience and which is increasingly viewed as a necessary condition for securing the safety and pleasure of consumers and decent citizens—'Wicked people exist. Nothing avails except to set them apart.' Crime consciousness, with its dialectic of fear and defensive aggression, has come to be built into our daily environment.

It is within these private adaptations that we must locate some of the new ways of thinking about crime. The new criminologies of everyday life—rational choice theory, routine activity theory, crime as opportunity, situational crime prevention—that are coming to be so influential in the shaping of contemporary policy thinking, are usually credited to authors such as Ron Clarke, Marcus Felson, George Kelling, and James Q. Wilson. But it might be more accurate to attribute authorship of these ways of thinking and acting to the countless unnamed managers and security staff, whose job it has been to come up with practical solutions to counter the problem of crime as it affects their particular enterprise.

In what is a very Foucauldian story, this dispersed, disorganized, field of recipes and crime-control techniques—composed of a multitude of small-scale inventions, some of them ingenious, most of them quite mundane, all of them growing out of situated problem-solving activities rather than abstract analyses—come to be taken up and developed by criminological experts. Criminologists rationalized and systematized these ideas and techniques, creating new criminological theories, and persuading public agencies (the Home Office, the National Institute of Justice, the police) to adopt these ways of thinking. These theories are then fed back—through preventative partnerships and crime prevention advice[74]—into practical locales, where they help lay practitioners to systematize their practice, to become self-conscious about what they do, and to learn from accumulated data and proven best practice.

In much the same way that nineteenth-century penitentiary practice formed a surface of emergence for the science of criminology and was subsequently informed and influenced by the 'scientific' knowledge to which it had given rise,[75] the present-day world of private-sector crime prevention exists in a reflexive relationship to the theories and prescriptions of situational crime prevention. It is in this interchange—between the practical recipes of the commercial sector managers and the worked-out rationalities of criminologists and government policy-makers—that one must locate the strategy of preventative partnership and the habits of thought and action upon which it depends.

Private citizens, households, and communities

The adaptive reactions of private citizens, households, and communities to the new experience of crime take a similar trajectory and produce similar institutionalizing effects.[76] Over time, a pattern of response and adaptation emerged in which individuals began to take more routine precautions against crime.[77] Like most social changes, this shift was slow and unselfconscious at first, and led by small sections of the population—particularly the well-to-do, younger residents and middle-class home owners gentrifying down-market areas. But eventually the tendency to be more security conscious reached a threshold point where it became the collective pattern, shored up by the new common sense of home owners and tenants, and reinforced by the incentives and advice of insurance firms, building societies, tourist guides, and local police. This security consciousness was also encouraged by the commercial security industry, whose sales of security devices fuelled the public's fears and insecurities at the very moment that it claimed to allay them.[78]

Members of the public purchased insurance and security devices. They installed locks and bolts on their doors and windows, entry-phones in the entrances to their buildings, intruder alarms on their property, and removable radios and alarms in their cars. People, and particularly women, revised their daily routines in order to minimize their vulnerability to victimization.[79] They took time to lock doors, to hide valuables, to switch alarms on and off, leaving lights on in empty houses, not opening doors to strangers, limiting the amount of cash that they carried, and tightly constraining their conduct on streets and in public places, lest they draw attention to themselves as potential victims.[80] Many residents came together (with the active support of local police and, in the USA, foundation grants) to form neighbourhood watch schemes. Some went further and took part in citizen patrol groups and other forms of self-policing.[81]

These routine precautions often involved taking evasive action, much of which entailed a level of inconvenience and expense. Many city dwellers began to travel by car rather than public transport, avoided on-street parking or unsupervised parking lots, stayed off the streets at night, avoided parks after dusk, gave up going to football games, or city-center entertainment, and spent large amounts of time chauffeuring their children to school and elsewhere, rather than expose them to the risk of crime on the streets and on the buses and subways. Others took more drastic action, escaping to the suburbs, and even, when the suburbs themselves became more crime-prone (or merely too 'diverse'), to one of the 20,000 gated communities that have recently sprung up in the USA. A significant number of American households bought firearms as a defense against attack, bringing the war against crime back home in a way that must have had significant psychological effects.

At the same time, urban planners, architects, and construction companies began to adapt their designs to enhance the level of security that they offered to clients and residents. The most egregious example here is the 'gated community', which is now said to be the fastest growing mode of community living—though this overlooks the prison sector, which is a massive gated community, and a product of related social processes and sentiments operating over the same period.[82] But as Blakely and Snyder point out, 'gated living' is part of a broader shift towards security-oriented architecture and planning, a development that includes 'the full-service enclosed mall; public buildings and public plazas and parks bristling with security mechanisms; cookie-cutter hotels and convention centers; and skywalks and tunnels that allow tourists and downtown workers never to set foot on a city sidewalk'.[83] In this new urban architecture—pioneered in Los Angeles but now becoming evident in shopping malls and downtown business centres across America and Britain—the primary concern is to manage space and to separate out different 'types' of people.[84] And, as Shearing and Stenning have long since pointed out, the private character of these massive commercial spaces provides corporations with the legal authority and economic incentive to do their own policing—a dynamic that has done much to fuel the growth of private security.[85]

A related development is the huge growth in residential associations that has occurred over the last thirty years, especially in the USA. As David J. Kennedy points out, these associations, variously known as homeowners' associations, property owners' associations, and residents' associations are emerging as a major force in urban and suburban life, geared to enhancing security, improving the quality of life, and maintaining real estate values. In America in 1970 there were 10,000 of these organizations. By 1992, there were 150,000 of them, covering thirty-two million people, or roughly 12 per cent of the population.[86] Where security concerns, profit motives and property interests come together, private actors have responded vigorously to the perceived deficiencies of state provision.

The crime control effects of these private, low-level adaptations are difficult to guage and have never, to my knowledge, been carefully evaluated.[87] But what is more important for our purposes is that these shifts in daily routines eventually resulted in settled *cultural* effects. They changed how people think and feel, what they talk about and how they talk about it, their values and priorities, how they teach their children or advise newcomers to the neighbourhood. The fear of crime—or rather a collectively raised consciousness of crime—has gradually become institutionalized. It has been written into our common sense and the routines of our everyday life. It is woven into the text of our news programmes, our real estate categories and our insurance contracts, and, in more fantastic forms, in our urban myths and TV entertainment.[88]

'The crime complex': the culture of high crime societies

One might sum up this historical process by saying that a cultural formation has grown up around the phenomena of high crime rates and increased insecurity and that this formation now gives the experience of crime a settled institutional form. This cultural formation—which we might term the 'crime complex' of late modernity—is characterized by a distinctive cluster of attitudes, beliefs, and assumptions:

   (i) high crime rates are regarded as a normal social fact,[89]
  (ii) emotional investment in crime is widespread and intense, encompassing elements of fascination as well as fear, anger and resentment,
 (iii) crime issues are politicized and regularly represented in emotive terms
  (iv) concerns about victims and public safety dominate public policy
   (v) the criminal justice state is viewed as inadequate or ineffective
  (vi) private, defensive routines are widespread and there is a large market in private security
 (vii) a crime consciousness is institutionalized in the media, popular culture and the built environment.

Once established, this view of the world does not change rapidly. It is not much affected by year to year changes in the recorded crime rate, even when these involve reductions in real rates of criminal victimization. This explains the apparent absence of a relationship between crime trends and fear of crime sentiments. Our attitudes to crime—our fears and resentments, but also our common sense narratives and understandings—become settled cultural facts that are sustained and reproduced by cultural scripts and not by criminological research or official data.[90]

The development of a crime complex produces a series of psychological and social effects that exert an influence upon politics and policy.[91] Citizens became crime-conscious, attuned to the crime problem, and many exhibit high levels of fear and anxiety. They are caught up in institutions and daily practices that require them to take on the identity of (actual or potential) crime victims, and to think, feel and act accordingly. This enforced engagement with crime and crime prevention produces an ambivalent reaction. On the one hand a stoical adaptation that prompts new habits of avoidance and crime prevention routines. On the other, a measure of irritation, frustration and aggravation at the cumulative nuisance that crime represents for daily life. Substantial sections of the public became less willing to countenance sympathy for the offender, more impatient with criminal justice policies that were experienced as failing, and more viscerally identified with the victim. The posture of 'understanding' the offender—always a demanding and difficult attitude, and more readily attained by liberal elites unaffected by crime or else by professional groups who make their living out of it—gives way more and more to that of *condemning* him or her. The prospect of reintegrating the offender is more and more viewed as unrealistic and, over time, comes to seem less morally compelling.

The social and psychic investment that individuals have in issues of crime and punishment expands considerably. The sentiments involved come to be more deeply felt and more extensively distributed throughout the population. Members of the public increasingly express their fear, their aggravation at having to alter their life-styles and incur expenses, their dissatisfaction with the system that failed them. The daily tribulation of minor crime and disorder easily slides into a concern with 'crime as such', which in turn connotes violent predatory crime.[92] The trauma of powerlessness in the face of fear prompts the demand for action. The feeling that 'something must be done' and 'someone must be blamed' increasingly finds political representation and fuels political action.

It is this pattern of social routines, cultural practices, and collective sensibilities that formed the social surface on which was built the crime control strategies that dominate at the present time. It is a social ensemble, a collective experience, which sustains a new level of crime-consciousness, a new depth of emotional investment, and a new salience of crime in our everyday lives. The very different policies of preventative partnership and of punitive segregation should both be seen as politico-administrative initiatives that rest upon this social surface and are conditioned by its contours and characteristics. Far from being the exclusive creations of politicians or the media, these strategies depend—for their practical operation as well as for their political support—upon widespread habits of thought, routines of action, and structures of feeling that are have recently come to characterize civil society.

Of course the facts of national difference shape how these strategies have played out in their different locales. For example, the private, corporate anti-crime initiatives are more prominent in the US than in the UK, whereas the reverse ratio holds in respect of central government's crime prevention efforts. And the punitive and incapacitive thrust of American policies has been markedly greater, and sustained over a much longer period, than is the case in the UK. But the strategic patterns that characterize the crime control fields in both places are substantially the same, and have tended to persist even when Conservative and Republican administrations have given way to Labour and Democratic ones.

The primary themes of the new strategies—expressivity, punitiveness, victim-centredness, public protection, exclusion, enhanced control, loss-prevention, public–private partnership, responsibilization—are grounded in a new collective experience from which they draw their meaning and their strength, and in the new social routines that supply their techniques and practical supports. They are also rooted in a reactionary thematization of 'late modernity', produced by not just by crime but by the whole reactionary current of culture and politics that characterizes the present in terms of moral breakdown, incivility and the decline of the family, and urges the reversal of the 1960s revolution and the cultural and political liberation that it ushered in. The open, porous, mobile society of strangers that is late modernity has given rise to crime control practices that seek to make society less open and less mobile: to fix identities, immobilize individuals, quarantine whole sections of the population, erect boundaries, close off access.[93] And while these strategies are by no means *determined* by the social field that I have described, they are strongly conditioned by that field and probably inconceivable without it.

The New Culture of Crime Control

My analysis so far has been from the point of view of action, particularly the problem-solving actions of politicians and administrators and the every-day actions of large social groups. I want to shift now to a more structural perspective, and to focus on the crime control field that has emerged as a result of these converging, conflicting actions and decisions. I want to reflect on the character of the field as a whole, to specify how it differs from the penal-welfarism of mid-century, and to comment on the overall impact of the transformations I have described. But before proceeding with that account, I want briefly to address two analytical issues.

The first concerns the problem of complexity and how to tame it. The field being described here is composed of a multiplicity of different agencies, practices and discourses, and is characterized by a variety of policies and practices, some of which are quite contradictory. Its general character is best conveyed by plotting the distribution of elements, the organizing principles that relate them, and the fault lines around which conflicts are ranged, rather than seeking to identify a single essence and having it stand for the field as a whole. Characterizing the field in this way lacks the immediate impact of essentialist analyses with their powerful simplicity, just as it lacks the critical edge that is achieved by depicting the field in terms of its extreme values rather than its central tendencies. But essences and extremes tend to be a poor guide to social reality. Even in its heyday, the penal-welfare field was not typified by highly developed correctional facilities: the modal sanctions were actually fines and probation, and most local jails offered little rehabilitative treatment.[1] In the same way, the contemporary field cannot be accurately portrayed if we focus only upon extremes such as the 'three strikes' laws or crime prevention partnerships and ignore the other practices that make up the field.

The second point concerns the relation of the past to the present. Up until now I have been concerned to describe and explain the new developments that have been emerging in crime control. My analysis has been trained upon those ideas and practices that break with the established penal-welfare arrangements, with a view to characterizing change and identifying its sources. But when considering the field as a whole, we need to bear in mind that these new practices and mentalities co-exist with the residues and continuations of older arrangements. Our focus upon the new and the transformative should not lead us to neglect these older practices and institutions. History is not the replacement of the old by the new, but the more or less extensive modification of one by the other. The *intertwining* of the established and the emergent is what structures the present, and our analyses should reflect that fact.

How then, ought we to describe the field of crime control and criminal justice that has taken shape over the last thirty years? What are its organizing principles, its strategic rationales, and its recurring contradictions? What are the political values, cultural sensibilities, and criminological conceptions that guide its practices and give them meaning? And how do these crime control arrangements relate to other social developments occurring in America and Britain over the course of the last thirty years, particularly to the 'reformed' welfare state and to the social organization of late modernity?

The crime control apparatus

The historical change that we have been studying is not a transformation at the level of institutional forms. This is not an era in which the old institutions and practices are being abandoned and new ones are being legislated into existence. There has been no process of abolition and reconstruction, such as occurred when the scaffold and gallows were dismantled and penitentiaries were built in their place. Nor has there been an extensive process of institution building that would compare with the creation of the juvenile court, the probation service and the individualization of sentencing that occurred one hundred years ago. The institutional architecture of penal modernity remains firmly in place, as does the state apparatus of criminal justice. It is their deployment, their strategic functioning and their social significance that have been transformed.

There have been changes in size and emphasis of course. Between 1970 and the present, the criminal justice systems in both countries have massively expanded in terms of caseloads, employment, and overall expenditure, and in the last two decades the biggest prison building programme since the Victorian age has occurred.[2] There has also been a reversal of a long-term tendency for custodial sentences to decline as a proportion of all sentences in favour of fines and community supervision. Since the 1980s, in both the USA and the UK, sentences of imprisonment have increased in length, average time served has increased, custodial sentences have been used in a larger proportion of cases, and the likelihood of being returned to custody from parole has greatly increased.[3] There has thus been a shift—more pronounced in the USA than the UK, but present in both countries—towards a much greater and more intensive use of custody. This more punitive trend is echoed in America by the increased frequency of judicial executions, which have recently reached levels not seen since the 1950s. These shifts of penal emphasis have had important effects—on the numbers of people in custody, the size of the prison industry, the racial composition of the prison population, and on the political and cultural significance of punishment. But they have been changes in deployment rather than more basic alterations in the types of sanctions or institutional forms.

Similarly, in the policing sector, there has been a shift of emphasis away from reactive strategies and '911' policing, towards more proactive community policing efforts, and, more recently, to the more intensive policing of disorder, incivilities, and misdemeanours. Problem-oriented policing, community policing, order-maintenance policing, quality-of-life policing—these new strategies redefine how police forces are deployed and how they interact with the public. Policing has become 'smarter', more targeted, more attuned to local circumstance, more responsive to public pressure, more willing to work with the community and to emphasize prevention. Information technology and new management techniques have been combined to produce tighter control of resources and more directed, problem-solving conduct. Police have begun to move into the post-bureaucratic phase of organization, and to develop flexible links with other partners, seeking to join up strategically rather than to monopolize the effort.[4] So the stated purposes of police have changed, sometimes quite dramatically, and new tactics increasingly define how they deploy their resources. But studies of police budgets and working practices suggest that the daily practices of most police forces have not changed so drastically as this would suggest.[5] And, moreover, these new priorities and tactics have not, as yet, led to any basic reorganization of the police as a public agency. As a legal and organizational entity, funded by tax-payers and charged with law enforcement, the public police look much the same today as they did thirty years ago.

The fore-grounding of the figure of the victim has certainly altered the processes of criminal justice in a number of significant respects. The recognition of victims' rights; the introduction of victim impact statements and 'victim opinions' in respect of sentencing and parole; the growth of victim support groups; and the routine referral of victims to such organizations by the police—these have changed not only the routines of criminal justice, but also the relative status and worth of the various parties involved. But with the exception of victim support organizations, these shifts have not entailed the development of new apparatuses, nor led to the emergence of new sanctions. It is true that new arrangements for reparation and mediation have begun to appear, filtering suitable cases out of the regular system, bringing offenders and victims together, and promoting 'restorative' rather than punitive outcomes wherever possible. And in the last few years there has been a remarkable upsurge of interest in this style of doing justice—on the part of academics, reformers, and even government ministers. But at present these restorative justice initiatives play only a tiny role at the shallow end of the system, and are more notable for the reforming enthusiasm that they attract than for the frequency of their use or their impact upon criminal justice.[6]

Most surprisingly perhaps, the correctionalist apparatus associated with penal-welfarism is, for the most part, still in place. Sentencing law has been thoroughly transformed, particularly in the USA, and indeterminate sentences are now much less common. But most of the distinctive technologies, powers and knowledges developed by the penal-welfare movement are still in daily use. The juvenile court and the probation service continue to expand their range and their activities. Social and psychiatric experts are still employed to prepare social inquiry reports, provide diagnostic services, and to help manage and treat offenders. In fact the 1990s saw a quite significant increase in the numbers of treatment programmes provided to offenders in the community and in prisons.[7] Individuals are still assessed and classified; treatment prospects and risk factors are still identified; the judicial power to punish continues to be overlaid with a psycho-social framework of diagnosis and remedy. If we inhabit a 'post-rehabilitative' era, as the conventional wisdom assumes, it is not because the structures for assessing individuals and delivering rehabilitation have been dismantled and removed.

The third sector: policing, penality—and prevention

The most significant development in the crime control field is not the transformation of criminal justice institutions but rather the development, alongside these institutions, of a quite different way of regulating crime and criminals. Alongside policing and penality there has grown up a third 'governmental' sector—the new apparatus of prevention and security. As we saw in Chapter 5, this small but expanding sector is made up of crime prevention organizations, public–private partnerships, community policing arrangements, and multi-agency working practices that link together the different authorities whose activities bear upon the problems of crime and security. Unlike the other two sectors with their solid buildings, large staffs and sizeable budgets, this sector has a more fragile, virtual existence. It consists mainly of networks and co-ordinating practices—local authority panels, working groups, multi-agency forums, and action committees—whose primary task is to link up the activities of existing actors and agencies and direct their efforts towards crime reduction. This new sector occupies an intermediate, borderline position, poised between the state and civil society, connecting the criminal justice agencies with the activities of citizens, communities and corporations. And while its budgets, staff lists, and organizations are relatively small (particularly compared to overall police or prisons expenditure) the development of this new infrastructure significantly extends the field of 'formal' crime control and its potential for organized action.[8]

A key consequence of this development is that the formal boundaries of the crime control field are no longer marked out by the institutions of the criminal justice state. That field now extends beyond the state, engaging the actors and agencies of civil society, allowing crime control practices to be organized and directed at a distance from the state agencies. Crime control is coming to be the responsibility not just of criminal justice specialists but of a whole series of social and economic actors. Two centuries after Patrick Colquhoun, and at the end of a period during which the crime control function was concentrated within differentiated state bureaucracies and increasingly monopolized by state officials, a small but significant movement towards de-differentiation has now begun.

The development of this new sector has begun to alter the overall balance of the field. Its very existence exerts a small but insistent pressure that tends to push policy away from retribution, deterrence, and reform and towards a concern with prevention, harm-reduction, and risk management. Instead of pursuing, prosecuting and punishing individuals, it aims to reduce the supply of criminal events by minimizing criminal opportunities, enhancing situational controls, and channelling conduct away from criminogenic situations. Rather than treating criminal dispositions or punishing guilty individuals, it concentrates on preventing the convergence of factors that precipitate criminal events. Whereas the criminal justice state relies upon the deployment of penal powers, or the threat thereof, this new apparatus seeks to activate the preventive action of the host of actors and agencies that make up civil society. Community safety becomes the chief consideration and law-enforcement becomes merely a means to this end, rather than an end in itself. Fear-reduction, harm and loss-reduction and cost-control become foreground considerations. And insofar as this new prevention sector is linked into the older ones of policing and penality—particularly through the police and probation agencies—these preventative concerns have come to be felt across the whole field.

Over the last twenty years we have begun to see the appearance of a series of new specialists who staff this still rather inchoate and ill-defined set of arrangements. Crime prevention advisers, co-ordinators, inter-agency workers, systems analysts, crime auditors, risk managers, design experts, and community police officers—still small in numbers but of increasing significance—make up the staff of this sector. Ideas derived from situational crime prevention, routine activity theory and environmental criminology increasingly shape their thinking and inform their actions. Instead of concentrating upon individual offenders, the preventative sector targets criminogenic situations that can be altered in ways that make them less vulnerable to criminal events, less inviting to potential offenders. It analyses flows of people and the distribution of criminal events, identifying 'hot spots', 'hot products', and repeat victimization patterns and making them the focus for action. And while policing and penal solutions are part of its repertoire, the preferred remedy is to put in place situational controls and channel conduct away from temptation, rather than to bring prosecutions and punish offenders. To the extent that 'the government' succeeds in organizing, augmenting, and directing the social control capacities of citizens, corporations, and communities, it simultaneously extends its governmental reach and transforms its mode of exerting control.[9]

The declining autonomy of criminal justice

The field of organized crime control has thus been extended, even if the institutional architecture of the criminal justice state remains largely in place. In the process, the relationship of criminal justice to its social and political environment has undergone a series of significant shifts.

Criminal justice is now less autonomous than it was three decades ago, and more forcefully directed from the outside. Criminal justice actors and agencies are now less capable of directing their own fate and shaping their own policies and decisions. This is partly a result of the need to work with other 'providers', and the concern to be more responsive to the public and to other 'customers'. But the primary reason for this loss is that the field's relations to the public and to the political process have changed. A new relationship between politicians, the public and penal experts has emerged in which politicians are more directive, penal experts are less influential, and public opinion becomes a key reference point for evaluating options. Criminal justice is now more vulnerable to shifts of public mood and political reaction. New laws and policies are rapidly instituted without prior consultation with the criminal justice professionals, and expert control of the policy agenda has been considerably reduced by a populist style of policy making.

The populist current in contemporary crime policy is, to some extent, a political posture or tactic, adopted for short-term electoral advantage.[10] As such, it can quickly be reversed if 'popular' initiatives cease to coincide with calculations of political gain. But we should be aware that this populist moment has been accompanied by a retooling of the mechanisms of political action in this field—a change that will have continuing consequences for how policy is made and for the capacity of politicians to shape the practices of criminal justice. With the coming of mandatory minimum sentencing and other tools for micro-managing penal decision-making—such as sentencing guidelines, truth in sentencing requirements, national standards for probation and community service, performance indicators in prisons, etc.—legislatures and government ministers have acquired more direct and unimpeded means of shaping practical outcomes. In the area of sentencing, the legal and administrative arrangements now in place significantly reduce the scope for professional decision-making and for the discretionary review of offender's sentences. There is, as Nils Christie might put it, a more streamlined system of pain-delivery, with fewer intervening obstacles between the political process and the allocation of individual punishments. Public demands for greater punishments are now more easily and instantly translated into increased sentences and longer jail terms.

A similarly streamlined dynamic increasingly characterizes the process of legislation as well. The current rules of political engagement ensure that governments and legislatures are highly attuned to public concerns, particularly to the sentiment that offenders are being insufficiently punished or dangerous individuals inadequately controlled, and there is a great pressure to enact measures that express and relieve these concerns. Governments today are on a war footing in respect to drug abuse, sex offending, and violent crime, and they are expected to produce an instant response whenever this is called for. In the 1990s the pattern was for high visibility crime cases to become the focus of a great deal of media attention and public outrage, issuing in urgent demands that something be done. These cases typically involve a predatory individual, an innocent victim (often a child), and a prior failure of the criminal justice system to impose effective controls—their regularity reflecting the structure of middle-class fears and mass media news values rather than the statistical frequency of such events.[11] Almost inevitably, the demand is for more effective penal control. Megan's law, Three Strikes, the Violent Sexual Predator laws, the reintroduction of children's prisons in the wake of James Bulger's murder, the Home Office clamp-down on prison conditions and bail restrictions following highly publicized breaches of security—these are only the best known examples of the rapid response system that now characterizes policymaking in this field.[12] What this amounts to is a kind of retaliatory law-making, acting out the punitive urges and controlling anxieties of expressive justice. Its chief aims are to assuage popular outrage, reassure the public, and restore the 'credibility' of the system, all of which are political rather than penological concerns. It is hardly surprising that these measures often fly in the face of expert penological advice.

The extent and nature of structural change

These then, are what one might describe as the structural or morphological changes that have occurred in the field of crime control over the last quarter century. The field has not been transformed from end to end, nor has the criminal justice state been completely made over. What has happened is that criminal justice institutions have altered their emphases and the field of crime control has expanded in new directions, as state agencies and civil society have adapted to the growth of crime and insecurity that accompanied the coming of late modernity. The result is that the criminal justice state is larger than before, but it occupies a relatively smaller place in the overall field because of the growth of private security and the organized activities of communities and commercial organizations.

The political culture of crime control now takes it for granted that the state will have a huge presence, while simultaneously claiming this presence is never enough. The paradoxical outcome is that the state strengthens its punitive forces and increasingly acknowledges the inadequate nature of this sovereign strategy. Alongside an increasingly punitive sentencing structure, one also sees the development of new modes of exercising power by which the state seeks to 'govern at a distance' by forming alliances and activating the governmental powers of non-state agencies.[13] In this context, the criminal justice state no longer claims a monopoly position in respect of crime control, and no longer holds itself out as the sole or even the main provider of security. The state now operates in a mixed economy of security provision and crime control, and its agencies have to accommodate the private security arrangements that have grown up over the last thirty years.[14]

The modern institutions of criminal justice have shown themselves to be quite resilient in the face of change. They have exerted an inertia of their own, an ability to withstand shocks and to defuse the impact of externally imposed change. As a consequence, they have changed more slowly and more subtly than most penological commentary would suggest.[15] At the structural level, change has been a matter of *assimilating new elements* (the victim, crime prevention, restorative justice); *altering balances and relations* (between punishment and welfare, state provision, and commercial provision, instrumental means and expressive ends, the rights of offenders and the protection of the public); and *changing the field's relation to its environment* (above all its relation to the political process, to public opinion, and to the crime-control activities of civil society).

The institutional and cultural changes that have occurred in the crime control field are analogous to those that have occurred in the welfare state more generally. Talk of the 'end of welfare' and the 'death of the social'—like talk of the demise of rehabilitation—should be understood as a kind of counter-rhetoric, not as empirical description. The infrastructures of the welfare state have not been abolished or utterly transformed. They have been overlaid by a different political culture, and directed by a new style of public management.[16] In the process they have become more restrictive and means-tested, more concerned to control the conduct of claimants, more concerned to transmit the right incentives and discourage 'dependency'. Like the criminal justice reforms of the last twenty years, current social policies are shaped by the perceived dysfunctions and pathologies of the institutions of welfarism.[17] The solution has become the problem. Penal-welfarism shares the fate of the welfarist social arrangements that brought it into existence. Its destiny is not to be dismantled, but to become the problematic institutional terrain upon which new strategies and objectives are continually built.

The changes that have occurred in the crime control field have mainly been a matter of redeploying and redirecting the practices of existing institutions. It has been a process not of inventing new institutions or instituting new practices but of redefining those that already exist, giving them a different force and significance, and putting them to different uses. The frameworks that direct crime control and penal practices have been altered, giving rise to new aims and objectives, new forms of calculation, and new priorities. New forms of knowledge and styles of reasoning have grown up that subtly alter how we think about crime and criminals, how we understand the problems that they present, and how we act upon these problems and entities. An altered structure of legal rules and managerial reasoning has changed the day-to-day decision making of crime control professionals. And a new set of symbols, images and representations has formed up around these practices, evoking cultural meanings that are very different from those that used to prevail.

The new culture of crime control

One might sum up this complex process by saying that although the structures of control have been transformed in important respects, the most significant change is at the level of the *culture* that enlivens these structures, orders their use, and shapes their meaning. A reworked pattern of cognitive assumptions, normative commitments, and emotional sensibilities is now inscribed in the field, motivating the actions of crime control agencies, giving new purpose and meaning to their practices, and altering the practical effects and symbolic significance of their conduct. Without a pre-formed design or explicit articulation, the cultural co-ordinates of crime control have gradually been changed, altering the way that penal agents think and act, giving new meaning to what they say and do. Together with the revised legal provisions that now regulate police and penal practice, it is this new culture that has done most to change how we think and act in relation to crime and insecurity. This new culture of crime control has formed around three central elements: (i) a re-coded penal-welfarism; (ii) a criminology of control; (iii) an economic style of reasoning.

The transformation of penal-welfarism

In the day to day practices of criminal justice, there has been a marked shift of emphasis from the welfare to the penal modality. As we have seen, sentencing law and practice give greater priority to retributive, incapacitative, and deterrent aims. Probation represents itself as a punishment in the community, not as a social work alternative to conviction. Juvenile courts in the USA routinely waive young offenders up to the adult courts for harsher sentencing, while they and their equivalents in England increasingly stress guilt and individual responsibility, and give greater weight to public safety.[18] Custodial institutions for children and young people stress security rather than education or rehabilitation, and become increasingly indistinguishable from adult prisons. Parole agencies downplay their traditional re-integrative functions, prioritize the close monitoring of released offenders, link up more closely with the police, and more frequently return offenders to custody.

In the course of these developments, both 'penal' and 'welfare' modalities have changed their meaning. The penal mode, as well as becoming more prominent, has become more punitive, more expressive, more security-minded. Distinctively *penal* concerns such as less eligibility, the certainty and fixity of punishment, the condemnation and hard treatment of offenders,[19] and the protection of the public have been prioritized. The welfare mode, as well as becoming more muted, has become more conditional, more offence-centred, more risk conscious. The offenders dealt with by probation, parole, and the juvenile court are now less likely to be represented in official discourse as socially deprived citizens in need of support. They are depicted instead as culpable, undeserving and somewhat dangerous individuals who must be carefully controlled for the protection of the public and the prevention of further offending. Rather than clients in need of support they are seen as risks who must be managed. Instead of emphasizing rehabilitative methods that meet the offender's needs, the system emphasises effective controls that minimize costs and maximize security.

Rehabilitation redefined

Where rehabilitative interventions are undertaken today their character is rather different than before. They focus more upon issues of crime control than upon individual welfare, and are more 'offence centred' than 'client-centred'. The offence is no longer taken to be a superficial presenting symptom; it is instead the thing itself, the central problem to be addressed. Where once the individual's personality or social relations formed the object of transformative efforts, that object is now offence behaviour and the habits most closely associated with it. The immediate point is no longer to improve the offender's self-esteem, develop insight, or deliver client centred services, but instead to impose restrictions, reduce crime, and protect the public. These shifts in practice, together with the recent revival of less-eligibility concerns, prompt treatment programmes to hold themselves out as being for the benefit of future victims rather than for the benefit of the offender. It is future victims who are now 'rescued' by rehabilitative work, rather than the offenders themselves.[20]

The practice of rehabilitation is increasingly inscribed in a framework of risk rather than a framework of welfare. Offenders can only be 'treated' (in drug-abuse programmes, anger-management groups, offence-reduction programmes, etc.) to the extent that such treatment is deemed to be capable of protecting the public, reducing risk, and being more cost-effective than simple, unadorned punishment. Rehabilitation is thus represented as a targeted intervention inculcating self-controls, reducing danger, enhancing the security of the public. In the new framework rehabilitation is viewed as a means of managing risk, not a welfarist end in itself.[21] If the treatment programme does not work, one can revert to other, more effective means, such as close supervision or prison custody. The contemporary emphasis upon rigorous 'breach' procedures (that return probationers and parolees to court if they violate their licences) serves precisely this function.

Rehabilitation no longer claims to be the overriding purpose of the whole system, or even of traditionally welfarist agencies such as probation and parole. It is now one aim among others, delivered as a specialist provision, and no longer accompanied by any great amount of idealism or expectation. The rehabilitation of offenders is no longer viewed as a general all-purpose prescription, but instead as a specific intervention targeted towards those individuals most likely to make cost-effective use of this expensive service. It is treated as an investment rather than a standard entitlement, and like all investments, is closely monitored and evaluated to ensure that it produces returns. In that respect, the 'What Works' movement currently influencing penal policy in the UK bears the marks of the post-Martinson scepticism and reflexivity: it is not a return to rehabilitative optimism. Whether the offender is being punished or being treated, the key concerns are now to protect the public, reduce the risk of further victimization and to do so with a minimum of resources. If the official aim of penal-welfare was the promotion of social welfare the overriding concern today is, quite unashamedly, the efficient enhancement of social control.

Probation repositioned

For much of the twentieth century, probation was a core institution of criminal justice. Extensively used, in the vanguard of penal progress, it was often regarded as the exemplary instance of the penal-welfare approach to crime control. In today's criminal justice world, probation occupies a position that is much more conflicted and much less secure. Over the last thirty years, probation has had to struggle to maintain its credibility, as the ideals upon which it was based have been discredited and displaced. Under pressure from government it has tightened its procedures, highlighted its supervisory capacities, downplayed its social work affiliations, intensified its controls, and represented itself as a community punishment. 'Intensive probation orders' have been developed, involving heavier restrictions and reporting requirements, and probation supervision has increasingly been 'blended' with more explicitly penal measures, such as curfews, partial custody, and fines. As one English Chief Probation Officer put it, 'The Probation Service has absorbed the politics of punishment, entered the market place, mirrored the private sector [and] taken its managers through a grand renaming ceremony.'[22] Despite all this upheaval, the courts and the public remain unconvinced that probation is a 'real' punishment and a credible means of control.[23]

Probation has moved away from its original mission, sometimes described as being to 'assist, advise and befriend' deserving offenders, and settled upon priorities that reflect the new penological climate: changing offenders' behaviour; reducing crime, achieving safer communities; protecting the public; supporting victims.[24] Revised training courses, operations manuals and performance indicators continue to push further in this direction, as do the legal changes that have deemed probation a compulsory court punishment rather than a voluntary measure in lieu of conviction. Probation practice increasingly embraces new forms of close monitoring, including tagging, tracking, curfews, and drug testing. And where once probation officers would offer supervision to anyone who seemed capable of benefiting from it, probation resources are now much more carefully dispensed. 'Match input to risk' is the new gate-keeping rule. 'Offer intensive supervision only to those offenders who score high on the scale of risk and on the scale of responsivity.'[25] The management of risks and resources has displaced rehabilitation as the organization's central aim.

The reinvented prison

In the penal-welfare system, the prison functioned as the deep end of the correctional sector, dealing with those offenders who failed to respond to the reformatory measures of other institutions. In theory if not in practice, it represented itself as the last-resort terminus on a continuum of treatment. Today it is conceived much more explicitly as a mechanism of exclusion and control.[26] Treatment modalities still operate within its walls, and lip service is still paid to the ideal of the rehabilitative prison. But the walls themselves are now seen as the institution's most important and valuable element. The old penal-welfare ideal of the permeable prison, of the open prison that lowers the barrier between custody and the community, of reintegrating prisoners and their families by means of furloughs and home leaves and paroles—these ideals are now much less in evidence. Instead the walls have been fortified, literally and figuratively. Perimeter security has been enhanced, and early release is more restrictive, more strictly controlled, more closely supervised.[27]

The prison is used today as a kind of reservation, a quarantine zone in which purportedly dangerous individuals are segregated in the name of public safety. In the USA, the system that is taking form resembles nothing so much as the Soviet gulag—a string of work camps and prisons strung across a vast country, housing two million people most of whom are drawn from classes and racial groups that have become politically and economically problematic.[28] The prison-community border is heavily patrolled and carefully monitored to prevent risks leaking out from one to the other. Those offenders who are released 'into the community' are subject to much tighter control than previously, and frequently find themselves returned to custody for failure to comply with the conditions that continue to restrict their freedom. For many of these parolees and ex-convicts, the 'community' into which they are released is actually a closely monitored terrain, a supervised space, lacking much of the liberty that one associates with 'normal life'.

This transformation of the prison–community relationship is closely related to the transformation of work. The disappearance of entry-level jobs for young 'underclass' males, together with the depleted social capital of impoverished families and crime-prone neighbourhoods, has meant that the prison and parole now lack the social supports upon which their rehabilitative efforts had previously relied. Work, social welfare, and family support used to be the means whereby ex-prisoners were reintegrated into mainstream society. With the decline of these resources, imprisonment has become a longer-term assignment from which individuals have little prospect of returning to an unsupervised freedom.[29]

Like the pre-modern sanctions of transportation or banishment, the prison now functions as a form of exile, its use shaped less by a rehabilitative ideal and more by what Rutherford calls an 'eliminative' one.[30] Like the Soviet gulag or the American urban ghetto this internal exile has social and economic effects as well as penological ones.[31] In the USA today the prison system contains a massive population of working-age adults whose structural exclusion from the workforce is routinely forgotten in economic analyses and unemployment statistics.[32] Large-scale incarceration functions as a mode of economic and social placement, a zoning mechanism that segregates those populations rejected by the depleted institutions of family, work, and welfare and places them behind the scenes of social life. In the same way, though for shorter terms, prisons and jails are increasingly being used as a *faute de mieux* repository for the mentally ill, drug addicts, and poor, sick people for whom the depleted social services no longer provide adequate accommodation.[33] Most recently, 'zero tolerance' and 'quality of life' policing have begun to extend this coercive zoning, using aggressive arrest practices to exclude 'disorderly' individuals from public spaces wherever they are seen as interfering with commercial interests or the 'quality of life' demanded by more affluent residents.[34] Private security forces have long done the same thing for private or commercial space.

The new individualization and 'punishment-at-a-distance'

In the penal-welfare framework, the offending individual was centre-stage: the primary focus of criminological concern. Sentencing was to be individualized to meet the offender's particular needs and potential for reform. Biographical accounts were assembled. Social and psychological reports were prepared. The individual characteristics of the offender were, in theory if not always in practice, to be the key determinant of all penal action. In vivid contrast, the individual victim featured hardly at all. For the most part, he or she remained a silent abstraction: a background figure whose individuality hardly registered, whose personal wishes and concerns had no place in the process.

In contemporary penality this situation is reversed. The processes of individualization now increasingly centre upon the victim. Individual victims are to be kept informed, to be offered the support that they need, to be consulted prior to decision-making, to be involved in the judicial process from complaint through to conviction and beyond. Victim impact statements are introduced to court in order to individualize the impact of the crime, to show how the offence affected this particular victim, in all her particularity, in all her human specificity. Several American states now permit individual victims to make recommendations to the judge prior to sentencing, and to put their views to the parole board prior to the release of 'their' offender.[35]

Meanwhile in the perspective of the new sentencing laws, the offender is rendered more and more abstract, more and more stereotypical, more and more a projected image rather than an individuated person. 'Just deserts' sentencing begins to have this effect, particularly where standard sentences are mechanically imposed. Sentencing guidelines take the process further. Mandatory minimum sentences go all the way, completely undoing any element of individualization at the point of sentencing.[36] These methods of fixing sentences well in advance of the instant case extend the distance between the effective sentencer (in reality, the legislature, or the sentencing commission) and the person upon whom the sentence is imposed. The individualization of sentencing gives way to a kind of 'punishment-at-a-distance' where penalty levels are set, often irreversibly, by political actors operating in political contexts far removed from the circumstances of the case. The greater this distance, the less likely it is that the peculiar facts of the case and the individual characteristics of the offender will shape the outcome.[37] The treatment of offenders thus becomes increasingly less individuated at precisely the moment when the victim is brought into full human focus and given an individual voice. Michel Foucault described how the coming of disciplinary institutions shifted the 'axis of individualization' away from the great personages and brought it to bear upon the lowly deviant.[38] Today that axis is shifting once again, this time from the delinquent in the dock to the victim in the witness box.

The society–offender relation

The penal-welfare approach proceeded as if the interests of society and the interests of the offender could be made to coincide. Rehabilitating offenders, reforming prisons, dealing with the roots of crime—these were in the interests of everyone. Money spent on treating the offender and improving social conditions would be repaid by falling rates of crime and a better-integrated citizenry. The treatment of offenders was a positive sum game. Today the interests of convicted offenders, insofar as they are considered at all, are viewed as fundamentally opposed to those of the public. If the choice is between subjecting offenders to greater restriction or else exposing the public to increased risk, today's common sense recommends the safe choice every time.[39] In consequence, and without much discussion, the interests of the offender and even his or her legal rights, are routinely disregarded.[40]

The same lack of balance and mutuality shapes the relationship between offender and victim that penal policy projects. The interests of victim and offender are assumed to be diametrically opposed: the rights of one competing with those of the other in the form of a zero sum game. Expressions of concern for the offender and his needs signal a disregard for the victim and her suffering.[41] The standard response to those who campaign for prisoners' rights or better treatment for offenders, is that they should direct their compassion and concern towards the innocent victim, not the guilty offender.

This declining respect for the rights of offenders and the absolute priority given to public safety concerns can be seen quite clearly in the growing practice of disclosure and notification. In today's information society, criminal justice agencies come under increasing pressure to share their information with members of the public, particularly where this concerns security risks and potential dangers. Community notification laws and paedophile registers are prominent instances of the new willingness to disclose information that would once have been confidential.[42] So too is the practice of correctional agencies (such as the Florida Department of Corrections) that now post internet websites giving personal details of all the prisoners who are released from their custody. This new practice is in sharp contrast to the thinking embodied in the Rehabilitation of Offenders Acts and 'expungement laws' that were passed in the 1960s and 1970s, which made it illegal to disclose information about an ex-offender's criminal record after a certain time had elapsed.[43] The assumption today is that there is no such thing as an 'ex-offender'—only offenders who have been caught before and will strike again. 'Criminal' individuals have few privacy rights that could ever trump the public's uninterrupted right to know.

Finally, one sees this shifting balance in the way that 'stigma' has taken on a renewed value in the punishment of offenders. In the penal-welfare framework, stigma was viewed as a harmful and unnecessary aspect of criminal justice. Stigmatizing an offender was liable to be counterproductive insofar as it lessened the offender's self-esteem and prospects of reintegration. Correctional institutions such as juvenile justice, children's hearings, probation and reformatories were carefully designed to avoid stigmatizing effects and even prison regimes came to abandon the use of demeaning symbols such as the convict haircut or the broad stripe uniform. Today stigma has become useful again. Doubly useful in fact, since a public stigma can simultaneously punish the offender for his crime and alert the community to his danger. Community notification schemes, paedophile registers, prisoners and community service workers dressed in distinctive uniforms, chain gangs in the southern states of the USA, and 'scarlet letter' penalties requiring offenders to proclaim their criminality with signs and pictures—all of these involve the public marking of the offender. Whether for punitive effect or public protection, or both, the deliberate stigmatizing of offenders is once again a part of the official penal repertoire.[44]

As the offender's perceived worth tends towards zero, victims' interests expand to fill the gap. One sees this in the changed attitude towards minor offences and what used to be called 'crimes without victims'. Today there is no such thing as victimless crime. If no one in particular is harmed by the conduct in question, this does not prevent the invocation of a collective victim—'the community' and its 'quality of life'—that is deemed to suffer the ill-effects that must always flow from prohibited behaviour, however trivial. Public drinking, soft drug use, graffiti, loitering, vagrancy, begging, sleeping rough, being 'uncivil': these cease to be tolerable nuisances or pricks to the middle-class conscience and become the disorderly stuff upon which serious crime feeds. In current police thinking, in the new city ordinances that are being passed in the UK and USA, and of course in the world of commercialized private security, victimless crime is a thing of the past.[45] Every minor offence, every act of disorderly conduct—particularly if committed by poor people in public spaces—is now regarded as detrimental to the quality of life. In the high crime society, tiny crimes are viewed cumulatively and 'the community' is the collective, all-purpose victim. The public's fears and insecurities, its heightened awareness of the problem, its scepticism about liberal policies, its lack of concern for the offenders themselves—all of these have prompted us to find victims where there were once only violations.

How could this be? How could offenders have been so thoroughly deprived of their citizenship status and the rights that typically accompany it? How could an overweening concern for 'the victim' block out all consideration of the wrongdoer, as if the two categories were mutually exclusive? Perhaps because we have become convinced that certain offenders, once they offend, are no longer 'members of the public' and cease to be deserving of the kinds of consideration we typically afford to each other. Perhaps because we already assume a social and cultural divide between 'us', the innocent, long-suffering middle-class victims, and 'them', the dangerous undeserving poor. By engaging in violence, or drug abuse, or recidivism, they reveal themselves for what they are: 'the dangerous other', the underclass. 'Our' security depends upon 'their' control. With this equation, we allow ourselves to forget what penal-welfarism took for granted: namely, that offenders are citizens too and their liberty interests are our liberty interests. The growth of a social and cultural divide between 'us' and 'them', together with new levels of fear and insecurity, has made many complacent about the emergence of a more repressive state power.[46] In the 1960s, critics accused penal-welfare institutions of being authoritarian when they wielded their correctional powers in a sometimes arbitrary manner. Today's criminal justice state is characterized by a more unvarnished authoritarianism with none of the benign pretensions.

The criminology of control

Over the last twenty years there has been a marked diversification of criminological thought. In particular, two new currents have emerged that contrast sharply with one another and with the older social welfare criminology that once dominated official thinking. The older ideas—which view criminality as the dispositional outcome of social deprivation—still circulate and command respect. They have no more been abolished than have the institutions of penal-welfarism. In more or less revised form, they still form the core viewpoint of many academics and practitioners. But increasingly these welfarist ideas find themselves in competition with two quite different criminologies, both of which developed in critical reaction to the perceived failure of penal modernism, both of which are attractive to political actors and policymakers.

One reaction to the problems of penal modernism—the new criminologies of everyday life—might be described as *late modern* in character and orientation. Frameworks such as situational crime prevention, routine activity theory and the rest continue the modernist themes of correctionalist criminology insofar as they stress instrumentally rational, morally neutral, knowledge-based, pragmatic solutions. But they develop these modernist themes in new ways, stressing the modification of situations and opportunity structures rather than the reform of deviant individuals; prescribing situational engineering in place of social engineering. This is a less idealistic, less utopian modernism, more attuned to the way we live now, more aware of the limits of governmental schemes, more modest in its ambitions for human improvement.

If we reflect upon the social implications of this way of thinking, there is an interesting contrast with the logic of penal-welfare practice that can best be brought out by using the sociological distinction between social integration and system integration.[47] Penal-welfare practices and the criminologies that informed them aimed to enhance social order by doing the work of *social* integration. They aimed to change the values and attitudes of offenders in ways that brought them into line with the prevailing normative codes. They envisioned social order as a problem of value consensus and they aimed to bring deviants back into that order by means of moral education and reformative practices that changed beliefs and behaviour.

In contrast, the criminologies of everyday life approach social order as a problem of *system* integration. It isn't people who most need to be integrated, but the social processes and arrangements that they inhabit. Instead of addressing human beings and their moral attitudes or psychological dispositions, the new criminologies address the component parts of social systems and situations. They consider how different situations might be redesigned so as to give rise to fewer opportunities for crime, how interacting systems (transport systems, schools, shops, leisure areas, housing . . .) might be made to converge in ways that create fewer security weaknesses or criminological hot spots. For these frameworks, social order is a matter of aligning and integrating the diverse social routines and institutions that compose modern society. It is a problem of ensuring co-ordination—getting the trains to run on time—not of building normative consensus.

The criminologies of everyday life thus offer an approach to social order that is, for the most part, amoral and technological.[48] They bypass the realm of values and concentrate on the routine ways in which people are brought together in time and space. Their conception of social order is a matter not of shared values but of smart arrangements that minimize the opportunities for disruption and deviance. This is a very self-conscious, very sophisticated approach to social order in a complex, differentiated society. It flies in the face of traditionalist ideas that see order as emerging out of moral discipline and obedience to authority. But it also subverts the old welfare state belief, that for society to work, solidarity must extend to all of its members who must be made part of an all-encompassing civic union.

Such an approach sits easily with social and economic policies that exclude whole groups of people, so long as segregation of this kind makes the social system work more smoothly. It also has obvious affinities with 'zero tolerance' policing policies that tend to be associated with low-level repression, discriminatory use of police powers, and the violation of the civil liberties of the poor and minorities. On the other hand, it is not impossible to imagine a socialized version of situational crime prevention in which the poorest, most vulnerable groups are provided with crime prevention resources and improved levels of community safety, though such a scheme would require that this criminology be uncoupled from the commercial imperatives and market settings with which it is often associated.

In terms of its self-representation, this framework cultivates a neutral, apolitical, demeanour, seeking only to *repair* the social and economic relations that give rise to criminogenic outcomes, never to *reject* them as socially unjust or unacceptable. In the present political climate, this criminology's very practical emphasis upon control, and its silence on the question of how offenders should be sanctioned, mean that it offers one of the few routes to a non-punitive policy that is not vulnerable to the charge of being 'soft on crime'.

Today's other emergent criminology—the criminology of the other—might properly be described as *anti-modern* in character. It reacts to the failures of penal modernism and to the social arrangements of late modern society by questioning that society's normative codes and seeking to transform the values upon which they are built. This is the criminology of the dangerous other, a criminological echo of the culture wars and neo-conservative politics. If the criminology of everyday life de-dramatizes crime, treating it as a routine part of the normal scheme of things, this other criminology re-dramatizes it—depicting it in melodramatic terms, viewing it as a catastrophe, framing it in the language of warfare and social defence.[49] According to proponents of this criminology the problem with penal modernism, and with the modern society that spawned it, is that they have suffered a failure of moral nerve. They are unwilling to judge, reluctant to condemn, overly sensitive about matters of punishment and discipline.[50] They have distrusted the 'natural' sentiments of retributive justice and the common sense of ordinary people and have replaced them instead with the professional nostrums of liberal elites and sociological ideologies. In consequence, they have failed to uphold law and order or maintain respect for authority, and have unleashed the flood of crime, disorder and social problems that have characterized the late modern period.

This criminology is decidedly anti-modern in its central themes: the upholding of order and authority, the assertion of absolute moral standards, the affirmation of tradition and common sense. It is also deeply illiberal in its assumption that certain criminals are 'simply wicked' and in this respect intrinsically different from the rest of us. This view of the criminal has both has ontological and epistemological implications. Being intrinsically evil or wicked, some offenders are not like us. They are dangerous others who threaten our safety and have no calls on our fellow feeling. The appropriate reaction for society is one of social defence: we should defend ourselves against these dangerous enemies rather than concern ourselves with their welfare and prospects for rehabilitation. As the title of a John DiIulio article once put it, we should simply 'Let 'em rot'.[51] Their intrinsic otherness has implications for our understanding also. Intrinsic evil defies all attempts at rational comprehension or criminological explanation. There can be no mutual intelligibility, no bridge of understanding, no real communication between 'us' and 'them'. To treat them as understandable—as criminology has traditionally done—is to bring criminals into our domain, to humanize them, to see ourselves in them and them in ourselves. The criminology of the other encourages us, in the words of a British Prime Minister, to be prepared 'to condemn more and to understand less'.[52] It prompts us to treat them as 'opaquely monstrous creatures beyond or beneath our knowing'— which helps still the conscience of anyone who might be have qualms about incapacitating millions of people, and even killing a few, all in the name of public safety.[53]

Criminology's usual concern has been to shift discussion away from moral questions of responsibility towards scientific questions of causation and prevention; to replace the urge to punish with the will to understand. The criminology of the other does the opposite. Aware, perhaps, that the death penalty and mass imprisonment depend upon our refusal to comprehend the human beings we so completely condemn, it reinstates an older, metaphysical conception that depicts the offender as evil-doer, and the criminal act as unconditioned evil choice.[54] Whether the offender's character is the result of bad genes or of being reared in an anti-social culture, the outcome is the same—a person who is beyond the pale, beyond reform, outside the civil community. In this anti-modern perspective, social order necessitates social consensus, but it is consensus of a pre-modern, mechanical kind—based upon a shared set of values not a pluralism of tolerated differences. Those who do not or cannot fit in must be excommunicated and forcibly expelled.[55]

Such a criminology is, of course, quite opposed to the criminology of everyday life. But we should note that its vision of the offender is also completely at odds with the politics of solidarity that underpinned the welfare state and the sociological criminology that dominated at mid-century. The popularity today of this kind of criminological reasoning, in the USA and to a lesser extent in the UK, is a measure of how far we have moved from that earlier inclusive vision.

The characteristics of these the two new criminologies are different in most respects, as are their constituencies and sources of social support. But they share a focus upon *control,* an acknowledgement that *crime has become a normal social fact,* and a *reaction against* the criminological ideas and penal policies associated with *penal-welfarism.* The one is late-modern, taking the amoral social science approach even further than correctionalism did, viewing crime as the predictable outcome of normal social routines rather than of skewed dispositions. The other is anti-modern and anti-social science, adopting an absolutist, moralizing approach to crime, and insisting that criminal actions are voluntary, the bad choices of wicked individuals.

These new criminologies also signal how far we have moved from the project of integration through individual correction and social reform—a project that was the hallmark of criminal justice in the welfare state. One criminology takes late modern society as it finds it and suggests how we might adapt. The other is appalled by contemporary culture and the new social arrangements and calls for them to be dismantled. One argues that social and economic arrangements routinely generate criminal events and suggests ways of modifying how these arrangements are put together. The other asserts that an immoral underclass is the source of the problem and suggests ways of excluding and policing it. Despite these profound differences, however, both of the new criminologies share a fundamental feature: they each respond to, and further entrench, the culture of control that has increasingly taken hold in public discourse about social and criminal issues.

In contrast to the correctionalist criminology, with its concern for prevention through reform, these new currents have a quite different conception of their task. Both afford priority to control and to public protection, though each has a very different method of instituting these aims. The first proposes the piecemeal development of a network of unobtrusive situational controls, retrofitted to modify existing routines. It wants to inscribe controls into the warp and weft of social life, aiming to channel conduct in orderly ways without disturbing the flow of social events. The other exerts an excess of control and cares little for the social costs and penal consequences. It imposes control from the outside in the form of legal threats and moral exhortations, and condemns and excludes all those who fail to take heed. Deter, punish, incapacitate—and hang the expense.

These two criminologies are reactions against the culture of welfarism and the related criminology of correctionalism. They are twinned reactions that diverge from that earlier orthodoxy in opposite ways. The emergence of these reactions at this time is neither accidental nor arbitrary, and their appeal to politicians and administrators is not in the least surprising. For these opposing ways of thinking and acting upon crime are precisely aligned with the two poles of the cultural ambivalence that has grown up around crime. One position says, 'crime is normal, get used to it'. 'Be realistic, adapt, protect, survive.' The other sees crime's pervasiveness is a catastrophe for which someone must be blamed, a plague that afflicts a degenerate society and acts as a sign that we should return to more traditional and perhaps more God-fearing way of life.[56] These new ways of thinking about crime are, in that sense, grounded in our culture. As Foucault showed decades ago, our social sciences are destined to 'discover' precisely those cultural themes that gave rise to these forms of knowledge and to the objects that they study.

The shifting emphases of criminology and crime control

What are the practical effects of these new criminologies? And how do they differ from the social criminologies that preceded them? As we saw in Chapter 2, the social criminologies associated with mid-century correctionalism displayed a particular pattern of emphases and silences. These discursive characteristics fitted well with the structure and culture of penal-welfarism, and echoed the institutional arrangements and political commitments of that period. The most striking feature of recent criminological discourse is the way that it has highlighted the silences and blindspots that characterized the older criminological scheme.

The social criminologies that dominated prior to the 1970s had no programme of policing, no substantive interest in crime events, and no theory of the social and economic routines that generate criminal opportunities and criminogenic situations. Nor were they interested in primary or secondary crime prevention, since preventive effects were presumed to flow from general social reforms rather than specific criminological interventions. Questions of motivation took precedence over questions of control, for the simple reason that criminal acts were taken as signs of an underlying pathology rather than merely a lack of effective controls.

The social criminologies also downplayed the idea of deterrence, despite the fact that this notion had formed the crucial link between traditional punishment and crime control. Criminologists before the 1970s were highly sceptical about the effectiveness of legal threats, and tended to regard deterrent policies as little more than a cover for more basic retributive concerns. This attitude had its roots in epistemological as well as ideological commitments. Since it was typically conservatives who stressed the need for tough, deterrent penalties, the liberal bias of most welfare state criminologists made them wary of this approach. But more fundamentally, it was the distinctive mind-set of welfarist criminology that led most experts and practitioners to be sceptical about the utility of deterrent punishments. If crime was a symptom of underlying pathologies, if it was shaped by long-term, at-a-distance processes of causation, then it made little sense to focus upon the immediacies of the situation and the impact of threats and disincentives. The basic premises of penal-welfare criminology tended to undercut the idea of deterrence, not as an empirical matter but in a more fundamental, *a-priori* fashion.

In contrast, recent criminologies have revived interest in the whole question of deterrents and disincentives, and have encouraged policy-makers to adopt deterrent measures, ranging from mandatory minima for drug dealing and organized crime to aggressive stop and search measures to reduce the frequency of casual gun carrying. As a consequence, the practical distinction between the normal and the pathological has been revised. In penal-welfare criminology, the pathological offender was the focus for analysis and for correctional intervention: it was a criminological category that was widely defined and constantly expanding. In contrast, normal, rational offenders formed a theoretically more marginal category, of little professional interest. Today, there has been a shift of attention and priority. The mundane, opportunist offender now stands much closer to centre-stage in criminological study and crime control practice and the needy, pathological offender is much less prominent.

These new criminologies also give much greater prominence to the crime-reducing potential of the police and to policing activity in general. In the new criminology of control, the police play a much more central role, and social or psychological interventions recede into the background. The police are deemed capable of crime reduction in a variety of ways—by deterrence, by prevention, by building partnerships, by aggressive policing. Indeed the most talked about developments of contemporary policing—the 'broken windows' and the 'zero-tolerance' approaches—imply a complete inversion of the old criminological assumptions. In today's criminology, minor offending matters, situational controls shape conduct, and deterrent penalties are a central resource for crime control. This much is common ground for the criminologies of everyday life and the more punitive criminology of the other.

From a 'social' to an 'economic' style of reasoning

In any institutional setting there are basic recipes that shape thinking and guide decision-making. These recipes are not articulated theories or legal guidelines but instead habits of thought and routine styles of reasoning that are embedded in the precedents and practices of the institution. New recruits learn these ways of thinking 'on the job'. They become the common sense of the actors, prompted by the structures and culture of the organization. These recipes become ingrained in institutions and individuals and tend not to change rapidly: once learned they are hard to unlearn. But they can be changed over time, and in the last thirty years a new way of thinking has been gradually inscribed in the habits of crime control actors.

For much of the twentieth century, most crime policy and criminal justice decisions were underpinned by a *social* style of reasoning. Crime problems had a social cause and a social solution. The particular problems that emerged were to be placed in their social context, traced to their social roots, and dealt with by the most appropriate social means, such as social counselling and case-work, social provision, or social reform. Recently, however, a different way of approaching problems has emerged, a style that might be described as 'economic' rather than social. This way of thinking has shaped how criminal justice practitioners make decisions, how they allocate resources and how they deploy their powers. It has changed how institutions control their staffs and how they manage their internal actions. It has even affected how criminal justice authorities regard the conduct of offenders, probationers and prisoners. In short, it has become a shaping force in criminological thought and action, both inside and outside the criminal justice agencies.[57]

Of course, justice has always depended upon resources, and crime control has always had its costs. There has never been a time when police and penal administrators did not complain that their budgets were inadequate, or when politicians did not accuse them of wasting taxpayers' money. But issues of costs and effectiveness are foregrounded in policy decisions today to an extent never seen before, and the police, the court and the various penal agencies are costed and audited more thoroughly today than at any time in their history. Over the last twenty years, the pressure to attain 'value-for-money', together with the effects of specific mechanisms of fiscal restraint and managerial discipline, have given rise to a framework of economic thinking that has become increasingly pervasive and powerful.

Today, the practitioners of crime control and criminal justice are required to talk the economic language of 'cost–benefit', 'best value' and 'fiscal responsibility'. Managerialism—with its portable, multi-purpose techniques for accountability and evaluation and its 'can-do' private sector values—has flowed into the vacuum created when the more substantive, more positive content of the old social approach lost credibility. The crime control field—from crime prevention work and policing to the prison regimes and the practice of parole—has become saturated with technologies of audit, fiscal control, measured performance, and cost–benefit evaluation. The old language of social causation has been displaced by a new lexicon (of 'risk factors', 'incentive structures', 'supply and demand', 'stocks and flows', 'crime costing' and 'penalty pricing') that translates economic forms of calculation into the criminological field. The costs of crime are now routinely calculated, but so too are the costs of prevention, policing, prosecution, and punishment, and the comparative figures that are produced help shape policy choices and operational priorities.[58] The chief virtue of new policies such as private prison contracting or 'punishment in the community' is their claim to be economically rational alternatives to previous arrangements. And priority setting by criminal justice agencies is increasingly a matter of 'targeting' or 'gatekeeping', or 'smart sentencing' in ways that use least resources to achieve maximum effect.

Despite its formalistic character, this way of thinking has substantive consequences. As the critics of managerialism point out, it can limit experimentation, favour 'outputs' over 'outcomes', skew practice to fit performance indicators, limit the discretion of field staff, and diminish an agency's real effectiveness in order to maximize the practices that are most easily measurable. But this increasingly influential rationality has also helped to change how the system thinks about crime and criminals—encouraging a more costed, conception of social harm and a conception of the offender that emphasizes rational choice and calculation. The institutionalization of this style of reasoning in criminal justice institutions has increased the resonance and appeal of some criminological conceptions as opposed to others. For example, this economic framework has clear affinities with criminological analyses that view crime as an externality of normal social transactions or which conceive crime as the outcome of reasoned, opportunistic choices. The same might be said of the new image of the victim as a supplier of criminal opportunities, and the idealized figure of *homo prudens* projected by official crime prevention literature.[59]

Each of these new (or revived) conceptions contrasts markedly with the social criminologies that previously shaped our thinking. They strip away the sociological and psychological layers in which twentieth century criminology had clothed its conception of the criminal offender, and seem at first to be a puzzling return to the naive criminology of Jeremy Bentham and his utilitarian followers. This reversion appears less puzzling in the light of the institutional forces that now pull in that direction. Of course the revival of the 'rational criminal' in official criminology, and the concern to govern this figure by manipulating incentives and risks, would certainly have been encouraged by the general culture of choice and consumerism that characterizes late modernity. But the close affinity of these criminological ideas with the managerial and auditing processes of the criminal justice institutions have greatly increased their appeal. Criminal justice staffs increasingly seek to control offenders using the same techniques they use to control themselves.

The utilization of economic ideas to think about crime probably occurred first in the private sector—in the practices of insurance companies, private security firms, and commercial enterprises seeking to reduce those costs of crime that fall on them. Their preferred way of approaching the problem was to focus on reducing or displacing the costs of crime, upon prevention rather than punishment, and upon minimizing risk rather than ensuring justice. The willingness of firms to weigh the costs of crime against the costs of its prevention—and their tendency to take preventative action only where it pays to do so—led to the elaboration of a 'managerial' approach to crime that was rather different from that employed by governments.

The emergence of this rationality is, like the disciplinary prison, a conjunctural outcome that was not pre-planned. The old social language 'didn't work' and became discredited both as a practical matter and as a political proposition. In contrast, economic modes of reasoning were available, transferable, and appeared to work, or at least to satisfy funding authorities who increasingly demand that the activities they financed be monitored and assessed in this way. The political parties in power during the 1980s and 1990s emphatically favoured 'market solutions', 'private sector' values, and managerial solutions, and encouraged state agencies to adopt this way of thinking. The declining credibility of social service professionals and the unwillingness of politicians to devolve penal power encouraged the use of techniques to control decision-making from the outside.[60] Trust and grants of discretionary power were increasingly replaced by the detailed specification of performance and close evaluation. Over time, criminal justice agencies were drawn into 'the audit society' and came to share the 'new public management' working practices that had already become standard elsewhere in the public sector.[61]

The economic style of reasoning, like the social one that preceded it, has a thematic and cultural coherence—the success of an exemplar, everywhere applied—rather than a strict logic or tight conceptual structure. It is, in effect, a ragbag of techniques, models, analogies, and recipes for action that are loosely bound up together by their appeal to economic rationality. As writers such as Gary Becker or Richard Posner have shown, this kind of reasoning can be applied in all kinds of domains, though its poor fit with the substantive rationality of 'doing justice' has meant that it has provoked greater resistance in this field than in some others. The economic rationality is, above all, a language for doing and representing. It has been superimposed upon practices that sometimes seem quite limited in their rationality and quite removed from economic considerations (such as the conduct of offenders, the choices of prisoners, the behaviour of victims, etc.) and upon practitioners who are hostile to it (probation officers, social workers, judges). That is has taken root in this setting is not a reflection of the economic character of crime and justice, or even of the intrinsic power of economic models. It is the effect of a particular politico-cultural environment operating through the institutions through which we construct 'crime' and 'justice' as social entities.

The political limits of economic reasoning

Economic habits of thought may have become the default style of decision making in crime control, but they are displaced at certain points by a very different way of thinking which presses the imperatives of punishing criminals and protecting the public, 'whatever the cost'. This alternative modality contrasts sharply with the economic framework. It is 'value rational' rather than purpose-rational, expressive rather than calculating, and absolutist rather than strategic in its approach. Where the economic mode of reasoning is managerial, relativistic, cost-conscious, and oriented to the bottom-line, the expressive mode is more overtly moralistic, uncompromising, and concerned to assert the force of sovereign power.[62] The penal measures associated with this expressive, sovereign approach tend to be fuelled by collective outrage and a concern for symbolic statement rather than by careful calculations of cost and effect.

It hardly needs to be said that this way of responding to crime confounds the cost-effectiveness considerations of the economic framework. The War on Drugs is a prominent example of this. So too are the mandatory sentences of the California Three Strikes laws, the recent 'prison works' policy of the UK government, and zero tolerance policing policies, all of which are very costly and, in crime control terms, of doubtful effectiveness. The adoption of a war mentality altogether defeats economic reasoning.

The process of switching between these contradictory rationalities, of moving from one discursive register to another, is very much a *political* process. It is governed not by any criminological logic but instead by the conflicting interests of political actors and by the exigencies, political calculations and short-term interests that provide their motivations. In its detailed configuration, with all its incoherence and contradictions, the field is thus a product of the decidedly aleatory history of political manoeuvres and calculations.

The clash between the institutional logic of cost-effectiveness and the sovereign state gestures of the 'war against crime' is thus a clash of irreconcilable principles. Hence the barely concealed frustration of cost-conscious administrators and agency chiefs when confronted with the absolutism of the War on Drugs or the demand that violent predators be locked up indefinitely to protect the public. It is true, of course, that penal measures are frequently presented in terms that appear to function on both registers—as economic *and* expressive measures. For example mandatory minimum sentences are represented by their proponents as being liable to save money in the long run by incapacitating large numbers of offenders and hence reducing crime. But in this instance and in others, the supposed economic rationale is bogus, and is backed up by little in the way of statistical cost estimates, offender profiling or actuarial data. Punitive policies such as the War on Drugs, 'prison works', and the death penalty, may claim to be cost-effective forms of risk management but the calculations involved are far from actuarial. Rather, they are motivated by an unstated but well-understood sentiment that views the offenders targeted by such acts (recidivists, career criminals, 'sexually violent predators', drug dealers, paedophiles) as wicked individuals who have lost all legal rights and all moral claims upon us. The motivating mind-set here is not actuarial prediction or careful risk-management. It is a hard, self-righteous intolerance produced by stereotypical images of danger and negative evaluations of moral worth.

The prevailing attitude is that it is better to keep a known criminal locked up for ever than to risk the life or property of another innocent victim. Perhaps if offenders had more political importance or social status they might command the actuarial attention required by programmes of selective incapacitation or bifurcated sentencing. As it is, politicians often speak the language of risk only to bowdlerize its terms and confound its logic. If it relates to the release of a convicted offender, then any level of risk is unacceptable. Their calculations are simple—the liberty interests of the prisoner are set at zero if his or her release might expose the public to avoidable danger, or require the responsible official to run any substantial political risk. In today's political climate, a record of prior offending affects the individual's perceived moral status rather more than it changes their actuarial risk.

8

Crime Control and Social Order

The crime control landscape that has emerged in America and Britain at the end of the twentieth century has surprised experts and defied historical predictions. I have argued that one can best understand these developments—in policing, sentencing, punishment, penal philosophy, penal politics, private security, crime prevention, criminological theory, the treatment of victims, and so on— by regarding them as interrelated aspects of a social field that is itself being restructured. I have tried to show how the field of crime control and criminal justice has been affected by changes in the social organization of the societies in which it functions, by the distinctive problems of social order characteristic of that form of social organization, and by the political, cultural, and criminological adaptations that have emerged in response to these distinctive problems. By way of a conclusion, I want to show how my explanation bears upon some specific issues that still need to be addressed, and to indicate some of the consequences that follow if my interpretation is correct.

Today's world of crime control and criminal justice was not brought into being by rising crime rates or by a loss of faith in penal-welfarism, or at least not by these alone. These were proximate causes rather than the fundamental processes at work. It was created instead by a series of adaptive responses to the cultural and criminological conditions of late modernity—conditions which included new problems of crime and insecurity, and new attitudes towards the welfare state. But these responses did not occur outside of the political process, or in a political and cultural vacuum. On the contrary. They were deeply marked by the cultural formation that I have described as the 'crime complex'; by the reactionary politics that have dominated Britain and America during the last twenty years; and by the new social relations that have grown up around the changing structures of work, welfare and market exchange in these two late modern societies.

During the 1980s and the 1990s the political culture that articulated these social relations was quite different from that which had prevailed in the heyday of the welfare state. In its emphases if not in every respect, this culture was more exclusionary than solidaristic, more committed to social control than to social provision, and more attuned to the private freedoms of the market than the public freedoms of universal citizenship. The institutions of crime control and criminal justice have shifted in this same general direction. They have adjusted their policies, practices and representations in order to pursue the social objectives and invoke the cultural themes that now dominate in the political domain.

The specific policies and practices that have emerged are adaptations to the world in which crime control now operates and to the practical predicaments that this world creates. As we have seen, these new practices typically emerge as local solutions to the immediate problems encountered by individuals and organizations as they go about their daily routines. But what they add up to is a process of institutional adaptation in which the whole field of crime control gradually adjusts its orientation and functioning. In terms of that bigger picture, the adjustments that have occurred are structural, and concern the relationship between crime control and social order. Over time, our practices of controlling crime and doing justice have had to adapt to an increasingly insecure economy that marginalizes substantial sections of the population; to a hedonistic consumer culture that combines extensive personal freedoms with relaxed social controls; to a pluralistic moral order that struggles to create trust relations between strangers who have little in common; to a 'sovereign' state that is increasingly incapable of regulating a society of individuated citizens and differentiated social groups; and to chronically high crime rates that co-exist with low levels of family cohesion and community solidarity. The risky, insecure character of today's social and economic relations is the social surface that gives rise to our newly emphatic, overreaching concern with control and to the urgency with which we segregate, fortify, and exclude. It is the background circumstance that prompts our obsessive attempts to monitor risky individuals, to isolate dangerous populations, and to impose situational controls on otherwise open and fluid settings. It is the source of the deep-seated anxieties that find expression in today's crime-conscious culture, in the commodification of security, and in a built environment designed to manage space and to separate people.

I have described how the new crime control developments have 'adapted' and 'responded' to the late modern world, and to its political and cultural values. But these developments also, in their turn, play a role in *creating* that world, helping to constitute the meaning of late modernity. Crime control today does more than simply manage problems of crime and insecurity. It also institutionalizes a set of responses to these problems that are themselves consequential in their social impact. In America and Britain today, 'late modernity' is lived—not just by offenders but by all of us—in a mode that is more than ever defined by institutions of policing, penality, and prevention.[1]

This desire for security, orderliness, and control, for the management of risk and the taming of chance is, to be sure, an underlying theme in any culture. But in Britain and America in recent decades that theme has become a more dominant one, with immediate consequences for those caught up in its repressive demands, and more diffuse, corrosive effects for the rest of us.[2] Spatial controls, situational controls, managerial controls, system controls, social controls, self-controls—in one social realm after another, we now find the imposition of more intensive regimes of regulation, inspection and control and, in the process, our civic culture becomes increasingly less tolerant and inclusive, increasingly less capable of trust.[3] After a long-term process of expanding individual freedom and relaxing social and cultural restraints, control is now being re-emphasized in every area of social life—with the singular and startling exception of the economy, from whose deregulated domain most of today's major risks routinely emerge.

The rise to dominance of this cultural theme has the character of a reaction, a backlash, an attempted undoing of accumulated historical change. The 1950s, 1960s, and 1970s were decades of rapid social and economic change during which families and communities were severely dislocated, even as individuals and social groups enjoyed new freedoms, more varied lifestyles, and an enhanced range of consumer choices. That earlier phase subsequently gave way to a wave of anxiety about the breakdown of family, the relaxation of institutional disciplines, and the collapse of informal norms of restraint. In the closing decades of the twentieth century the pursuit of freedom has come to be overshadowed by a new sense of disorder and of dangerously inadequate controls. As we have seen, a reactionary politics has used this underlying disquiet to create a powerful narrative of moral decline in which *crime* has come to feature—together with teenage pregnancies, single parent families, welfare dependency, and drug abuse—as the chief symptom of the supposed malaise. This call for a return to order has led to the imposition of extensive new disciplines and controls, though it has been a feature of these developments that they have been targeted against particular social groups rather than universally imposed. The 1980s and 1990s have seen a return to restraint, a retrofitting of controls, an attempt to put the lid back on a newly disordered world. But despite these efforts, the clocks have not been turned back. There has been no return to a world in which all individuals are more hemmed in by the communal controls of local belonging, steady work, and tight-knit family. What has happened is that the individual freedoms granted by late modern morals and markets have been shored up by a new structure of controls and exclusions, directed against those groups most adversely affected by the dynamics of economic and social change—the urban poor, welfare claimants, and minority communities.

Convinced of the need to re-impose order, but unwilling to restrict consumer choice or give up personal freedoms; determined to enhance their own security, but unwilling to pay more taxes or finance the security of others; appalled by unregulated egoism and anti-social attitudes but committed to a market system which reproduces that very culture, the anxious middle classes today seek resolution for their ambivalence in zealously controlling the poor and excluding the marginal.[4] Above all, they impose controls upon 'dangerous' offenders and 'undeserving' claimants whose conduct leads some to suppose that they are incapable of discharging the responsibilities of the late modern freedom. The most vehement punishments are reserved for those guilty of child abuse, illegal drug use, or sexual violence—precisely the areas in which mainstream social and cultural norms have undergone greatest change and where middle-class ambivalence and guilt are at their most intense.

Punishment and welfare in late modernity

This study has focused on the effects of the new social relations and political culture in the field of crime control. But the same kinds of effects can also be seen in other areas of social and economic policy, above all, in the treatment of the poor. In political discourse and government policy the poor are once again viewed as undeserving and treated accordingly. Their poverty is attributed to their supposed lack of effort, their feckless choices, their distinctive culture, and chosen conduct.[5] In the increasingly prosperous world of the 1990s and since, these persistently poor populations are easily viewed as 'different' and not merely 'disadvantaged'. Like persistent offenders and 'career criminals', they are conveniently regarded as an alien culture, a class apart, a residuum left behind by the fast-paced, high-tech processes of the globalized economy and the information society.[6] The themes that dominate crime policy—rational choice and the structures of control, deterrents, and disincentives, the normality of crime, the responsibilization of individuals, the threatening underclass, the failing, overly lenient system—have come to organize the politics of poverty as well. The same premises and purposes that transformed criminal justice are evident in the programmes of 'welfare reform' that have been adopted by governments (and opposition parties) on both sides of the Atlantic and in the restructured social policy to which these have given rise.

Beginning in the 1980s benefits levels have been steadily reduced, even in periods when the numbers of out-of-work claimants greatly increased.[7] The provision of welfare has been skirted round with work conditions and disciplinary restrictions. 'Choice' and 'responsibility' have been emphasized, 'dependency' anathematized, and 'the market' has come to be viewed as a providential force of nature rather than a set of social relations that requires careful regulation and moral restraint. The termination of benefits is increasingly used as a means to force claimants off the rolls—usually into low-paid work but no doubt also into the alternative economy of drugs and crime. Unemployed workers have had to demonstrate that they are 'active jobseekers' before they can claim benefits. A recognition that social and economic processes can create undeserved hardship has given way to a more moralistic account of labour market success and failure, in much the way that determinist criminologies have been displaced by the moralism of rational choice. Solidarity with the victims of social and economic dislocation has given way to a more condemnatory view of claimants, many of whom are now viewed as members of a culturally distinct and socially threatening 'underclass', in which all of the pathologies of late modern life are concentrated. At the same time, chronic unemployment for certain social groups has come to be seen as a normal fact of economic life, quite beyond the reach of government policy or regulatory control. In the new economic order, only entrepreneurial conduct and prudent risk-management can offset the threat of insecurity: the state no longer acts as the insurer of last resort; citizenship no longer guarantees security. Like the system of criminal justice, the benefits structure of the welfare state has come to be viewed as a generator of problems and pathologies rather than a cure for them. Reform efforts focus upon reducing costs, strengthening disincentives, surrounding benefit payments with controls and restrictions, and 'getting people off welfare'. Less effort is directed to addressing the structural sources of unemployment, poverty, and ill-health. The parallels with the new field of crime control are impossible to miss.

During the last twenty years, the combined effect of 'neo-liberal' and 'neo-conservative' policies—of market discipline and moral discipline—has been to create a situation in which more and more controls are imposed on the poor, while fewer and fewer controls affect the market freedoms of the rest. Tax cuts for upper income groups, housing and pensions subsidies for the middle classes, the deregulation of the finance and credit industries, the privatization of major industries, and a prolonged stock market boom—these have ensured that those in well-paid work have enjoyed increased living standards, enhanced consumer freedom, and ever-fewer state controls on their economic conduct. The widening gap between rich and poor that these policies have created, together with the meanness of state benefits, have prompted those who can afford it to look to private, market-based provision of goods when it comes to housing, health, education, and pensions. A thriving market in commodified services has grown up parallel to the welfare state, in precisely the same way that the new market in private policing and security has appeared alongside the criminal justice system. The predictable consequence has been that the middle classes have become less inclined to view state welfare as a system that works to their benefit. Instead, it comes to be seen as a costly and inefficient government bureaucracy redistributing the hard-earned income of people in employment to an undeserving mass of idle and feckless recipients. With welfare, as with crime, large sections of the middle and working classes see themselves as victimized by the poor and by a system that reproduces the problem it is supposed to solve.[8] The more punitive, more demanding welfare-to-work structures that have put in place in recent years are the direct expression of this new sentiment. What Galbraith called a culture of contentment has increasingly given way to an anti-welfare politics in which the market freedoms and economic interests of the middle and upper classes dictate a more restrictive and less generous policy towards the poor.[9] In the prosperous 1990s these policies succeeded in reducing welfare rolls and limiting the growth of social spending. It remains to be seen how they will function once the economy falters and unemployment levels once more begin to rise.

The dialectic of freedom and control

Historians have pointed to a recurring pattern of social development in which the upheaval and disruption characteristic of periods of social change subsequently give way to efforts at consolidation and the re-imposition of order and control.[10] This dialectic between freedom and control could be said to have characterized the last thirty years. In certain respects, the social liberation of the 1960s and the market freedoms of the 1980s are now being paid for in the coin of social control and penal repression. Where the liberating dynamic of late modernity emphasized freedom, openness, mobility, and tolerance, the reactionary culture of the end of the century stresses control, closure, confinement, and condemnation. The continued enjoyment of market-based personal freedoms has come to depend upon the close control of excluded groups who cannot be trusted to enjoy these freedoms. So long as offenders and claimants appear as 'other', and as the chief source of their own misfortune, they offer occasions for the dominant classes to impose strict controls without giving up freedoms of their own. In contrast to a solidaristic social control, in which everyone gives up some personal freedom in order to promote collective welfare, market individualism is the freedom of some premised upon the exclusion and close control of others.

When we impose control upon offenders today, we take pains to affirm their supposed freedom, their moral responsibility, and their capacity to have acted otherwise. The criminologies and sentencing assumptions that have become influential in the 1980s and 1990s—criminologies of choice and control—are precisely those that echo today's cultural norms and socio-political imperatives. We live in a social world built upon the imperatives of individual choice and personal freedom. Criminological accounts that slight free choice and stress social determinants now lack the kind of resonance and ideological appeal that they exerted in the heyday of the welfare state. Those accounts that highlight rational choice and the responsiveness of offenders to rewards and disincentives chime with today's common sense and with the individualistic morality of our consumer culture. Offenders must be deemed to be free, to be rational, to be exercising choice, because that is how we must conceive of ourselves. 'Crime is a decision not a disease' is the new conventional wisdom.[11] More precisely put, crime is taken to be a freely chosen act, a rational decision, except in these cases where it is actually the determined outcome of a constitutional pathology. If individuals are to be deemed irresponsible, if impersonal forces are to account for their actions, then these must be forces that do not act upon the rest of us—causes with their roots in biological, psychological, and cultural difference. If we are to see ourselves as the uncaused causes of our own actions and choices, as the moral individualism of market society teaches us to do, then those not fully in control of their own conduct must appear different in some extra-social sense. Their otherness is a condition of their exculpation. What is missing today, what is actively suppressed by our cultural commitments, is the excluded middle that lies between complete freedom and irresistible compulsion—the old welfarist notion that individual decisions and choices are themselves socially structured, as are the capacities and opportunities for realizing them.

In the middle decades of the last century, the criminal justice system formed part of a broader solidarity project. Its programmatic response to crime was part of the welfare state's programmatic response to poverty and destitution. Criminal justice was shaped by the politics of social democracy, and its ideals were the re-integrative ideals of an inclusive welfare state society. And if its actual practices fell far short of these ideals, as they typically did, they could at least be criticized by reference to these ideals, and reformed in ways that lessened the gap. Today, welfare state institutions still play a supporting role in economic and social life, just as penal-welfare institutions still underpin criminal justice. But that solidarity project no longer dominates the rhetoric of policy or the logic of decision-making. The high ideals of solidarity have been eclipsed by the more basic imperatives of security, economy, and control. Crime control and criminal justice have come to be disconnected from the broader themes of social justice and social reconstruction. Their social function is now the more reactionary, less ambitious one of re-imposing control on those who fall outside the world of consumerist freedom. If penal-welfare conveyed the hubris and idealism of twentieth-century modernism, today's crime policies express a darker and less tolerant message.

The social roots of crime control

The explanation for some of the more puzzling facts of contemporary crime control can be found if we trace their connections to the kinds of social organization and political culture that dominate in Britain and America today.

Why has the prison moved from being a discredited institution destined for abolition, to become an expanded and seemingly indispensable pillar of late modern social life? Not because it was the centrepiece of any penal programme that argued the need for mass imprisonment. There was no such programme. Imprisonment has emerged in its revived, reinvented form because it is able to serve a newly necessary function in the workings of late modern, neo-liberal societies: the need for a 'civilized' and 'constitutional' means of segregating the problem populations created by today's economic and social arrangements. The prison is located precisely at the junction point of two of the most important social and penal dynamics of our time: risk and retribution.[12] With the absolutist logic of a penal sanction, it punishes and protects, condemns and controls. Imprisonment simultaneously serves as an expressive satisfaction of retributive sentiments and an instrumental mechanism for the management of risk and the confinement of danger. The sectors of the population effectively excluded from the worlds of work, welfare and family—typically young urban minority males—increasingly find themselves in prison or in jail, their social and economic exclusion effectively disguised by their criminal status. Today's reinvented prison is a ready-made penal solution to a new problem of social and economic exclusion.

Why do governments so quickly turn to penal solutions to deal with the behaviour of marginal populations rather than attempt to address the social and economic sources of their marginalization? Because penal solutions are immediate, easy to implement, and can claim to 'work' as a punitive end in themselves even when they fail in all other respects. Because they have few political opponents, comparatively low costs, and they accord with common sense ideas about the sources of social disorder and the proper allocation of blame. Because they rely upon existing systems of regulation, and leave the fundamental social and economic arrangements untouched. Above all, because they allow controls and condemnation to be focused on low-status outcast groups, leaving the behaviour of markets, corporations and the more affluent social classes relatively free of regulation and censure.

Why have we made such massive new investments in private security and created such thriving markets in commodified control? Because the old fashioned sovereign state can deliver punishment but not security, and this has become apparent to economic actors who have a real stake in the process. Because affluent sectors of the population have become accustomed to insuring themselves and their property and are increasingly willing to spend money on the pursuit of personal safety. Because these same groups are acutely aware of the social and racial divisions that characterize today's society and resort to defensive space and fortified property as ways of warding off threatening outsiders. And because in high crime societies, the problems of personal security, crime prevention and penal provision have created commercial opportunities that have been vigorously exploited by the private interests and market forces that neo-liberalism has so effectively liberated.

Why is the emphasis now shifting to situational crime prevention and away from the social reform programmes that used to dominate the field? Because unlike earlier efforts to build social prevention programmes, job creation schemes, and community regeneration, the new situational methods do not appear to benefit the undeserving poor, to imply a social critique, or to disturb market freedoms. Their implementation can proceed outside of a politics of solidarity and collective sacrifice, and in the absence of support for redistributive welfare programmes. Their growing appeal rests on the fact that they can be distributed through the market as customized commodities, rather than delivered by state agencies. Like private policing and commercial security, these methods mesh with the dynamics of market society, adapting themselves to individuated demand, slotting into the circuits of profitable supply and private consumption.

Why is the image of the suffering victim now so central to the crime issue and our responses to it? Because in the new morality of market individualism, public institutions lack compelling force and the state's law lacks independent authority. Whatever mutuality and solidarity exists is achieved through the direct identification of individuals with one another, not with the polity or the public institutions to which they each belong. In a world in which moral sentiments are increasingly privatized along with everything else, collective moral outrage more easily proceeds from an individualized basis than from a public one. A declining faith in public institutions now means that only the sight of suffering 'individuals like us' can be relied upon to provoke the impassioned responses needed to supply the emotional energy for punitive policies and a war upon crime. In the individualistic culture of consumer capitalism, the law more and more relies upon identifications of an individual kind. Justice, like the other public goods of the post-welfare society, is increasingly rendered in the currency of consumer society, increasingly adapted to individuated demand. The new importance attributed to the figure of the 'victim' is created not by the reality of victimhood—there has always been plenty of that—but by the new significance of visceral identification in a context where few sources of mutuality exist.[13]

Finally, why do contemporary crime policies so closely resemble the anti-welfare policies that have grown up over the precisely the same period? Because they share the same assumptions, harbour the same anxieties, deploy the same stereotypes, and utilize the same recipes for the identification of risk and the allocation of blame. Like social policy and the system of welfare benefits, crime control functions as an element in a broader system of regulation and ideology that attempts to forge a new social order in the conditions of late modernity.

That future is not inevitable

I have argued that today's crime control strategies have a certain congruence, a certain 'fit' with the structures of late modern society. They represent a particular kind of response, a particular adaptation, to the specific problems of social order produced by late modern social organization.[14] But such policies are not inevitable. The social surface upon which crime control institutions are built poses certain problems, but does not dictate how these will be perceived and addressed by social actors and authorities. These responses are shaped by political institutions and cultural commitments. They are the products of a certain style of politics, a certain conjuncture of class forces, a particular historical trajectory. They are the outcome (partly planned, partly unintended) of political and cultural and policy choices—choices that could have been different and that can still be rethought and reversed.[15]

The general explanation that I have set out here necessarily involves two kinds of accounts: a *structural* account that points to the general characteristics of a certain kind of social organization, and a *conjunctural* account that identifies the choices and contingencies that shaped how particular social groups adapted to these structures and mediated their social consequences. In narrating these historical developments I have tried to distinguish these different levels of analysis, and to differentiate structural characteristics from political or cultural adaptations. I have tried to argue that the reconfigured field of crime control is structurally related to the conditions of late modernity, while emphasizing that 'structurally related' is not the same as 'strictly determined'. But in the real world there is no clear separation between 'social structure' and 'political response': the two come bundled together. Only comparative analyses allow us to show how the same structural co-ordinates can support quite different political and cultural arrangements. This study has chosen to consider the UK and the USA together, in an effort to point up the structural similarities that mark their social, political and penological trajectories. But Britain is not America. Its penal regime is not so repressive, its social and racial divisions are not so deep, its recent history has not been so explosive. Nor are the competing political parties the same in every respect—Clinton is not Bush and Blair is not Thatcher, and the differences that distinguish their governments' policies have had real consequences for people's lives. My claim is not that there are no differences that matter. My claim is that there are now important structural similarities in the patterns of thought and organizational strategies that shape practice in these two late modern societies, no matter which party is currently in power. A more extensive work of international comparison could have shown how other societies, such as Canada, Norway, the Netherlands, or Japan, have experienced the social and economic disruptions of late modernity without resorting to these same strategies and levels of control.[16]

But even if the present study cannot show this conclusively, its analyses do suggest points at which different choices might have been made, different policies pursued, and different outcomes made more likely.[17] As we have seen, political actors in Britain and America have repeatedly chosen to respond to widespread public concern about crime and security by formulating policies that punish and exclude. They have assumed the posture of a sovereign state deploying its monopoly of force to impose order and punish law-breakers. As I have argued, this attempt to create social order through penal means is deeply problematic, particularly in late modern democracies. Instead of working to build the complex institutions of governance and integration needed to regulate and unify today's social and economic order, these penal policies have set up a division between those groups who can be allowed to live in deregulated freedom, and those who must be heavily controlled. Instead of reversing the processes of economic marginalization and social exclusion that are endemic in today's globalized economy, the new emphasis upon punishment and policing has overlaid and reinforced these very processes. Instead of addressing the difficult problem of social solidarity in a diverse, individuated world, our political leaders have preferred to rely upon the certainties of a simpler, more coercive, Hobbesian solution.

But other possibilities exist for the control of crime and the shaping of orderly conduct, as we saw when we considered the adaptive responses developed by administrative agencies. Efforts to share responsibility for crime control, to embed social control into the fabric of everyday life, to reduce the criminogenic effects of economic transactions, to protect repeat victims—these are possibilities that already exist and could be given much more prominence in government policy. As compared to penal solutions, these other possibilities are better adapted to the social arrangements of the late modern world, more realistic about the limits of the sovereign state and its criminal justice mechanisms, and less liable to reinforce existing social divisions.

We have seen that the American and British publics today are highly attuned to the crime issue, and that political actors feel compelled to respond directly to these concerns. To be out of touch with public sentiment on this issue is to invite negative headlines and political disaster. But the emotional involvement that many people now have with this issue need not always result in the expression of punitive sentiments. The public demands that something should be done about crime, that their property and persons should be protected, that offenders should be adequately punished and controlled, and that the system should operate reliably and efficiently. But these recurring concerns are capable of being met in a variety of ways. Public attitudes about crime and control are deeply ambivalent.[18] They leave room for other resolutions. Politicians have tended to take the easy route here, to opt for segregation and punishment rather than try to embed social controls, regulate economic life, and develop policies that will enhance social inclusion and integration. If late modern societies are to uphold the ideals of democracy, equal rights for all, and a minimum of economic security for the whole population, they will need to ensure that moral regulation and social control are extended to the mainstream processes of economic decision-making and market allocation—not confined to the world of offenders and claimants.

Nor is it just our politicians who will need to revise their attitudes. As we have seen, the cumulative choices of individuals and households make a difference too, and form the basis upon which social structures emerge. Today's enormous market in private security and defensive space is a consequence of these choices. So too, is the widening gap between those who can afford to protect themselves and those who cannot. Precisely because choices that seem rational from an individual viewpoint can produce irrational outcomes when repeated on a massive scale, the market in security is one that also needs to be subjected to collective regulation and moral restraint. Today's governmental authorities may be obliged to operate alongside this private sector, and in conjunction with it, but they are not obliged to stand back and allow its unregulated consequences to fall where they may.

The new iron cage

At the beginning of the twenty-first century, the USA is experiencing an unprecedented economic boom, with low unemployment levels, rising standards of living, a federal surplus and healthy state budgets. The UK is also enjoying an extended economic recovery. Crime rates fell steadily in both places during the 1990s, with the USA recording declines in every year between 1992 and the present, and England and Wales experiencing five consecutive years of decrease until the reported increase of the year ending 1999.[19] Yet despite these positive trends, there is every sign that the shift towards punitive justice and a security build-up is continuing unabated.[20] As the market in private security expands, the delivery of penal legislation speeds up, and the crime complex reproduces itself, we face the real possibility of being locked into new 'iron cage'. Max Weber long ago described how the capitalist rationality outlived the spiritual vocation that originally gave it impetus and meaning. The new culture of crime control, born of the fears and anxieties of the late twentieth century, could well continue long after its originating conditions have ceased to exist. After all, such arrangements spawn institutional investments and produce definite benefits, particularly for the social groups who are at the greatest distance from them. They entail a way of allocating the costs of crime—unjust, unequal, but feasible none the less. Penal solutions may be expensive, but the last twenty-five years have shown that their financial costs can be borne even where taxpayers are notoriously reluctant to meet the costs of other public expenditure.

The new crime-control arrangements do however involve certain social costs that are, over the long term, less easily accommodated. The hardening of social and racial divisions, the reinforcement of criminogenic processes; the alienation of large social groups; the discrediting of legal authority; a reduction of civic tolerance; a tendency towards authoritarianism—these are the kinds of outcomes that are liable to flow from a reliance upon penal mechanisms to maintain social order.[21] Mass imprisonment and private fortification may be feasible solutions to the problem of social order, but they are deeply unattractive ones. A large population of marginalized, criminalized poor may lack political power and command little public sympathy, but in aggregate terms they would have the negative capacity to make life unpleasant for everyone else. It is no accident that the dystopian images of the 1980s movie 'Blade Runner' have had such powerful cultural resonance.[22] Gated communities and the purchase of private security may be options for the rich, but they cannot offer a general social solution to the problems of crime and violence—not least because full private protection is beyond the means of most middle-class households who will continue to rely on the public police and state provision.[23] Mass imprisonment may continue to be affordable for 'law and order' states, a provider of much-needed jobs for rural communities, and a source of profit for commercial corrections companies. But over the long term it is probable that its conflict with the ideals of liberal democracy will become increasingly apparent, particularly where penal exclusion (and the disenfranchisement it entails) is so heavily focused upon racial minorities. A government that routinely sustains social order by means of mass exclusion begins to look like an apartheid state.

These social and political costs make it less likely that such policies will continue indefinitely. The recent reduction in crime rates has made the issue of crime control slightly less urgent, slightly less prominent in political discourse. The costs of mass imprisonment are beginning to be apparent. In the USA, there is currently a public debate prompted by evidence of faulty convictions in a high percentage of death penalty cases, and at least one governor has called a moratorium on executions pending the results of further inquiries. Some of the most conservative figures in crime policy are beginning to back away from the prospect of continued mass incarceration.[24] The policy is beginning to be the problem, not the solution. If these shifts continue, there is a prospect that current trends will be tempered and perhaps eventually reversed.

But the most fundamental lesson of the twentieth century is not a political one but a structural one. The problem of crime control in late modernity has vividly demonstrated the limits of the sovereign state. The denials and expressive gestures that have marked recent penal policy cannot disguise the fact that the state is seriously limited in its capacity to provide security for its citizens and deliver adequate levels of social control. The lesson of the late twentieth-century experience is that the nation state cannot any longer hope to govern by means of sovereign commands issued to obedient subjects, and this is true whether the concern is to deliver welfare, to secure economic prosperity, or to maintain 'law and order'. In the complex, differentiated world of late modernity, effective, legitimate government must devolve power and share the work of social control with local organizations and communities. It can no longer rely upon 'state knowledge', on unresponsive bureaucratic agencies, and upon universal solutions imposed from above. Social and political theorists have long argued that effective government in complex societies cannot rely upon centralized command and coercion.[25] Instead it must harness the governmental capacities of the organizations and associations of civil society, together with the local powers and knowledge that they contain. We are discovering—and not before time— that this is true of crime control as well.

Appendix

The four figures that follow are intended to provide a simple, 'at-a-glance' summary of crime and imprisonment trends over time in the USA and in England and Wales. The US and the UK data are not, however, strictly comparable. The US 'index offenses' include murder, robbery, rape, aggravated assault, burglary, motor vehicle theft, larceny, and arson. The English category of 'notifiable offences' is much more comprehensive, including all of those offence categories and other, less serious ones, such as simple assault and criminal damage. Similarly, the US prison population data includes only Federal and State prison inmates and thus excludes the inmates of local jails serving sentences of one year or less. The prison population data for England and Wales includes all imprisoned offenders.

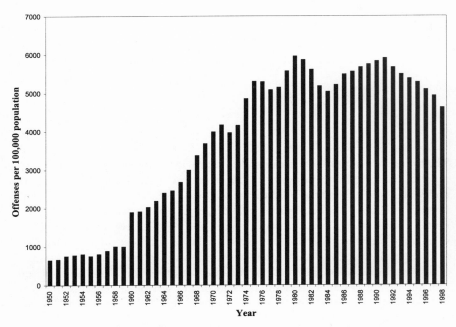

FIG. 1: Index offenses known to police per 100,000 population United States, 1950–1998

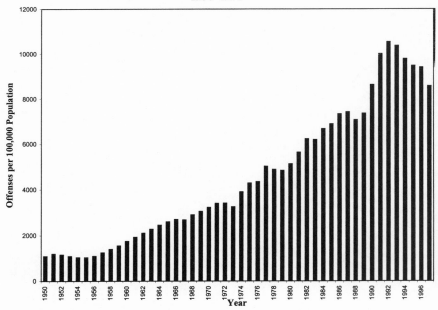

FIG. 2: Notifiable offenses recorded by the police per 100,000 population England and Wales, 1950–1997

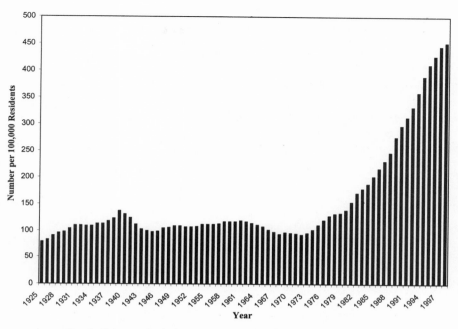

FIG. 3: Prison population per 100,000 residents United States, 1925–1998

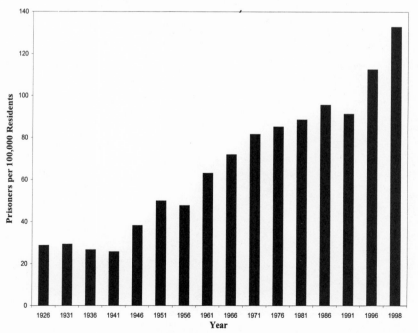

FIG. 4: Prison population per 100,000 residents England and Wales, 1926–1998

Notes

Chapter 1   A History of the Present

1 For representative statements of official US and UK policy in the 1960s, see Home Office, *The War Against Crime* (London: HMSO, 1964) and The President's Commission on Law Enforcement and Administration, *The Challenge of Crime in a Free Society Report* (Washington DC: US Government Printing Office, 1967). For a statement of American sentencing assumptions in that period, see The American Law Institute, *The Model Penal Code* (1962), sections 6 and 7 and H. Wechsler, 'Sentencing, corrections and the Model Penal Code', 109 *University of Pennsylvania Law Review* (1961 no 6), 465–93. For evidence of the rehabilitative ideologies of high-ranking US prison officials in the 1970s, see R. Berk and P. Rossi, *Prison Reform and State Elites* (Cambridge, MA: Ballinger, 1977). For discussions of British attitudes and expectations, see Lord Windlesham, *Responses to Crime, Vol 2: Penal Policy in the Making* (Oxford: Clarendon Press, 1993), chs. 2 and 3 and A. E. Bottoms and S. Stephenson, ' "What Went Wrong?" Criminal Justice Policy in England and Wales, 1945–70' in D. Downes (ed) *Unravelling Criminal Justice* (Basingstoke: Macmillan, 1992). As an indication of the difference between then and now, consider the following: In 1972, after a two-decade downward trend in executions, the US Supreme Court in *Furman v Georgia*, 408 US 238 (1972) held that capital punishment, as then administered, violated the Eighth Amendment's prohibition of 'cruel and unusual punishments.' Between 1920 and 1970 the US incarceration rate remained stable at approximately 110 state and federal prisoners per 100,000 US residents. So pronounced was this pattern that theories were developed to explain it—see A. Blumstein and J. Cohen, 'A Theory of the Stability of Punishment', *Journal of Criminology, Criminal Law and Police Science* (1973), 63(2), 198–207. In 1973 a US Commission recommended that 'no new institutions for adults should be built and existing institutions for juveniles should be closed' and concluded that 'the prison, the reformatory, and the jail have achieved only a shocking level of failure': National Advisory Commission on Criminal Justice Standards and Goals, *A National Strategy to Reduce Crime: Final Report* (Washington DC: Government Printing Office, 1973), 358 and 597.

2 This approach is, of course, inspired by the work of Michel Foucault. On the idea of a 'history of the present' see M. Foucault, *Discipline and Punish* (London, Allen Lane 1977), 31. For a discussion, see M. Dean, *Critical and Effective Histories* (London: Routledge, 1994) and J. Goldstein (ed), *Foucault and the Writing of History* (Oxford: Blackwell, 1994).

3 The idea of a social field—a differentiated domain of social practice—is taken from the work of Pierre Bourdieu. The best summary of Bourdieu's conception is provided by Loic Wacquant: 'in advanced societies, people do not face an undifferentiated social space. The various spheres of life, art, science, religion, the economy, politics, and so on, tend to form distinct microcosms endowed with their own rules, regularities and forms of authority—what Bourdieu calls fields. A field is, in the first instance,

a structured space of positions, *a force field* that imposes its specific determinations upon all those who enter it. Thus she who wants to succeed as a scientist has no choice but to acquire the minimal "scientific capital" required and to abide by the mores and regulations enforced by the scientific milieu of that time and place', L. Wacquant, 'Pierre Bourdieu' in R. Stones (ed), *Key Sociological Thinkers* (New York: New York University Press, 1998), 215–29 at 221.

4 For a discussion of how the various traditions of historical sociology have understood punishment and penal history, see D. Garland, *Punishment and Modern Society* (Oxford: Oxford University Press, 1990).

5 Some of the most salient differences for my purposes are these: In mid-year 1999, the US imprisonment rate, including jail inmates, was 682 per 100,000 residents, which was about six times that of the UK. See A. J. Beck, *Prison and Jail Inmates at Midyear 1999: Bureau of Justice Statistics Bulletin* (Washington DC: US Department of Justice, April 2000). A majority of American states sentence offenders to death—a practice that has been outlawed in Britain for more than thirty years. And while both nations have developed public–private crime prevention partnerships in recent years, in Britain the government has taken the main initiative in this, while in the USA, the private sector has played the leading part. Behind these contrasts, lie important differences in crime patterns, social relations, and political institutions. Although crime rates for most offences are not greatly different between the USA and the UK, homicide rates are more than six times higher in the former than the latter. Firearms were used in 41 per cent of US robberies, compared to 5 per cent of English robberies. See P. A. Langan and D. P. Farrington, *Crime and Justice in the United States and in England and Wales, 1981–1996* (Washington DC: US Department of Justice, Bureau of Justice Statistics, 1997) and F. E. Zimring and G. Hawkins, *Crime is Not the Problem* (New York: Oxford University Press, 1997). America's extraordinary level of lethal violence, the widespread availability of handguns, and its intensely pursued 'war on drugs' help explain some of the differences of size and intensity that mark off the US response to crime. So too do the deep racial divisions that still characterize American society, the more marked economic inequality of the US income distribution, and America's traditional of minimising welfare provision for the 'undeserving poor.' See A. Hacker, *Two Nations: Black and White, Separate, Hostile, Unequal* (New York: Ballantine Books, 1992); W. J. Wilson, *The Truly Disadvantaged* (Chicago: University of Chicago Press, 1987) and P. J. Cook and M. H. Moore, 'Gun Control', in J. Q. Wilson and J. Petersilia (eds), *Crime* (San Francisco: ICS Press, 1995). Important differences in the policy-making processes and political institutions of the two countries also have a major impact on crime-control policy. For example, the centralized administrative powers of the British Home Office have allowed it to develop policies—such as crime prevention partnerships—with greater speed and coherence than has been possible in the USA. And direct ballot voter initiatives and the election of criminal justice officials make populism a more pronounced feature of American policy making than it has been in the UK.

6 For a discussion of how different European nations have experienced late modernity, see G. Therborn, *European Modernity and Beyond* (London: Sage, 1995).

7 F. A. Allen, *The Decline of the Rehabilitative Ideal* (New Haven: Yale University Press, 1981).

8 P. Gendreau and R. Ross, 'Revivication of Rehabilitation: Evidence from the 1980s', *Justice Quarterly* (1987), vol 4, no 3, 349–407; J. McGuire, *What Works? Reducing*

Reoffending (New York: Wiley, 1995); G. Gaes, 'Correctional Treatment' in M. Tonry (ed), *The Handbook of Crime Punishment* (New York: Oxford University Press, 1998). For a flavour of how rehabilitation has been reworked into the contemporary political idiom, see Visiting Committee of the Correctional Association of New York *Rehabilitation that Works: Improving and Expanding Shock Incarceration in New York State* (New York: Correctional Association of New York, April 1996)

9 For an example of the impact on policy-makers, see the statement by John Croft, Head of the Home Office Research and Planning Unit, 'The reformation of the criminal . . . has been central to the English approach to criminal justice since the end of the nineteenth century . . . But penological research carried out over the last twenty years or so suggests that penal 'treatments' as we significantly describe them, do not have any reformative effect, whatever other effects they may have. The dilemma is that a considerable investment has been made in various measures and services, of which the most obvious examples are custodial institutions for young adult offenders and probation and after-care services in the community for a wide variety of offender. Are these services simply to be abandoned on the basis of the accumulated research evidence?' J. Croft, Research in Criminal Justice, *Home Office Research Study No. 44* (London: HMSO, 1978), 4. For evidence about changing public opinion in the USA, see G. Pettinico, 'Crime and Punishment: America Changes its Mind', *The Public Perspective*, September/October 1994. Pettinico presents time series polling data that suggests a marked shift in public attitudes from pro-rehabilitation to pro-punishment and incapacitation in the period 1971 to 1993.

10 See A. von Hirsch, *Censure and Sanctions* (Oxford: Clarendon Press, 1993) and A. Ashworth, *Sentencing and Criminal Justice*, 2nd edn (London: Weidenfeld & Nicolson, 1995).

11 See J. Pratt, 'The Return of the Wheelbarrow Men', *British Journal of Criminology* (2000), vol 40, no 1, 127–45; J. Pratt, 'Emotive and Ostentatious Punishments', *Punishment & Society* (2000), vol 2(4), 416–38; B. Hebenton and T. Thomas, 'Sexual Offenders in the Community: Reflections on Law, Community and Risk Management in the USA, England and Wales', *International Journal of Sociology of Law* (1996), vol 24, 427–43; P. Finn, *Sex Offender Community Notification*, Research in Action, February 1997, NIJ, US Department of Justice; A. S. Book, 'Shame on You: An Analysis of Modern Shame Punishment as an Alternative to Incarceration', *William and Mary Law Review* (1999), vol 40, 653–86; M. Tonry, 'Rethinking Unthinkable Punishment Policies in America,' *UCLA Law Review* (1999), vol 46, no 6, 1751–91; K. Barry, 'Chain Gangs' (1997), unpublished paper on file with the author. For an example of the reintroduction of corporal punishment, see the legislation introduced in Mississippi in 1999: Mississippi House Bill No 327 (1999 MS HB 327 (SN)). For a discussion of the English policy of 'austere prisons', see R. Sparks, 'Penal Austerity and Social Anxiety', in L. Wacquant (ed), *From Social State to Penal State* (New York: Oxford University Press, forthcoming).

12 On punitive language, see A. E. Bottoms, 'The Philosophy and Politics of Punishment and Sentencing', in C. Clark and R. Morgan (eds), *The Politics of Sentencing Reform* (Oxford: Clarendon Press, 1995); D. Lewis, *Hidden Agendas: Politics, Law and Disorder* (London: Hamish Hamilton, 1997); and *Federal Sentencing Reporter*, March/April 1998, vol 10, no 5, Special Issue on 'Sentencing in England: The Rise of Populist Punishment'. On the new retributivism in juvenile justice see S. Singer, *Recriminalizing Delinquency* (Cambridge: Cambridge University Press, 1996) and

D. Bishop, 'Juvenile Offenders in the Criminal Justice System', *Crime & Justice*, vol 27 (forthcoming). For an example of official efforts to represent community penalties as punishments, see Home Office, *Punishment, Custody and the Community* (London: HMSO, 1988) and the announcement by Home Office Minister Paul Boateng of 1 December 1999 of his plan to rename the Probation Service as the 'Community Punishment and Rehabilitation Service'.

13 See R. A. Duff, 'Penal Communications: Recent Work in the Philosophy of Punishment', M. Tonry (ed), *Crime and Justice, An Annual Review of Research*, 20 (1995)

14 On restorative justice in the US context, see L. Kurki, 'Restorative and Community Justice in the United States', M. Tonry (ed), *Crime and Justice*, vol 27 (2000). More generally, see J. Braithwaite, 'Restorative Justice', in M.Tonry (ed), *The Handbook of Crime and Punishment* (New York: Oxford University Press, 1998), 323–44. The Labour government in Britain describes its introduction of reparation orders in the Crime and Disorder Act, 1998 as an example of restorative justice. See J. Quin, Minister of State at the Home Office, 'The Labour Government's New Approach to Criminal Justice', *Policy Studies*, vol 19, no 3/4 (December 1998), 188. After describing reparation orders in this way, Quin adds, 'We are . . . very conscious that restorative justice, while having a very useful part to play, needs to be used in a way that works with, and not against, the interests of the victim.'

15 A Report in *American Demographics* makes the historical contrast: 'Crime concern is broad-based, suggesting that law and order will continue to be foremost in people's minds. Crime is the number-one problem most often cited by people of virtually all ages and household incomes. That's a very different picture than the early 1970s, when crime was much more likely to be seen as a problem by older Americans, Republicans, the poor, and people in the Northeast, the South and big cities', Roper Reports Editors, 'The Big Picture: Crime Fears', *American Demographics* (July 1997).

16 The British Home Office's *British Crime Survey* and the US Department of Justice's *Bureau of Justice Statistics Sourcebook*, regularly report findings on public fear of crime. For discussions, see M. Hough, *Anxiety About Crime: Findings From the 1994 British Crime Survey* (1995), London: Home Office; C. Hale, 'Fear of Crime: a Review of the Literature', *International Review of Victimology* (1996), vol 4, 79–150. When, in 1992, a UK Commission on Social Justice presented its updated version of the Beveridge Report (the document that founded the post-war British welfare state) the Commissioners argued that 'fear of crime' should be added to the list of giant evils that social policy had to confront.

17 See Julian Roberts, 'Public Opinion, Crime and Criminal Justice', *Crime and Justice*, vol 16 (1992); T. J. Flanagan and D. R. Longmire (eds), *Americans View Crime and Justice* (Thousand Oaks, CA: Sage, 1996); M. Hough and J. Roberts, *Attitudes to Punishment: Findings from the 1996 British Crime Survey* (London: Home Office, 1998).

18 See F. E. Zimring, 'The New Politics of Criminal Justice', in D. Garland (ed), *Mass Imprisonment in the USA* (London: Sage, forthcoming).

19 Many victims groups avoid becoming involved with issues of punishment, preferring to focus upon the demand for victims' rights, compensation, support, information, etc. This is true, for example of the Britain's National Association of Victim Support Schemes (now called Victim Support). See P. Rock, *Helping Victims of Crime*

(Oxford: Clarendon Press, 1990). In the USA, there has been a closer association between the victims' rights movement and the politics of 'law and order', but even there, political representations of victims' needs are often at odds with the declared concerns of actual victims: see R. Elias, *Victims Still: The Political Manipulation of Crime Victims* (Thousand Oaks: Sage, 1993). For evidence that victims of crime are not especially punitive in their attitude to offenders, see J. Roberts, 'Public Opinion, Crime and Criminal Justice', *Crime and Justice*, vol 16 (1992) and M. Hough and D. Moxon, 'Dealing with Offenders: Popular Opinion and the View of Victims', *Howard Journal* (1985), vol 24, 160–75. Restorative justice initiatives embody a view of the relationship of offender and victim that contrasts with the dominant zero-sum vision I have described.

20 See for example, the Presidents Task Force on Victims of Crime, *Final Report* (Washington DC: Government Printing Office, 1982). The opening lines of the Report are: 'Something insidious has happened in America: crime has made victims of us all.' President Reagan echoed this theme in his 1985 State of the Union address when he stated, 'Of all the changes in the past 20 years, none has more threatened our sense of national well-being than the explosion of violent crime. One does not have to be attacked to be a victim. The woman who must run to her car after shopping at night is a victim. The couple draping their door with locks and chains are victims: as is the tired, decent cleaning woman who can't ride the subway home without being afraid.' See too the British Labour Party policy statement of 1995 entitled *Everyone's a Victim* (London: Central Office, 28 March 1995). Outlining New Labour's strategy to fight crime, party spokesman (and later Home Secretary) Jack Straw said, 'Not long ago crime was seen as something that happened to someone else. Now, particularly since the doubling in recorded crime over the last decades and a half, crime is something that affects us all', J. Straw, 'The Criminal Justice Crisis', *Criminal Justice Matters*, no 26, Winter 96/97. US Attorney General Janet Reno told a victims' rights conference in 12 August 1996, 'I draw the most strength from the victims for they represent America to me', quoted in B. Shapiro, 'Victims & Vengeance: Why the Victims' Rights Amendment is a Bad Idea', *The Nation* (10 Feb. 1997). More than half the American states now have amended their state constitutions to include victim's rights language.

21 For an example of how the exclusionary rule has recently been limited in the USA, see *Pennsylvania Board of Probation & Parole v. Scott* 524 US 357, which found that the federal exclusionary rule does not bar the introduction at parole hearings of evidence seized in violation of parolees' Fourth Amendment rights. In England and Wales, a defendant's 'right to silence' was greatly restricted by the *Criminal Justice and Public Order Act 1994*, sections 34–6. For a discussion, see A. F. Jennings, 'More resounding silence', in *New Law Journal* (1999), vol 149, no 6899, 1180.

22 F. E. Zimring, 'Populism, Democratic Government, and the Decline of Expert Authority: Some Reflections on "Three Strikes" in California', *Pacific Law Journal* 28 (Fall 1996), 243–56. S. Pillsbury, 'Why are we Ignored? The Peculiar Place of Experts in the Current Debate About Crime and Justice', *Criminal Law Bulletin*, July/August 1995, 305–36. A. K. Bottomley, *Crime and Penal Politics: The Criminologists' Dilemma* (England: Hull University Press, 1989). The Labour government's recent promise of an 'evidence-led' crime policy marks a recognition of this trend and indicates an intention to move away from it—or at least a wish to characterize itself, in Bill Clinton's terms, as 'smart' as well as 'tough'.

23 The crime policy aspects of John Major's 'back to basics' programme are discussed in I. Dunbar and A. Langdon, *Tough Justice* (London, Blackstone, 1998), at p. 118. The Home Secretary of that time declared, 'We should have no truck with trendy theories that try to explain away crime by blaming socio-economic factors. Criminals . . . should be held to account for their actions and punished accordingly.' See too the comments of Charles Murray, *Sunday Times*, 20 January 1997 and Jack Straw, *The Times*, 8 April 1998. For examples of this in US penal politics, see K. Beckett, *Making Crime Pay* (New York: Oxford University Press, 1997), 49.

24 For an overview of these developments in the USA, see M. Tonry, *Sentencing Matters* (New York: Oxford University Press, 1996). On similar, though less pronounced, trends in the UK, see R. Hood and S. Shute, 'Protecting the Public: Automatic Life Sentences, Parole and High Risk Offenders', *Criminal Law Review*, November 1996, 788–800.

25 For a discussion of UK government efforts to reduce the prison population, see A. E. Bottoms, 'Limiting Prison Use: Experience in England and Wales', *Howard Journal* (1987), vol 26, no 3, 177–202. On the US experience, see N. Morris and M. Tonry, *Between Prison and Probation* (New York: Oxford University Press, 1990). On the growth of the US prison population after 1973, see A. Blumstein and A. Beck, 'Population Growth in US Prisons 1980–1996', in M. Tonry and J. Petersilia (eds), *Prisons* (Chicago: University of Chicago Press, 1999). On the recent UK prison policy, see I. Dunbar and A. Langdon, *Tough Justice* (London: Blackstone, 1998). For prison rates in the USA and in England and Wales, see Appendix, Figures 3 and 4.

26 For data on the US prison population increase, see T. Caplow and J. Simon, 'Understanding Prison Policy and Population Trends' in M. Tonry and J. Petersilia (eds), *Prisons, Crime and Justice*, vol 26 (Chicago: University of Chicago Press, 1999), 63. For an analysis of the ratio of prison sentences to crime committed, and the recent reversal of this first in the USA, and later in England and Wales, see P. A. Langan and D. P. Farrington, *Crime and Justice in the United States and in England and Wales, 1981–1996 Bureau of Justice Statistics Executive Summary* (Washington DC: US Department of Justice, 1997). The Uniform Crime Reports also shows recorded rates of property crime in the USA declining steadily from 1982 onwards. After dipping and then rising sharply again in the 1980s, recorded rates of violent crime declined steadily after 1992.

27 In the UK, the idea that 'prison works' remains controversial, having been introduced by Home Secretary Michael Howard in the early 1990s in sharp opposition to the position adopted by his predecessors that 'imprisonment is an expensive way of making bad people worse'. For discussions of this policy reversal, see E. Baker, 'From "Making Bad People Worse" to "Prison Works": Sentencing Policy in England and Wales in the 1990s', *Criminal Law Forum* (1996), vol 7, no 3, 639–71; Lord Windlesham, *Responses to Crime, vol 3: Legislating with the Tide* (Oxford: Oxford University Press, 1996); and I. Dunbar and A. Langdon, *Tough Justice: Sentencing and Penal Policies in the 1990s* (London: Blackstone, 1998). But the value of imprisonment as a method of retribution and containment is now more firmly established in political debate than it was twenty years ago. The Labour Government's approach to this issue is deliberately ambiguous: see the speech by Home Secretary Jack Straw, *Making Prisons Work,* Prison Reform Trust Annual Lecture, December 1998. As Straw put it on another occasion, 'reducing the prison population cannot be more important than protecting the public.' J. Straw, *Open Letter to Penal Affairs*

Consortium (August 1997). In the USA, politicians express little doubt about the efficacy of imprisonment as a response to crime..

28 For an overview, see P. Rock (ed), *The History of Criminology* (Aldershot: Dartmouth, 1994), part IV.

29 For leading examples see T. Hirschi, *Causes of Delinquency* (Berkeley: University of California Press, 1969); M. Gottfredson and T. Hirschi, *A General Theory of Crime* (Stanford, CA: Stanford University Press); J. Q. Wilson, *Thinking About Crime* (1983); C. Tittle, *Control Balance: Towards a General Theory of Deviance* (Boulder CO: Westview Press, 1995); R. V. Clarke, 'Situational Crime Prevention: Its Theoretical Basis and Practical Scope', in M. Tonry and N. Morris (eds), *Crime and Justice: An Annual Review of Research*, vol 4 (1983), 225–56. For a more politicized version, see W. Bennett, J. J. DiIulio Jr., and J. P. Walters, *Body Count: Moral Poverty and How to Win America's War Against Crime and Drugs* (New York: Simon & Schuster, 1996).

30 On routine activity, see L. E. Cohen and M. Felson, 'Social Change and Crime Rate Trends: A Routine Activity Approach', in *American Sociological Review* (1979) vol 44, no 4, 588–608 and M. Felson, *Crime and Everyday Life*, 2nd edn (Thousand Oaks, CA: Pine Forge Press, 1998). On lifestyle and victimization, see M. Hindelang, M. Gottfredson, and J. Garafalo, *Victims of Personal Crime* (Cambridge, MA: Ballinger, 1978). M. Maxfield, 'Lifestyle and Routine Activities Theories of Crime: Empirical Studies of Victimization, Delinquency and Offender Decision-Making', *Journal of Quantitative Criminology* (1987), vol 3, no 4, 275–82. On rational choice, see R. V. Clarke and D. Cornish (eds) *The Reasoning Criminal: Rational Choice Perspectives on Offending* (New York: Springer-Verlag, 1986).

31 On UK developments, see A. Crawford, *The Local Governance of Crime* (Oxford: Oxford University Press, 1997) and Crawford *Crime Prevention and Community Safety* (London: Longman, 1998). On US developments, see R. C. Ellickson, 'Controlling Chronic Misconduct in City Spaces: Of Panhandlers, Skid Rows, and Public-Space Zoning', *Yale Law Journal* (1996), 105: 1165; J. R. Pack, 'BIDs, DIDs, SIDs, SADs: Private Governments in Urban America' *The Brookings Review*, Fall 1992, 18–21. T. M. Seamon, 'Private Forces for Public Good' *Security Management*, September 1995, 92–7. For a dystopian critique, see M. Davis, 'Beyond Blade Runner: Urban Control—the Ecology of Fear', *Open Magazine Pamphlet Series #23* (1992), Open Magazine: Open Media.

32 For examples, see D. Garland, 'Limits of the Sovereign State', *British Journal of Criminology* (1996), vol 36, no 4 and M. H. Moore, 'Public Health and Criminal Justice Approaches to Prevention', in M. Tonry and D. P. Farrington (eds), *Building a Safer Society* (Chicago: University of Chicago Press, 1995), 237–62.

33 On private policing and the security industry, see T. Jones and T. Newburn, *Private Security and Public Policing* (Oxford: Clarendon Press, 1998). L Johnston, *The Rebirth of Private Policing* (London: Routledge, 1992) and C. Shearing, 'The Relation Between Public and Private Policing', in M. Tonry and N. Morris (eds), *Modern Policing* (Chicago: University of Chicago Press, 1992). On the development of private prisons, see R. Harding, 'Private Prisons', in M. Tonry (ed), *The Handbook of Crime and Punishment* (New York: Oxford University Press, 1998).

34 See J. W. Raine and M. J. Willson, *Managing Criminal Justice* (London: Harvester Wheatsheaf, 1993); C. Jones, 'Auditing Criminal Justice', *British Journal of Criminology* (1993), vol 33, no 2, 187–202; A. J. Fowles, 'Monitoring Expenditure on

the Criminal Justice System: The Search for Control', *The Howard Journal* (1990), vol 29, no 2, 82–100; N. Lacey, 'Government as Manager, Citizen as Consumer: The Case of the Criminal Justice Act of 1991', *The Modern Law Review* (1994), 57: 534–54; S. Walker, *Taming the System* (New York: Oxford University Press, 1993); W. Heydebrand and C. Seron, *Rationalizing Justice* (Albany: SUNY Press, 1990).

35   The Willie Horton case in the USA is perhaps the best-known example of this, see D. C. Anderson, *Crime and the Politics of Hysteria* (New York: Times Books, 1995). In the UK, recurring scandals about 'bail bandits' and prison escapes produced the same kind of reaction. The phenomenon of 'zero-tolerance' policing—the very name of which indicates the more relaxed policies against which it reacts—is at once a political and an organizational backlash against policies that were widely adopted in the 1970s and 1980s in the face of high crime rates. The new popularity of mandatory sentences and more restrictive rules for bail, repeat cautioning, and early release are reactive in the same way.

36   For a discussion, see A. E. Bottoms and R. H. Preston, *The Coming Penal Crisis* (Edinburgh: Scottish Academic Press, 1981). In 1980 the British Home Office Permanent Secretary told a Department seminar that 'on a gloomy view, we seem to be locked into negative forces and negative results. The police and prison service require more and more men and more and more money. But crime increases steadily and becomes nastier and the prison population rises'. Quoted in P. Rock, 'The Organization of a Home Office Initiative', *European Journal of Crime, Criminal Law and Criminal Justice* (1994), 2(2), 142. See also A. E. Bottoms and S. Stevenson, ' "What Went Wrong?": Criminal Justice Policy in England and Wales, 1945–70', in D. Downes (ed), *Unravelling Criminal Justice* (London: Routledge, 1992). The former research director of the LEAA, Gerald Chaplan, offered an equally defeatist analysis of American crime policy in 1981: 'First, we have more crime than any other place in the world, more this year than last, and much, much more than we had in 1964 when Senator Goldwater became the first presidential candidate to argue that the Federal government must do something about crime in the streets. Second, most of the increase occurred in the midst of high employment and unprecedented affluence and during a period when the Federal government launched a new, multi-billion dollar anti-crime program . . . [T]oday, virtually no one—scholars, practitioners and politicians alike—dares to advance a program which promises to reduce crime substantially in the near future', quoted in J. Rosch, 'Crime as an issue in American Politics', in E. S. Fairchild and V. J. Webb (eds), *The Politics of Crime and Criminal Justice* (New York: Sage 1985), 19

37   M. Foucault, 'Structuralism and Post-Structuralism: An Interview with Michel Foucault' (with G. Raulet), in *Telos*, no 55, Spring 1983, 195–211.

38   On the idea of a 'new penology', see M. Feeley and J. Simon, 'The New Penology: Notes on the emerging strategy of corrections and its implications', *Criminology* (1992), vol 30, no 4, 449–74. For a discussion of modernism and postmodernism in penality, see D. Garland, 'Penal Modernism and Postmodernism', in T. Blomberg and S. Cohen (eds), *Punishment and Social Control* (New York: Aldine de Gruyter, 1995).

39   See S. Hall *et al.*, *Policing the Crisis: Mugging, the State and Law and Order* (London: MacMillan, 1978); F. A. Allen, *The Decline of the Rehabilitative Ideal* (New Haven: Yale University Press, 1981); A. E. Bottoms, 'Neglected Features of Contemporary Penal Systems', in D. Garland and P. Young (eds), *The Power to Punish* (Aldershot: Gower, 1983) and Bottoms, 'The Philosophy and Politics of Punishment and

Sentencing', in C. Clark and R. Morgan (eds), *The Politics of Sentencing Reform* (Oxford: Clarendon Press, 1995); S. Cohen, *Visions of Social Control* (Oxford: Polity Press, 1985); M. Feeley and J. Simon, 'The New Penology: Notes on the emerging strategy of corrections and its implications', *Criminology* (1992), vol 39, no 4, 449–74; J. Simon and M. Feeley, 'True Crime: The New Penology and the Public Discourse on Crime', in T. Blomberg and S. Cohen (eds), *Punishment and Social Control* (New York: Aldine de Gruyter, 1995); P. O'Malley, 'Post-Keynesian Policing', *Economy and Society* (1996), 25(2), 137–55; 'Risk, Power, and Crime Prevention', *Economy and Society* (1992), 21, 252–75, 'Volatile and Contradictory Punishment', *Theoretical Criminology* (1999), 3(2), 175–96; A. Crawford, *The Local Governance of Crime* (Oxford: Oxford University Press, 1997); E. Girling, I. Loader, and J. R.Sparks, *Crime and Social Order in Middle England* (London: Routledge, 2000); S. Scheingold, *The Politics of Street Crime* (Philadelphia: Temple University Press, 1991), 'Politics, Public Policy, and Street Crime' *ANNALS, AAPSS,* May 1995, and 'Constructing the New Political Criminology: Power, Authority and the Post-Liberal State', in *Law and Social Inquiry* (forthcoming). The present book has emerged out my engagement with these works and others like them.

40 On the relationship between actors' choices and the social fields in which they exercise them, as mediated by the actor's *habitus*, see P. Bourdieu, 'Social space and symbolic power', *Sociological Theory*, 7(1), June 1989. For a different statement of this fundamental sociological issue, see A. Giddens, *The Constitution of Society* (Oxford: Policy Press, 1984).

41 The term 'working social categories' is taken from P. Hirst, 'The Concept of Punishment', in R. A. Duff and D. Garland (eds), *A Reader on Punishment* (Oxford: Oxford University Press, 1994).

Chapter 2   Modern Criminal Justice

1 For analyses of the formation of the penal-welfare state in Britain, see D. Garland, *Punishment and Welfare: A History of Penal Strategies* (Aldershot: Gower, 1985); M. Wiener, *Reconstructing the Criminal* (Cambridge: Cambridge University Press, 1990); L. Radzinowicz and R. Hood, *A History of the English Criminal Law and its Administration*, vol 5 (Oxford: Clarendon Press, 1990). On the USA, see D. Rothman, *Conscience and Convenience* (Boston: Little Brown, 1980). Most of the key correctionalist ideas were already being discussed by reformatory supervisors in 1871: see the 'Statement of Principles' in National Congress on Penitentiary and Reformatory Discipline, *Transactions of the National Congress on Penitentiary and Reformatory Discipline 1871* (Albany NY: Weed Parsons, 1871), 541–7.

2 In the 1949 US Supreme Court case of *Williams v. People of State of New York,* 337 US 241, 69 S.Ct.1079, Justice Black, speaking for the majority, referred to the 'prevalent modern philosophy of penology that the punishment should fit the offender and not merely the crime' and stated further that 'Retribution is no longer the dominant objective of the criminal law. Reformation and rehabilitation have become important goals of criminal jurisprudence.' See also the American Friends Service Committee, *Struggle for Justice* (New York: Hill and Wang, 1971), 37: 'The individualized treatment model . . . has, for nearly a century been the ideological spring from which almost all actual or proposed reform in criminal justice has been derived. It would be hard to exaggerate the power of this idea or the extent of its influence', M. Tonry,

Sentencing Matters (New York: Oxford University Press, 1996) notes that between 1930 and the mid-1970s, American sentencing law was predominantly based upon the indeterminate sentencing model. In 1973 high ranking correctional personnel in several states said that they regarded rehabilitation of offenders to be a goal of the highest priority: see R. A. Berk and P. Rossi, *Prison Reform and State Elites* (Cambridge MA: Ballinger, 1977). For a survey of 'liberal opinion' on crime between 1945 and 1975, see R. Bayer, 'Crime, Punishment and the Decline of Liberal Optimism' in *Crime and Delinquency* (April 1981), 169–90. For evidence of the UK commitment to this framework, Scottish Home Department, *The Scottish Borstal System* (Edinburgh: HMSO, 1947); Home Office, *Prisons and Borstals: England and Wales* (London: Home Office, 1950); Home Office, *Penal Practice in a Changing Society* (London: HMSO, 1959).

3 See L. Blom-Cooper, *Progress in Penal Reform* (Oxford: Oxford University Press, 1974).

4 On early modern state-formation, see C. Tilly (ed), *The Formation of National States in Western Europe* (Princeton: Princeton University Press, 1975) and N. Elias, *The Civilizing Process*, vol 2 (Oxford: Blackwell, 2000). On the criminal justice institutions of colonial America, see E. Monkkonen (ed) , *Crime and Justice in American History* (Westport: Meckler, 1991)

5 On the emergence of the criminal justice state in Britain, see D. Philips, ' "A New Engine of Power and Authority": The Institutionalization of Law-Enforcement in England, 1780–1830', in V. A. C. Gatrell *et al.* (eds), *Crime and the Law: The Social History of Crime in Western Europe Since 1500* (London: Europa Publications, 1980), and P. Rock, 'Introduction' to P. Rock (ed), *History of Criminology* (Aldershot: Dartmouth, 1996). On the American history, see L. Friedman, *Crime and Punishment in American History* (New York: Basic Books, 1993) and S. Walker, *Popular Justice: A History of American Criminal Justice*, 2nd edn (New York: Oxford University Press, 1998). On the development of policing, see D. H. Bayley, 'The Police and Political Development in Europe', in C. Tilly (ed), *The Formation of National States* (Princeton: Princeton University Press, 1975) and *Patterns of Policing* (New Brunswick, NJ: Rutgers University Press, 1985). For a discussion of contemporary police organization in Britain and America and their differences, see P. Manning, *Police Work: The Social Organization of Policing*, 2nd edn (Prospect Heights, Il:, Waveland Press, 1997).

6 T. Hobbes, *Leviathan* (London: J. M. Dent. originally 1651).

7 P. Colquhoun, *Treatise on the Police of the Metropolis explaining the various Crimes and Misdemeanours which are at present felt as a pressure upon the Community, and suggesting Remedies for their Prevention, by a Magistrate*, 2nd edn (London: H. Fry for C. Dilly, 1796). On the early modern idea of 'police' see M. Foucault, 'Governmentality', in G. Burchell *et al.* (eds), *The Foucault Effect: Studies in Governmentality* (London: Harvester Wheatsheaf, 1991); P. Pasquino, 'Theatrum Politicum: The Genealogy of Capital—Police and the State of Prosperity', in G. Burchell *et al.* (eds). *The Foucault Effect*; F.-L. Knemeyer, 'Polizei', *Economy and Society*, 9:2, 172–96 and G. Oestreich, *Neostoicism and the Early Modern State* (Cambridge: Cambridge University Press. 1982). For a discussion of British writing in this tradition, see L. Radzinowicz, *A History of the English Criminal Law and its Administration*, vol 3 (London: Stevens, 1956, 417–23.

8 See D. Garland, 'The Limits of the Sovereign State', *British Journal of Criminology*, vol 34, no 4, 1996 and J. L. McMullan, 'The Arresting Eye: Discourse, Surveillance

and Disciplinary Administration in Early English Police Thinking', in *Social & Legal Studies*, 7: 97–128.

9 See T. A. Critchley, *A History of Police in England and Wales*, 2nd edn (London: Constable, 1978) and C. Reith, *British Police and the Democratic Ideal* (Oxford: Oxford University Press, 1943). The original charter of Peel's Metropolitan Police in 1829 charged them with preventing crime, maintaining public tranquillity, and only finally, apprehending criminals. But this preventive function came be interpreted as the deterrent effect of a police presence ('the scarecrow function'), and the apprehension of offenders eventually took operational priority. See D. Gilling, 'Crime Prevention Discourses and the Multi-Agency Approach', *International Journal of the Sociology of Law* (1993), vol 21, 145–57. As for urban police in the USA, Eric Monkkonen desribes their original nineteenth-century function as being 'civil servants of last resort, called on to run soup kitchens, inspect boilers, standardize weights and measures, and recover lost children. Not until the end of the nineteenth century did they begin to focus more narrowly on crime control; in doing so they diminished varied range of social services, which included the overnight housing of thousands of homeless people.' E. H. Monkkonen, 'History of Urban Police', in *Crime and Justice: A Review of Research*, vol 15 (Chicago: University of Chicago Press, 1992). The tension between general 'order maintenance' functions and narrower 'crime control' is one that continues to affect modern policing. Sociological researchers have repeatedly discovered that police conceive of themselves in terms of the latter role but spend most of their time in the former. See D. Bayley, *Police for the Future* (New York: Oxford University Press, 1994), ch. 2 and R. Reiner, *The Politics of the Police*, 2nd edn (Hemel Hemstead: Harvester Wheatsheaf, 1995).

10 See C. Emsley, 'The History of Crime and Crime Control Institutions', in M. Maguire *et al.* (eds), *The Oxford Handbook of Criminology*, 2nd edn (Oxford: Oxford University Press, 1997).

11 On the importance of informal social control in reducing crime and violence in the USA, see R. Lane, *Murder in America: A History* (Columbus: Ohio State University Press, 1997) and in Britain see M. Clarke, 'Citizenship, Community and the Management of Crime', *British Journal of Criminology*, 1987, 27 (4), 384–400. For a criminological discussion, see J. Q. Wilson, 'Crime and American Culture', in his *Thinking About Crime*, 2nd edn (New York: Vintage, 1983).

12 Of course, informal crime control and private justice continued to play a part in the production of 'law and order' throughout the nineteenth and much of the twentieth centuries. This is particularly true of the USA, some of which was still a frontier society for much of this period, see J. P. Reid, *Policing the Elephant: Crime, Punishment and Social Behavior on the Overland Trail* (San Marino, CA: Huntington Library, 1997). And then there was lynching—an institution that killed almost 3,000 people (mostly African Americans) between 1882 and 1930. See S. E. Tolney and E. M. Beck, *A Festival of Violence: An Analysis of Southern Lynchings, 1882–1930* (Urbana: University of Illinois Press, 1995). But for much of the twentieth century, the balance between private and public crime control did shift towards the latter, see L. Johnston, *The Rebirth of Private Policing* (London: Routledge, 1992). Citing US and UK sources, Engstad and Evans note the 'gradual shifting of responsibility for crime control (and the 'handling' of a vast array of social problems) from citizens to the police . . . The police have generally welcomed the growth of their sphere of responsibility and concomitant increase in their powers . . . whether acquired by default, though

active lobbying or through legislative acts . . . Correspondingly, citizens appear to have been willing to relinquish responsibility for crime control', P. Engstad and J. L. Evans, 'Responsibility, competence and police effectiveness in crime control', in R. V. Clarke and M. Hough (eds), *The Effectiveness of Policing* (Aldershot: Gower, 1980).

13 As Robert Reiner has argued, 'the rise of *the* police—a single professional organisation for handling the policing function of regulation and surveillance, with the state's monopoly of legitimate force as its ultimate resource—was itself, a paradigm of the modern. It was predicated upon the project of organising society around a central, cohesive, notion of order', R. Reiner, 'Policing a Postmodern Society', *The Modern Law Review*, vol 55, no 6, November 1992.

14 See V. A. C. Gatrell, 'Crime, Authority and the Policeman-State' in F. M. L. Thompson (ed), *Cambridge Social History of Britain, 1750–1950, Vol 3: Social Agencies and Institutions* (Cambridge: Cambridge University Press, 1992). On the decline in crime and violence in late nineteenth-century Britain, see V. A. C. Gatrell, 'The Decline of Theft and Violence in Victorian and Edwardian England', in V. A. C. Gatrell *et al.* (eds), *Crime and the Law: The Social History of Crime in Western Europe Since 1500* (London: Europa 1980) and M. Clarke, 'Citizenship, Community and the Management of Crime'; M. Wiener, *Reconstructing the Criminal: Culture, Law and Policy in England, 1830–1914* (Cambridge: Cambridge University Press, 1990) and L. Radzinowicz and R. Hood, *A History of the English Criminal Law and its Administration*, vol 5 (Oxford: Clarendon Press, 1990). On the USA, see R. Lane, 'Urban Police and Crime in Nineteenth Century America', in *Crime and Justice: An Annual Review of Research*, vol 2 (1980), id. *Murder in America: A History*, and T. R. Gurr, 'Historical Trends in Violent Crime: Europe and the United States', in T. R. Gurr (ed), *Violence in America, Vol 1: The History of Crime* (Beverley Hills, CA: Sage, 1989).

15 For historical evidence about increasing levels of informal social control in the Victorian period, see R. Lane, *Murder in America* (Columbus: Ohio State University Press, 1997), M. Clarke, 'Citizenship, Community and the Management of Crime' and J. Q. Wilson, 'Crime and the American Character'. For an analysis of broad trends in social control, see F. Fukuyama, *The Great Disruption: Human Nature and the Reconstitution of Social Order* (New York: The Free Press, 1999).

16 Politicians probably share this sense that the political fortunes of penal-welfare measures depend upon a perception that crime is under control. See A. E. Bottoms and S. Stevenson, '"What Went Wrong?": Criminal Justice Policy in England and Wales, 1945–1970', in D. Downes (ed), *Unravelling Criminal Justice* (Basingstoke: MacMillan, 1992). They quote British Home Secretary R. A. Butler's memorandum commenting on the draft of *Penal Practice in a Changing Society*, a landmark document in the rise of penal-welfarism: '[The final drafts] must have some reference to the present success of the police . . . I am in doubts as to whether the idealistic portions of this document designed to chart the way into the future will appear in their proper setting unless some comfort is given at some stage in the [first] paragraphs about the efficiency of the police force and the present operation of the criminal law' (p. 12).

17 On the importance of informal social control and community action in containing crime rates prior to the 1950s, see M. Clarke, 'Citizenship, Community and the Management of Crime'; and L. Johnson, *The Rebirth of Private Policing*. For ethnographic descriptions of these community controls, see N. Elias and J. Scotson, *The*

Established and the Outsiders (London: Cass, 1965). On the history of interactions between the police and working class communities in Britain in the first half of the twentieth century, see P. Cohen, 'Policing the Working Class City', in R. Fine *et al.* (eds), *Capitalism and the Rule of Law* (London: Hutchinson, 1979).

18 Scottish Conservative Party, *Tomorrow Scotland: Better with the Conservatives* (Edinburgh: Scottish Conservative and Unionist Party Central Office, 1970).

19 A good example of the modern reliance upon state agencies rather than social processes is to be found in the American Presidents Crime Commission Report, a central document of crime policy in the penal-welfare period. In his retrospective analysis of the Report, Mark Moore points to the 'fundamentally reactive' view of crime control that was implicit in the Report. '[I]n focusing attention on the publicly supported agencies of the criminal justice system, it necessarily de-emphasized the role that private individuals and institutions of civil society—families, community groups, churches, merchant associations—play in controlling crime, both by themselves and as adjuncts to the criminal justice system. The [Report] did not emphasize the central role played by victims and witnesses in activating and focusing the attention of criminal justice agencies on particular crimes, nor did it point to the important role played by citizens who make individual and collective efforts to guard their own property and intervene with fellow citizens who are behaving badly. Similarly the Crime Commission did not draw attention to the role that local merchants play in seeking to enforce orderly conditions on the streets that front their stores or in providing jobs to neighborhood kids. It did not emphasize the role of church groups in giving support to single parents struggling to supervise and raise their children. Such private efforts were viewed as beyond the boundaries of criminal justice', M. H. Moore, 'The Legitimation of Criminal Justice Policies and Practices' *Perspectives on Crime and Justice, 1996–97 Lecture Series* (Washington DC: NIJ, 1997).

20 On this use of 'high modernism' see J. C. Scott, *Seeing Like a State* (New Haven: Yale University Press, 1998). According to Scott, high modernism 'is best conceived as a strong, one might even say muscle-bound, version of the self-confidence about scientific and technical progress, the expansion of production, the growing satisfaction of human needs, the mastery of nature (including human nature) and, above all, the rational design of social order commensurate with the scientific understanding of natural laws . . . There was, to put it mildly, an elective affinity between high modernism and the interests of many state officials' (pp. 4–5). Scott's discussion relies in part upon D. Harvey, *The Condition of Post-Modernity: An Inquiry into the Origins of Social Change* (Oxford: Basil Blackwell, 1989), 35. On 'government knowledge' see D. Yergin and J. Stanislaw, *The Commanding Heights*. The authors contrast 'government knowledge—the collective intelligence of decision makers at the center' to 'market knowledge—the dispersed intelligence of private decision makers and consumers in the marketplace' (p. 11).

21 See D. Garland, *Punishment and Welfare*, 242. Had it not been for the increased numbers of offenders processed, the prison population in both countries would have steadily declined for much of the twentieth century. The shift of emphasis from treatment in custody to community corrections is clearly evident in the Presidents Commission on Law Enforcement and the Administration of Justice, *The Challenge of Crime in a Free Society* (Washington DC: Government Printing Office, 1967). The US Law Enforcement Administration Agency, created by the Omnibus Crime Control Act of 1968, particularly emphasized 'de-institutionalization' and community measures in

its funding and project development. See also the US National Advisory Commission on Criminal Justice Standards and Goals, *A National Strategy to Reduce Crime: Final Report* (Washington DC: Government Printing Office, 1973), 187: 'States should refrain from building any more State institutions for juveniles: States should phase out present institutions over a 5-year period. They should also refrain from building more State institutions for adults for the next ten years, except where total institution planning shows that the need is imperative.' The Juvenile Justice and Delinquency Prevention Act of 1974 was also concerned to 'discourage the use of secure incarceration and detention' and promote 'community based alternatives to juvenile detention and correctional facilities.' See A. Pisciotta, 'A Retrospective Look at the Task Force Report on Juvenile Delinquency and Youth Crime', in J. A. Conley (ed), *The 1967 President's Crime Commission Report: Its Impact 25 Years Later* (Cincinatti: Anderson, 1994).

22 See E. Goffman, *Asylums* (London: Penguin Books, 1961*)*, 80–1: 'It is widely appreciated that total institutions typically fall far short of their official aims. It is less well appreciated that each of these official goals or charters seems admirably suited to provide a key to meaning—a language that the staff, and sometimes the inmates, can bring to every crevice of action in the institution . . . Paradoxically, then, while the while total institutions seem the least intellectual of places, it is nevertheless here, at least recently, that concern about words and verbalised perspectives has come to play a central and feverish role.'

23 On the incapacitative aspects of penal-welfare measures, see D. Garland, *Punishment and Welfare*, 241–2. For a discussion of 'predictive restraint' laws in the USA, see A. Von Hirsch, 'Review of F. Allen's Decline of the Rehabilitative Ideal', *University of Pennsylvania Law Review* (1983), vol 131, at p. 822.

24 See Michael Serrill comment on the gap between declared sentence and actual time served: 'There are signs posted on the counters of branches of the Chemical Bank in New York which read, in large capital letters, "bank robbery is punishable by 20 years in federal prison". The signs are a deception. But their impact would be more than a little diminished if they were more accurate, and read: "The symbolic penalty for bank robbery is 20 years in prison. The actual penalty for bank robbery is amorphous, in that it can be anything from probation up to 20 years, depending on the nature of the plea bargain worked out between the offender and the prosecutor, the personal policy of the judge toward bank robbery, the severity of overcrowding in the federal prisons, and the opinion of the parole hearing officers on the exent of the rehabilitation and/or dangerousness of the criminal" ', M. Serrill, 'Determinate Sentencing: The History, the Theory, the Debate' *Corrections Magazine* (1977), vol 3: 3–13.

25 Home Office, *The War Against Crime* (London: HMSO, 1964). For a discussion of various American initiatives to develop a criminological research base for policy making, see L. Radzinowicz, *The Need for Criminology* (London: Heinemann, 1965) and *Adventures in Criminology* (London: Routledge 1999), ch. 16.

26 'A good correctional institution is more than a gleaming edifice . . . It is a workshop of a team of skilled people concerned to turn social failures into useful citizens', T. Morris, 'Social Values and the Criminal Act', *The Nation*, 4 July 1959.

27 On the contradiction between penal purpose and social work mentalities, see M. D. Jacobs, *Screwing the System and Making it Work: Juvenile Justice in the No-Fault Society* (Chicago: University of Chicago Press, 1990). For a discussion of the impact

of social work thinking upon American parole practice, see J. Simon, *Poor Discipline: Parole and the Social Control of the Underclass* (Chicago: University of Chicago Press, 1993), ch. 3.

28 On the central role of experts in American crime policy from the Presidents Crime Commission of the late 1960s to the determinate sentence reforms of the early 1980s, see S. Pillsbury 'Why Are We Ignored? The Peculiar Place of Experts in the Current Debates about Crime and Justice', *Criminal Law Bulletin* (July–August 1995), 313. On the UK, see L. Radzinowicz, *Adventures in Criminology* (London: Routledge, 1998), ch. 13.

29 On broad bipartisan support for penal-welfarism in Britian, see L. Radzinowicz, *Adventures in Criminology* (London: Routledge, 1999), ch. 13 and Lord Windlesham, *Responses to Crime, Vol. 2: Penal Policy in the Making* (Oxford: Oxford University Press, 1993), 105–6. Evidence of a similar situation in the USA can be found in the Republican campaign platform of 1968. Although the Republicans sought to make 'crime in the streets' a national issue, their commitment to penal-welfarism remained firmly in place. The official platform called for 'Increased research into the causes and prevention of crime, juvenile delinquency and drug addiction' and 'a new approach to the problem of chronic offenders, including adequate staffing of the corrections system and improvement of rehabilitative techniques'. The 1972 Republican campaign platform was equally affirmative: 'We have given the rehabilitation of criminal offenders more constructive, top-level attention than it has received at any time in the Nation's history': D. B. Johnson, *National Party Platforms, Vol. II, 1960–1976* (Urbana: University of Illinois Press, 1978), at pp. 751 and 869.

30 See for example the Presidents Crime Commission, *The Challenge of Crime in a Free Society* (1967), 6: 'Warring on poverty, inadequate housing and unemployment is warring on crime. A civil rights law is a law against crime. Money for schools is money against crime. Medical, psychiatric and family-counseling services are services against crime. More broadly and more importantly every effort to improve life in America's "inner cities" is an effort against crime.' In the UK, the high point of this approach is the Kilbrandon Report of 1964 in which the penal and welfare elements blend completely into one another—see Lord Kilbrandon, *Children and Young Persons in Scotland* (Edinburgh: HMSO, 1964). The Social Work (Scotland) Act of 1968, which followed on from Kilbrandon's Report, abolished separate probation departments making probation supervision a function of generic social work departments. The Act also set up the Children's Hearing System—a welfare-oriented tribunal, run by social workers and lay volunteers that blended juvenile justice with child welfare.

31 On the utilitarian penal theories of Cesare Beccaria and Jeremy Bentham, see J. Heath, *Eighteenth Century Penal Theory* (Oxford: Oxford University Press, 1963).

32 For a vivid statement of this position in the USA, see K. Messinger, *The Crime of Punishment* (New York: Viking, 1968) and in Britain, J. R. Rees, *Mental Health and the Offender* (London: Clarke Hall Fellowship, 1947). For a critique of its arguments and evidence, see B. Wootton, *Social Science and Social Pathology* (London: Allen & Unwin, 1959). For a discussion of the formation of modernist criminology, see D. Garland, 'The Criminal and his Science', *British Journal of Criminology* (1985), vol 25, no 2, 109–37.

33 From the First World War until the late 1980s, very few British government publications or statutes used the word 'punishment' in their titles. Those that did were typically restricting or repealing prior laws on corporal or capital punishment.

34 See N. Elias, *The Civilising Process* (London: Blackwell, 1999), D. Garland, *Punishment and Modern Society* (Oxford: Oxford University Press, 1990) and A. Rutherford, *Criminal Justice and the Pursuit of Decency* (Oxford: Oxford University Press, 1993).

35 See P. J. Young, 'Punishment, Money and Legal Order', unpublished Ph.D. thesis (Edinburgh: University of Edinburgh, 1987).

36 For an analysis of this theoretical drift away from social processes towards individual ones, see D. Garland, *Punishment and Welfare*.

37 On the relationship between criminology and government, see D. Garland, 'Of Crime and Criminals: The Development of Criminology in Britain', in M. Maguire *et al.* (eds), *The Oxford Handbook of Criminology*, 2nd edn (Oxford: Oxford University Press, 1997) and 'Criminological Knowledge and its Relation to Power: Foucault's Genealogy and Criminology Today', *British Journal of Criminology* (1992), vol 32, no 4, 403–22. For an insider's account, see L. Radzinowicz, *The Cambridge Institute: Its Background and Scope* (London: HMSO, 1988).

38 On the development of criminological theory in Britain over the course of the twentieth century, see P. Rock (ed), *A History of British Criminology* (Oxford: Oxford University Press, 1988). On criminological theory in the USA, see G. B. Vold and T. Bernard, *Theoretical Criminology*, 2nd edn (New York: Oxford University Press, 1979).

39 The most important writings in this tradition were R. K. Merton, 'Social Structure and Anomie', in R. K. Merton, *Social Theory and Social Structure*, rev. edn (New York: Free Press, 1968); A. Cohen, *Delinquent Boys: The Culture of the Gang* (New York: Free Press, 1955); R. A. Cloward and L. E. Ohlin, *Delinquency and Opportunity* (New York: Free Press, 1960) and D. Downes, *The Delinquent Solution* (London: Routledge & Kegan Paul, 1966). Theories of anomie, blocked opportunity and frustrated expectations resonated with policy makers and politicians: Cloward and Ohlin's work was taken up by the federal government's Mobilization for Youth Program in the mid-1960s, see M. B. Katz, *The Undeserving Poor: From the War on Poverty to the War on Welfare* (New York: Pantheon, 1989), 96–7. In Britain, the ideas of Merton and Cohen appear in the political party crime policy documents of the late 1960s. See Conservative Party, *Crime Knows No Boundaries* (London: Conservative Party Central Office, 1966); Labour Party, *Crime: A Challenge To Us All* (*The Longford Report*) (London: Labour Party, 1964). The 1970 Manifesto of the Scottish Conservative Party, *Tomorrow Scotland: A Better Future with the Conservatives*, identifies the 'root causes' of crime as lying in 'social problems, educational inadequacies, and economic frustrations'.

40 See U. Beck, *The Risk Society: Towards a New Modernity* (London: Sage, 1992). Beck discusses the classic problems of modern industrial societies and the solutions developed to deal with them. He contrasts these with the more reflexive problems, perceptions and solutions of late modernity and the 'risk society'.

41 See generally, E. Hobsbawm, *The Age of Extremes* (London: Michael Joseph, 1994) and D. Yergin and J. Stanislaw, *The Commanding Heights*.

42 My discussion of the Hobbesian, Marxist and Durkheimian versions of the problem of social order draws upon D. Wrong, *The Problem of Order* (New York: Free Press, 1994).

43 For a discussion of the different forms that the welfare state took in the USA and the UK, see G. Esping-Anderson, *The Three Worlds of Welfare Capitalism* (Cambridge:

Polity, 1990). On the growing convergence of UK and US social policy in the 1980s and 1990s, see J. Holmwood, 'The Americanization of British Social Policy' (unpublished paper, on file with the author). For an account of the distinctive structure of the American welfare state, which is more localized than that of the UK, more clearly split between public assistance and social insurance, and relies more upon private agencies for service delivery, see M. B. Katz, *Improving Poor People* (Princeton, NJ: Princeton University Press, 1995), ch. 1. On the UK, see A. Digby, *British Welfare Policy: Workhouse to Workfare* (London: Faber & Faber, 1989).

44 Here one ought to distinguish the impact of New Deal measures such as the Social Security Act 1935, that operated 'to prevent the non-poor from falling into poverty' from Great Society legislation, such as Economic Opportunity Act of 1964 that 'were mainly concerned with helping the poor rise in the world.' See C. Jencks, *Rethinking Social Policy* (Cambridge, MA: Harvard University Press, 1992), 3. On the economic effects of social legislation, see T. Cutler, K. Williams, and J. Williams, *Keynes, Beveridge and Beyond* (London: Routledge & Kegan Paul, 1986) and D. Yergin and J. Stanislaw, *The Commanding Heights* (New York: Simon & Schuster, 1998). As Paul Pierson puts it, 'In all the advanced democracies, the welfare state was a central part of the postwar settlement that ushered in a quarter century of unprecedented prosperity . . . Social expenditure was a key instrument of macroeconomic and microeconomic policy. The welfare state was considered a powerful tool, producing deficits during recessionary periods and (at least in theory) surpluses during boom times. At a microeconomic level, social-welfare programs served to partially offset important market failures. Decent health care, housing, and a modicum of economic security can all contribute to the productive potential of workers, yet firms often view these factors as public goods. Welfare states offset the private sector's tendency to underinvest in its own workforce', P. Pierson, *Dismantling the Welfare State* (New York: Cambridge University Press, 1994), 2–3. As late as 1971 American policy was still being shaped by Keynesian policies. See D. Yergin and J. Stanislaw, *The Commanding Heights*, 60 for a discussion of Nixon's Keynesianism and the 'full employment' budget of that year. On the rise and fall of Keynesianism in Britain, see ch. 4 of P. Hall, *Governing the Economy* (Cambridge: Polity, 1986).

45 See H. J. Aaron, *Politics and the Professors: The Great Society in Perspective* (Washington DC: Brookings Institute, 1978); M. Weir, A. S. Orloff, and T. Skocpol (eds), *The Politics of Social Policy in the United States* (Princeton NJ: Princeton University Press, 1988); M. B. Katz, *The Undeserving Poor* (New York: Pantheon, 1989) ch. 3, 'The Intellectual Foundations of the War on Poverty'.

46 For comparative evidence about middle-class support for welfare state measures, see P. Baldwin, *The Politics of Solidarity: Class Bases of the European Welfare State* (New York: Cambridge University Press, 1990) and R. E. Goodin and J. Le Grand (eds), *Not Only the Poor: The Middle Classes and the Welfare State* (London: Allen & Unwin, 1987). For US evidence, see C. Howard, *The Hidden Welfare State: Tax Expenditures and Social Policy in the United States* (Princeton, NJ: Princeton University Press, 1997). J. K. Galbraith points out that it was only in the 1970s, when a wealthier middle class began to question that public benefits they received in return for their taxes, that these welfare state arrangements came to be seriously challenged: J. K. Galbraith, *The Culture of Contentment* (London: Sinclair-Stevenson, 1992). For evidence that, despite this challenge, the core programmes of the welfare state have survived more or less intact, see P. Pierson, *Dismantling the Welfare State: Reagan,*

Thatcher and the Politics of Retrenchment (New York: Cambridge University Press, 1994).

47 J. Rawls, *A Theory of Justice* (Oxford: Clarendon Press, 1962). Rawls's highly technical arguments and difficult prose were influential beyond the world of professional philosophy because his approach expressed the dominant social ethos of the time.

48 On this form of social governance, see J. Donzelot, *The Policing of Families* (London: Hutcheson, 1980); G. Steinmetz, *Regulating the Social: The Welfare State and Local Politics in Imperial Germany* (Princeton NJ: Princeton University Press, 1993); P. Hirst, 'The Genesis of the Social', in *Politics and Power*, vol 3 (London: Routledge & Kegan Paul), 67–82. On the significance of social insurance as an economic and political institution, see F. Ewald, *L'Etat Providence* (Paris: B. Grasset, 1986).

49 H. Perkin, *The Rise of Professional Society* (London: Routledge, 1989): 'Titmuss's remark in 1965 could have applied to any part of the twentieth century: "during the last twenty years, whenever the British people have identified and investigated a social problem there has followed a national call for more social work and more trained social workers" ' (p. 349).

50 On the US history see A. J. Polsky, *The Rise of the Therapeutic State* (Princeton: Princeton University Press, 1991). For UK evidence, see H. Perkin, *The Rise of Professional Society*.

51 See J. Simon, *Poor Discipline* (Chicago: University of Chicago Press, 1993).

52 See F. Fukuyama, *The Great Disruption* and W. G. Skogan, *Disorder and Decline: Crime and the Spiral of Decay in American Neighborhoods* (New York: Free Press, 1990).

53 See L. Radzinowicz, 'Public Opinion and Crime', in *Medicine, Science and Law*, 1961, vol 2, no 1, 24–32 and F. Zimring and G. Hawkins, *Capital Punishment and the American Agenda* (New York: Cambridge University Press, 1986), ch. 1.

Chapter 3   The Crisis of Penal Modernism

1 M. Foucault, *Discipline and Punish* (London: Allen Lane, 1977); M. Ignatieff, *A Just Measure of Pain* (London: MacMillan, 1978).

2 The American Friends Service Committee, *Struggle for Justice* (San Francisco: Hill and Wang, 1971), 12.

3 Ibid. 23.

4 Ibid. 171.

5 The criminological arguments of David Matza's *Delinquency and Drift* (Englewood Cliffs, NJ: Prentice Hall, 1964) had implied a similar critique of juvenile court, though not a fully explicit one. See also N. Kittrie, *The Right to be Different: Deviance and Enforced Therapy* (Baltimore: The Johns Hopkins Press, 1971) and E. Goffman, *Asylums* (New York: Anchor Books, 1961). Goffman was a signatory to the *Doing Justice* Report.

6 David Greenberg, one of the authors of *Struggle for Justice*, later wrote: 'The understanding that the criminal justice system is sometimes used for political repression came at the end of a decade in which Southern sheriffs clubbed, hosed, cattle prodded and jailed civil rights activists; demonstrators clashed with police on campuses and in the streets; and the FBI and local law enforcement agencies tapped telephones, burglarized apartments and offices, opened mail and used infiltrators and provocateurs to disrupt and destroy radical organizations and programs', D. F. Greenberg

and D. Humpries, 'The Cooptation of Fixed Sentencing Reform', *Crime and Delinquency* (1980), vol 26, 206–25.

7 F. A. Allen, *The Borderland of Criminal Justice* (Chicago: University of Chicago Press, 1964); K. C. Davis, *Discretionary Justice* (Urbana: University of Illinios, 1969). See also L. Radzinowicz and R. Hood, 'The American *volte face* in sentencing thought and practice', in C. Tapper (ed), *Crime, Proof and Punishm*ent (London: Butterworths, 1981).

8 The 'little man' quote is from *Struggle for Justice*, 31. For a cultural history of the USA in this period, see T. Gitlin, *The Sixties: Years of Hope, Days of Rage* (New York: Bantam Books, 1987). On the reaction in philosophy, see J. Kleinig, *Punishment and Desert* (The Hague: Martin Nijhoff, 1973); H. Morris, 'Persons and Punishment', *The Monist* (1968), vol 52, 475–501; J. Murphy, 'Marxism and Retribution', *Philosophy and Public Affairs* (1973), vol 2, 217–43, H. L. A. Hart, 'Prolegomenon to the Principles of Punishment', in H. L. A. Hart, *Punishment and Responsibility* (Oxford: Oxford University Press, 1968).

9 See D. Lipton *et al.*, *The Effectiveness of Correctional Treatment* (New York: Praeger, 1975); W. Bailey, 'Correctional Outcome: An Evaluation of 100 Reports', *Journal of Criminal Law, Criminology, and Police Science*, June 1966, 53–160; J. Robinson and G. Smith, 'The Effectiveness of Correctional Programs', *Crime and Delinquency*, January 1971, 67–80; L. Sechrest *et al.*, *The Rehabilitation of Criminal Offenders: Problems and Prospects* (Washington DC: National Academy of Science, 1979). British studies include S. R. Brody, *The Effectiveness of Sentencing: A Review of the Literature, Home Office Research Study No. 35* (London: HMSO, 1976) and M. S. Folkard, *Intensive Matched Probation and After-Care Treatment Home Office Research Study No. 24* (London: HMSO, 1974).

10 J. Mitford, *Kind and Usual Punishment: The Prison Business* (New York: Random House, 1973); N. Morris, *The Future of Imprisonment* (Chicago: University of Chicago Press, 1974).

11 M. Frankel, *Criminal Sentences: Law Without Order* (New York: Hill and Wang, 1973); A. Von Hirsch, *Doing Justice: The Choice of Punishments—Report of the Committee for the Study of Incarceration* (New York: Hill and Wang, 1976) Twentieth Century Fund Task Force, *Fair and Certain Punishment* (New York: Wiley, 1976); D. Fogel, *We Are The Living Proof . . . the Justice Model of Corrections* (Cincinnati: Anderson Pub., 1975).

12 The discomfort that liberals experienced in adopting this position is apparent in Rothman and Willard's 'Introduction' to *Doing Justice* which describes their choice as a product of despondency not enthusiasm, and insists that commensurate punishments ought to be fixed at the lowest possible levels. The Report argues that prison should be reserved for cases involving bodily harm or the threat thereof, with fines and other measures used for lesser offences. Five years' imprisonment was viewed as the top of the new penal scale, except for the crime of murder.

13 von Hirsch, *Doing Justice*, 134. Leslie Wilkins and Don Gottfredson had earlier shown how a two axis grid of this kind could be used to guide parole decision making.

14 J. Q. Wilson, *Thinking About Crime* (New York: Vintage Books, 1975). Much of this work had previously been published in popular periodicals such as *Atlantic Monthly, The Public Interest, Commentary, New York Times Magazine,* and *The Washington Post*, which greatly increased its impact.

15 Unlike Van Den Haag, Wilson drew back from openly endorsing the death penalty, though his discussion of the topic was designed to discomfit its opponents. See Andrew von Hirsch's response to these illiberal developments in his *Past or Future Crimes?* (Manchester: Manchester University Press, 1985).

16 On the alliance of forces, see M. S. Serrill, 'Determinate Sentencing: The History, the Theory, the Debate', in *Corrections Magazine* (1977), vol 3, 3–13. For examples of similar calls for sentencing reform in Britain see R. Hood, *Tolerance and the Tariff: Some Reflections on Fixing the Time Prisoners Serve in Custody* (London: NACRO, 1974); Howard League, *Whose Discretion? Fairness and Flexibility in the Penal System* (London: Howard League for Penal Reform, 1975); L. Taylor *et al.*, *In Whose Best Interests?* (London: Cobden Trust, 1980) extended the critique to deal with juvenile justice in England. For a British echo of the critique of rehabilitation, followed by an argument for retibutive punishment, see P. Bean, *Rehabilitation and Deviance* (London: Routledge & Kegan Paul, 1976) and P. Bean, *Punishment* (London: MacMillan, 1981).

17 See M. Tonry *Sentencing Matters* (New York: Oxford University Press, 1996). For a history of this reform process, see L. Radzinowicz and R. Hood, 'The American *volte face*'.

18 The government policy statement read: 'The aim of the Government's proposals is better justice through a more consistent approach to sentencing, so that convicted criminals get their "just desserts" [*sic*]. The severity of the sentence of the court should be directly related to the seriousness of the offence', Home Office, *Crime, Justice and Protecting the Public* (London: HMSO, 1990), 2. For another example of 'just deserts' sentencing reform, see the Swedish Sentencing Statute of 1988, discussed in A. von Hirsch and A. Ashworth (eds), *Principled Sentencing: Readings on Theory and Policy*, 2nd edn (Oxford: Hart Publishing, 1998), 240–52.

19 In Britain, a government prisons report of 1979 commented that 'the rhetoric of "treatment and training" has had its day and should be replaced', Home Office, *Report of the Committee of Inquiry into the UK Prisons Services* (*The May Report*) (Cmnd 7673) (London: HMSO, 1979). See also Scottish Home and Health Department, *Parole and Related Issues in Scotland* (*The Kincraig Report*) (Edinburgh: HMSO, 1989). At p. 2 the report states, 'It is probably now generally accepted that a custodial sentence is unlikely in itself to achieve rehabilitation, and thus rehabilitation may no longer be an aim which sentencers have in mind in sending a person to prison.' For an early attempt to rethink probation in Britain following the loss of faith in rehabilitation, see A. E. Bottoms and W. McWilliams, 'A Non-Treatment Paradigm for Probation Practice', *British Journal of Social Work* (1979), vol 9, 159–202. On the shift in US parole practice from a clinical to a management model, see J. Simon, *Poor Discipline* (Chicago: University of Chicago Press, 1993). On the new role of probation officers under the US sentencing guidelines, see S. M. Bunzel, 'The Probation Officer and the Federal Sentencing Guidelines: Strange Philosophical Bedfellows', *Yale Law Journal*, vol 104, Jan 1995, 933–66. On the reduction of funding for prison treatment programs following Martinson, see C. Riveland, 'Prison Management Trends, 1975–2025', in M. Tonry and J. Petersilia (eds), *Prisons* (Chicago: University of Chicago Press, 1999), at p. 167. On changes in American juvenile justice, see B. Feld, *Bad Kids* (New York: Oxford University Press, 1998) and on Britain, L. Gelsthorpe and A. Morris, 'Juvenile Justice, 1945–1992', in M. Maguire *et al.* (eds), *The Oxford Handbook of Criminology* (Oxford: Oxford University Press, 1994).

20 Mandatory sentences for drug offences, and later for crimes of violence, sex offences and repeated offending proceeded apace despite extensive research that showed no discernible effect on drug use or crime levels. See M. Tonry, *Sentencing Matters*, 141 ff.

21 The very process of enacting the new sentencing laws tended to politicize the issue of punishment. When state legislatures in the 1970s and 1980s held open debates about the appropriate levels of punishment, it was against a background of rising crime and public disquiet. In these circumstances, the enactment of tough new sentencing laws was a predictable outcome.

22 'I believe we may accomplish more by frankly adopting a "failure model", by recognizing our inability to achieve such heady and grandiose goals as eliminating crime and remaking the offender. Let us accept failure and pursue its implications', D. Rothman, 'Prisons: The Failure Model', *The Nation*, 21 Dec 1974, 657. On the ineffectiveness of probation, see M. S. Folkard, *Intensive Matched Probation and After-Care Treatment Home Office Research Study No. 24* (London: HMSO, 1974). On the limited effect of deterrent sentencing, see D. Beyleveld, *The Effectiveness of General Deterrents Against Crime* (Cambridge: Institute of Criminology, 1978) and A. Blumstein *et al.* (eds), *Deterrence and Incapacitation: Estimating the effects of Criminal Sanctions in Crime Rates* (Washington DC: National Academy of Sciences, 1978). On the limits of social programmes as crime control, see J. Q. Wilson, *Thinking About Crime*. For an influential critique of Great Society social programmes, see D. P. Moynihan, *Maximum Feasible Misunderstanding* (New York: Free Press, 1969).

23 On the limited effectiveness of policing, see R. V. Clarke and M. Hough (eds), *The Effectiveness of Policing* (Aldershot: Gower, 1980); R. V. Clarke and K. H. Heal, 'Police effectiveness in dealing with crime: some current British research', in *The Police Journal* (1979), vol 52, 24–41; H. Goldstein, 'Improving policing: A problem-oriented approach', *Crime and Delinquency* (1979), vol 25, 236–58; D. Bayley, *Police for the Future* (New York: Oxford University Press, 1994); G. Kelling *et al.*, *The Kansas City Preventive Patrol Experiment* (Washington DC: Police Foundation, 1974).

24 J. Young, 'The failure of criminology: The need for a radical realism', in R. Matthews and J. Young (eds), *Confronting Crime* (London: Sage, 1986). Croft's statement was as follows: 'Criminological research however has not solved the problem of crime and, insofar as research is an element of technological management . . . has been a failure.' 'There was a mismatch between the expectations of those who commissioned the research, the objectives of the investigations themselves and the available technology. On these circumstances it has been difficult to maintain the credibility of criminological research—at least as an aid to policy formation', J. Croft, *Managing Criminological Research, Home Office Research Study No. 69* (London : Home Office, 1981), 3.

25 See for instance, M. Cavadino and J. Dignan, *The Penal System: An Introduction* (London: Sage, 1992), 49–51 and S. Christianson, *With Liberty for Some: 500 Years of Imprisonment in America* (Boston: Northeastern University Press, 1998), 277–8. F. A. Allen, *The Decline of the Rehabilitative Ideal* (New Haven: Yale University Press, 1981) offers a richer sociological account of rehabilitation's decline.

26 R. Aron, *Main Currents in Sociological Thought*, vol 1 (New Brunswick, NJ: Transaction Books, 1998), 313.

27 See for instance F. A. Allen, 'Legal values and the rehabilitative ideal', *Journal of Criminal Law, Criminology and Police Science* (1959), vol 50, 226–32; C. S. Lewis, 'The Humanitarian Theory of Punishment', *Res Judicatae*, vol 6 (1953). For a response, see N. Morris and D. Buckle, 'The Humanitarian Theory of Punishment: A Reply', *Res Judicatae*, vol 6 (1953), 231–7.

28 J. Langbein, *Torture and the Law of Proof* (Chicago: University of Chicago Press, 1976).

29 For early evidence of failure, see B. McKelvey, *American Prisons: A History of Good Intentions* (originally publ. 1936, repr. Montclair, NJ: Patterson Smith, 1979) and B. Wootton, *Social Science and Social Pathology* (London: Allen & Unwin, 1957). David Rothman describes how supporters of correctionalism shrugged off such criticism: 'Failure, they believed, reflected faulty implementation, not underlying problems with theory or politics; incompetent administrators and stingy legislators, not basic flaws within the design . . . Reformers responded to disappointment in a one-note fashion: they urged better training for probation and parole officers, better programs for prisons and training schools, more staff for juvenile courts and more attendants for mental hospitals. Do more of the same so that the promise of the innovations would be realised', D. Rothman, *Conscience and Convenience* (Boston: Little Brown & Co., 1980), 9. As Ronald Bayer notes, 'the history of penal reform shows that during the period of rehabilitation's popularity, each failure prompted a demand for more experimentation, more expertise, more resources', R. Bayer, 'Crime, Punishment and the Decline of Liberal Optimism', *Crime and Delinquency*, April 1981, 169–90.

30 For an early counter-critique, see T. Palmer, 'Martinson Revisited', *Journal of Research in Crime and Delinquency*, 1975, vol 12, 133–52. For Martinson's reformulation, see R. L. Martinson, 'New Findings, New Views: A Note of Caution Regarding Sentencing Reform', *Hofstra Law Review* (1979), vol 7, 242–58. On the history of the empirical debate, and the methodology of meta-analysis, see P. Gendreau and R. Ross, 'Revivification of Rehabilitation: Evidence from the 1980s', in *Justice Quarterly*, Sept 1987, vol 4, no 3, 349–407.

31 N. Morris, *The Future of Imprisonment* ; N. Walker, *Treatment and Justice in Penology and Psychiatry: The 1976 Sandoz Lecture* (Edinburgh: Edinburgh University Press, 1976). For other defences, see F. Hussey, 'Just Deserts and Determinate Sentencing: Impact on the Rehabilitative Ideal', *The Prison Journal*, vol LIX, no 2 (1980).

32 Self-report studies of delinquency began in the USA in the late 1950s: see J. F. Short and F. I. Nye, 'Extent of unrecorded delinquency: Some tentative conclusions', *Journal of Criminal Law, Criminology and Police Science* (1958), vol 49, 296–302. By the mid-1960s such data had become widely used in the study of juvenile delinquency.

33 Jock Young pointed to these tensions and omissions as early as 1975, only two years after he had published, with Taylor and Walton, the paradigm text of radical deviancy theory, *The New Criminology* (London: Routledge & Kegan Paul, 1973). See J. Young, 'Working Class Criminology', in Taylor *et al.* (eds), *Critical Criminology* (London: Routledge, 1975). In the USA, already becoming a high crime society by the mid-1970s, the utopianism of the British radicals was more apparent. See E. Currie's review of *The New Criminology*, in *Crime and Social Justice*, vol. 2 (1974), 109–13 and T. Platt and P. Takagi, 'Intellectuals for Law and Order: A Critique of the New "Realists"', *Crime and Social Justice*, vol 8 (Fall–Winter,

1977), 8. Platt and Takagi argued that 'street crime is a serious and demoralizing problem that depreciates the quality of life in working class communities and fosters racism and other divisions.' By the mid-1980s, this 'left realist' view was increasingly adopted by radical criminologists in Britain as well.

34 The difficulties of combining radical theory and practice are discussed in S. Cohen, 'Its All Right for You to Talk: Political and Social Manifestos for Social Work Action', in R. Bailey and M. Brake (eds), *Radical Social Work* (London: Edward Arnold, 1975), 76–95. For an example of a closer relationship between radical deviancy theory and radical politics, see T. Mathiesen, *The Politics of Abolition* (London: Martin Robertson, 1974).

35 The rapid expansion of academic criminology in the early 1970s made it possible for the younger generation of radical deviancy theorists to have a prominent voice in the discipline, particularly in Britain, where academic criminology was a small and relatively recent development. This generation tended to define itself in opposition to the correctionalist attitudes and positivistic methods of its forerunners, and to be critical of criminology's close relationship with the criminal justice state. See P. Rock, 'The Present State of Criminology in Britain', in Rock (ed), *A History of British Criminology* (Oxford: Oxford University Press, 1988).

36 See the British sources in note 18 above.

37 Michel Foucault, who brilliantly articulated the radical wisdom of the time, did just this. For a critical discussion of Foucault's account see D. Garland, *Punishment and Modern Society* (Oxford: Oxford University Press, 1990), ch. 7 and id., 'Criminological Knowledge and its Relation to Power: Foucault's Genealogy and Criminology Today', in *British Journal of Criminology* (1992), vol 32, no 4, 403–22.

38 A. Hirschman, *The Rhetoric of Reaction: Perversity, Futility, Jeopardy* (Cambridge, MA: Harvard University Press, 1991).

39 As Michael Serrill pointed out, even the basic idea of reducing discretion meant very different things to different people. 'Today it is difficult to find a prominent member of the academic, prison reform or liberal political community who does not favor a drastic reduction in the amount of discretion exercised within the criminal justice system. But when one begins to discuss specific proposals, the brickbats begin to fly', M. S. Serrill 'Determinate Sentencing: The History, the Theory, the Debate' *Corrections Magazine* (1977), vol 3: 3–13.

Chapter 4   Social Change and Social Order

1 Other nation-states in Europe and Scandinavia reacted differently to the forces of late modernity, doing more to secure their working populations against the threat of mass unemployment and poverty produced by the world-wide slump of the 1980s and the impact of globalized markets. Many of these same states also avoided the more punitive forms of crime control and welfare policies now existing in the Anglo-American world. See G. Therborn, *Why Some Peoples Are More Unemployed Than Others* (London: Verso, 1986); M. Mauer, *Americans Behind Bars: US and International Use of Incarceration*, 1995 (Washington DC: The Sentencing Project, 1996) and J. Lynch, 'Crime in International Perspective', in J. Q. Wilson and J. Petersilia (eds), *Crime* (San Francisco: Institute of Contemporary Studies, 1995, 11–39.

2 See E. Hobsbawm, *The Age of Extremes* (London: Michael Joseph, 1994) and also G. Therborn, *European Modernity and Beyond* (London: Sage, 1995). The first part of this chapter draws extensively upon Hobsbawm's account of the post-war period.

3 K. Marx and F. Engels, *The Communist Manifesto* (New York: Verso, 1998, originally published in 1848), 38–9.

4 See E. Hobsbawm, *The Age of Extremes*, and D. J. Smith, 'Living conditions in the Twentieth Century', in M. Rutter and D. J. Smith (eds), *Psycho-Social Disorders in Young People: Time Trends and Their Causes* (London: Wiley, 1995). As Hobsbawm notes, even in these 'golden years', unemployment among blacks in the USA remained at high levels.

5 J. K. Galbraith, *The Affluent Society* (Boston: Houghton Mifflin, 1998); J. Goldthorpe *et al.*, *The Affluent Worker in the Class Structure* (London: Cambridge University Press, 1969).

6 H. Perkin, *The Rise of Professional Society: England Since 1880* (London: Routledge, 1989); S. Brint, *In An Age of Experts: The Changing Role of Professionals in Politics and Public Life* (Princeton NJ: Princeton University Press, 1994). On the rise of consumer capitalism, see D. Bell, *The Cultural Contradictions of Capitalism* (New York: Basic Books, 1976), ch. 1.

7 T. H. Marshall, 'Citizenship and Social Class', in Marshall, *Sociology at the Crossroads* (London: Heinemann, 1963); D. Yergin and J. Stanislaw, *The Commanding Heights: The Battle Between Government and the Marketplace that is Remaking the World* (New York: Simon & Schuster, 1998).

8 P. Baldwin, *The Politics of Social Solidarity* (New York: Cambridge University Press, 1990). T. Gitlin, *The Sixties: Years of Hope, Days of Rage* (New York: Bantam Books, 1987).

9 D. Yergin and J. Stanislaw, *The Commanding Heights*, ch. 5; E. Hobsbawm, *The Age of Extremes*, ch. 14.

10 In the USA, between 1970 and 1990, manufacturing employment as a percentage of total employment fell from 25.9 per cent to 17.5 per cent. In Britain it fell from 38.7 per cent to 22.5 per cent, M. Castells, *The Rise of the Network Society* (Malden Mass: Blackwell, 1996). See also F. Fukuyama, *The Great Disruption*, 105 and A. Amin (ed), *Post-Fordism: A Reader* (Oxford: Blackwell, 1994).

11 R. Crompton, *Women and Work in Modern Britain* (Oxford: Oxford University Press, 1997), 31–5. V. Beechey and T. Perkins, *A Matter of Hours: Women, Part-Time Work and the Labor Market* (Minneapolis: University of Minnesota Press, 1987); D. R. Williams, 'Women's Part-Time Employment', *Monthly Labor Review*, April 1995, 36–44.

12 See W. Hutton, *The State We're In* (London: Jonathan Cape, 1995), ch. 2; C. Oppenheim, *Poverty: The Facts Revised Edition* (London: Child Poverty Action Group, 1993), ch. 9. On US trends, see L. M. Mead, *The New Politics of Poverty* (New York: Basic Books, 1992), 75 and T. B. Edsall, *Chain Reaction: The Impact of Race, Rights and Taxes on American Politics* (New York: Norton, 1991), 23.

13 E. Hobsbawm, *The Age of Extremes*, 308. For a discussion of the impact of these developments on African American communities, see W. J. Wilson, *When Work Disappears: The World of the New Urban Poor* (New York: Knopf, 1997). For its impact upon gender relations in Britain's working class communities, see B. Campbell, *Goliath: Britain's Dangerous Places* (London: Methuen, 1993).

14 E. Hobsbawm, *The Age of Extremes*, 310; R. Crompton, *Women and Work in Modern Britain* (Oxford: Oxford University Press, 1997), 25. US Bureau of Labor statistics show that married women's labour force participation rate increased to just under 60 per cent in 1990. Over the period 1948 to 1987, male participation fell from

89 per cent to 78 per cent. Between 1969 and 1987 the fraction of American married women who were housewives fell from 30 per cent to 15 per cent. See J. B. Schor, *The Overworked American: The Unexpected Decline of Leisure* (New York: Basic Books, 1992), 25–8 and 36.

15 On the decline in fertility rates, see, R. Crompton, *Women and Work*, 74–6. Crompton states that the British post-war fertility rates peaked at 2.95 in 1964 and then fell rapidly to a low point in 1.69 in 1977. In 1994 the figure was 1.75. On the feminization of poverty, see L. Morris, *Dangerous Classes: The Underclass and Social Citizenship* (London: Routledge, 1994), 113–16.

16 E. Hobsbawm, *The Age of Extremes*, 321. According to *Social Trends*, The UK rate of divorcing per 1000 married persons in a given year increased from 2.1 in 1961 to 12.7 in 1989—see T. Griffin (ed), *Social Trends* (London: HMSO, 1991). US divorce rates are discussed by F. Fukuyama, *The Great Disruption*, 41: 'The American divorce rate has increased every year since the Civil War, but the rate of change began to accelerate sharply beginning in the mid-1960s.' Births to unmarried women have also trended sharply upwards: 'Births to unmarried women as a proportion of live births for the United States climbed from under 5 per cent to 31 per cent from 1940 to 1993. Illegitimacy rates vary significantly by race and ethnicity. In 1993 the ratio for whites was 23.6 per cent and for African Americans 68.7 per cent'; F. Fukuyama, *The Great Disruption*, 42–3. For details of UK trends, see L. Morris, *Dangerous Classes*: 'The changes in family structure which have been documented in America appear to be under way here, with single parent families growing from 8 per cent of all families in 1971, to 16 per cent in 1988 . . . The principal reason for single motherhood in Britain is divorce, which accounted for 40 per cent of single mothers in 1986, with separation accounting for 19 per cent, and never-married mothers accounting for 23 per cent. This last percentage has risen from 15 per cent in 1972' (p. 119).

17 According to the US Bureau of the Census, *Statistical Abstracts of the United States* for 1978 and 1996, the number of households with two or more cars in the US increased from 20 per cent in 1960 to 60 per cent in 1996. In 1975, over 80 per cent of households with children cared for those children in their own house, with the care given by the child's parent. By 1995 this number had halved to 40 per cent. The shift to day-care and or centre-based childcare was dramatic in this period (US Bureau of the Census: Statistical Abstracts for 1996 and US National Center for Educational Statistics, *Statistics in Brief*, 1996). On increased stress, see A. R. Hochschild, *The Time Bind* (New York: Metropolitan Books, 1997) and J. B. Schor, *The Overworked American*. On the rise of dual-earner and one-parent families, see D. Hernandez and D. E. Myers, 'Revolutions in Chidren's Lives', in A. Skolnick and J. Skolnick (eds), *Family in Transition*, 10th edn (New York: Longman, 1999): 'The rise in the proportion of children living in dual earner or one-parent families [in the USA] was extremely rapid . . . the increase from 15–20 per cent to 50 per cent required only 30 years. . . . By 1980, nearly 60 percent of children lived in dual earner or one-parent families, by 1989 about 70 percent lived in such families, and by the year 2000 . . . the proportion . . . may exceed 80 per cent' (p. 240).

18 E. Hobsbawm, *The Age of Extremes*, 322. See also L. Hess, 'Changing Family Patterns in Western Europe', in M. Rutter and D. J. Smith (eds), *Psycho-Social Disorders*, 123.

19 US Bureau of the Census, *Statistical Abstracts of the United States 1978 and 1996*. The rate of car ownership per thousand population in the UK went up from 46 in 1950 to

366 in 1989. In the US, the rate was already 266 per thousand in 1950, and rose to 589 in 1989. See G. Therborn, *European Modernity and Beyond* (London: Sage, 1995), 142.

20　Between 1940 and 1970, the proportion of US metropolitan residents who lived in suburban areas rose from one third to a half—see D. S. Massey and N. A. Denton, *American Apartheid: Segregation and the Making of the Underclass* (Cambridge, MA: Harvard University Press, 1993), 44. See also K. T. Jackson, *Crabgrass Frontier: The Suburbanization of the United States* (New York: Oxford University Press, 1985): Jackson argues that 'racial prejudice and cheap housing' (p. 287) were the primary causes of residential deconcentration in the USA. As Wilson argues, the US government policies of mortgage subsidy and tax relief played a major role in this segregation process: 'By manipulating market incentives, the federal government drew middle-class whites to the suburbs and, in effect, trapped blacks in the inner cities. Beginning in the 1950s, the suburbanization of the middle class was facilitated by a federal transportation and highway policy, including the building of freeway networks through the hearts of many cities, mortgages for veterans, mortgage-interest tax exemptions and the quick, cheap production of massive amounts of tract housing', W. J. Wilson, *When Work Disappears: The World of the New Urban Poor* (New York: Knopf, 1997), 46.

21　W. J. Wilson, *The Truly Disadvantaged: The Inner City, the Underclass and Public Policy* (Chicago: University of Chicago Press, 1987) and D. S. Massey and N. A. Denton, *American Apartheid*. On UK housing patterns, see A. Murie, 'Linking Housing Changes to Crime', in C. J. Finer and M. Nellis (eds), *Crime and Social Exclusion* (Oxford: Blackwell, 1998), 22–36.

22　'The ecology of American society has been altered drastically by the process of suburbanization. It has sorted the population along race and class lines, concentrating in large cities the poor and the unemployed. It has left large, dense central cities, a deteriorated physical plant which is cheaper to abandon than to repair, peopled by working class whites and blacks and Latinos of various classes who are unable to escape. The middle classes, reacting rationally to the availability of cheap, safe housing with handy connections to freeways, has acted to escape the taxes, politics, and litter which plague them', W. G. Skogan, 'The Changing Distribution of Big-City Crime', *Urban Affairs Quarterly*, 1977, vol 13, no 1, 33–48 at 43.

23　'[S]ince 1980, a fundamental shift in the federal government's support for basic urban programs has aggravated the problems of joblessness and social organization in the new poverty neighborhoods. The Reagan and Bush administrations—proponents of the New Federalism—sharply cut spending on direct aid to cities, including general revenue sharing, urban mass transit, public service jobs and job training, compensatory education, social service block grants, local public works, economic development assistance, and urban development action grants', W. J. Wilson, *When Work Disappears: The World of the New Urban Poor* (New York: Knopf, 1997), 49. See also D. N. Massey and N. A. Denton, *American Apartheid*, 45. On Mrs Thatcher's local government policies, see P. Hirst, *After Thatcher* (London: Collins, 1989).

24　J. Meyrowitz, *No Sense of Place: The Impact of Electronic Media on Social Behavior* (New York: Oxford University Press, 1985, 133; J. B. Thompson, *Ideology and Modern Culture* (Cambridge: Policy Press, 1990), 184. See also J. R. Sparks, *Television and the Drama of Crime* (Buckingham: Open University Press, 1992). For details of American television viewing trends, see R. Putnam, *Bowling Alone* (New York: Simon & Schuster, 2000), ch. 13.

25 J. Meyrowitz, *No Sense of Place*, 133.

26 Ibid. 133.

27 'With the advent of electronic media and especially television . . . communicating individuals become *personalities* with a voice, a face, a character and a history, personalities with whom recipients can sympathize, or empathize, whom they can dislike, detest or revere', J. B. Thompson, *Ideology and Modern Culture*, 228.

28 E. Goffman, *The Presentation of Self in Everyday Life* (Harmondsworth: Penguin Books, 1969), ch. 3. J. Meyrowitz, *No Sense of Place*, ch. 14. On the implications of media scrutiny for prison management, see S. Cohen and L. Taylor, *Prison Secrets* (London: NCCL, 1978) and J. B. Jacobs, *Stateville: The Penitentiary in Mass Society* (Chicago: University of Chicago Press, 1977).

29 J. Meyrowitz, *No Sense of Place*, p. viii

30 As Meyrowitz points out, the growth of national systems of electronic mass media amplified this egalitarian, democratizing current. 'Information integration makes social integration seem more possible and desirable. Distinctions in status generally require distinctions in access to situations. The more people share similar information-systems, the greater the demand for consistency of treatment', J. Meyrowitz, *No Sense of Place*, p. 133.

31 R. Miliband, 'A State of Desubordination', *British Journal of Sociology*, 1978, vol 29, no 4, 399–409. De-subordination would also have consequences for criminal behaviour, to the extent that it involves a diminished respect for social authorities and their right to govern: see G. LaFree, *Losing Legitimacy: Street Crime and the Decline of Social Institutions in America* (Boulder: Westview, 1998).

32 A. de Swaan, *The Management of Normality* (London: Routledge, 1990), 150–61.

33 On the eclipse of expert authority in social policy, see N. Glazer, *The Limits of Social Policy* (Cambridge: Harvard University Press, 1983), ch. 7.

34 A. de Swaan, *The Management of Normality*; C. Wouters, 'Changing Patterns of Social Controls and Self Controls', *British Journal of Criminology*, vol 39, no 3 (1999), 416–32.

35 T. Newburn, *Permission and Regulation: Law and Morals in Postwar Britain* (London: Routledge, 1992); D. Halpern, 'Values, Morals and Modernity', in M. Rutter and D. J. Smith (eds), *Psycho-Social Disorders*, 324–88.

36 T. Newburn, *Permission and Regulation*; T. Gitlin, *The Twilight of Common Dreams: Why America is Wracked by Culture Wars* (New York: Metropolitan Books, 1995).

37 This, of course, formed the socio-cultural and epistemological basis for the criminological changes described in ch. 3. Foucault's *Discipline and Punish* (London: Allen Lane, 1977) formed the intellectual bridge between this wider cultural and philosophical movement, and the specific criminological critique of penal-welfare.

38 E. Hobsbawm, *The Age of Extremes*, 338: 'The old moral vocabulary of rights and duties, mutual obligations, sin and virtue, sacrifice, conscience, rewards and penalties, could no longer be translated into the new language of desired gratification. Once such practices were no longer accepted as part of a way of ordering society that linked people to each other and ensured social co-operation, most of their capacity to structure human social life vanished. They were reduced simply to expressions of individuals' preferences.' See also, F. Fukuyama, *The Great Disruption*, 'Anyone who lived through the decades between the 1950s and the 1990s in the United States or any other Western country can scarcely fail to recognize the massive value changes that

have taken place over this period. These changes in norms and values are complex, but can be put under the general heading of *increasing individualism. . . .* In modern societies, options for individuals vastly increase, while the ligatures binding them into webs of social obligation are greatly loosened' (p. 47). For a discussion of this morality in the sphere of crime control, see H. Boutellier, *Crime and Morality: The Significance of Criminal Justice in Post-modern Culture* (London: Kluwer, 2000).

39 L. Radzinowitz and J. King, *The Growth in Crime: The International Experience* (Harmondsworth: Penguin Books, 1977); D. J. Smith, 'Youth crime and Conduct Disorders: Trends, Patterns and Causal Explanations', in M. Rutter and D. J. Smith, *Psycho-Social Disorders in Young People: Time Trends and Their Causes* (London: Wiley, 1995).

40 See Appendix, Figures 1 and 2 for details of recorded crime trends in the USA and in England and Wales. Readers should bear in mind that crime recorded by the police represents about one-third of all crime that takes place, though recorded crime rates have a special significance insofar as they are the rates most often discussed in the media. As David Smith points out, the increase in recorded crime since 1950 was considerably less in Scotland than it was in England and Wales; see D. J. Smith, 'Less Crime Without More Punishment', *Edinburgh Law Review* (1999), vol 3, 294–316: '[B]etween 1950 and 1995, recorded robberies increased by 15 times in Scotland compared with 67 in England; serious assault increased by 17 times in Scotland, compared with 39 times in England; sexual assaults rose by 5 times in Scotland, whereas rapes increased by 20 times in England; and housebreaking increased by less than 3 times in Scotland, whereas burglaries increased by over 13 times in England' (p. 310). Recorded crime in Northern Ireland also rose steeply in the post-war decades, see J. Brewer, B. Lockhart, and P. Rodgers, *Crime in Ireland, 1945–1995* (Oxford: Clarendon Press, 1997).

41 Gary LaFree's analysis of US trends in 'street crime' from 1946 to 1995—analysing UCR data on murder, rape, robbery, burglary, aggravated assault, larceny, and motor vehicle theft—shows that seven of these crimes exhibit similar historical patterns, with low points in the early part of the post-war period, and high points near the end. As LaFree points out, this finding 'suggests that whatever caused crime to increase in the postwar United States probably had very broad-gauged effects, influencing murder as well as larceny, rape as well as motor vehicle theft', G. LaFree, *Losing Legitimacy*, 27.

42 The evidence from all of the developed countries, with the important exception of Japan, points to this pattern. See D. J. Smith, 'Youth Crime and Conduct Disorders', in M. Rutter and D. Smith, *Psycho-Social Disorders*, 401; F. Fukuyama, *The Great Disruption*, ch. 2.

43 See M. Felson and L. E. Cohen, 'Human Ecology and Crime: A Routine Activity Approach', *Human Ecology* (1980), vol 8, no 4, 389–406: L. E. Cohen and M. Felson, 'Social Change and Crime Rate Trends: A Routine Activity Approach', *American Sociological Review* (1979), vol 44, no 4, 588–608; G. LaFree, *Losing Legitimacy* and A. E. Bottoms and P. Wiles, 'Crime and Insecurity in the City', in F. Fijnaut, J. Goethals, T. Peters, and L. Walgrave (eds), *Changes in Society, Crime and Criminal Justice in Europe*, vol. 1 (The Hague: Kluwer, 1995).

44 See M. Felson and M. Gottfredson, 'Social Indicators of Adolescent Activities Near Peers and Parents', *Journal of Marriage and the Family* (Aug 1984, 709–15. According to M. Rutter and D. J. Smith, *Psycho-Social Disorders*, this generation of

young people also experienced higher rates of other 'psycho-social disorders' such as abuse of alcohol and drugs, suicide, depression, and eating disorders. The presence of another 'at risk' category—that of the mentally ill—also increased during the 1970s and 1980s, as policies of de-institutionalization put thousands of mentally ill people back on the streets, often without adequate support or housing. Partly as a result, homelessness increased fourfold in the USA between 1979 and 1994—see C. Jencks, *The Homeless* (Cambridge, MA: Harvard University Press, 1994). In Britain, the numbers of homeless people rose every year between 1979 and 1994, W. Hutton, *The State We're In*, 210.

45 Tim Hope notes the criminological implications of these ecological changes: 'Corresponding to this evolution of built-form, human activities likewise become dispersed—property is dispersed at low building densities, people are dispersed among more households, travellers into more vehicles, and social activities into more sites away from the home. And each form of dispersal reduces intimate encounters, weakens social bonds, heightens anonymity and lowers restraints', T. Hope (book review) *British Journal of Criminology* (1997), vol 37, no 1, 151–3.

46 Several highly modernized societies, most notably Japan and Korea, have developed in ways that have preserved informal social controls and community restraints, and have not experienced Western levels of crime and disorder. See F. Fukuyama, *The Great Disruption*, ch. 7.

47 H. Goldstein, *Problem-Oriented Policing* (New York: McGraw Hill, 1990) comments: 'In the vast majority of police departments, the telephone, more than any policy decision by the community, or by management, continues to dictate how police resources will be used' (p. 21). The spread of motor car ownership also altered relations between the police and the middle-class public, with more middle-class citizens coming into unwelcome contact with the police. The motorization of police patrols in the 1960s in Britain and America tended to distance the police from the communities they served, with adverse consequences that were later widely acknowledged.

48 See J. Simon, *Poor Discipline: The Social Control of the Underclass, 1890–1990* (Chicago: University of Chicago Press, 1993).

49 On the 'crisis' of the welfare state, see C. Offe, *Contradictions of the Welfare State* (London: Hutchinson, 1984) and C. Pierson, *Beyond the Welfare State?* (Cambridge: Polity Press, 1991).

50 '[T]he percentage of all Americans receiving welfare increased dramatically from about 2 per cent in the mid-1960s to about 6 per cent in the mid-1970s, while aggregate spending on welfare more than doubled, from 0.24 per cent of GNP in 1965 to 0.60 in 1975', M. Gilens, *Why Americans Hate Welfare* (Chicago: University of Chicago Press, 1999), 122. As a percentage of GDP, British social expenditure increased from 12.4 per cent in 1960 to 19.6 per cent in 1975. In the USA it increased from 9.9 per cent to 19.7 per cent over the same period, C. Pierson, *Beyond the Welfare State* (Cambridge: Polity Press, 1991), 128.

51 Glazer describes how democratic politics contributes to the 'revolution of rising expectations', N. Glazer, *Limits of Social Policy*, 4. In pointing out these problems, commentators rarely emphasized the fact that the population was gradually becoming healthier, better housed, better nourished and educated. Contemporary problems crowded out the longer-term historical perspective.

52 A. Selsdon, *Wither the Welfare State* (London: Institute of Economic Affairs, 1981), 11. The same phenomena has been described in the USA by J. K. Galbraith, *The*

Culture of Contentment and R. Reich, 'The Secession of the Successful' *The New York Times Magazine*, 20 Jan 1991.

53 J. K. Galbraith, *The Culture of Contentment*; T. Edsall, *Chain Reaction*.

54 See M. Ignatieff, 'Citizenship and Moral Narcissism', *The Political Quarterly* (1988), vol. 59; R. Rosenblatt, 'Social Duties and the Problem of Rights in the American Welfare State', in D. Kairys (ed), *The Politics of Law*, rev. edn (New York: Pantheon Books, 1990), 90–114.

55 See G. Himmelfarb, 'Preface' to D. Anderson (ed), *This Will Hurt: The Restoration of Virtue and Civic Order* (London: Social Affairs Unit, 1995), p. ix: 'The state—and more specifically the welfare state—is now seen as part of the problem rather than the solution.' In his State of the Union addresses in the mid-1980s, President Reagan regularly attacked the welfare state in these terms: 'Welfare is a narcotic, a subtle destroyer of the human spirit. And we must now escape the spider's web of dependency' (1986). 'Some years ago, the Federal government declared war on poverty, and poverty won' (1988).

56 See N. Glazer, 'Towards a Self Service Society', *The Public Interest*, no 70 (Winter 1983), 66–90. Hayek's free market views had been circulating since the war, but without much political resonance, see Yergin and Stanislaw, *The Commanding Heights*.

57 See for instance, the President's Commission on Law Enforcement, *The Challenge of Crime in a Free Society* (Washington: US Government Printing Office, 1967).

58 For details, see P. A. Langan and D. P. Farrington, 'Crime and Justice in the United States and in England and Wales, 1981–96,' *Bureau of Justice Statistics Executive Summary* (Washington: US Department of Justice, Bureau of Justice Statistics, 1997).

59 S. Hall *et al.*, *Policing the Crisis* (London: MacMillan, 1978); T. Edsall, *Chain Reaction*; P. Schrag, *Paradise Lost: California's Experience, America's Future* (Berkeley, CA: University of California Press, 1998).

60 For a description of these events, and an account of their political consequences, see S. Hall, *The Hard Road to Renewal: Thatcherism and the Crisis of the Left* (London: Verso, 1988) and T. Edsall, *Chain Reaction* (1992). According to Edsall, the Watts riots of 1965, which broke out the week after the Voting Rights Act was signed into law, was 'the first of a chain of events that would push a substantial segment of the American electorate to the right, producing nearly a decade of intense ideological, social, and racial conflict. This chain of events included: ghetto riots; the emergence of a separatist black power movement; the abrupt rise of black crime and illegitimacy; the shift of civil rights protests to the North, where traditionally democratic voters polarized on issues of busing and open housing; an uprising among the nation's college-educated youth that challenged the Vietnam War, conventions of academic discipline, and the traditional restrictions surrounding sex and drugs; the emerging women's movement and the broader rights revolution; the surfacing of white backlash as a powerful political force; the fostering of conflict by the War on Poverty between white elected officials and black protest leaders; an unprecedented surge in the number of applicants for welfare; intensified demands by blacks for jobs in two besieged institutions under the control of white Democrats—the labor unions and City Hall' (pp. 48–9).

61 Edsall notes that 'The meaning of taxes . . . was transformed. No longer the resource with which to create a beneficent federal government, taxes had come for many voters to signify the forcible transfer of hard-earned money away from those who worked, to those who did not. Taxes had come to be seen as the resource financing a liberal fed-

eral judiciary, granting expanded rights to criminal defendants, to convicted felons, and, in education and employment, to "less qualified" minorities', T. Edsall, *Chain Reaction*, 214. See also, M. B. Katz, *The Undeserving Poor: From the War on Poverty to the War on Welfare* (New York: Pantheon, 1989): 'By emphasizing the obligations of the poor instead of their entitlement to public benefits, the appeal of the new authoritarianism diffused beyond conservative circles; in Congress, it even became the intellectual foundation of a bipartisan approach to welfare reform' (p. 125).

62 'States no longer commit themselves to full employment: they do not believe it to be possible. Instead they crave price stability and the approval of the global bond markets for their fiscal rectitude. Independent central banks are worshipped as guardians of monetary order and low inflation. It is no surprise that if the unemployed in the industrialized world numbered 35 million in 1994, a record post-war high, then inflation, at under 3 per cent, was at a thirty-year low. This is the conscious choice of the world's leading industrialised countries', W. Hutton, *The State We're In* (London: Jonathan Cape, 1995), 16. This policy is also, however, an acknowledgement that the nation state is no longer in full control. Unemployment comes to be represented as an inevitable effect of the actions of others. This denial of (government) responsibility would become a prominent theme in the economic social policies of the 1980s, at a time when individual responsibility was being heavily emphasized, D. Yergin and J. Stanislaw, *The Commanding Heights*, 116 quote Thatcher cabinet minister John Wakeham as saying, 'One of the real driving forces for privatization was the consensus among bureaucrats that they did not know how to determine anything anymore. Planning, nationalization, and so on—it had all failed. The state-owned industries were running massive deficits. There was a willingness to try something new. You found that the response within the bureaucracy to the new conservative government was that "it could not get any worse than it had already got." ' On the same shift in the USA, Thomas Edsall comments: 'From 1978 to 1980, during the Carter years, the central claim of the post-New Deal Democratic party, that it could manage the economy and produce sustained growth—collapsed under the weight of inflation, escalating oil prices, unemployment, high interest rates, and industrial stagnation', T. Edsall, *Chain Reaction*, 134.

63 Ibid.; P. Pearson, *Dismantling the Welfare State: Reagan, Thatcher and the Politics of Retrenchment* (New York: Cambridge University Press, 1994); E. Hobsbawm, *The Age of Extremes*, ch. 14; D. Yergin and J. Stanislaw, *The Commanding Heights*, chs. 4 and 12.

64 On the meaning of 'reactionary' politics, see A. Hirschman, *The Rhetoric of Reaction* (Cambridge, MA: Harvard University Press, 1991). For details of such policies, see P. Pierson, *Dismantling the Welfare State?* (New York: Cambridge University Press, 1994) and D. Yergin and J. Stanislaw, *The Commanding Heights* (New York: Simon & Schuster, 1998), chs. 4 and 12.

65 See A. Gamble, *The Free Economy and the Strong State* (Basingstoke: MacMillan, 1988). As we will see, the tensions within this combination of market liberalism and moral conservatism were reproduced in criminal and penal policy. The neo-liberal demand to get value for money, to apply business and market disciplines to government, to curtail public expenditure, to think in utilitarian terms was countered by the more deontological retributivism prompted by moral conservatives. This tension between market and moral discipline was to be a shaping contradiction in criminal justice throughout the last decades of the century.

66 See M. Magnet, *The Dream and the Nightmare: The Sixties Legacy to the Underclass* (New York, Encounter Books, 1993). For a critique of this line of argument, see H. Dean and P. Taylor-Gooby, *Dependency Culture: The Explosion of a Myth* (London: Harvester Wheatsheaf, 1992).

67 See generally, R. Keat and N. Abercrombie (eds), *Enterprise Culture* (London: Routledge, 1991).

68 See Commission on Social Justice, *Social Justice: Strategies for Renewal* (London: Vintage, 1994), 28–9: 'For nearly forty years after the Second World War, the income gap between the richest and the poorest in the UK gradually narrowed. That progress has now been reversed. Today, the gap between the earnings of the highest-paid and those of the lowest-paid workers is greater than at any time since records were first kept in 1886', see also W. Hutton, *The State We're In*, ch. 2; C. Oppenheim, *Poverty: The Facts Revised Edition* (London: Child Poverty Action Group, 1993) ch. 9. On US trends, see L. M. Mead, *The New Politics of Poverty* (New York: Basic Books, 1992), 75 and T. Edsall, *Chain Reaction*. Edsall notes: 'In terms of straightforward economic rewards, the Republican-dominated decade of the 1980s produced one of the most dramatic redistributions of income in the nation's history. While overall family *after-tax* income rose by 15.7 per cent, the income of families in the bottom decile fell by 10.4 per cent, from $4,791 to $4,295 (in constant 1990 dollars) while the income of those in the top one per cent rose by 87.1 per cent, from $213,675 to $399,697' (p. 23).

69 C. Murray, *Losing Ground: American Social Policy, 1950–1980* (New York: Basic Books, 1984); N. Glazer, *The Limits of Social Policy* (Cambridge, MA: Harvard University Press, 1988); L. M. Mead, *The New Politics of Poverty* (New York: Basic Books, 1992); W. Bennett, J. DiIulio, and J. Walters, *Body Count: Moral Poverty and How to Win America's War Against Crime and Drugs* (New York: Simon & Schuster, 1996); G. Himmelfarb, *The Demoralization of Society: From Victorian Virtues to Modern Values* (New York: Knopf, 1995); N. Dennis, *Rising Crime and the Dismembered Family* (London: Institute of Economic Affairs, 1993); N. Dennis, *The Invention of Permanent Poverty* (London: Institute of Economic Affairs, 1997); C. Murray, *The Emerging British Underclass* (London: Institute for Economic Affairs, 1990); D. Anderson (ed), *This Will Hurt: The Restoration of Virtue and Civic Order* (London: Social Affairs Unit, 1995). In her Preface to Anderson, Gertrude Himmelfarb sounds this anti-modern sentiment: 'It is evident that we are suffering from a grievous moral disorder. "Social pathology" is the familiar term for the syndrome of crime, violence, promiscuity, illegitimacy, drug addiction, and welfare dependency: "moral pathology" would be more accurate. And that moral pathology requires strenuous moral purgatives and restoratives' (p. x).

70 See A. Gamble, *The Free Economy and the Strong State*.

71 See W. Hutton, *The State We're In*, ch. 7; P. Pierson, *Dismantling the Welfare State?*

72 B. Campbell, *Goliath*.

73 É. Durkheim, *Professional Ethics and Civic Morals* (London: Routledge, 1992). See also P. Hirst, *Associative Democracy* (Cambridge: Polity, 1994).

74 Concluding her analysis of American public opinion on social issues, in which she finds evidence of increasing toleration of 'lifestyle difference', but decreasing toleration of crime, Kathlyn Gaubatz speculates that: 'Many Americans have decided to tolerate behavior they nevertheless find bothersome. Thus they go about their lives, still carrying the burden of feeling that their fellow citizens are engaging in activities

that are somehow distasteful, unnatural, sinful, dangerous, immoral, or uppity. But they choose not to release that psychological burden into advocacy of prohibitions on these activities. What I am suggesting is that gradually over the years many Americans were developing a pool of insufficiently actualized negative feelings, and that they needed some place to put them. What better place than in strenuous opposition to the acts of criminal offenders?', K. T. Gaubatz, *Crime in the Public Mind* (Ann Arbor: University of Michigan Press, 1995), 162.

75 See C. Oppenheim, *Poverty: The Facts, Revised Edition* (London: Child Poverty Action Group, 1993), ch. 9; W. J. Wilson, *When Work Disappears*.

76 For details of the 'dualized society', see M. Piore and C. Sabel, *The Second Industrial Divide* (New York: Basic Books, 1984). On 'Thirty, thirty, forty society', see W. Hutton, *The State We're In*, 105–10, referring to the 30 per cent of the population disadavantaged (long-term unemployed), the 30 per cent marginal and insecure (in part-time, or temporary employment) and the 40 per cent privileged (high wage, more secure employment). On the 'seduced and repressed', see Z. Bauman, *Legislators and Interpreters* (Oxford: Polity, 1987). On American apartheid, see D. S. Massey and N. A. Denton, *American Apartheid*.

77 A *Sunday Times* editorial of 26 November 1989 gives a sense of this: 'The underclass spawns illegitimate children without a care for tomorrow and feeds on a crime rate which rivals the United States in property offences. Its able-bodied youths see no point in working and feel no compulsion either. They reject society while feeding off it; they are becoming a lost generation giving the cycle of deprivation a new spin. . . . No amount of income redistribution or social engineering can solve their problem, Their sub-lifestyles are beyond welfare benefit rises and job creation schemes. They exist as active social outcasts, wedded to an anti-social system.'

78 For US data on property and violent crime trends, see US Department of Justice, *Crime in the United States 1995* (Washington, DC: US Government Printing Office, 1995). For data on England and Wales, see Home Office, *Digest 4* (London: Home Office, 1999). See also A. Norrie and S. Adelman, ' "Consensual Authoritarianism" and Criminal Justice in Thatcher's Britain', *Journal of Law and Society* (1989), vol 16, no 1, 112–28; R. J. Terrill, 'Margaret Thatcher's Law and Order Agenda', *The American Journal of Comparative Law* (1989), vol 37, 429–56.

79 As Ronald Reagan put it, 'the American people have lost patience with liberal leniency and pseudo-intellectual apologies for crime', quoted in K. Beckett, *Making Crime Pay: Law and Order in Contemporary American Politics* (New York: Oxford University Press, 1997), 49.

80 On the increasing tendency to represent street crime as a problem of black youth, see M. H. Barlow, 'Race and the Problem of Crime in Time and Newsweek Cover Stories, 1946 to 1995' *Social Justice* (1998), vol 25, no 2, 149–83; C. West, *Race Matters* (New York: Vintage Books, 1994) and S. Hall *et al.*, *Policing the Crisis: Mugging, the State and Law and Order* (London: MacMillan, 1978). Martin Gilens has shown how American media representation of poverty highlight white people in periods of when policy is sympathetic towards the plight of the poor, and highlight black people when public attitudes and policies are more hostile. M. Gilens, *Why Americans Hate Welfare* (Chicago: University of Chicago Press, 1999). Like media images of crime, these welfare images, which have made 'welfare' a codeword for 'race' in the USA, are highly misleading: 'For most Americans, the most powerful images of poverty are undoubtedly the black urban ghettos. These concentrations of

poverty represent the worst failures of our economic, educational and social welfare systems. Yet they also represent a minuscule proportion of all the American poor. Only 6 per cent of all poor Americans are blacks living in urban ghettos' (p. 132).

Chapter 5   Policy Predicament: Adaptation, Denial, and Acting Out

1 For detailed accounts of policy-making, readers should consult the following studies: On the UK: Lord Windlesham, *Responses to Crime, vol 2: Penal Policy in the Making* (Oxford: Oxford University Press, 1993) and *vol 3: Legislating With the Tide* (Oxford: Oxford University Press, 1996); I. Dunbar and A. Langdon, *Tough Justice: Sentencing and Penal Policy in the 1990s* (London: Blackstone, 1998); P. Rock, *Helping Victims of Crime* (Oxford: Oxford University Press, 1990); On the USA, H. Chernoff *et al.*, 'The Politics of Crime', *Harvard Journal of Legislation* (1996), vol 33, 527–79; Lord Windlesham, *Politics, Punishment, and Populism* (New York: Oxford University Press, 1998).

2 See, for instance, reports on the limited impact of 'Three Strikes' laws, outside of California. J. Austin *et al.*, 'The Impact of "three strikes and you're out"', *Punishment & Society* (1999), vol 1, no 2, 163–86.

3 In the UK, the tendency for the prison population to drift upwards throughout the 1970s and 1980s occurred despite constant government efforts to contain it. In 1993 however, government ministers deliberately relaxed this effort, which resulted in dramatic rise in the population. See I. Dunbar and A. Langdon, *Tough Justice*. For analyses of the forces that produced the current levels of imprisonment in the USA, see D. Garland (ed), *Mass Imprisonment in the USA* (London: Sage, forthcoming).

4 M. M. Feeley and A. D. Sarat, *The Policy Dilemma: Federal Crime Policy and the Law Enforcement Assistance Administration* (Minneapolis: University of Minnesota Press, 1980) analyse the 'policy dilemma' faced by the US crime policy in the 1960s and 1970s in similar terms. 'Government today is caught in a policy dilemma, a dilemma in which constant and continuing demands for government services are matched by a growing recognition of the inefficiency and ineffectiveness of much of what the government does' (p. 11).

5 For crime rate trends in the USA and in England and Wales, see Appendix, Figures 1 and 2. For Scottish crime trends over the same period, see D. J. Smith, 'Less Crime Without More Punishment', *Edinburgh Law Review* (1999), vol 3, 294–316. For Northern Ireland, see J. Brewer *et al.*, *Crime in Ireland, 1945–1995: 'Here Be Dragons'* (Oxford: Clarendon Press, 1997).

6 Rural and affluent areas that are, in fact, low-crime areas often view themselves as distinguished and defined by this favourable contrast. But they are also threatened by the incursion of criminal elements—the spread of crime from the big city. In this respect, crime consciousness and fear of crime has a broader grip than crime itself. See E. Girling *et al.*, *Crime and Social Change in Middle England* (London: Routledge, 2000).

7 The constant presence of crime is emphasized in the FBI's annual crime reports which carry a picture of the 'Crime Clock' indicating the frequency of index crimes by reference to time intervals: 'One violent crime every 21 seconds', 'One property crime every 3 seconds'. US Federal Bureau of Investigation, *Crime in the United States: Uniform Crime Reports 1987* (Washington DC: Government Printing Office, 1988), 6. A 1994 National Institute of Justice Report, begins with the following sentence:

'Today, like every other day in the United States this year, 65 persons will be murdered, and 264 women will be raped. In the next hour, 120 persons will be assaulted. In the time it takes to read this paragraph—49 seconds—another person will be robbed', F. E. Earls and A. J. Reiss, *Breaking the Cycle: Predicting and Preventing Crime* (Washington DC: NIJ, 1994).

8 See J. Roberts and J. Stalans, *Public Opinion, Crime and Criminal Justice* (New York: Westview, 1997).

9 Presidents Commission, *The Challenge of Crime in a Free Society* (Washington DC: US Government Printing Office, 1967).

10 See Paul Rock's account of the climate of opinion at the Home Office in the early 1980s: 'The diagnosis was bleak. Despite an abundance of "myths and nostrums", no one appeared to know much about the causes of crime. Most crime resisted formal control. Offenders resisted rehabilitation. The Home Office's own special domain was detection, arrest, and punishment, and those activities appeared to be less and less useful in tackling the root causes of criminality. The police were not considered to be demonstratively effective: patrolling achieved modest results, criminal investigation was not always skilfully conducted, and increased police staffing had not led to an increased clear-up rate. Prisons did not reform inmates. Non-custodial penalties had not emptied the prisons, sentences did not have a deterrent effect, and reconviction rates had not improved. There was, said one prominent member of the [Research and Planning Unit] in 1984, "a perception of the limitations of conventional intervention through sentencing, policing, imprisonment"', P. Rock, *Helping Victims*, 256. The Head of the Home Office Research and Planning Unit noted in 1991 that the Home Office is increasingly drawn to a 'management model . . . based on the insight that crime is inevitable in any society and conceives the task as being to manage, reduce or prevent the amount of crime so as to make its occurrence as little damaging to society as possible', M. Tuck, 'Community and the Criminal Justice System', *Policy Studies*, vol 12, no 3 (Autumn 1991), 22–7 at 23.

11 Hough and Roberts, *Public Opinion, Crime and Criminal Justice*; D. C. Anderson, *Crime and the Politics of Hysteria* (New York: Times Books, 1995).

12 See S. Brody, *The Effectiveness of Sentencing: A Review of the Literature* (London: Home Office, 1976); J. Burrows and R. Tarling *Clearing Up Crime* (London: Home Office, 1982); K. Heal *et al.*, *Policing Today* (London: Home Office, 1985); A. Blumstein *et al.* (eds), *Deterrence and Incapacitation: Estimating the Effects of Criminal Sanctions in Crime Rates* (Washington DC: National Academy of Sciences, 1978); L. Sechrest *et al.*, *The Rehabilitation of Criminal Offenders: Problems and Prospects* (Washington DC: National Academy of Science, 1979), R. L. Martinson, 'What Works? Questions and Answers in Prison Reform', *The Public Interest* (1974) vol 35; G. L. Kelling *et al.*, *The Kansas City Preventive Patrol Experiment* (Washington DC: Police Foundation, 1974).

13 Home Office, *Criminal Justice: A Working Paper* (London: Home Office, 1986); Commissioner of the Police of the Metropolis, *Report for the Year 1986*, Cm 158, (London : HMSO, 1987. See the comments of former head of the LEAA, Patrick Caplan, stated, 'We have learned that the conditions that really make a difference in crime control lie largely outside governmental authority', quoted in T. E. Cronin, *US v. Crime in the Streets*, 179. In March 1982, the Lord Chief Justice said, in the House of Lords, 'Neither police, not courts, nor prisons can solve the problem of the rising crime rate', quoted in G. Laycock and K. Heal, 'Crime prevention: The British

Experience', in D. J. Evans and D. T. Herbert (eds), *The Geography of Crime* (London: Routledge, 1989), 315–30 at 317. In 1983, a senior Home Office official stated that 'the general impression must be that crime in this country has increased very considerably in the last twenty years; that it is still increasing; that the forces of law and order are under great pressure; and even that they are fighting a losing battle', David Faulkner, quoted in P. Rock, *Helping Victims of Crime* (Oxford: Oxford University Press, 1990), 255.

14 See S. Strange, *The Retreat of the State: The Diffusion of Power in the World Economy* (Cambridge: Cambridge University Press, 1996); P. Hirst, *Associative Democracy* (Oxford: Polity, 1994); S. Lash and J. Urry, *The End of Organised Capitalism* (Cambridge: Polity Press, 1987).

15 As Barry Goldwater put it in 1964, 'security from domestic violence, no less than foreign aggression, is the most elementary and fundamental purpose of any government, and a government that cannot fulfil this purpose cannot long command the loyalty of its citizens', quoted in T. E. Cronin *et al.*, *US v. Crime in the Streets* (Bloomington, Ind.: Indiana University Press, 1981), 18. A British Prime Minister made the same point in 1994: 'A primary responsibility of any government at home is to take action to protect people from crime . . . *the guarantee of law and order* is essential to the British way of life', John Major, 9 September 1994 (emphasis in the original).

16 This is a classic example of what Robert Merton described as 'sociological ambivalence'—see R. K. Merton, *Sociological Ambivalence* (New York: Free Press, 1976), 8. In the UK, the late 1980s and early 1990s saw the emergence of a series of carefully planned policy initiatives (most notably the Criminal Justice Act of 1991 and the government's prison reform programme following the Woolf Report) which were quite suddenly undercut by shifts of political mood. For details of this erratic pattern of policy development, see R. Reiner and M. Cross, *Beyond Law and Order: Criminal Justice Policy and Politics into the 1990s*, (London: MacMillan, 1991); A. Ashworth and B. Gibson, 'Altering the Sentencing Framework' *Criminal Law Review*, Feb 1994, 101–9; Lord Windlesham, *Responses to Crime vol 3*. For an account—and a criticism—of the US government's recent criminal law-making activities, see the recent Meese Report of the American Bar Association Task Force entitled *The Federalization of Criminal Law* (Washington, DC: American Bar Association, Criminal Justice Section, 1998).

17 For insider accounts, see Lord Windlesham, *Responses to Crime Vol 2: Penal Policy in the Making* (Oxford: Oxford University Press, 1993), ch. 1; D. Lewis, *Hidden Agendas*; P. Rock, *A View From the Shadows*. For a discussion, see M. Hill, *The Policy Process in the Modern State*, 3rd edn (London: Harvester Wheatsheaf, 1997) 78 ff.

18 See W. G. Skogan, *Disorder and Decline* (New York: Free Press, 1990) on the 'tremendous upsurge in the volume of crime reported to the police. It began in the mid-1960s. In US cities with a population of over 250,000, the number of recorded (Part 1) offences grew from fewer than 1 million in 1960 to 2.2 million in 1970, and to 3.8 million by 1980. Police budgets expanded in response, but not fast enough to catch up—the crimes per officer ratio almost doubled during each decade, from 10 to 19 during the 1960s, and from 19 to 34 between the beginning and the end of the 1970s' (86–7). Skogan goes on to describe how the police reorganized by developing centralized dispatching systems and focusing upon 911 services.

19 See A. Blumstein, 'Coherence, Coordination and Integration in the Administration of Criminal Justice', in J. van Dijk (ed), *Criminal Law in Action* (Deventer: Kluwer,

1988). On the shift to a 'technocratic administration of justice' in the USA, see W. Heydebrand and C. Seron, *Rationalizing Justice* (Albany, NY: State University of New York Press, 1990). A. J. Fowles, 'Monitoring Expenditure on the Criminal Justice System: The Search for Control', *The Howard Journal*, vol 29, no 2 (1990), 82–100; C. Jones, 'Auditing Criminal Justice', *British Journal of Criminology* (1993), vol 33, no 2, 187–202

20 For British evidence, see Lord Windlesham, *Responses to Crime*, vol 2. In the USA, rates of growth in probation case loads have, since 1980, have been similar to rates of prison population growth. On the USA, see T. R. Clear and A. A. Braga, 'Community Corrections', in J. Q. Wilson and J. Petersilia (eds), *Crime* (San Francisco: Institute for Contemporary Studies, 1995), 421–44.

21 Lord Windlesham cites Home Office figures on police expenditure, which rose (in 1993 pounds) from 1,629 million pounds in 1964/5 to 3,545 million in 1979/80 and 5,862 million in 1992/3 (1996, p. 80). On probation see Audit Commission, *The Probation Service: Promoting Value for Money* (London: Audit Commission, 1989) and Audit Commission, *Going Straight: Developing Good Practice in the Probation Service* (London: Audit Commission, 1991).

22 On the spread of audit and associated management techniques, see M. Power, *The Audit Explosion* (London: Demos, 1994).

23 S. Walker, *Taming the System: The Control of Discretion in Criminal Justice, 1950–1990* (New York: Oxford University Press, 1993). As Jacobs points out, a major dynamic in the rationalization of prison management has been the impact of successful prisoners' rights litigation and court oversight provisions. J. B. Jacobs, 'The Prisoners Rights Movement and its Impacts, 1960–1980', in N. Morris and M. Tonry (eds), *Crime and Justice: An Annual Review of Research*, vol 2 (Chicago: University of Chicago Press, 1980), 429–70. In the 1990s the US courts have pulled back from this role, and Congress has legislated to limit the extent to which prisoners' rights claims can be pursued: see for example the Prison Litigation Reform Act of 1996.

24 J. W. Raine and M. J. Willson, *Managing Criminal Justice* (London: Harvester Wheatsheaf, 1993); A. James and J. Raine, *The New Politics of Criminal Justice*, ch. 4; Humprey, 1991; S. Walker, *Taming the System*; J. Simon, *Poor Discipline*.

25 R. Harding, 'Private Prisons' in M. Tonry (ed), *The Handbook of Crime and Punishment* (New York: Oxford University Press, 1998), 626–58; J. R. Lilly and P. Knepper, 'The Corrections-Commercial Complex', *Crime and Delinquency*, vol 39, no 2 (1993), 150–66. P. Young, *The Prison Cell: The Start of a Better Approach to Prison Management* (London: Adam Smith, 1987).

26 Clifford Shearing notes that the Rand study of private security in the mid-1970s shifted the issue, 'from a question of politics and sovereignty to be responded to in absolute terms to a matter of economics and efficiency', C. D. Shearing, 'The Relation between Public and Private Policing', in M. Tonry and N. Morris (ed), *Modern Policing* (Chicago: University of Chicago Press, 1992), 410. See also T. Jones and T. Newburn, *Private Security and Public Policing* (Oxford: Oxford University Press, 1998); L. Johnston, *The Rebirth of Private Policing* (London: Routledge, 1992).

27 Hence the new practice of conducting surveys and market research to identify local public opinion and to identify community concerns and policing priorities. See D. Bayley, *Police for the Future* (New York: Oxford University Press, 1994); Commissioner of the Police of the Metropolis *Report for the Year 1986* (Cm 158) (London: HMSO, 1987).

28 See D. P. Moynihan, 'Defining Deviancy Down', *The American Scholar* (1992), 17–30. Moynihan coined the phrase to criticise a shift in levels of cultural toleration, and what he referred to as the tendency to 'normalize' the (high) crime levels of the 1970s and 1980s. I use the term here to describe a specific bureaucratic strategy.

29 The lack of scrutiny that facilitates 'defining down' measures also facilitates their unwanted side-effects, such as the dilution of due process. See S. Cohen, *Visions of Social Control* (Oxford: Policy, 1985).

30 On the use of prosecution discretion to define deviance down in England and Wales, see D. Rose, *In the Name of the Law* (London: Jonathan Cape, 1996), ch. 4. As Rose notes, the Criminal Justice Act of 1988 redefined whole categories of offending (car theft became 'taking without owner's consent') and moved them from the Crown Court to the lower magistrates' court. See the Home Office Working Paper, *A Review of Criminal Justice Policy 1976* (London: HMSO, 1977): 'consideration needs to be given to ways of limiting the input into the system, for example through slimming the scope of the criminal law, more selective prosecution policy, the development of penalties that do not require the involvement of the penal agencies to enforce them, and modification of the criminal process' (paragraph 16). For US evidence, see Vera Institute, *Felony Arrests: Their Prosecution and Disposition in New York City's Courts* (New York: Vera Institute, 1977). The major mechanism of defining deviance down is, of course, the plea-bargaining system that has been institutionalized in the USA and more recently the UK. On diversion and decriminalization in American juvenile justice, see the Juvenile Delinquency Prevention and Control Act of 1968 and the Juvenile Delinquency Prevention Act of 1974. For British developments, see the Social Work (Scotland) Act 1968 and the Children and Young Persons Act 1969. For other evidence of defining deviance down in the USA, see R. C. Ellickson, 'Controlling Chronic Misconduct in City Spaces: Of Panhandlers, Skid Rows and Public-Space Zoning', *Yale Law Review*, vol 105 (1996), 1165–248

31 On police cautioning, see J. Ditchfield, *Police Cautioning in England and Wales* (London: Home Office, 1976) and R. Taylor, *Forty Years of Crime and Criminal Justice Statistics, 1958 to 1997* (London: Home Office, 1998) which reports an eleven fold increase in cautioning between 1958 and 1997. On diversion from prosecution and the use of summary and fixed penalties, see Stewart Committee, *Keeping Offenders Out of Court: Further Alternatives to Prosecution* (Cmnd 8958) (Edinburgh: HMSO, 1983) and the Thompson Committee Reports in Scotland. On the reduced use of imprisonment relative to crime in the UK between 1950 and 1990, see C. Nuttall and K. Pease, 'Changes in the Use of Imprisonment in England and Wales 1950–1991', *Criminal Law Review* (1994). D. P. Farrington, *Understanding and Preventing Youth Crime* (York: J. Rowntree Foundation, 1996) points to the increase in non-formal warnings by the police and the downgrading of offences such as theft from motor vehicles from indictable to summary offences.

32 '[I]n the face of limited resources, not every demand can be met', Commissioner of Police of the Metropolis, *Report for the Year 1986* (Cm 158) (London: Home Office, June 1987), 13. 'To prevent the Force being submerged under a flood-tide of demands, I have introduced systems to prioritize and filter them', 11.

33 Wesley Skogan describes how US police practice adapted. 'Departments had to meet these growing demands in the face of shrinking resources, for by the beginning of the 1980s, many big-city departments were smaller than they were a decade earlier. With efficiency in mind, police managers adopted call-prioritising schemes which guaran-

teed a rapid response to "man with a gun", "burglary in progress", and other emergencies, but put most complaints concerning disorder at the bottom of the stack. Many stoutly resisted providing services that were not "productive"—which did not give them wide area coverage and speed their response time, or did not generate arrests. One early victim of productivity was foot patrol', Skogan, *Disorder and Decline*, 88. Skogan goes on to note 'the decline in arrests in the "big four" disorder categories: drunkenness, disorderly conduct, vagrancy, and suspicion. In 1960 there were 2.3 million of these arrests, and they constituted 52 percent of all non-traffic arrests in the United States. In 1985 (when the population had grown considerably) there were only 1.4 million arrests in these categories and they made up only 16 percent of the total (Federal Bureau of Investigation yearly statistics). Both absolutely and relatively, the police appear to be paying less formal attention to major classes of disorder' (p. 89). For UK evidence, see the Audit Commission, *Helping With Enquiries: Tackling Crime Effectively* (London: HMSO, 1993) and P. Amey *et al.*, *Proactive policing: An evaluation of the Central Scotland Police management model* (Edinburgh: Scottish Office, 1996). 'Traditionally the practice of Central Scotland Police was to visit every victim and every crime scene. The project tested whether resources could be used more effectively by conducting a thorough investigation of a large number of minor crimes over the telephone, with officers attending only if the telephone investigation showed that this was necessary' (p. 2).

34 'In 1958 over 142,000 persons were sentenced for indictable offences in England and Wales. This figure rose steadily to peak at over 474,000 in 1982. The number of persons sentenced by the courts has gradually declined since 1982 to stand at just over 318,000 in 1997', R. Taylor, *Forty Years of Crime and Criminal Justice Statistics, 1958 to 1997* (London: Home Office, 1998), 24.

35 See F. Fessenden and D. Rohde, 'Dismissed by Prosecutors Before Reaching Court, Flawed Arrests Rise in New York City', *New York Times*, 23 August 1999.

36 '[O]ur strategy has to take account of . . . the limited ability of police over the next two decades to make a real impact on random and opportunistic crimes by their own unaided efforts', Commissioner of Police of the Metropolis, *Report for the Year 1986* (Cm 158) (London: Home Office, June 1987), 2. See L. Sherman, 'Attacking Crime: Police and Crime Control', in M. Tonry and N. Morris (eds), *Modern Policing* (Chicago: University of Chicago Press, 1992), 159–230; D. Bayley, *Police for the Future*; R. Reiner, *The Politics of the Police*, 2ne edn (Hemel Hempstead: Wheatsheaf, 1992).

37 'It is . . . one of the consequences of the pressures placed upon the Prison Service by excessive demands and inadequate resources that we have become increasingly unable to meet virtually any of the objectives expected of us other than simple 'incapacitation' of the offender for the period of his sentence', HM Prison Department, *Report of the Work of the Prison Department 1981* (London: HMSO, 1982), 5. See the Learmont Report of 1995, which defined 'custody' as the dominant aim of the prison service. Sir John Learmont, *Review of Prison Service Security in England and Wales* (Cm 3020) (London: HMSO, 1995) and I. Dunbar and A. Langdon, *Tough Justice*. On US developments, see F. E. Zimring and G. Hawkins, *Incapacitation: Penal Confinement and the Restraint of Crime* (New York: Oxford University Press, 1995), ch. 1.

38 On the changing character of community penalties in America, see D. R. Gordon, *The Justice Juggernaut* (New Brunswick, NJ: Rutgers, 1991), ch. 5. On UK changes,

see I. Brownlee, *Community Punishment: A Critical Introduction* (London: Longman, 1998) ch. 4. See for instance, the Home Office Memo to the Chief Probation Officers of England and Wales, *Tackling Offending: An Action Plan* (17 August 1988): 'Programmes should always focus on working with offenders to confront their offending and to examine, with them, the circumstances of their offending and the effects on their victims, their families, their friends, the community and themselves', Annex A.

39 See Scottish Prison Service, *Opportunity and Responsibility* (Edinburgh: Scottish Prison Service, 1990); D. Nelkin, 'Discipline and Punish: Some Notes on the Margin', *Howard Journal* (1989) 28/4, 245–254; A. E. Bottoms, 'Intermediate Punishments and Modern Societies', *Paper presented at the American Society of Criminology Meeting* (Miami: November 1994).

40 We may now be seeing the beginnings of a reaction against this. The best publicized example is the New York Police Department, which recently began to claim responsibility for crime reduction outcomes, and to measure its own performance in these terms, but there are signs that a similar shift is beginning to occur in the UK as well. For most of the 1990s, the performance measures used by the Prison Service in England and Wales were internal measures such as 'number of hours prisoners spend per week engaged in purposeful activity' or 'time unlocked' to indicate programme effectiveness, rather than external ones such as recidivism rates. In the year 2000–1, the Service plans to introduce a new measure—'rate of reconviction compared with level predicted'. See Her Majesty's Prison Service, *Framework Document* (London: Prison Service, 1999), Annex A. On the recent history of prisons policy in England and Wales, see R. D. King and K. McDermott, *The State of Our Prisons* (Oxford: Oxford University Press, 1995).

41 Commissioner of Police for the Metropolis, *Report for the Year 1986* (Cm 158) (London: HMSO, 1987); R. Ericson and K. Haggerty, *Policing the Risk Society* (Toronto: University of Toronto Press, 1997); D. Bayley, *Police for the Future*. The New York Police Department has recently been a newsworthy exception to this pattern, claiming an ability to reduce crime, inviting the public to judge the organization in these terms, and imposing crime-reduction goals upon precinct commanders. But in doing so the NYPD was self-consciously reacting against the strategy I describe in the text, which it had hitherto adopted. The department's new slogan, 'We're not Report-takers, we're the Police' encapsulates this previous history and the negative connotations it had developed—with the public and with the police themselves.

42 On the recent history of sentencing reform in the USA, see K. Stith and J. A. Cabranes, *Fear of Judging: Sentencing Guidelines in the Federal Courts* (Chicago: University of Chicago Press, 1998), M. Tonry, *Sentencing Matters* (New York: Oxford University Press, 1996). In the UK, see I. Dunbar and A. Langdon, *Tough Justice*.

43 '[A]udit in a range of different forms has come to replace the trust once accorded to professionals both by their clients—now users and consumers—and the authorities which employ, legitimate and constitute them. The constant demands for audit both gives expression to and contributes to the erosion of trust, and the expertise and positive knowledge of human conduct on which it was based', N. Parton, 'Social Work, Risk and "the Blaming System" ', in N. Parton (ed), *Social Theory, Social Change and Social Work* (London: Routledge 1996), 112.

44 See Home Office, *A Review of Criminal Justice Policy 1976* (London: HMSO, 1976).

45 For details see M. Maguire, 'The Needs and Rights of Victims', in M. Tonry (ed),

Crime and Justice: A Review of Research, vol 14 (Chicago: University of Chicago Press, 1991), 363–433; P. Rock, *Helping Victims of Crime* (Oxford: Oxford University Press, 1990). By 1997, twenty-nine American states had amended their state constitutions to guarantee various rights to victims: see B. Shapiro, 'Victims and Vengeance', *The Nation*, 10 February 1997, 11–19.

46 M. Maxfield, *Fear of Crime in England and Wales* (London: HMSO, 1984); T. H. Bennett, *Tackling Fear of Crime: A Review of Policy Options* (Cambridge: Institute of Criminology, 1989); C. Hale, 'Fear of Crime: A Review of the Literature', *International Review of Victimology*, vol 4 (1996), 79–150; J. Garofalo, 'The Fear of Crime: Causes and Consequences', *Journal of Criminal Law and Criminology*, vol 72, no 2 (1981), 839–58.

47 For an account of the Home Office's attempts to use fear of crime research findings in this way, see P. Rock, *Helping Victims*, 262 ff.

48 As Home Secretary Douglas Hurd put it in 1986, 'All would agree that the criminal justice system on its own cannot hope to succeed in reversing the upward trend in crime figures. The underlying causes of crime lie within society itself', D. Hurd, 'Foreword' to Home Office, *Criminal Justice: A Working Paper* (London: HMSO, 1986).

49 S. Cohen, *Visions of Social Control* (Oxford: Policy, 1985); D. R. Karp (ed), *Community Justice: An Emerging Field* (New York: Rowman and Littlefield, 1998).

50 T. Jones *et al.*, *Democracy and Policing* (London: Policy Studies Institute, 1997). This is particularly so in the USA, now that the federal government provides subsidies for community oriented policing. See *Criminal Justice Newsletter*, vol 29, no 24, 15 December 1998, quoting the Justice Dept Inspector General 'It has been our experience that the COPS office accepts virtually any activity related to law enforcement as community policing' (p. 1).

51 The term 'responsibilize' is used by Pat O'Malley to describe the effort on the part of authorities to render others responsible—a trend that he was among the first to identify. See P. O'Malley 'Post-Keynesian Policing' *Economy and Society* (1996), 25(2): 137–55 and O'Malley, 'Risk, Power, and Crime Prevention', *Economy and Society*, (1992), 21: 252–75. O'Malley locates this process within a broader 'neo-liberal' shift that affects pensions, welfare, health care, etc. as the post-Keynesian state seeks to shift responsibility to the individual and the market.

52 See the UK Government's *Interdepartmental Circular on Crime Prevention* which opened with the declaration that: 'A primary objective of the police has always been the prevention of crime. However, since some of the factors affecting crime lie outside the control or direct influence of the police, crime prevention can not be left to them alone. Every individual citizen and all those agencies whose policies and practices can influence the extent of crime should make their contribution. Preventing crime is a task for the whole community', Home Office, *Crime Prevention, Circular 8/1984* (London: Home Office, 1984).

53 On these developments in the UK, see generally A. Crawford, *The Local Governance of Crime* (Oxford: Oxford University Press, 1997). On crime prevention beyond the criminal justice system, see D. Gilling, *Crime Prevention: Theory, Policy and Practice* (London: UCL Press, 1997), ch. 6. On US developments, see D. R. Rosenbaum, *Community Crime Prevention* (Beverly Hills: Sage, 1986); C. Murray, 'The Physical Environment', in J. Q. Wilson and J. Petersilia (eds), *Crime* (San Francisco: Institute for Contemporary Studies, 1995); and R. V. Clarke (ed), *Situational Crime*

Prevention: Successful Case Studies, 2nd edn (Albany, NY: Harrow and Heston, 1997), chs. 19 and 22.

54 R. Engstad and J. L. Evans, 'Responsibility, Competence and Police Effectiveness in Crime Control' in R. Clarke & M. Hough (eds), *The Effectiveness of Policing* (Aldershot: Gower, 1980), 6–7.

55 D. Garland, 'Governmentality and the Problem of Crime: Foucault, Sociology, Criminology', *Theoretical Criminology* (1997), vol 1, no 2, 173–214. M. Foucault, 'Governmentality' in Burchell *et al.* (eds), *The Foucault Effect* (Hemel Hempstead: Harvester Wheatsheaf, 1992).

56 The first two quotations are from D. Riley, and P. Mayhew, *Crime Prevention Publicity: An Assessment*, Home Office Research Study, No. 63, (London: Home Office, 1980), p. 15. The third is from M. Foucault, 'Governmentality'.

57 M. Hough *et al.*, 'Introduction' to R. Clarke and P. Mayhew (eds), *Designing Out Crime* (London: HMSO, 1980), 16.

58 See the pamphlets entitled *Partners Against Crime* (London: Home Office, Sept 1994) and *Preventing Crime Together in Scotland* (Edinburgh: Scottish Office, nd) that were mailed to households by the British government in the mid-1990s. A Scottish Office brochure, aimed at the business community describes the government's thinking about crime prevention: 'Crime prevention was in the past regarded as predominantly the province of the police. The complacency towards crime prevention this engendered in the population at large inhibited progress in this important area. The new strategy seeks to heighten individual and collective responsibility for crime prevention activity by encouraging wider participation and greater community involvement. It aims to build an inter-agency approach', *Preventing Crime Together: A Guide to Good Practice in Business* (Edinburgh: Scottish Office, nd). For details of American crime prevention practices, see National Crime Prevention Council website.

59 '[I]t is now widely recognised that crime cannot be prevented by an exclusive reliance on the police and other criminal justice agencies, the bodies to which the community has traditionally delegated responsibility. Rather, it depends on co-ordinated action by a wide range of agencies', Home Office, *A Practical Guide to Crime Prevention for Local Partnerships* (London: HMSO, 1993), p. iii.

60 As John Patten, Minister of State at the Home Office put it, 'our crime prevention needs to go beyond fitting stouter locks and bolts, and attempt to restore a framework of informal but effective controls. Perhaps politicians and professionals fight shy of mentioning the need to exercise "control", "Social control", "community control"— whatever label you want to use—means responsible adults and active citizens, all of us, not just the police or the probation service, acting individually and together to prevent young men and women from drifting into crime when possible. Government alone cannot perform this task . . . . Inspiring and enlisting the active citizen in all walks of life is the key', J. Patten, 'Crime: A Middle Class Disease?', *New Society* 13 May 1988.

61 On Business Improvement Districts and their crime-control activities, see J. R. Pack, 'BIDs, DIDs, SIDs and SADs', Brookings Review (Fall 1992), 18–21 and T. M. Seamon, 'Private Forces for Public Good', *Security Management* (September 1995), 92–7. Seamon reports that, in 1995, there were estimated to be more than 1,000 BIDS in the USA and Canada. On the development of BIDs in Britain, see C. Sharman, 'Writing on the Wall for Graffiti', *The Daily Telegraph*, 23 February 1998.

62 See M. Hough *et al.*, 'Introduction' to R. V. Clarke and P. Mayhew (eds), *Designing Out Crime* (London: HMSO, 1980), 14; R. V. Clarke, *Hot Products: Understanding, anticipating and reducing demand for stolen goods* (London: Home Office, Research, Development and Statistics Directorate, 1999)

63 See J. Kooiman, *Modern Governance: New Social-Governmental Interactions* (London: Sage, 1993). In an important sense, the US Federal authorities necessarily 'govern-at-a-distance' in respect of crime, because of the constitutional division of jurisdiction. Traditionally, their method of influencing crime policy at the state level has been to make funding available to those state and local authorities prepared to undertake federally approved projects, such as system-co-ordination, 'truth in sentencing' or community policing. Frustration with this indirect form of action, and the wish to be seen to do something about crime, has prompted the 'federalization' of criminal law in recent decades.

64 R. V. Clarke and D. Cornish (eds) *The Reasoning Criminal: Rational Choice Perspectives on Offending* (New York: Springer-Verlag, 1986), M. Felson, *Crime and Everyday Life* (London: Pine Forge Press/Sage, 1994); K. Heal and G. Laycock (eds), *Situational Crime Prevention: From Theory to Practice* (London: HMSO, 1986); R. V. Clarke and P. Mayhew (eds), *Designing Out Crime* (London : HMSO, 1980); M. J. Hindelang *et al.*, *Victims of Personal Crime: An Empirical Foundation for a Theory of Victimization* (Cambridge MA: Ballinger, 1978).

65 N. Walker, 'Introduction', K. Heal and G. Laycock (eds) *Situational Crime Prevention* (London: HMSO, 1986), p. v.

66 D. Cornish and R. V. Clarke, 'Introduction' to R. V. Clarke and D. Cornish (eds), *The Reasoning Criminal: Rational Choice Perspectives on Offending* (New York: Springer-Verlag, 1986*a*), 4.

67 J. Q. Wilson, *Thinking About Crime* , rev. edn (New York: Vintage, 1983), ch. 7.

68 As van Dijk puts it; 'offenders are seen as the consumers of criminal gains and victims as the reluctant suppliers of criminal opportunities' and 'property offences are transactions completed by consumers without the suppliers' permission', J. J. M. van Dijk, 'Understanding Crime Rates: On the interactions between the rational choices of victims and offenders', *British Journal of Criminology* (1994), vol 34, no 2, 105–21 at 105 and 106.

69 '[T]he policy analyst is led to act as if crime were the product of a free choice . . . The radical individualism of Bentham and Beccaria may be scientifically questionable but prudentially necessary', J. Q. Wilson, *Thinking About Crime*, 51.

70 This claim is stated in the concluding paragraph of ibid. 260.

71 In Freudian terms, 'denial' is a psychic defence mechanism by means of which some painful experience or reality is refused access to consciousness. 'Hysterical' behaviour is conduct entailing 'conversion-symptoms' that disguise the psychic problem that lie at their root. The implication is that the observed phenomena should not be taken at their face value and that they are intended to draw or distract attention. 'Acting out' is a form of expressive, impulsive activity, prompted by internal conflicts in individuals who lack the capacity for inhibition. See C. Rycroft, *A Critical Dictionary of Psychoanalysis* (Harmondsworth: Penguin Books, 1968). I use these terms in the text to suggest the underlying conflicts and ambivalence that shape institutional action. No strict application is intended.

72 The statement that prison is 'an expensive way of making bad people worse' is from Home Office, *Crime, Justice and Protecting the Public* (London: HMSO, 1990).

Home Secretary Howard's declaration that 'prison works' was in his Speech to the Conservative Party Conference 6 October 1993—a speech that was preceded by the appearance on the platform of a victim of a sexual attack who spoke harrowingly about her ordeal. See I. Dunbar and A. Langdon, *Tough Justice*, and E. Baker, 'From "Making Bad People Worse" to "Prison Works": Sentencing Policy in England and Wales in the 1990s', *Criminal Law Forum*, vol 7, no 3 (1996). *The Crime (Sentences) Bill of 1997* introduced new provisions on mandatory minimum sentences and the electronic tagging of juveniles, permitted the naming of juvenile offenders appearing in youth courts, and abolished the statutory requirement that an offender should consent to probation, community service and curfew orders. Despite widespread protests from the judiciary and criminal justice professionals, the Labour opposition did not oppose these measures, and went on to implement them once in government.

73 See M. Tonry, *Malign Neglect* (New York: Oxford University Press, 1995), ch. 3. Readers should bear in mind that the decreased American crime rates of the 1990s leave out of account drug offences, which are not included in the FBI's Uniform Crime Reports. By the end of the 1990s, drug arrests had increased to an all-time high: see *Drug and Crime Facts* at the US Department of Justice, Bureau of Statistics website www.ojp.usdoja. gov/bjs.

74 D. C. Anderson, *Crime and the Politics of Hysteria* (New York: Times Books, 1995).

75 For an insider's account, see the memoirs of the former Director of the English Prison Service, D. Lewis, *Hidden Agendas, Politics, Law and Disorder* (London: Hamish Hamilton, 1997). Lewis describes how Home Secretary Howard's 'political imperative' prevented him from consulting the prison service about the far-reaching sentencing proposals he introduced (p.198). See also M. Tonry, *Sentencing Matters*, 159: 'Officials who support mandatory penalties often do not much care about problems of implementation, foreseeable patterns of circumvention, or the certainty of excessive and unjustly severe penalties for some offenders. Their interests are different, as recent policy debates demonstrate. According to a *New York Times* article about mandatory proposals offered by US Senator Alfonse D'Amato of New York, "Mr. D'Amato conceded that his two successful amendments, which Justice Department officials say would have little practical effect on prosecution of crimes, might not solve the problem." 'But', he said, "it does bring about a sense that we are serious.' " '(p. 159). A statement by Republican Senator Orrin Hatch gives the same impression: 'It's no use kidding ourselves; some of these tough on crime amendments may not have tremendous effect', quoted in W. Kaminer, *Its All the Rage* (New York: Addison Wesley), 196.

76 On recent American shaming statutes, see A. S. Book, 'Shame on You: An Analysis of Modern Shame Punishment as an Alternative to Incarceration', *William and Mary Law Review*, vol 40 (1999), 653–86. On chain gangs, see the Amnesty International Report, *United States of America Florida Reintroduces Chain Gangs* (London: Amnesty International, January 1996).

77 On supermax prisons, see C. Riveland, *Supermax Prisons: Overview and General Considerations* (Washington DC; NIJ, 1999) and R. D. King, 'The Rise and Fall of Supermax: An American Solution in Search of a Problem?' *Punishment & Society*, vol 1, no 2 (1999). On sexual predator laws, see D. Denno, 'Life Before the Modern Sex Offender Statutes,' *Northwestern University Law Review* (1998), vol 92, no 4, 1317–414. For details of sex offender community notification in the USA, see P. Finn, *Sex Offender Community Notification* (Washington DC: NIJ, February 1997) and in

the UK, see B. Hebenton and T. Thomas, 'Sexual Offenders in the Community', *International Journal of the Sociology of Law*, vol 24 (1996), 427–43; on electronic monitoring see, E. Mortimer and C. May, *Electronic Monitoring of Curfew Orders: Research Findings, No 66* (London: Home Office Research and Statistics Directorate, 1998) on mandatory sentencing, see R. Hood and S. Shute, 'Protecting the Public: Automatic Life Sentences, Parole and High Risk Offenders', *Criminal Law Review* (November 1996), 788–800.

78 M. Foucault, *Discipline and Punish* (London: Allen Lane, 1977).

79 A British Home Secretary's speech about the need to abolish the right to silence gives a sense of the conflict between the niceties of professional (in this case legal) expertise and the demands of the public: 'As I talk to people up and down the country, there is one part of our law in particular that makes their blood boil. . . . It's the so-called right to silence. . . . The so-called right to silence will be abolished. The innocent have nothing to hide.' M. Howard, *Speech to the 110th Conservative Party Conference*, Blackpool, 6 October 1993. On the politics of 'expressive justice' see D. C. Anderson, *Crime and the Politics of Hysteria*.

80 Two former members of the English Prison Board wrote in 1998, 'this country is slipping into an ever-greater reliance on the use of imprisonment, at an escalating and underestimated resource cost, with serious consequences for the prison system, with at best only marginal improvement in public protection in the short term and with a real prospect of reduced public protection in the longer term. To our mind, exactly the wrong lessons have seem to have been learnt from the USA . . .' I. Dunbar and A. Langdon, *Tough Justice: Sentencing and Penal Policy in the 1990s* (London: Blackstone, 1998), 3. Strong and very public expressions of judicial opposition greeted the Crime (Sentences) Bill of 1997, which introduced mandatory minimum sentences for repeat offenders: see A. Ashworth, *Sentencing in the 80s and 90s: The Struggle for Power* (London: ISTD, 1997). The *Criminal Justice Newsletter* of 1 November 1994 reports that the American Correctional Association criticized the 1994 Crime Act, declared its opposition to mandatory sentences and expressed the view that 'the law places too much emphasis on incarceration' (p. 2). See also the report in *Criminal Justice Newsletter*, vol 24, no 14 (15 July 1993) headed '30 organizations call for shift in criminal justice policy', at p. 3.

81 See D. Shichor and D. K. Sechrest (eds), *Three Strikes and You're Out: Vengeance as Public Policy* (Thousand Oaks, CA: Sage, 1996).

82 A statement in the 1987 Conservative Party Manifesto betrayed this tension: 'Conservatives have always believed that a fundamental purpose of government is to protect the security of the citizen under the rule of law. There can be no half-heartedness, no opting out in the fight against crime and violence.' Conservative Party, *The Next Moves Forward* (London: Conservative Central Office, 1987).

83 British examples include the sudden turn against policies of 'punishment in the community', police cautioning, bail release, and non-custodial juvenile sentencing. See the letter from the Editor of the *Daily Mail*, 14 September 1993, 'The crux of the changing mood is the realisation that legislation and changes in prosecuting practice designed to ease prison overcrowding have only succeeded in deepening the exasperation of those who suffer the effects of crime', quoted in Lord Windlesham, *Responses to Crime*, vol 3 (Oxford: Oxford University Press, 1996), 47. See also *The Times* criticisms of police cautioning and home leave for prisoners, also quoted there, and Labour Prime Minister Tony Blair's invoking of 'zero tolerance' in his speech of

29 September 1998. Adaptive responses to the normality of crime are the target of the much quoted remark by Raymond Kelly, former New York City Police Commissioner: 'A number of years ago there began to appear, in the windows of automobiles parked on the streets of American cities, signs which read: "No radio". Rather than express outrage, or even annoyance at the possibility of a car break-in, people tried to communicate with the potential thief in conciliatory terms. The translation of "no radio" is: "Please break into someone else's car, there's nothing in mine." These "no radio" signs are flags of urban surrender. They are handwritten capitulations. Instead of "no radio", we need new signs that say "no surrender" ', cited in D. P. Moynihan, 'Towards a New Intolerance' *The Public Interest*, no 112 (Winter 1993), 122 and in W. Bennett *et al.*, *Body Count*, 193.

84 As Susan Sontag points out, 'War making is one of the few activities that people are not supposed to view "realistically"; that is, with an eye to expense and practical outcome. In all-out war, expenditure is all-out, unprudent—war being defined as an emergency in which no sacrifice is excessive', quoted in J. Best, *Random Violence: How We Talk About New Crimes and New Victims* (Berkeley, CA: University of California Press), 147.

85 On the USA, see M. Mauer, *The Race to Incarcerate* (New York: The New Press, 1998) and A. Sarat (ed), *The Killing State: Capital Punishment in Law, Politics and Culture* (New York: Oxford University Press, 1999). Referring to England and Wales, Dunbar and Langdon note that in the post 1993 period, 'the courts are using prison more freely than at any time in living memory, and they are passing much longer sentences than would have been considered normal 20 or 30 years ago. The explosion in prison numbers is due to an absolutely extraordinary step change in sentencing norms over a very short period', I. Dunbar and A. Langdon, *Tough Justice*, 153.

86 Some examples: 'we are terrified by the prospect of innocent people being gunned down at random, without warning, and almost without motive, by youngsters who afterwards show us the blank, unremorseful face of a feral, pre-social being', J. Q. Wilson, 'Crime and Public Policy', in J. Q. Wilson and J. Petersilia (eds), *Crime* (San Francisco: Institute of Contemporary Studies, 1995), 492. 'America is now home to thickening ranks of juvenile "superpredators"—radically impulsive, brutally remorseless youngsters, including ever more preteenage boys, who murder, assault, rape, rob, burglarize, deal deadly drugs, join gun-toting gangs, and create communal disorders', Bennett *et al.*, *Body Count*, 27. Charles Murray's articles on 'The Emerging British Underclass' talked about 'the new rabble' and young males who are 'essentially barbarians'. C. Murray, *Underclass: The Crisis Deepens* (London: IEA in association with *The Sunday Times*, 1994), 18 and 26. As Adam Sampson points out, sex offenders are frequently discussed in this demonic idiom. 'A crude stereotype of a violent, calculating and perpetually dangerous offender has been built up in the popular press, and . . . in the 'respectable' writing about sexual crime', A. Sampson, *Acts of Abuse: Sex Offenders and the Criminal Justice System* (London: Routledge, 1994).

87 M. Douglas, *Risk and Blame : Essays in Cultural Theory* (London: Routledge, 1992); N. Christie, 'Suitable Enemies', in H. Bianchi and R. van Swaaningen (eds), *Abolitionism: Towards a Non-Repressive Approach to Crime* (Amsterdam: Free University Press, 1986).

88 J. Q. Wilson and R. J. Herrnstein, *Crime and Human Nature: The Definitive Study of the Causes of Crime* (New York: Simon & Schuster, 1986); L. Mead, *The New*

Politics of Poverty; C. Murray, *The Emerging British Underclass* (London: The IEA Health and Welfare Unit, 1990); C. Murray, *Underclass: The Crisis Deepens* (London: IEA Health and Welfare Unit, in association with *The Sunday Times*, 1994); W. Bennett *et al.*, *Body Count* (New York: Simon & Schuster, 1996).

89 President Ronald Reagan, quoted in K. Beckett, *Making Crime Pay* (New York: Oxford University Press, 1997), 47.

90 For details of these contradictory elements in the crime policy of the Clinton administration, see Lord Windlesham, *Politics, Punishment and Populism* (New York: Oxford University Press, 1998), 30 ff. and H. Chernoff *et al.*, 'The Politics of Crime', *Harvard Journal of Legislation* (1996), vol 33, 527–79. On the oscillations of UK policy, see Lord Windlesham, *Responses to Crime vol 3: Legislating with the Tide* (Oxford: Oxford University Press, 1996).

Chapter 6   Crime Complex

1 As I noted in the Preface, I proceed here on the assumption that there are structural similarities (as well as extensive examples of imitation and borrowing) that make it worthwhile to discuss the UK and the USA together. To do so is, of course, to gloss over important dissimilarities. This is exacerbated by the fact that discussions of 'US' crime control gloss over the great variation that marks off the fifty different states, the District of Columbia, and the federal system, and 'UK' developments mask the differences that set off Scotland and Northern Ireland from England and Wales. What I take to be interesting, and worth trying to explain, is the fact that similar patterns of punishment and crime control have recently emerged in both of these countries. My argument will allude to differences of content, timing and context where these are significant in respect of this structural level of analysis.

2 Readers should bear in mind that such measures are still not the standard means of dealing with convicted offenders—most of whom are convicted of minor offences or misdemeanours and are dealt with by less expensive, less penal, and less expressive measures such as fines and probation and discharge. My concern at this point is to describe and explain these new strategies. Chapter 7 will discuss the field as a whole.

3 W. G. Skogan, 'Community Organizations and Crime,' in M. Tonry and N. Morris (eds), *Crime and Justice: An Annual Review of Research* (Chicago: University Press of Chicago, 1988); D. Rosenbaum, 'Community Crime Prevention: A Review and Synthesis of the Literature', *Justice Quarterly* (1988), vol 5, 323–95; P. N. Grabowsky, 'Law Enforcement and the Citizen: Non-Governmental Participants in Crime Prevention and Control', *Policing and Society* (1992), vol 2, 249–71. A. Crawford, *The Local Governance of Crime* (Oxford: Clarendon Press, 1997).

4 Details of these measures can be found in the literature cited in Chapter 4. For a discussion of chain gangs, which were re-instituted in Alabama in 1995 and subsequently in several other southern states, see K. Barry, 'Chain Gangs' (unpublished paper on file with the author). Bills to permit the corporal punishment of juveniles were introduced in the state legislatures of Mississippi (where the bill passed into law), Oklahoma, New York, and California between 1994 and 1997. On 'no frills prisons' see P. Finn, 'No-Frills Prisons and Jails', Federal Probation (September 1996), vol 60, 35–44 and J. Nossiter, 'Making Hard Times Harder.' *New York Times*, 17 September, 1994, sect 1, p. 1 which describes the reintroduction of striped uniforms and reduced privileges in southern state prisons. On Sex Offender Orders in Britain, as well as Anti-Social Behaviour Orders and mandatory minimum sentences,

see D. Downes, 'Toughing it Out: From Labour Opposition to Labour Government', *Policy Studies*, (1998), 19 (3/4).

5 Clearly the USA has gone further in this direction than has the UK, and there are major differences of scale and intensity that mark off one jurisdiction from the other. There are also more recent differences of emphasis that distinguish recent Democratic and New Labour initiatives from those undertaken by the Republican and Conservative administrations that preceded them. But what is striking, and most relevant for the structural account developed here, is the extent to which the strategic patterns, discursive themes, political debates, and policy choices of the two nations and their two governing parties have come to be so closely aligned in recent years.

6 F. E. Zimring, 'Populism, Democratic Government, and the Decline of Expert Authority: Some Reflections on "Three Strikes" in California', *Pacific Law Journal*, 28 (1996), 243–56; Federal Sentencing Reporter, *Special Issue on 'Sentencing in England: The Rise of Populist Punishment'* (Vera Institute of Justice, California: University of California Press, 1998); A. E. Bottoms, 'The Philosophy and Politics of Punishment and Sentencing', in C. Clark and R. Morgan (eds), *The Politics of Sentencing Reform*, (Oxford: Clarendon Press, 1995).

7 D. Lewis, *Hidden Agenda* (London: Hamish Hamilton, 1997); S. Pillsbury, 'Why Are We Ignored? The Peculiar Place of Experts in the Current Debate About Crime and Justice', *Criminal Law Bulletin* (July/August 1995).

8 Recent statements by Britain's New Labour government to the effect that it will develop 'evidence-led' crime policies mark the recognition of this tendency. It remains to be seen whether these statements will, in fact, herald its herald its reversal. In July 2000, and without prior consulation with either the police or Home Office researchers, Prime Minister Tony Blair announced his intention to introduce a new police power to impose summary 'on-the-spot' fines upon disorderly individuals. The next day, the Prime Minister's office withdrew the proposal in the face of overwhelmingly negative reactions from the press and criminal justice professionals.

9 See W. Kaminer, *Its All the Rage: Crime and Culture* (New York: Addison-Wesley, 1995), 71.

10 For a discussion of the crime victim in contemporary culture, see J. M. Boutellier, *Crime and Morality: The Significance of Criminal Justice in Post-Modern Culture* (London: Kluwer, 2000).

11 Labour Party, *Everyone's a Victim* (London: Central Office, 28 March 1995); President's Task Force on Victims, *Final Report* (Washington, DC: Government Printing Office, 1982) pp. vii and 3.

12 The quotation is from W. Kaminer, *It's All the Rage*, 71.

13 On this, see J. Best, *Random Violence: How We Talk About New Crimes and New Victims* (Berkeley, CA: University of California Press, 1999), ch. 5.

14 On the idea of expressive justice and punitive reactions as 'therapy', see D. C. Anderson, *Crime and the Politics of Hysteria* (New York: Times Books, 1995).

15 L. Friedman, *Crime and Punishment in American History* (New York: Basic Books, 1993); H. Chernoff et al., 'The Politics of Crime', *Harvard Journal of Legislation* (1996), vol 33, 527–79; H. Jacob, 1984. *The Frustration of Policy* (Boston: Little, Brown and Co, 1984); D. Downes and R. Morgan, ' "Hostages to Fortune"? The Politics of Law and Order in Post-War Britain', in M. Maguire et al. (eds), *The Oxford Handbook of Criminology* (Oxford: Clarendon Press, 1994); K. Beckett, *Making Crime Pay* (New York: Oxford University Press, 1997).

16 Lord Windlesham, *Responses to Crime*, vol 2 (Oxford: Oxford University Press, 1993).

17 M. Hough and J. Roberts, 'Sentencing Trends in Britain: Public Knowledge and Public Opinion', *Punishment & Society* (1999), 1 (1), 11–26.

18 As Stuart Hall states, '[populism] is no rhetorical device or trick. . . . Its success and effectivity do not lie in its capacity to dupe unsuspecting folk but in the way it addresses real problems, real and lived experiences, real contradictions.' S. Hall, *The Hard Road to Renewal* (London: Verso, 1988), 56.

19 The best study of this issue is K. Beckett, *Making Crime Pay* which appears to demonstrate a high degree of malleability. Beckett's data suggest that public opinion and concern about crime follow the lead of media headlines and political initiatives. But in fact her data is such that it is always liable to produce such a finding, because she uses polls that ask 'What is the biggest problem facing the country?'—an inquiry that prompts responses intended to indicate a knowledge of what is happening in national politics, rather than revealing personal feelings and localized concerns. Note that Beckett also points out that the discourse of law and order resonates with 'important cultural themes and sentiments' (p. 11).

20 S. Donziger (ed), *The Real War on Crime* (New York: Harper Perennial, 1996); Her Majesty's Prison Service, *Audit of Prison Resources* (London: HM Prison Service, 1996).

21 M. Miller, 'Cells vs. Cops vs. Classrooms', in L. Friedman and G. Fisher (eds), *The Crime Conundrum*, (New York: Westview Press, 1997), 127–62.

22 See J. R. Sparks, *Television and the Drama of Crime* (Milton Keynes: Open University Press, 1992): '[I]f these [crime] stories do . . . relate in any way worth mentioning to the feelings, sympathies and attitudes of their audiences, they can only do so by first being sufficiently successful in gaining attention, holding interest and providing pleasure' (p. 149).

23 In the UK, 1992 was the peak year for recorded crime rates. The Home Office (1996) reported that 'There were 5.0 million offences recorded by the police in 1996, 1 per cent fewer than in 1995. This was the fourth consecutive annual fall, the first such occurrence this century', *Criminal Statistics for England and Wales* (p. 16). Note though that the 1996 British Crime Survey report suggests an increase of 4 per cent in crimes against individuals and their property between 1993 and 1996. In the USA, according to UCR data, recorded crime peaked in 1980, when it reached a record high of 5950 per 100,000. Thereafter the rate steadily dropped until 1984, rose again until 1990, and sharply decreased during the 1990s. See US Department of Justice, Federal Bureau of Investigation Uniform Crime Reports, *Crime in the United States 1995* (Washington, DC: US Government Printing Office, 1995). The NCVS surveys suggest that the victimization rate peaked in 1981. See United States Department of Justice, *Criminal Victimization* (Washington, DC: US Government Printing Office, 1994 and 1996). See Appendix, Figures 1 and 2.

24 For Michel Foucault's use of the term 'experience', from which I derive this conception, see M. Foucault, 'Preface to the History of Sexuality, Volume II', in P. Rabinow (ed), *The Foucault Reader* (New York: Pantheon, 1984).

25 D. Garland, *Punishment and Welfare* (Aldershot: Gower, 1985); M. Weiner, *Reconstructing the Criminal* (New York: Cambridge University Press, 1990).

26 For information on the distribution of victimization in the USA by race, Hispanic origin, household income, region and home ownership of households victimized, see

United States Department of Justice, *Criminal Victimization in the United States: 1973–1992 Trends* (Washington, DC: US Government Printing Office, 1994), 7–8. For data on England and Wales, see M. Hough, *Anxiety About Crime: Findings From the 1994 British Crime Survey* (London: Home Office ,1995).

27 See T. G. Taylor *et al.*, 'Salience of Crime and Support for Harsher Criminal Sanctions', *Social Problems* (1979), vol 26, no 4: 'It is clear that support for harsher sanctions is (at least sometimes) an ideological position and that holding this position is related to the salience of crime in the environment. . . . Measuring the environmental salience of the crime issue is more difficult. Salience is only partly a result of changes in objective phenomena (e.g. crime rates). It is clearly influenced by media, political campaigns and all of the other diffuse sources of cultural information and cultural change . . .' (p. 423).

28 Both T. Tyler and R. J. Boeckmann, '"Three Strikes and You Are Out", But Why? The Psychology of Public Support for Punishing Rule Breakers,' *Law and Society Review* (1997), vol 331, no 2 and K. Beckett, *Making Crime Pay* summarize polling data evidence suggesting that the US public has become more punitive over recent decades. See also G. Pettinico, 'Crime and Punishment; America Changes Its Mind', *The Public Perspective* (September/October 1994); P. B. Ellsworth and S. R. Gross, 'Hardening of the Attitudes: Americans' Views on the Death Penalty', *Journal of Social Issues* (1994), vol 50, no 2, 19–52. On attitudes to punishment in Britain, see M. Hough and J. Roberts, 'Sentencing Trends in Britain'.

29 Given the lack of directly relevant empirical evidence about these developments, I should emphasize the suggestive character of the analysis that follows.

30 A. Rutherford, *Criminal Justice and the Pursuit of Decency* (Oxford: Oxford University Press, 1993).

31 J. B. Jacobs, *Stateville* (Chicago: University of Chicago Press, 1977); Lord Windlesham, *Responses to Crime*, vol 3 (Oxford: Oxford University Press, 1996).

32 S. Brint, *In An Age of Experts* (Princeton, NJ: Princeton University Press, 1994); P. Baldwin, *The Politics of Social Solidarity* (New York: Cambridge University Press, 1990); C. Pierson, *Beyond the Welfare State* (Oxford: Polity, 1994).

33 H. Perkin, *The Rise of Professional Society* (London: Routledge, 1989). These economic interests and educational credentials mark off the professional middle classes and especially those employed in the public sector from the commercial and business middle classes. See S. Brint, *In An Age of Experts* for an account of the differences.

34 See S. Ranulf, *Moral Indignation and Middle Class Psychology* (New York: 1964) on the punitive attitudes of the lower middle classes and their social roots.

35 R. Fishman, *Bourgeois Utopias* (New York: Basic Books, 1987); N. Elias and J. Scotson, *The Established and the Outsiders* (London: Cass, 1965).

36 The Labour Government Home Secretary makes just this point in support of Labour's tough new crime policy. 'For many years, the concern of those who lived in areas undermined by crime and disorder were ignored or overlooked by people whose comfortable notions of human behaviour were matched only by their comfortable distance from its worst excesses', J. Straw, 'Crime and Old Labour's Punishment', *The Times*, 8 April 1998.

37 N. Glazer, 'Towards a Self-Service Society', *Public Interest* (1987), no 70, 66–90; J. Hopkins, 'Social Work Through the Looking Glass', in N. Parton (ed), *Social Theory, Social Change and Social Work* (London: Routledge, 1996); D. Yergin and J. Stanislaw, *The Commanding Heights* (New York: Simon & Schuster, 1998).

38 '[F]ew persons with an extensive criminal justice background serve as close policy advisors to elected executives. Nor are such experts brought in to consult in a serious way when criminal justice policy is formulated. Can we imagine major legislative decisions on health policy being made without careful consultation of doctors, insurance executives, and health care administrators?', S. Pillsbury, 'Why Are We Ignored?', 313.

39 A. E. Bottoms, 'Introduction to the Coming Penal Crisis', in A. E. Bottoms and R. H. Preston (eds), *The Coming Penal Crisis* (Edinburgh: Scottish Academic Press, 1981); F. A. Allen, *The Decline of the Rehabilitative Ideal* (New Haven: Yale University Press, 1981).

40 M. Foucault, *Discipline and Punish* (London: Allen Lane, 1977), 247; J. B. Jacobs, 'The Prisoners' Rights Movement and its Impacts, 1960–1980', in N. Morris and M. Tonry (eds), *Crime and Justice: An Annual Review of Research* (Chicago: University of Chicago Press, 1980); M. Maguire *et al.*, *Accountability and Prisons* (London: Tavistock, 1985).

41 J. Simon, *Poor Discipline* (Chicago: University of Chicago Press, 1993); N. Parton, 'Social Work, Risk and "the Blaming System"', in N. Parton (ed), *Social Theory, Social Change and Social Work* (London: Routledge, 1996).

42 R. Bayer, 'Crime, Punishment and the Decline of Liberal Optimism', in *Crime and Delinquency* (April 1981), 169–90; B. Ehrenreich, *Fear of Falling: The Inner Life of the Middle Class* (New York: Perennial, 1989); K. B. Bottomley and J. G. Johnstone, 'Labour's Crime Policy in Context', *Policy Studies* (1998), vol 19, no 3–4, 173–84; K. Beckett, *Making Crime Pay*. The emergence of 'left realism' as an influential position among radical criminologists, especially in the UK, is another important indicator of the collapse of older left-liberal positions. For a discussion of the context in which this shift occurred, see I. Taylor, 'Left Realist Criminology and the Free Market Experiment in Britain', J. Young and R. Matthews (eds), *Rethinking Criminology: The Realist Debate* (London: Sage, 1992).

43 A. E. Bottoms, 'Introduction to the Coming Penal Crisis'; F. A. Allen, *The Decline of the Rehabilitative Ideal*.

44 D. Greenberg and D. Humpries, 'The Co-Optation of Fixed Sentencing Reform', *Crime and Delinquency* (1980), vol 26, 205–25.

45 See Appendix, Figures 1 and 2. '[Recorded] Crime has risen over ninefold since 1950. The rate per 100,000 population increased from about 1,100 in 1940 to 9,400 in 1996. The average annual percentage increase over the past 40 years has been about 6 per cent', Home Office, *Criminal Statistics for England and Wales* (London: HMSO, 1996), 16. See also United States Department of Justice, *Criminal Victimization in the United States: 1973–1992 Trends* (Washington, DC: US Government Printing Office, 1994).

46 W. G. Skogan and M. Maxfield, *Coping With Crime* (Beverly Hills: Sage, 1981); M. Hough, *Anxiety About Crime: Findings From the 1994 British Crime Survey* (London: Home Office, 1995); C. Mirrlees-Black *et al.*, *The 1996 British Crime Survey* (London: HMSO, 1996).

47 See the Presidents Task Force on Victims, *Final Report* (Washington DC: Government Printing Office, 1982); Research and Forecasts Inc, *America Afraid: How Fear of Crime Changes the Way We Live: The Figgie Reports* (New York: NAL.Research and Forecasts, 1983). In the USA, especially after the 1960s, fear of crime came to be heavily overlaid by racial antagonisms and anxieties, to the extent

that political discourse about 'the crime problem' often carried a powerful subtext that spoke to interracial hostilities: see T. Edsall, *Chain Reaction*, 224. As Stuart Hall has argued, the UK is by no means free of this kind of racial division, but the scale and intensity of the problem is quite different. See Hall *et al.*, *Policing the Crisis* (London: MacMillan, 1978). Poor minorities are typically at greatest risk of victimization. The *Criminal Justice Newsletter* of 15 June 1994 reports that 'Residents of black households are about three times as likely to be concerned about crime in their neighborhood as residents of white households, and the gap is widening, according to a Justice Department Study.' According to the 1991 census, 5.5 per cent of the UK population is non-white; the equivalent US figure is 25.8 per cent.

48 '[M]ost urban dwellers cannot get through a day without being touched by [crime] in one way or another', W. G. Skogan and M. Maxfield, *Coping With Crime* (Beverly Hills: Sage, 1981), 11. D. C. Anderson, *Crime and the Politics of Hysteria* argues that recent policies have been driven by a public perception that crime increasingly involved 'random violence against innocent middle-class victims, committed by criminals the system might have controlled better' (p. 55). He quotes Mike Reynolds, who campaigned for a tough sentencing law after the murder of his daughter: 'What these crimes have done is show people that you can do all the right things and it doesn't matter. You can lock your door, stay in the right neighborhoods . . . When bad guys are killing bad guys, that's one thing. But when they start killing regular people, that's where you draw the line in the sand. That's what's driving people crazy' (p. 12).

49 I. Taylor, *Crime in Context* (Oxford: Policy, 1999); D. C. Anderson, *Crime and the Politics of Hysteria* (New York: Times Books, 1995); C. Hay, 'Mobilization Through Interpellation: James Bulger, Juvenile Crime and the Construction of a Moral Panic', *Social and Legal Studies* (1995), 4 (2).

50 B. Campbell, *Goliath:Britain's Dangerous Places* (London: Methuen, 1993); K. Beckett, *Making Crime Pay*.

51 On fear, see C. Hale, 'Fear of Crime: a Review of the Literature', *International Review of Victimology,* (1996, vol 4, 79–150. On exclusion, see W. J. Wilson, *The Truly Disadvantaged* (Chicago: Chicago University Press, 1987) and *When Work Disappears* (New York: Knopf, 1997); B. Campbell, *Goliath*; L. Morris, *The Dangerous Classes: The Underclass and Social Citizenship* (London: Routledge, 1994).

52 There are, of course, many varieties of family and household in contemporary Britain and America, and a great diversity of lifestyles, even within a single class. My discussion here is intended to sketch a rough trajectory of change, and to suggest some of the typical domestic consequences of these social trends.

53 A. R. Hochschild, *The Time Bind* (New York: Metropolitan Books, 1997); J. B. Schor, *The Overworked American* (New York: Basic Books, 1992); P. Hewitt, *About Time: The Revolution in Work and Family Life* (London: Institute of Public Policy Research, 1993).

54 For a discussion of the 'separation of time and space' and 'disembedding' see A. Giddens, *The Consequences of Modernity* (Oxford: Polity Press, 1990). A telling example of how these ecological changes impact upon the daily lives of families is the data on the journey to school. 'In 1971 . . . 80 per cent of seven and eight year old children in England travelled to school on their own, unaccompanied by an adult. By 1990, this figure had dropped to 9 per cent; the questionnaire survey disclosed that the parents' main reason for not allowing their children to travel independently was fear

of traffic', J. Adams, *Risk* (London: UCL Press, 1995), 13. For data on the changing workload of American families, see J. B. Schor, *The Overworked American*.

55 That arrangement, of course, produced serious pathologies and forms of oppression of its own. My point is not to celebrate the inequality and sexism of the old nuclear family, but instead to point to some of the hidden consequences of its subsequent transformation.

56 The phrase 'ontological insecurity' is from A. Giddens, *The Consequences of Modernity*. On the changing nature of work in what he calls 'the new capitalism', see R. Sennett, *The Corrosion of Character* (New York: Norton, 1998). For an empirical study of the connection between these concerns and support for punitive measures, see T. R. Tyler and R. J. Boeckmann, 'Three Strikes and You Are Out, But Why? The Psychology of Public Support for Punishing Rule Breakers', *Law and Society Review* (1997), vol 331, no 2.

57 The rather different stresses and insecurities of working-class and poor households are, if anything, even more intense, and have been exacerbated by the neo-liberal policies and 'welfare reforms' of the 1980s and 1990s. My focus here is on middle class attitudes because shifts in the political orientation of this group played a key role in facilitating the movement away from penal-welfare policies.

58 L. E. Cohen and D. Cantor, 'The Determinants of Larceny in the United States: Life-Style and Demographic Factors Associated with the Probability of Victimization', *Journal of Research in Crime and Delinquency* (1981), vol 18, 113–27; M. Felson, *Crime and Everyday Life*, 2nd edn (Thousand Oaks, Ca.: Pine Forge Press, 1998).

59 I. Taylor, 'Private Homes and Public Others', *British Journal of Criminology* (1995), vol 35, no 2, 63–285.

60 A. Giddens, *The Consequences of Modernity*.

61 Girling *et al.* put it well: 'in speaking of crime, people routinely register its entanglement with other aspects of economic, social and moral life; attribute responsibility and blame; demand accountability and justice, and draw lines between "us" and various categories of "them" . . . "fear of crime" research is at its most illuminating when it addresses the various sources of in/security that pervade people's lives (and the relationships between them), and when it makes explicit (rather than suppresses) the connections the "crime-related" anxieties of citizens have with social conflict and division, social justice and solidarity', E. Girling *et al.*, *Crime and Social Change in Middle England* (London: Routledge, 2000, 170.

62 As Albert Biderman put it, as early as 1967: 'We have found that the attitudes of citizens regarding crime are less affected by their past victimization experiences than by ideas about what is going on in their community—fears about a weakening of social controls on which they feel their safety and the broader fabric of social life is ultimately dependent', quoted in W. G. Skogan, *Disorder and Decline* (Chicago: University of Chicago Press, 1990), 76.

63 Peter Schrag argues that changing demographics (i.e. the increased size of what used to be 'minority' groups) exacerbated this sense of unease among middle-class whites in California—a state that has led the country prison expansion and in the fortification of cities. P. Schrag, *Paradise Lost: California's Experience, America's Future* (Berkeley, CA: University of California Press, 1998). See also T. R. Tyler and R. J. Boeckmann, 'Three Strikes and You Are Out, But Why?'.

64 Could it be that the extraordinary public fears and hostilities in respect of certain crimes against children stem from the residual guilt and ambivalence that families feel

about their own choices and the vulnerabilities that they seem to cause? If so, the pae-dophile and the drug dealer are screens upon which we project our guilt as well as our anxieties.

65 D. C. Anderson, *Crime and the Politics of Hysteria* provides many telling examples.

66 J. R. Sparks, *Television and the Drama of Crime* (Milton Keynes: Open University Press, 1992); R. Ericson *et al.*, *Representing Order: Crime, Law and Justice in the News Media* (Buckingham: Open University Press, 1991); D. Duclos, *The Werewolf Complex: America's Fascination with Violence* (New York: Oxford University Press, 1998); R. Reiner *et al.*, 'Discipline or Desubordination: Changing Images of Crime in the Media Since World War II', paper presented to the ISA World Congress, Montreal, July 1998.

67 '[T]hree findings from the literature are inescapable: the public overestimate crime rates, particularly violent crime rates; the public cite the news media as their primary source of information about criminal justice; crimes of violence are considerably overrepresented in the news media', J. V. Roberts, 'Public opinion, crime and crimi-nal justice', in M. Tonry and N. Morris (eds), *Crime and Justice* (Chicago: University of Chicago Press, 1992).

68 An illustration of this is the fact that a majority of US and UK respondents believe that sentencers are typically too lenient, but when faced with a series of actual sen-tencing decisions, the respondents themselves choose sentences that are the same, or more lenient than, those actually given by judges. See M. Hough and J. Roberts, 'Sentencing Trends in Britain: Public Knowledge and Public Opinion', *Punishment & Society* (1999), 1 (1).

69 If proof of this is needed, we should remind ourselves that in the period between 1960 and 1975, when recorded crime rates were rising precipitously in both the UK and the US, the penal policies and practices of both countries continued to develop in pre-cisely the opposite direction, becoming increasingly 'liberal' and 'non-punitive'.

70 M. Foucault, *Discipline and Punish*.

71 M. Felson and R. V. Clarke (eds), *Business and Crime Prevention*, (Monsey, NY: Criminal Justice Press, 1997). Felson and Clarke note however, 'We should not exag-gerate the degree of business innovation in crime prevention. Most businesses put security systems in late, rather than early, relying on expensive technology or guards rather than inexpensive situational prevention. Many guards seek to catch people in the act of stealing rather than designing systems that prevent stealing in the first place. This is why business itself has something to learn' (p. 7). Clifford Shearing points to the role of private policing in developing the community-oriented, problem-solving strategies that have become popular with the public police, C. Shearing, 'The unrecognised origins of the new policing: Linkages between private and public police', in M. Felson and R. V. Clarke (eds), *Business and Crime Prevention*, 219–30.

72 'Whereas the drive to persuade the individual citizen to protect him or herself from crime has many notable landmarks—in the form of ministerial pronouncements, cir-culars and campaigns—business has moved into a state of substantial self-sufficiency in crime prevention without much debate or dissension. In most medium to large size companies, internal security departments now have a history spanning several decades.' J. Burrows, *Making Crime Prevention Pay: Initiatives from Business*, Crime Prevention Unit Papers 27 (London: Home Office, 1991), 1. L. Johnston, *The Rebirth of Private Policing* (London: Routledge, 1992); T. Jones and T. Newburn, *Private Security and Public Policing* (Oxford: Clarendon Press, 1998).

73 A. Beck and A. Willis, *Crime and Security: Managing the Risk to Safe Shopping*, (Leicester: Perpetuity Press, 1995).

74 A. Crawford, *The Local Governance of Crime* (Oxford: Oxford University Press, 1997).

75 M. Foucault, *Discipline and Punish* (London: Allen Lane, 1977): D. Garland, *Punishment and Welfare* (Aldershot: Gower, 1985).

76 H. Krahn and L. W. Kennedy, 'Producing Personal Safety: The Effects of Crime Rates, Police Force Size, and Fear of Crime', *Criminology* (1985), vol 23, no 4, 697–710; R. Warren *et al.*, 'Coproduction, Equity and the Distribution of Safety', *Urban Affairs Quarterly* (1984), vol 19, 447–64.

77 S. Riger *et al.*, 'Coping With Urban Crime: Women's Use of Precautionary Behaviors', *American Journal of Community Psychology* (1982), vol 10, no 4, 369–86; W. G. Skogan and M. Maxfield, *Coping With Crime*; F. DuBow *et al.*, *Reactions to Crime: A Critical Review of the Literature* (Washington, DC: National Institute of Law Enforcement, 1979); W. Conklin, *The Impact of Crime* (New York: MacMillan, 1975); A. L. Schneider and P. B. Schneider, *Private and Public-Minded Citizen Responses to a Neighborhood-Based Crime Prevention Strategy* (Eugene, Ore.: Institute of Policy Analysis, 1977).

78 See Girling *et al.*, *Crime and Social Change in Middle England* (London: Routledge, 2000), ch. 7 for evidence of public ambivalence on the subject of security, especially in respect of CCTV surveillance. These authors note that middle-class respondents were more liable to voice concerns about home security and take steps to establish routine precautions against it than were residents of council house estates.

79 E. Stanko, *Everyday Violence: How Women and Men Experience Sexual and Physical Danger* (London: Pandora's Press, 1990). The role of women in the new politics of crime control is pivotal: in the victims movement, in the fear of crime policy, in everyday adaptations, and in pressure group campaigns for protection against domestic violence, sex offending, drunk driving, and child abuse.

80 Research and Forecasts, *America Afraid*; V. H. Sacco and H. Johnson, *Patterns of Criminal Victimization in Canada* (Canada: Minister of Supply and Services, 1990); T J. Flanagan and K. Maguire, *Sourcebook of Criminal Justice Statistics* (1994) (Table 2.42, 'Reported Self-Protective Measures Taken as a Result of Concern about Crime'). See E. Anderson, *Streetwise: Race, Class and Change in an Urban Community* (Chicago: University of Chicago Press, 1990), ch. 8 for an ethnographic account of crime avoidance by poor blacks in a inner city community.

81 P. N. Grabowsky, 'Law Enforcement and the Citizen: Non-governmental participants in crime prevention and crime control', *Policing and Society* (1992), vol 2, 249–71. 'Collective action for crime prevention by citizen groups ranks with the growth of the private security industry as one of the more distinctive developments in the United States . . . in recent years. Inspired in part by the perception that police resources were insufficient to provide patrol coverage in residential neighbourhoods, and encouraged by law enforcement agencies themselves, the most common model of this activity is neighbourhood watch . . .' (p.253). See also L. Johnston, *The Rebirth of Private Policing*, chs. 7 and 8.

82 See S. Christopherson, 'The Fortress City: Privatised Spaces, Consumer Citizenship', in A. Amin (ed), *Post-Fordism: A Reader* (Oxford: Blackwell, 1994), 409–10. Christopherson points out that: 'Contemporary defensive design responds to the connection between profit and safety. It also reflects an awareness that property values are significantly affected by security . . .' (p. 420).

83 E. Blakely and M. G. Snyder, *Fortress America* (Washington: Brookings Institute, 1997, 28. On the militarization of city life in Los Angeles, see M. Davis, *City of Quartz* (London: Vintage, 1990). On safe shopping, see A. Beck and A. Willis, *Crime and Security*. On 'geographies of exclusion', see D. Sibley, *Geographies of Exclusion* (London: Routledge, 1995). On fear of crime in women's lives, see E. Madriz, *Nothing Bad Happens to Good Girls: Fear of Crime in Women's Lives* (Berkeley, CA: University of California Press, 1997).

84 Christopherson,'The Fortress City': 'While . . . streetscapes continue to exist as sideshows, the dominant design tendency is to construct larger, highly managed commercial and consumption environments. These . . . are designed to insulate and isolate, to buffer and protect so-called 'normal users' in the space. The highly managed character of these spaces is as much defined by what is excluded as by what is included' (p. 417).

85 C. D. Shearing, 'The Relation between Public and Private Policing', M. Tonry and N. Morris, *Crime and Justice* (1992), 423.

86 D. J. Kennedy, 'Residential Associations as State Actors' *Yale Law Journal*, vol 105 (1995, 761–93 at 765.

87 On the measurement of routine precautions, see United States Department of Justice, *Sourcebook of Criminal Justice Statistics 1995* (Washington, DC: US Government Printing Office, 1996), 173, Table 2.42, 'Reported self-protective measures taken as a result of concern about crime'. More formal, collective action, such as neighbourhood watch schemes, has been evaluated: see T. H. Bennett, *Evaluating Neighbourhood Watch* (Cambridge: Cambridge University Press. 1990) and W. G. Skogan, *Disorder and Decline*, ch. 6.

88 One ought not to overlook the pleasure that is to be had in crime and punishment as sources of entertainment—sometimes very directly, in 'real life' crime television shows such as 'Crime Stoppers', 'Crime Watch UK'—more often mediated through dramatic fiction. See J. R. Sparks, *Television and the Drama of Crime* (Milton Keynes: Open University Press, 1992).

89 'High' is, of course, a relative term. In the USA and the UK, today's rates of crime and violence remain at an historically high level despite recent decreases, and are widely perceived as such, particularly by older people who can recall the very different circumstances of the 1950s and early 1960s. For my purposes, a 'high' rate of crime is one where crime avoidance is a prominent organizing principle of everyday life.

90 Analysing data in respect of three criminal justice issues (in response to questions about the death penalty, the sentencing of offenders, and expenditure on crime control) between 1950s and the 1990s, Sharpe notes: '[S]ince the mid-1960s, there really have been only two phases of public opinion about crime and punishment: an initial phase (1966 to approximately 1980) of sharply increasing concern and punitiveness, and a second phase (1980–1993) in which the high-water mark of public concern from the first phase is sustained, relatively unchanged', E. B. Sharpe, *The Sometime Connection: Public Opinion and Social Policy* (Albany NY: State University of New York Press, 1999), 53. Sharpe's conclusion is that public opinion on this issue is not responsive to actual policy changes. Tyler and Boeckmann reach a similar conclusion, after having found a link between punitive attitudes and a specific set of social values: 'Since social values represent long-term political orientations they reflect a stable influence on public opinion and are unlikely to change in reaction to contemporary public events. Hence the strong influence they have over punitiveness suggests

that current levels of public support form punitiveness are not simply the result of recent highly visible events like the Polly Klaas kidnapping. Instead, they develop from underlying social values that are stable and will shape public views for the near future', T. R. Tyler and R. J. Boeckmann, 'Three Strikes and You Are Out. But Why?' (p. 257),

91 These effects do, of course, vary in character and expression. For example, the political meaning of 'the crime victim' in the UK is not the same as in the USA, where a part of the victims' movement has been drawn into the orbit of right wing, punitive politics. But in both countries, the figure of the victim has become prominent and is increasingly used to justify measures of punishment and public protection.

92 Zimring and Hawkins call this process 'categorial contagion', F. E. Zimring and G. Hawkins, *Crime is Not the Problem* (New York: Oxford University Press, 1997), 4.

93 Z. Bauman, 'The Social Uses of Law and Order', in D. Garland and J. R. Sparks (eds), *Criminology and Social Theory* (Oxford: Oxford University Press, 2000).

Chapter 7   The New Culture of Crime Control

1 For accounts of institutions that *were* heavily committed to a correctionalist ethos, see, see F. L. Carney, *Criminality and its Treatment: The Patuxent Experience* (Malabar, FL: Krieger Publishing Co, 1989) and E. Genders and E. Player, *Grendon: A Study of a Therapeutic Prison* (Oxford: Oxford University Press, 1995).

2 See K. Maguire and A. Pastore (ed), *Sourcebook of Criminal Justice Statistics 1998* (Washington, DC: Bureau of Justice Statistics) section 1 provides detailed information on the characteristics of the US criminal justice system, including employment, expenditure and workload. See also, C. G. Camp and G. M. Camp (eds), *The Corrections Yearbook* 1998 (Middletown, CN: Criminal Justice Institute 1998). For recent trends in England and Wales, see Home Office, *Digest 4: Information on the Criminal Justice System*, ed. G. C. Barclay and C. Travers (London: Home Office, 1999).

3 P. White *et al.*, *Projections of Long Term Trends in the Prison Population to 2006* (London: Home Office, 2000) report that 'Between 1992 and 1997 the custody rate at the Crown Court rose from 44% to 60%. The average sentence length for adults also increased, from 21.0 months to 23.9 months. . . . At the magistrates' courts the custody rate for indictable offences doubled from 5% to 10%' (p. 3). See also I. Dunbar and A. Langdon, *Tough Justice* (London: Blackstone, 1998), ch. 11, 143–33. For a detailed analysis of US trends in prison committals, average time served, and parole revocations between 1980 and 1996, see A. Blumstein and A. J. Beck, 'Population Growth in US Prisons, 1980–1996', in M. Tonry and J. Petersilia (eds), *Prisons* (Chicago: University of Chicago Press, 1999, 17–62.

4 P. Manning, *Police Work*, 2nd edn (Prospect Heights, Ill: Waveland Press, 1997); A. J. Reiss, 'Police organization in the Twentieth Century', in M. Tonry and N. Morris (eds), *Modern Policing* (Chicago: University of Chicago Press, 1992); R. Reiner, 'Policing a Postmodern Society', *The Modern Law Review* (1992), vol 55, 761–81.

5 T. Jones *et al.*, *Democracy and Policing*, (London: PSI, 1994); P. Manning, *Police Work*.

6 L. Kurki, 'Restorative and Community Justice in the United States', in M. Tonry (ed) *Crime and Justice* (Chicago: University of Chicago, 2000). In a different report,

Kurki notes the lack of systematic data on these initiatives: 'No one knows how many or what kinds of programs there are; how many offenders, victims and volunteers participate; the amounts of restitution paid or community service performed; or the effects on victims, communities and offenders.' L. Kurki, *Incorporating Restorative and Community Justice Initiatives into American Sentencing and Corrections*, Research in Brief, No 3 (Washington DC: US Department of Justice, 1999).

7 According to the US Department of Justice Bureau of Justice Statistics, *Census of State and Federal Correctional Facilities, 1995* (Department of Justice, Government Printing Office, 1996) in 1995, 'Over 97% of correctional facilities offered counselling. Drug and alcohol counselling was available in nearly 90% of facilities; psychological, life skills, and psychiatric counselling in 69%; community adjustment counselling in 67%; employment search counselling in 60%; and parenting and child rearing in nearly 49%.' According to BJS figures, a large increase in staff and types of programme occurred in the period 1990 to 1995. Between 1984 and 1990, the percentage of inmates/residents enrolled in counselling programs increased from 14.2% to 30.8%.

8 'In 1993–4, £9.42 billion was spent on the criminal justice agencies [in England and Wales]. Only £240 million (0.37%) is spent by government directly on prevention', J. Bright, *Turning the Tide: Crime, Community and Prevention* (London: Demos, 1997). For details of crime prevention organizations and practices, see A. Crawford, *The Local Governance of Crime* (Oxford: Oxford University Press, 1997); A. Crawford, *Crime Prevention and Community Safety* (London: Longman, 1998) and M. Tonry and D. P. Farrington (eds), *Building a Safer Society* (Chicago: University of Chicago Press, 1995).

9 In Britain, the Crime and Disorder Act 1998, places local, partnership-based, crime reduction efforts on a statutory basis. For details, see the guidelines issued by the Home Office to local authorities: Home Office, *Guidance on Statutory Crime and Disorder Partnerships* (1998) www.home office.gov.uk/cdact/index.htm

10 'Populism' is more extensive and more endemic in the American context because the political institutions of the USA are more populist in design and tend to be more responsive to public pressure than those of the UK. Many US states permit the periodic popular election of justice officials (sheriffs, prosecutors, judges) which gives these officials reason to be attentive to local public opinion. Several states have direct voter initiatives that allow legislation to be framed by voters and subjected to referendum vote. In contrast, the punitive populism of recent British policy is less structurally determined. The most populist Home Secretary of recent times—Michael Howard—was preceded in that office by Douglas Hurd, whose style was a mix of patrician and mandarin, and whose policies of 'punishment in the community' and crime prevention followed the advice of criminological researchers rather than popular opinion. The crime complex may promote populism, but British political institutions tend to inhibit it.

11 D. C. Anderson, *Crime and the Politics of Hysteria* (New York: Times Books, 1995).

12 See J. R. Sparks, 'Risk and blame in criminal justice controversies', in M. Brown and J. Pratt (eds), *Dangerous Offenders: Criminal Justice and Social Order* (London: Routledge, 2000).

13 '[T]he task of government in contemporary, complex societies, is to influence social interactions in such ways that political governing and social self-organisation are

made complementary', J. Kooiman, *Modern Governance: New Social-Governmental Interactions*, (London: Sage, 1993), 256.

14 In the face of private policing, private prisons, private security and the crime prevention activities of citizens, communities and corporations, the state's agencies have become increasingly self-conscious about their relationship to 'private providers'. The result has been the development of specific arrangements for regulating this public–private relationship, whether as voluntary partnerships (as with crime prevention) or as contractual agreements (as with private prisons and commercial provision of criminal justice services). See T. Jones and T. Newburn, *Public Private Security and Public Policing* (Oxford: Clarendon Press, 1998) for details.

15 See D. Garland, 'Penal Modernism and Postmodernism' in T. Blomberg and S. Cohen (eds), *Punishment and Social Control* (New York: Aldine de Gruyter, 1995) for a discussion of the literature on penal change and its social meaning.

16 See P. Pierson, *Dismantling the Welfare State?* (New York: Cambridge University Press, 1994).

17 'The discourse of welfare dependency defines welfare itself as the problem to be tackled, rather than poverty or unemployment, and Clinton, of course, promised to end welfare as we know it, not poverty', J. Peck, *The Guardian*, 7 August 1996.

18 The Scottish Children's Hearing system is an interesting exception to this pattern. See P. Duff and N. Hutton (eds), *Criminal Justice in Scotland* (Aldershot: Ashgate, 1999), ch. 14.

19 On penal austerity in England and Wales, see J. R. Sparks, 'Penal austerity and social anxiety at the century's turn: governmental rationalities, legitimation deficits and populism in English penal politics in the 1990s', in L. Wacquant (ed), *From Social State to Penal State* (New York: Oxford University Press, forthcoming). On 'no frills' prisons in the US, see P. Finn, 'No-Frills Prisons and Jails: A Movement in Flux', *Federal Probation*, vol 60 (September 1996), 35–44.

20 The Labour Government Home Secretary Jack Straw and his Conservative predecessor Douglas Hurd agree on this. In a recent speech, Straw quoted Hurd (now Chairman of the Prison Reform Trust) on the victim-related purpose of reform in prison: '[W]e can hardly be insensitive to the opportunities which the provision of well-targeted education in prison offers. As your Chairman wrote in an article in yesterday's *Daily Telegraph*, "it is inextricably linked to the future safety of the citizen"', J. Straw, *Making Prisons Work* (The Prison Reform Trust Annual Lecture, December 1998).

21 See H. Kemshall, 'Risk in Probation Practice: The Hazards and Dangers of Supervision', *Probation Journal*, vol 42, no 2 (June 1995), 67–71.

22 E. Wallis, 'A New Choreography: Breaking Away from the Elaborate Corporate Dance', in R. Burnett (ed), *The Probation Service: Responding to Change* (Oxford: Probation Studies Unit, Oxford University, 1997), 91–104 at 91.

23 On the 'credibility' of probation as a punishment in the UK, see H. Rees and E. H. Williams, *Punishment, Custody and the Community* (London: LSE, 1989) and I. Brownlee, *Community Punishment* (London: Longman, 1998). On the failures and credibility problems of US probation, see the Reinventing Probation Council, *Broken Windows Probation* (New York: Manhattan Institute, 7 August 1999).

24 Labour Government Minister Paul Boateng recently announced plans (later withdrawn) to rename the probation service: 'The new name, "Community Punishment and Rehabilitation Service" explains their purpose and signals the way ahead for this

vital service. The importance of their role in protecting the public by effective supervision of offenders in the community to reduce reoffending cannot be underestimated' (Home Office Press Release, 1 December 1999). The Press Release went on to say that 'the CPRS has a key role to play in delivering the Home Secretary's aims on effective sentencing and punishment that: the public is protected from dangerous offenders; offenders are properly punished and their sentences are rigorously enforced; punishments are made to work better both in prison and outside' (p. 1). In the USA, the Reinventing Probation Council makes the same point: 'Probation will be reinvented when the probation profession places public safety first, and works with and in the community', Reinventing Probation Council, *Broken Windows Probation*, 13).

25 H. Kemshall, *Risk in Probation Practice* (Aldershot: Ashgate, 1998) Over the last twenty years, probation in the US and the UK has been a troubled organization, constantly seeking to reinvent itself in a form more compatible with the changing penal climate in which it works. A recent set of proposals for change, offered by an American group of 'veteran practitioners and leading executives' calling themselves the 'Reinventing Probation Council', reflects this struggle to adapt perfectly. Calling its proposals 'Broken Windows Probation' it lists its key imperatives as follows: 'Public safety comes first'; 'Supervise probationers in the neighborhood, not the office'; 'Rationally allocate resources'; 'Enforce violations of probation conditions quickly and strongly'; 'Develop partners in the community'; 'Establish performance indicators'; 'leadership is crucial.'Reinventing Probation Council, *Broken Windows Probation*.

26 The Labour government Home Secretary recently defined his prison policy in these terms: 'First, our policy must be fundamentally about protecting the public. Assessing risk, reducing risk, and managing risk after release are the key elements of the task.' J. Straw, *Making Prisons Work* (The Prison Reform Trust Annual Lecture, December 1998).

27 On the latest phase in the build-up of American prison security, the supermax prison, see R. D. King, 'The rise and rise of supermax: An American solution in search of a problem?', *Punishment & Society*, vol 1, no 2 (1999), 163–86.

28 See N. Christie, *Crime Control as Industry: Towards Gulags Western Style* 2nd edn (London: Routledge, 1994). D. Garland (ed.), *Mass Imprisonment in the USA: Social Causes and Consequences* (London: Sage, forthcoming).

29 For an excellent account, see J. Simon, *Poor Discipline: Parole and the Social Control of the Underclass, 1890–1990* (Chicago: University of Chicago Press, 1993). See also W. J. Wilson, *When Work Disappears* (New York: Knopf, 1997); I. Taylor, *Crime in Context* (Cambridge: Polity Press, 1999), ch. 6; B. Campbell, *Goliath: Britain's Dangerous Places* (London: Methuen, 1993).

30 A. Rutherford, *Criminal Policy and the Eliminative Ideal* (Southampton: Institute of Criminal Justice, University of Southampton, 1996).

31 On the social, economic and penological functions of the American ghetto, see L. Wacquant, 'Deadly symbiosis: when ghetto and prison meet and merge,' *Punishment & Society*, vol 3, no 1 (2001), reprinted in D. Garland (ed), *Mass Imprisonment*.

32 See B. Western and K. Beckett, 'How Unregulated is the US Labor Market? The Penal System as a Labor Market Institution', *American Journal of Sociology*, 104 (January 1999, 1135–72.

33 See J. Gunn *et al.*, *Mentally Disordered Prisoners* (London: Institute of Psychiatry, 1991). One of the recurring features of neo-liberal societies where public services and socialized provision are minimized, is that the jail acts as an expensive institution of

last resort, filling up with individuals who were denied care elsewhere. The New York City jail system has the largest tuberculosis treatment unit in the USA, and one of the largest HIV treatment programmes. There is a tragic irony in this, and not much cost-effectiveness.

34 See B. Harcourt, 'Reflecting on the Subject: A Critique of the Social Influence Conception of Deterrence, the Broken Windows Theory, and Order-Maintenance Policing New York Style', *Michigan Law Review*, vol 97, no 2 (November 1998).

35 See Chapter 5 above. Britain's Labour government recently announced that a new advisory panel that will guide the Court of Appeal in its guideline sentencing decisions will include victims among its members. Home Office Press Release, 5 January 1998. In September 2000, the UK Home Secretary announced the planned introduction of victim impact statements for all victims in criminal cases.

36 Even non-discretionary sentences leave room for discretion—most often at the point of prosecution. Individuation may occur at that point, though the prosecutors concerns differ significantly from those of the judge, and are more often directed to securing a conviction rather than doing justice or obtaining the sentence that best fits the individual's needs and deserts.

37 See Christie, *Crime Control as Industry*, ch. 8. As Noam Chomsky observed in a different context, it is very much easier to unleash violent force against an enemy when you do not see your human targets up close. N. Chomsky, *American Power and the New Mandarins* (New York: Pantheon Books, 1969).

38 M. Foucault, *Discipline and Punish*. 'In certain societies . . . the more one possesses power or privilege, the more one is marked as an individual, by rituals, written accounts or visual reproductions. . . . In a disciplinary regime, on the other hand, individualization is 'descending': as power becomes more anonymous and more functional, those on whom it is exercised tend to be more strongly individualized. . . . In a system of discipline, the child is more individualized than the adult, the patient more than the healthy man, the madman and the delinquent more than the normal and the non-delinquent', 192–3.

39 'Ironically, once risk becomes institutionalised the ability and willingness of professionals to take risks—in the original sense of possible positive as well as negative outcomes—is curtailed', N. Parton, 'Social work, risk, and "the blaming system" ', in N. Parton (ed), *Social Theory, Social Change and Social Work* (London: Routledge, 1996, 113.

40 And not only the offender. The US Department of Housing and Urban Development currently has a policy which mandates that any drug-related or other serious crime by a member of a tenant's household is grounds for eviction from public housing. 'As President Clinton stressed in announcing the policy in 1996 . . . holding innocent tenants strictly responsible for the destructive conduct of members of their household . . . is essential to maintaining project safety', Center for the Community Interest, *CCI Friday Fax* (10 July 1998).

41 'Restorative justice' initiatives—endorsed by the 1998 Crime and Disorder Act, and used as an alternative to cautioning by many police forces—are an important contrast to this. At least in victim-offender mediation, the offender is intended to benefits from the process as well. See J. Braithwaite and S. Mugford, 'Conditions of Successful Degradation Ceremonies', *British Journal of Criminology* (1994), 34(2), 139–71; J. Hudson and B. Galaway (eds), *Restorative Justice: International Perspectives* (Monsey, NY: Willow Tree Press, 1996).

42 P. Finn, *Sex Offender Community Notification* (Washington DC: National Institute of Justice, Office of Justice Programs, 1997); B. Hebenton and T. Thomas, 'Sexual Offenders in the Community: Reflections on Problems of Law, Community and Risk Management in the U.S.A., England and Wales,' *International Journal of the Sociology of Law* (1996), 24: 427–443.

43 On the current status of these laws, see Home Office, *The Rehabilitation of Offenders Act 1974: A Consultation Paper* (London: Home Office, 1999) and M. D. Mayfield, 'Revisiting Expungement', *Utah Law Review* (1997), 1057.

44 For details, see J. Brilliant, 'The Modern Day Scarlet Letter: A Critical Analysis', *Duke Law Journal* (1989), 1357–85; D. Karp, 'The Judicial and Judicious Use of Shame Penalties', *Crime and Delinquency* (1998) 44: 277–94. T. Vinciguerra, 'The Clothes that Make the Inmate', *New York Times*, 1 October 2000.

45 R. C. Ellickson, 'Controlling Chronic Misconduct in City Spaces: Of Panhandlers, Skid Rows, and Public-Space Zoning,' *Yale Law Journal* (1996), 105: 1165–248.

46 'The generation that once feared a police state now lobbies for a cop on every corner', B. Carlen, 'Insecurity Complex', *California Lawyer* (June 1998), 85

47 On this, see D. Lockwood, 'Social Integration and System Integration', repr. in Lockwood, *Solidarity and Schism* (Oxford: Oxford University Press, 1992).

48 Recently, Ron Clarke has emphasized that 'stimulating conscience' should be regarded as one more technique of situational crime prevention—as when signs are posted pointing out that shoplifting is wrong as well as illegal. But moral appeal is only contingently and marginally involved in this approach—it is not necessary to it. R. V. Clarke, *Situational Crime Prevention: Successful Case Studies*, 2nd edn (Albany NY: Harrow and Heston, 1997), 24. For a critical discussion of the ethics of SCP, see A. von Hirsch, D. Garland and A. Wakefield (eds), *The Ethics of Situational Crime Prevention* (Oxford: Hart Publishing, 2000).

49 For a discussion, see J. Best, *Random Violence* (Berkeley, CA: University of California Press, 1999) and for a vivid example, see W. Bennett *et al.*, *Body Count*. As 'drug czar' in President Bush's administration, Bennett deplicitly sought to 'de-normalize' drug use, depicting drug users as criminals to be punished rather than 'people like us'. This strategy of 'othering' a form of behaviour that had become so widespread as to appear normal is what gives the War on Drugs its massive scope and ideological intensity.

50 See D. Anderson (ed), *This Will Hurt; The Restoration of Virtue and Civic Order* (London: The Social Affairs Unit, 1995); J. Q. Wilson, *Thinking About Crime* (New York: Vintage, 1983), ch. 12; Bennett *et al.*, *Body Count* (New York: Simon & Schuster, 1996); N. Dennis, *Rising Crime and the Dismembered Family* (London: IEA Health and Welfare Unit, 1993).

51 J. J. DiIulio Jr. 'Let 'em Rot', *The Wall Street Journal*, 26 January 1994, A14. Since this was a newspaper article, its title may have been the creation of a sub-editor. In any case, it appears that Mr. DiIulio has recently begun to relent: see his op-ed piece entitled 'Two Million Prisoners Are Enough', *The Wall Street Journal*, 12 March 1999, A14.

52 Prime Minister John Major, *The Sunday Times*, 21 February 1993.

53 The phrase comes from Daphne Markin's review of Inga Clendinnen's *Reading the Holocaust* in the *New York Times Book Review*, p. 17, 11 April 1999. She asks, should we view Nazis—or serious criminals—as 'heinous versions of the rest of us, rather than as opaquely monstrous creatures beyond or beneath our knowing'.

54 As Saint Augustine explained: 'A bad will is the cause of bad actions, but nothing is the cause of a bad will. For when the will abandons what is above itself and turns to what is lower, it becomes evil—not because that is evil to which it turns, but because the turning itself is wicked', St Augustine, *The City of God* (New York: Image Books, 1958).

55 There are unmistakable resonances here of Émile Durkheim's account of the repressive, 'mechanical solidarity' of pre-modern societies. See E. Durkheim, *The Division of Labor* (New York: Free Press, 1933), ch. 2.

56 The remedy for moral poverty and social breakdown offered by William Bennett and his co-authors is indicative: 'How do we restore these bonds? We believe the most obvious answer—and perhaps the only reliable answer—is a widespread renewal of religious faith, and the strengthening of religious institutions', Bennett *et al.*, *Body Count* (New York: Simon & Schuster, 1996), 208.

57 The idea of bringing a specifically economic framework to bear upon the analysis of crime and punishment has been proposed by various writers, most notably Gary Becker, Richard Posner, and Isaac Ehrlich. It is my impression, however, that an economic style of decision-making has first taken root as a result of practical, managerial developments, rather than as a result of academic writing.

58 As noted earlier, the 1998 Crime and Disorder Act requires all local authorities in Britain to conduct crime audits. For a discussion of related issues, in an explicitly economic idiom, see D. Pyle, *Cutting the Costs of Crime: The Economics of Crime and Criminal Justice* (London: IEA, 1995).

59 See J. van Dijk, 'Understanding Crime Rates: On the Interactions Between the Rational Choices of Victims and Offenders', *British Journal of Criminology* (1999), 34 (2): 105–21. On *homo prudens*, the 'zero risk man', who 'personifies prudence, rationality and responsibility', see J. Adams, *Risk* (London: UCL Press, 1995, 16).

60 Note that in the new field, it is not the case that all experts and professionals have been downgraded. Rather, it is those professional groups most clearly associated with the social rationality (probation officers, social workers, community workers, sociological criminologists) whose influence has declined, and the professionals associated with the new economic rationality (auditors, accountants, managers, information technicians) who are in the ascendant.

61 M. Power, *The Audit Explosion* (London: Demos, 1994).

62 To describe this as 'expressive' is to beg the question 'expressive of what?' For its proponents, the answer is that it is expressive of public sentiment. My use of the term is intended to highlight the emotionality and the deontological nature of this style of reasoning: its absolutism and its urgency.

Chapter 8   Crime Control and Social Order

1 On the cultural consequences of America's use of mass imprisonment and the death penalty, see D. Garland (ed), *Mass Imprisonment* (London: Sage, 2001) and A. Sarat (ed), *The Killing State* (New York: Oxford University Press, 1998).

2 P. Hirst, 'Statism, Pluralism and Social Control', and Z. Bauman, 'The Social Uses of Law and Order', both in D. Garland and J. R. Sparks (eds), *Criminology and Social Theory* (Oxford: Oxford University Press, 2000).

3 For a wide-ranging essay on the themes of inclusion and exclusion, see J. Young, *The Exclusive Society* (London: Sage, 1999).

4 '[F]rom everything we know about the opinions of most Americans, they want the benefits of orthodoxy in terms of community and social order, but they do not want

to give up any significant amount of personal freedom to achieve these ends. They deplore the loss of family values, but oppose the move away from no-fault divorce; they want friendly mom-and-pop stores but are enamored of low prices and consumer choice', F. Fukuyama, *The Great Disruption* (New York: Simon and Schuster, 1999), 90. Fukuyama is relying here on the empirical evidence set out in A. Wolfe, *One Nation, After All* (New York: Viking, 1998). Charles Leadbetter makes the same points about contemporary Britain: 'We want a free, diverse, open society but we also want a society that is ordered by older, more traditional virtues of civility, politeness and responsibility', C. Leadbetter, *The Self-Policing Society* (London: Demos, 1996).

5 See H. Dean and P. Taylor-Gooby, *Dependency Culture* (Hemel Hempstead: Harvester Wheatsheaf, 1992); M. B. Katz, *The Underserving Poor: From the War on Welfare to the War on the Poor* (New York: Pantheon, 1989); H. J. Gans, *The War Against the Poor: The Underclass and Antipoverty Policy* (New York: Basic Books, 1995).

6 See L. Morris, *Dangerous Classes: The Underclass and Social Citizenship* (London: Routledge, 1994); R. McDonald (ed), *Youth, 'the Underclass' and Social Exclusion* (London: Routledge, 1997); C. Jencks and P. E. Peterson (eds), *The Urban Underclass* (Washington DC: The Brookings Institute, 1991).

7 See H. Dean and P. Taylor-Gooby, *Dependency Culture* (Hemel Hempstead: Harvester Wheatsheaf, 1992) for an account of how UK social policy in the 1980s brought about 'a cut in benefits, a weakening of social welfare entitlement, a harsher regime of surveillance and a real increase in costs of living for [poor people of working age]' (p. 24). On US policies, see S. Danziger and P. Gottschalk, *America Unequal* (Cambridge, MA: Harvard University Press, 1995): 'Simply put, throughout the 1980s, economic growth did little to help poor and low-income workers, and government policies were not reoriented to counter . . . adverse changes in the labor market. Social programs lifted fewer families, especially families with children, out of poverty in the 1980s than the 1970s for two reasons. First, the percentage of the working poor served by the programs declined after Reagan's initial budget reductions. Second, real benefits continued to decline, as nominal benefit levels in many programs did not keep pace with the modest inflation of the 1980s' (p. 29).

8 M. Gilens, *Why Americans Hate Welfare: Race, Media and the Politics of Antipoverty Policy* (Chicago: University of Chicago Press, 1999).

9 J. K. Galbraith, *The Culture of Contentment* (London: Sinclair Stevenson, 1992). In his speech of 29 September 1998, Prime Minister Tony Blair set out New Labour's view of the welfare state: 'I challenge each and every one of us over the welfare state. We are spending more but getting less, failing to help those who need it and sometimes helping those who don't. Billions wasted every year through fraud and abuse.'

10 See, e.g., T. Raab, *The Struggle for Stability in Early Modern Europe* (New York: Oxford University Press, 1975); M. Wiener, *Reconstructing the Criminal* (New York: Cambridge University Press, 1990).

11 Prime Minister John Major used this phrase in his Speech on 9 September 1994 at Church House London.

12 Recent attempts in Britain and the USA to 'reinvent' probation and community penalties try to emulate this combination, but so far with little success. The cost advantages of 'community punishments', as compared with prison, make it likely that these attempts will continue, probably focusing on the penal possibilities of electronic monitoring and similar technologies.

13 The notion of crime control and criminal justice as commodities to be bought and sold by individual consumers is clearly set out in an Institute of Economic Affairs pamphlet. 'The real problem is that 'producers' in the criminal justice system are not directly answerable to their customers (the victims of crime). As a result, they can pursue their own interests which may conflict with those of the victims. The solution will be when the consumer can choose to buy protection in the market-place', D. Pyle, *Cutting the Costs of Crime: The Economics of Crime and Criminal Justice* (London: IEA, 1995), 61. On the criminal justice morality of late modern societies, see H. J. Boutellier, *Crime and Morality—The Significance of Criminal Justice in Post-modern Culture* (Dordrecht, Netherlands: Kluwer Academic, 2000). The other side of this individualized moral dynamic, is that offenders whom we do not recognize as being 'just like us' are more easily condemned to harsh punishment.

14 For an account of recent developments in Australian crime control and criminal justice, many of which follow the pattern I have described in the US and the UK, see R. Hogg and D. Brown, *Rethinking Law and Order* (Annandale, NSW: Pluto Press, 1998).

15 As Wesley Skogan notes in his discussion of crime and disorder: 'it should be clear that many factors that appear to engender disorder or may counter its spread are shaped by conscious decisions by persons in power. These decisions reflect the interests of banks, real-estate developers, employers, governmental agencies, and others playing for large economic and political stakes. None of these decisions are irreversible, although they obviously may be motivated by still larger economic and demographic forces' W. G. Skogan, *Disorder and Decline* (Chicago: University of Chicago Press, 1990), 179. For an insightful discussion of the importance of place and a detailed case study of how large-scale social forces are experienced (and addressed) in a specific locale, see E. Girling *et al.*, *Crime and Social Change in Middle England: Questions of Order in an English Town* (London: Routledge, 2000).

16 See S. Snacken *et al.*, 'Changing Prison Populations in Western countries: Fate or Policy?' *European Journal of Crime, Criminal Law and Criminal Justice*, vol 3, no 1 (1995), 18–53; J. Muncie and J. R. Sparks (eds), *Imprisonment: European Perspectives* (Hemel Hempstead: Harvester Wheatsheaf, 1991); M. Mauer, *Race to Incarcerate* (New York: The New Press, 1999), ch. 2.

17 Within the USA, research evidence suggests that the most punitive states, as measured by imprisonment rates, are also those with the least generous welfare policies and large racial minority populations. See K. Beckett and B. Western, 'Governing Social Marginality: Welfare, Incarceration and the Transformation of State Policy' in D. Garland (ed), *Mass Imprisonment* (London: Sage, forthcoming). Similar contrasts have been drawn in the UK between Scotland, with its stronger welfare traditions and its less punitive penal policies, and England and Wales. See L. McAra, 'The Politics of Penality: An Overview of the Development of Penal Policy in Scotland', in P. Duff and N. Hutton (eds), *Criminal Justice in Scotland* (Aldershot: Ashgate, 1999), 355–80 and D. J. Smith, 'Less Crime Without More Punishment', *Edinburgh Law Review* (1999). The contours of crime control may be socially structured, but the determination of policy is, in the end, a matter of political choice within social and cultural constraints.

18 For a summary discussion of public opinion and its ambivalence, see M. Tonry, 'Rethinking Unthinkable Punishment Policies in America', *UCLA Law Review* (1999), vol 46, no 6, 1751–91.

19 For US data, see K. Maguire and A. Pastore (eds), *Sourcebook of Criminal Justice Statistics, 1998*. On England and Wales, see Home Office, *Digest 4: Information on the Criminal Justice System*, ed. G. C. Barclay and C. Travers (London: Home Office, 1999) and D. Povey and J. Cotton, *Recorded Crime Statistics: England and Wales, October 1998 to September 1999* (London: Home Office, 18 January 2000): 'In the twelve months ending September 1999, the police in England and Wales recorded a total of 5.2 million offences. The trend in recorded offences shows a 2.2 per cent increase compared to the previous twelve months. This increase follows five consecutive falls for year ending September figures' (p. 3).

20 Setting out the re-election campaign themes for 1996, a leading political adviser to President Clinton listed these as follows: 'I came here to make America better. And, by the way we measure a better America, it is better. There are more people working than on the day I took office There are more people in prison cells than on the day I took office', James Carville, *The New Yorker*, 3 April 1995. While Tony Blair's claim has been to be 'tough on crime, tough on the causes of crime', Bill Clinton's aim is to be 'tough and smart'. 'Violent crime and the fear it provokes are crippling our society, limiting personal freedom and fraying the ties that bind us. The crime bill before Congress gives you a chance to do something about it—to be tough and smart', President Clinton, *State of the Union Address*, 26 January 1994.

21 Discussing the influence of capital punishment upon American political culture, Austin Sarat notes 'capital punishment is a tool of the powerful against dominated groups. As such, it appears as an enactment of the finality of state power, a finality that is quite at odds with the spirit and substance of democracy. The death penalty always calls us to certainty, and, in so doing, invites us to forget the limits of our reason', A. Sarat (ed), *The Killing State* (New York: Oxford University Press, 1999), 11.

22 Ridley Scott's film 'Blade Runner' was originally released in 1982. See M. Davis, 'Beyond Blade Runner: Urban Control—the Ecology of Fear', *Open Magazine Pamphlet Series #23* (Open Magazine: Open Media, 1992). On being elected in 1997, Prime Minster Tony Blair talked publicly about the need to avoid a 'Blade Runner' scenario developing in Great Britain.

23 See P. Hirst, 'Statism, Pluralism and Social Control, p. 130.

24 See J. J. Dilulio Jr., 'Two Million Prisoners are Enough', *The Wall Street Journal*, 12 March 1999. In January 2000, Governor George H. Ryan of Illinois announced a moratorium on the use of the death penalty in his state, pending an inquiry into why more death row inmates in his state had been exonerated than executed since capital punishment was reinstated in 1977. For details, see J. S. Liebman *et al.*, *A Broken System: Error Rates in Capital Cases, 1973–1995* (New York: The Justice Project, 2000). A Gallop poll conducted shortly after this event, reported that support for capital punishment had declined from 80 per cent in 1994, to 66 per cent—the lowest level in nineteen years. See B. Shapiro, 'Capital Offense', *The New York Sunday Times*, 26 March 2000. *Sourcebook of Criminal Justice Statistics 1998* reports that public concern about crime and violence has fallen off slightly from its peak in 1994 (Table 2.1).

25 J. C. Scott, *Seeing Like A State* (Yale: Yale University Press, 1998); P. Hirst, *Associative Democracy* (Cambridge: Polity, 1992); P. Selznick, *The Moral Commonwealth* (Berkeley, CA: University of California Press, 1992); J. Kooiman, *Modern Governance: New Social-Governmental Interactions,* (London: Sage, 1993).

Bibliography

AARON, H. J., *Politics and the Professors: The Great Society in Perspective* (Washington DC: Brookings Institute, 1978).

ADAMS, J., *Risk* (London: UCL Press, 1995).

ALLEN, F. A., 'Legal values and the rehabilitative ideal', *Journal of Criminal Law, Criminology and Police Science* (1959), vol 50, 226–32.

—— *The Borderland of Criminal Justice* (Chicago and London: University of Chicago Press, 1964).

—— *The Decline of the Rehabilitative Ideal* (New Haven: Yale University Press, 1981).

American Friends Service Committee, *Struggle For Justice: A Report on Crime and Punishment in America* (New York: Hill & Wang, 1971).

American Law Institute, *Model Penal Code (Proposed Official Draft)* (Philadelphia: American Law Institute, 1962).

AMEY, P., HALE, C. and UGLOW, S., 'Proactive Policing: An Evaluation of the Central Scotland Police Crime Management Model', *Crime and Criminal Justice Research Findings No. 10* (The Scottish Office Central Research Unit: HMSO, 1996).

AMIN, A. (ed), *Post-Fordism: a Reader* (Oxford: Blackwell, 1994).

Amnesty International, 'United States of America: Florida Reintroduces Chain Gangs' (New York, January 1996).

ANDERSON, D. (ed), *This Will Hurt: The Restoration of Virtue and Civic Order* (London: Social Affairs Unit, 1995).

ANDERSON, D. C., *Crime and the Politics of Hysteria: How the Willie Horton Case Changed American Justice* (New York: Times Books, 1995).

ANDERSON, E., *Streetwise: Race, Class and Change in an Urban Community* (Chicago: University of Chicago Press, 1990).

ARON, R., *Main Currents in Sociological Thought Vol 1* (New Brunswick, NJ: Transaction Books, 1978).

ASHWORTH, A., *Sentencing and Criminal Justice*, 2nd edn (London: Weidenfeld & Nicolson, 1995).

—— (1997) 'Sentencing in the 80's and 90's: The Struggle for Power', *The Eighth Eve Saville Memorial Lecture*, 21 May 1997 at King's College London, 1997.

—— and GIBSON B., 'Altering the Sentencing Framework', *Criminal Law Review*, February 1994, 101–9.

Audit Commission, *The Probation Service: Promoting Value for Money* (London: Audit Commission, 1989).

—— *Going Straight: Developing Good Practice in the Probation Service* (London: Audit Commission, 1991).

—— *Helping With Enquiries: Tackling Crime Effectively* (London: HMSO, 1993).

AUSTIN, J., CLARK, J., HARDYMAN, P. and HENRY, D. A., 'The Impact of "three strikes and you're out"', *Punishment & Society* (1999), vol 1, no 2, 163–86.

BAILEY, W., 'Correctional Outcome: An Evaluation of 100 Reports', *Journal of Criminal Law, Criminology and Police Science* (June 1966), 153–60.

BAKER, E., 'From "Making Bad People Worse" to "Prison Works": Sentencing Policy in England and Wales in the 1990s', *Criminal Law Forum: An International Journal* (1996), 7(3): 639–71.

BALDWIN, P., *The Politics of Solidarity: Class Bases of the European Welfare State 1875–1975* (Cambridge: Cambridge University Press, 1990).

BARLOW, M. H., 'Race and the Problem of Crime in Time and Newsweek Cover Stories, 1946 to 1995' *Social Justice* (1998), vol 25, no 2, 149–83.

BARRY, K., 'Chain Gangs', Unpublished paper, 1998 (on file with the author).

BAUMAN, Z., *Legislators and Interpreters* (Oxford: Polity Press, 1987).

—— 'The Social Uses of Law and Order', in D. Garland and J. R. Sparks (eds), *Criminology and Social Theory* (Oxford: Oxford University Press, 2000).

BAYER, R., 'Crime, Punishment and the Decline of Liberal Optimism', in *Crime and Delinquency* (April 1981), 169–90.

BAYLEY, D. H., 'The Police and Political Development in Europe', in C.Tilly (ed), *The Formation of National States* ((Princeton: Princeton University Press, 1975).

—— *Patterns of Policing* (New Brunswick, NJ: Rutgers University Press, 1985).

—— *Police for the Future* (New York: Oxford University Press, 1994).

—— and SHEARING, C. D., 'The Future of Policing', *Law & Society Review* (1996), 30 (3): 585–606.

BEAN, P. *Rehabilitation and Deviance* (London: Routledge & Kegan Paul, 1976).

—— *Punishment* (London: MacMillan, 1981).

BECK, A. and WILLIS, A., *Crime and Security: Managing the Risk to Safe Shopping* (Leicester: Perpetuity Press, 1995).

BECK, A. J., *Prison and Jail Inmates at Midyear 1999: Bureau of Justice Statistics Bulletin* (Washington DC: US Department of Justice, April 2000).

BECK, U., *The Risk Society: Towards a New Modernity* (London: Sage, 1992).

BECKETT, K., *Making Crime Pay* (New York: Oxford University Press, 1997).

—— and WESTERN, B., 'Governing Social Marginality: Welfare, Incarceration and the Transformation of State Policy', in D. Garland (ed), *Mass Imprisonment* (London: Sage, forthcoming).

BEECHEY, V. and PERKINS, T., *A Matter of Hours: Women, Part-Time Work and the Labor Market* (Minneapolis: University of Minnesota Press, 1987).

BELL, D., *The Cultural Contradictions of Capitalism* (New York: Basic Books, 1976).

BENNETT, T. H., *Tackling Fear of Crime: A Review of Policy Options* (Cambridge: Institute of Criminology, 1989).

—— *Evaluating Neighbourhood Watch* (Cambridge: Cambridge University Press, 1990).

BENNETT, W. J., DiIULIO, J. J., and WALTERS, J. P., *Body Count* (New York: Simon & Schuster, 1996).

BERK, R. A. and ROSSI, P. H., *Prison Reform and State Elites* (Cambridge, MA: Ballinger, 1977).

BEST, J., 'But Seriously Folks', in J. Hostein and G. Miller (eds), *Reconsidering Social Constructionism* (New York: Aldine de Gruyter, 1993).

—— *Random Violence: How We Talk About New Crimes and New Victims* (Berkeley, CA: University of California Press, 1999).

BEYLEVELD, D., *The Effectiveness of General Deterrents Against Crime* (Cambridge: Institute of Criminology, 1978).

BISHOP, D., 'Juvenile Offenders in the Criminal Justice System', *Crime & Justice*, vol. 27 (2000).

BLOM-COOPER, L., *Progress in Penal Reform* (Oxford: Oxford University Press, 1974).

BLAKELY, E. and SNYDER, M. G., *Fortress America* (Washington: Brookings Institute, 1997).

BLUMSTEIN, A.,'Coherence, Coordination and Integration in the Administration of Criminal Justice', in J. Van Dijk *et al.* (ed), *Criminal Law in Action: An Overview of Current Issues in Western Societies* (Deventer: Kluwer, 1986).

—— and BECK, A. J. 'Population Growth in US Prisons 1980–1996', in M. Tonry and J. Petersilia (eds), *Prisons* (Chicago: University of Chicago Press, 1999).

—— and COHEN, J. 'A Theory of the Stability of Punishment', *Journal of Criminology, Criminal Law and Police Science* (1973), 63(2), 198–207.

—————— and NAGIN, D. (eds), *Deterrence and Incapacitation: Estimating the Effects of Criminal Sanctions in Crime Rates* (Washington DC: National Academy of Sciences, 1978).

BOOK, A. S., 'Shame on You: An Analysis of Modern Shame Punishment as an Alternative to Incarceration', *William and Mary Law Review* (1999), vol 40, 653–86.

BOTTOMLEY, A. K., *Crime and Penal Politics: The Criminologists' Dilemma* (Hull: Hull University Press, 1989).

—— and JOHNSTONE, J. G., 'Labour's Crime Policy in Context', *Policy Studies* (1998), vol 19, no 3–4, 173–84.

BOTTOMS, A. E., 'Introduction to the Coming Penal Crisis', in A. E. Bottoms and R. H. Preston (eds), *The Coming Penal Crisis* (Edinburgh: Scottish Academic Press, 1980).

—— 'Neglected Features of Contemporary Penal Systems', in D. Garland and P. Young (eds), *The Power to Punish* (Aldershot: Gower, 1983).

—— 'Limiting Prison Use: Experience in England and Wales', *Howard Journal* (1987), vol 26, no 3, 177–202.

—— 'Intermediate Punishments and Modern Societies', paper presented at the American Society of Criminology Meeting, Miami, November 1994.

—— 'The Philosophy and Politics of Punishment and Sentencing', in C. Clark and R. Morgan (eds), *The Politics of Sentencing Reform* (Oxford: Clarendon Press, 1995).

—— and STEVENSON, S., ' "What Went Wrong?": Criminal Justice Policy in England and Wales, 1945–70', in D. Downes (ed), *Unravelling Criminal Justice* (Basingstoke: MacMillan, 1992).

—— and WILES, P., 'Crime and Insecurity in the City', in C. Fijnaut, J. Goethals, T. Peters and L. Walgrave (eds), *Changes in Society, Crime, and Criminal Justice in Europe*, vol. 1 (The Hague: Kluwer, 1995).

—— and McWILLIAMS, W., 'A Non-Treatment Paradigm for Probation Practice' *British Journal of Social Work* (1979), vol 9: 159–202.

BOURDIEU, P., 'Social space and symbolic power', *Sociological Theory*, 7(1) June 1989.

BOUTELLIER, H. J., *Crime and Morality—The Significance of Criminal Justice in Post-modern Culture* (Dordrecht, Netherlands: Kluwer Academic, 2000).

BOWER, W. J., VANDIVER, M. and DUGAN, P. H., 'A New Look at Public Opinion on Capital Punishment: What Citizens and Legislators Prefer', *American Journal of Criminal Law* (1994) 22: 77.

BRAITHWAITE, J. 'Restorative Justice', in M. Tonry (ed), *The Handbook of Crime and Punishment* (New York: Oxford University Press, 1998).

—— and MUGFORD, S., 'Conditions of Successful Degradation Ceremonies' *British Journal of Criminology* (1994), 34(2), 139–71.

BREWER, J., LOCKHART, B., and RODGERS, P., *Crime in Ireland, 1945–1995: 'Here Be Dragons'* (Oxford: Clarendon Press, 1997).

BRIGHT, J., *Turning the Tide: Crime, Community and Prevention* (London: Demos, 1997).

BRILLIANT, J. 'The Modern Day Scarlet Letter: A Critical Analysis', *Duke Law Journal* (1989), 1357–85.

BRINT, S., *In An Age of Experts: The Changing Role of Professionals in Politics and Public Life* (Princeton NJ: Princeton University Press, 1994).

BRODY, S., *The Effectiveness of Sentencing: A Review of the Literature*, Home Office Research Study, No 35 (London: Home Office, 1976).

BROWNLEE, I., *Community Punishment: A Critical Introduction* (London: Longman, 1998).

BUNZEL, S., 'The Probation Officer and the Federal Sentencing Guidelines: Strange Philosophical Bedfellows', *Yale Law Journal* (1994), 104, 933.

BURROWS, J., *Making Crime Prevention Pay: Initiatives from Business*, Crime Prevention Unit Papers 27 (London: Home Office, 1991).

—— and TARLING, R., *Clearing Up Crime*, Home Office Research Study No 73 (London: Home Office, 1982).

BUTLER, T. and SAVAGE, M., *Social Change and the Middle Classes* (London: UCL Press Limited, 1995).

CAMP, C. G. and CAMP, G. M. (eds), *The Corrections Yearbook 1998* (Middletown, CN: Criminal Justice Institute, 1998).

CAMPBELL, B., *Goliath: Britain's Dangerous Places* (London: Methuen, 1993).

Caplow, T. and SIMON, J., 'Understanding Prison Policy and Population Trends', in M. Tonry and J. Petersilia (eds), *Prisons* (Chicago: University of Chicago Press, 1999).

CARLEN, B., 'Insecurity Complex', *California Lawyer* (June 1998), 85.

CARNEY, F. L., *Criminality and its Treatment: The Patuxent Experience* (Malabar, FL: Krieger Publishing Co., 1989).

CASTELLS, M., *The Rise of the Network Society* (Malden Mass: Blackwell, 1996).

CAVADINO, M. and DIGNAN, J., *The Penal System: An Introduction* (London: Sage, 1992).

CHERNOFF, H. A., KELLY, C. M., and KROGER, J. R., 'The Politics of Crime' in *Harvard Journal of Legislation* (1996), vol 33, 527–79.

CHOMSKY, N., *American Power and the New Mandarins* (New York: Pantheon Books, 1969).

CHRISTIANSON, S., *With Liberty for Some: 500 Years of Imprisonment in America* (Boston: Northeastern University Press, 1998).

CHRISTIE, N., 'Conflicts as Property', *British Journal of Criminology* (1977), 1–15.

—— 'Suitable Enemies', in H. Bianchi amd R. van Swaaningen (eds), *Abolitionism: Towards a Non-Repressive Approach to Crime* (Amsterdam: Free University Press, 1986).

—— *Crime Control as Industry: Towards Gulags Western Style*, 2nd edn (London: Routledge, 1994).

CHRISTOPHERSON, S., 'The Fortress City: Privatized Spaces, Consumer Citizenship', in A. Amin (ed), *Post-Fordism: A Reader* (Oxford: Blackwell, 1994).

CLARKE, M., 'Citizenship, Community and the Management of Crime', *British Journal of Criminology* (1987), 27 (4): 384–400.

CLARKE, R. V., 'Situational Crime Prevention: Its Theoretical Basis and Practical Scope', in M. Tonry and N. Morris (eds), *Crime and Justice: An Annual Review of Research* (1983), vol 4, 225–6.

—— *Hot Products: Understanding, Anticipating and Reducing Demand for Stolen Goods*, Police Research Series Paper 112 (London: Home Office, Research, Development and Statistics Directorate, 1999).

—— and MAYHEW, P. (eds), *Designing Out Crime* (London: HMSO, 1980).

—— and CORNISH D., 'Introduction' in R. V. Clarke and D. Cornish (eds), *The Reasoning Criminal : Rational Choice Perspectives on Offending* (New York: Springer-Verlag, 1986).

———— (eds), *The Reasoning Criminal : Rational Choice Perspectives on Offending* (New York: Springer-Verlag, 1986).

—— and HEAL, K. H., 'Police effectiveness in dealing with crime: some current British research', in *The Police Journal* (1979), vol 52, 24–41.

CLEAR, T. R. and BRAGA, A. A., 'Community Corrections', in J. Q. Wilson and J. Petersilia (eds), *Crime* (San Francisco: Institute for Contemporary Studies, 1995), 421–44.

CLOWARD, R. A. and OHLIN, L. E., *Delinquency and Opportunity* (New York: Free Press, 1960).

COHEN, A., *Delinquent Boys: The Culture of the Gang* (New York: Free Press, 1955).

COHEN, L. E. and CANTOR, D., 'The Determinants of Larceny in the United States: Life-Style and Demographic Factors Associated with the Probability of Victimization', *Journal of Research in Crime and Delinquency* (1981), vol 18, 113–27.

—— and FELSON, M., 'Social Change and Crime Rate Trends: A Routine Activity Approach', *American Sociological Review* (1979), vol 44, issue 4, 588–608.

COHEN, P., 'Policing the Working Class City', in R.Fine, *et al.* (eds) *Capitalism and the Rule of Law* (London: Hutchinson, 1979).

COHEN, S., 'It's All Right for You to Talk: Political and Social Manifestoes for Social Work Action', in R. Bailey and M. Brake (eds), *Radical Social Work* (London: Edward Arnold, 1975), 76–95.

—— *Visions of Social Control* (Cambridge: Polity, 1985).

—— and TAYLOR, L., *Prison Secrets* (London: NCCL, 1978).

COLQUHOUN, P., *Treatise on the Police of the Metropolis explaining the various Crimes and Misdemeanours which are at present felt as a pressure upon the Community, and suggesting Remedies for their Prevention, by a Magistrate*, 2nd edn (originally published in 1795) (London: H. Fry for C. Dilly, 1796).

Commission on Social Justice, *Social Justice: Strategies for National Renewal* (London: Vintage, 1994).

Commissioner of the Police of the Metropolis, *Report for the Year 1986*, Cm 158 (London: HMSO, 1987).

CONKLIN, W., *The Impact of Crime* (New York: MacMillan, 1975).

Conservative Party, *Crime Knows No Boundaries* (London: Conservative Party Central Office, 1966).

—— *The Next Moves Forward* (London, Conservative Central Office 1987).

COOK, P. J. and MOORE, M. H., 'Gun Control', in J.Q.Wilson and J. Petersilia (eds), *Crime* (San Francisco: ICS Press, 1995).

CORNISH, D. and CLARKE, R., 'Introduction' to R. V. Clarke and D. Cornish (eds), *The Reasoning Criminal : Rational Choice Perspectives on Offending* (New York: Springer-Verlag, 1986).

CRAWFORD, A., *The Local Governance of Crime* (Oxford: Clarendon Press, 1997).

—— *Crime Prevention & Community Safety: Politics, Policies & Practices* (London: Longman, 1998).

Criminal Justice Newsletter (15 June 1994), vol 25. no 12.

Criminal Justice Newsletter (1 November 1994) 'ACA Says Crime Bill Focuses Too Much on Incarceration', vol 25, no 21.

Criminal Justice Newsletter (15 July 1993) '30 Organizations Call for Shift in Criminal Justice Policy', vol 24, no 14.

Criminal Justice Newsletter (15 December 1998), vol 29, no 24.

CRITCHLEY, T. A., *A History of Police in England and Wales*, 2nd edn (London: Constable, 1978).

CROFT, J., *Research in Criminal Justice*, Home Office Research Study, No 44 (London: Home Office, 1978).

—— *Managing Criminological Research, Home Office Research Study, No 69* (London: Home Office, 1981).

CROMPTON, R., *Women and Work in Modern Britain* (Oxford: Oxford University Press, 1997).

CRONIN, T. E., CRONIN, T. Z., and MILAKOVICH, M. E., *U.S. v. Crime in the Streets* (Bloomington: Indiana University Press, 1981).

CURRIE, E., Review of Taylor *et al.*, 'The New Criminology', in *Crime and Social Justice*, vol 2 (Fall/Winter 1974), 109–13.

CUTLER, T., WILLIAMS, K., and WILLIAMS, J., *Keynes, Beveridge and Beyond* (London: Routledge & Kegan Paul, 1986).

DANZIGER, S. and GOTTSCHALK, P. *America Unequal* (Cambridge, MA: Harvard University Press, 1995).

DAVIS, K. C., *Discretionary Justice* (Urbana: University of Illinois, 1969).

DAVIS, M., *City of Quartz: Excavating the Future in Los Angeles* (London: Vintage, 1990).

—— 'Beyond Blade Runner: Urban Control—the Ecology of Fear', *Open Magazine Pamphlet Series #23* (Los Angeles: Open Media, 1992).

DEAN, H. and TAYLOR-GOOBY, P., *Dependency Culture: The Explosion of a Myth* (Hemel Hempstead: Harvester Wheatsheaf, 1992).

DEAN, M., *Critical and Effective Histories: Foucault's Methods and Historical Sociology* (London: Routledge, 1994).

DENNIS, N., *Rising Crime and the Dismembered Family* (London: IEA Health and Welfare Unit, 1993).

—— *The Invention of Permanent Poverty* (London: The IEA Health and Welfare Unit, 1997).

DENNO, D., 'Life Before the Modern Sex Offender Statutes', *Northwestern University Law Review* (1998), vol 92, no 4, 1317–414.

DE SWAAN, A., 'Emotions in Their Social Matrix: The Politics of Agoraphobia', *The Management of Normality* (London: Routledge, 1990).

DIGBY, A., *British Welfare Policy: Workhouse to Workfare* (London: Faber and Faber, 1989).

DIIULIO, J. J. Jr., 'Let 'em Rot', *The Wall Street Journal*, 26 January 1994, A14.

—— 'Two Million Prisoners Are Enough', *The Wall Street Journal*, 12 March 1999, A14

DIJK, J. J. M. VAN, 'Understanding Crime Rates: On the Interactions Between the Rational Choices of Victims and Offenders', *British Journal of Criminology* (1994), 34 (2): 105–21.

DITCHFIELD, J., *Police Cautioning in England and Wales*, Home Office Research Study No 37 (London: Home Office, 1976).

DONZELOT, J., *The Policing of Families* (London: Hutcheson, 1987).

DONZIGER, S. (ed), *The Real War on Crime* (New York: Harper Perennial, 1996).

DOUGLAS, M., *Risk and Blame : Essays in Cultural Theory* (London: Routledge, 1992).

DOWNES, D., *The Delinquent Solution* (London: Routledge & Kegan Paul, 1966).

—— 'Toughing it Out: From Labour Opposition to Labour Government', *Policy Studies* (1998), 19 (3/4).

—— and MORGAN, R., ' "Hostages to Fortune"? The Politics of Law and Order in Post-War Britain', in M. Maguire, R. Morgan and R. Reiner (eds), *The Oxford Handbook of Criminology* (Oxford: Clarendon Press, 1994).

DuBow, F., McCABE, E., and KAPLAN, G., *Reactions to Crime: A Critical Review of the Literature* (Washington, DC: National Institute of Law Enforcement, US Department of Justice, 1979).

DUCLOS, D., *The Werewolf Complex: America's Fascination with Violence* (New York: Oxford University Press, 1998).

DUFF P. and HUTTON, N. (eds), *Criminal Justice in Scotland* (Aldershot: Ashgate, 1999).

DUFF, R. A.,'Penal Communications: Recent Work in the Philosophy of Punishment', *Crime and Justice, An Annual Review of Research* (1995), vol 20.

DUNBAR, I. and LANGDON, I., *Tough Justice* (London: Blackstone, 1998).

DURKHEIM, E., *The Division of Labor* (New York: Free Press, 1933).

—— *Professional Ethics and Civic Morals* (London: Routledge, 1992).

EARLS, F. J. and REISS, A. J. *Breaking the Cycle: Predicting and Preventing Crime* (National Institute of Justice, US Dept. of Justice, 1994).

EDSALL, T. B. with EDSALL, M. D., *Chain Reaction: The Impact of Race, Rights and Taxes on American Politics* (New York: Norton, 1991).

EHRENREICH, B., *Fear of Falling: The Inner Life of the Middle Class* (New York: Perennial, 1989).

EKBLOM, P., 'The conjunction of criminal opportunity', in K. Pease *et al.* (eds), *Key Issues in Crime Prevention* (London: Institute for Public Policy Research, forthcoming).

ELIAS, N., *The Civilizing Process: Volume 1 The History of Manners* (Oxford: Blackwell, 1978, originally published 1939).

—— *The Civilizing Process, Vol 2. State Formation and Civilization* (Oxford: Blackwell, 1982, originally published 1939).

—— and SCOTSON, J., *The Established and the Outsiders* (London: Cass, 1965).

Elias, R., *Victims Still: The Political Manipulation of Crime Victims* (Newbury Park: Sage Publications, 1993).

ELLICKSON, R. C., 'Controlling Chronic Misconduct in City Spaces: Of Panhandlers, Skid Rows, and Public-Space Zoning', *Yale Law Journal* (1996), 105: 1165.

ELLSWORTH, P. B. and GROSS, S. R., 'Hardening of the Attitudes: Americans' Views on the Death Penalty', *Journal of Social Issues* (1994), vol 50, no 2, 19–52.

EMSLEY, C.,'The History of Crime and Crime Control Institutions', in M. Maguire, R. Morgan, and R. Reiner, *The Oxford Handbook of Criminology* 2nd edn, Oxford (Oxford: University Press, 1997).

ENGSTAD, R. V. and EVANS, J. L., 'Responsibility, Competence and Police Effectiveness in Crime Control' in R. Clarke and M. Hough (eds), *The Effectiveness of Policing* (Aldershot: Gower, 1980).

ERICSON, R., BARANKEK, P., and CHAN, J., *Representing Order: Crime, Law and Justice in the News Media* (Buckingham: Open University Press, 1991).

ERICSON, R. and HAGGERTY, K., *Policing the Risk Society* (Toronto: University of Toronto Press, 1997).

ESPING-ANDERSON, G., *The Three Worlds of Welfare Capitalism* (Cambridge: Polity, 1990).

EWALD, F., *L'Etat Providence* (Paris, B. Grasset, 1986).

FARRINGTON, D. P., *Understanding and Preventing Youth Crime* (York: J. Rowntree Foundation, 1996).

Federal Sentencing Reporter, *Sentencing in England: The Rise of Populist Punishment,* Vera Institute of Justice (California: University of California Press, 1998).

FEELEY, M. and SARAT, A., *The Policy Dilemma* (Minneapolis: University of Minnesota Press, 1980).

—— and SIMON, J., 'The New Penology: Notes on the emerging strategy of corrections and its implications', *Criminology* (1992), vol. 30, no 4, 449–74.

FELD, B., *Bad Kids* (New York: Oxford University Press, 1998).

FELSON, M., *Crime and Everyday Life*, 2nd edn (Thousand Oaks, CA: Pine Forge Press, 1998).

FELSON, M. and CLARKE, R. V. (eds), *Business and Crime Prevention* (Monsey, NY: Criminal Justice Press, 1997).

—— and COHEN, L., 'Human Ecology and Crime: A Routine Activity Approach', *Human Ecology* (1980), vol 8, no 4, 389–406.

—— and GOTTFREDSON, M., 'Social Indicators of Adolescent Activities Near Peers and Parents', *Journal of Marriage and the Family*, August 1984, 709–15.

FESSENDEN, F. and ROHDE, D., 'Dismissed by Prosecutors Before Reaching Court, Flawed Arrests Rise in New York City', *New York Times*, 23 August 1999.

FINE, G. A., 'Scandal, Social Conditions and the Creation of Public Attention', in *Social Problems* (1997), vol 44, no 3, 297–323.

FINN, P., 'No-Frills Prisons and Jails: A Movement in Flux', *Federal Probation*, vol 60 (September 1996), 35–44.

—— *Sex Offender Community Notification* (Washington DC: National Institute of Justice, Office of Justice Programs, 1997).

FISHMAN, R., *Bourgeois Utopias: The Rise and Fall of Suburbia* (New York: Basic Books, 1987).

FLANAGAN, T. J. and LONGMIRE, D. R., *Americans View Crime and Justice: A National Public Opinion Survey* (Thousand Oaks, CA: Sage Publications, 1996).

—— and MAGUIRE, K., *Sourcebook of Criminal Justice Statistics* (Washington DC: Government Printing Office, 1994).

FOGEL, D., *We Are The Living Proof . . . the Justice Model of Corrections* (Cincinnati: Anderson Pub, 1975),

FOLKARD, M. S., *Intensive Matched Probation and After-Care Treatment Home Office Research Study, No 24* (London: HMSO, 1974).

FOUCAULT, M., *Discipline and Punish: The Birth of the Prison* (London: Allen Lane, 1977).

—— 'Structuralism and Post-Structuralism: An Interview with Michel Foucault' (with G. Raulet), *Telos*, no 55, Spring 1983, 195–211.

—— 'Preface to the History of Sexuality, Volume II', in P. Rabinow (ed), *The Foucault Reader* (New York: Pantheon, 1984).

—— 'Governmentality' in Burchell *et al.* (eds), *The Foucault Effect* (Hemel Hempstead: Harvester Wheatsheaf, 1991).

FOWLES, A. J., 'Monitoring Expenditure on the Criminal Justice System: The Search for Control', *The Howard Journal* (1990), 29 (2): 82–100.

FRANKEL, M., *Criminal Sentences: Law Without Order* (New York: Hill and Wang, 1973).

FRIEDMAN, L., *Crime and Punishment in American History* (New York: Basic Books, 1993).

FUKUYAMA, F., *The Great Disruption: Human Nature and the Reconstitution of Social Order* (New York: The Free Press, 1999).

GAES, G., 'Correctional Treatment', in M. Tonry (ed), *The Handbook of Crime and Punishment* (New York: Oxford University Press, 1998).

GALBRAITH, J. K., *The Culture of Contentment* (London: Sinclair Stevenson, 1992).

—— *The Affluent Society* (Boston: Houghton Mifflin, 1998).

GAMBLE, A., *The Free Economy and the Strong State: The Politics of Thatcherism* (Basingstoke: MacMillan, 1988).

GANS, H., *The War Against the Poor: The Underclass and Antipoverty Policy* (New York: Basic Books, 1995).

GARLAND, D., *Punishment and Welfare: A History of Penal Strategies* (Aldershot: Gower, 1985).

—— 'The Criminal and his Science', *British Journal of Criminology* (1985), vol 25, no 2, 109–37.

—— *Punishment and Modern Society: A Study in Social Theory* (Oxford: Clarendon Press, 1990).

—— 'Criminological Knowledge and its Relation to Power: Foucault's Genealogy and Criminology Today', in *British Journal of Criminology* (1992), vol 32, no 4, 403–22.

—— 'Of Crimes and Criminals: The Development of Criminology in Britain', in *The Oxford Handbook of Criminology*, ed. M. Maguire, R. Morgan, and R. Reiner (Oxford: Clarendon Press, 1994).

—— 'Penal Modernism and Postmodernism', in T. Blomberg and S. Cohen (eds), *Punishment and Social Control* (New York: Aldine de Gruyter, 1995).

—— 'The Limits of the Sovereign State: Strategies of Crime Control in Contemporary Society', *The British Journal of Criminology* (1996), 36(4): 445–71.

—— 'Governmentality and the Problem of Crime: Foucault, Criminology, Sociology', *Theoretical Criminology* (1997), vol 1, no 2, 173–214.

—— (ed), *Mass Imprisonment in the USA: Social Causes and Consequences* (London: Sage, forthcoming).

GAROFALO, J., 'The Fear of Crime: Causes and Consequences', *The Journal of Criminal Law & Criminology* (1981), vol 72, no 2, 839–57.

GATRELL, V. A. C., 'The Decline of Theft and Violence in Victorian and Edwardian England', in V. A. C. Gatrell, B. Lenman, and G. Parker (eds), *Crime and the Law* (London: Europa Publications Ltd, 1980).

—— 'Crime, Authority and the Policeman-State', in F. M. L. Thompson (ed), *Cambridge Social History of Britain 1750–1950, Vol 3, Social Agencies and Institutions* (Cambridge: Cambridge University Press, 1992).

GAUBATZ, K. T., *Crime in the Public Mind* (Ann Arbor, MI: University of Michigan Press, 1995).

GELSTHORPE, L. and MORRIS, A., 'Juvenile Justice 1945–1992', in M. Maguire, R. Morgan, and R. Reiner (eds), *The Oxford Handbook of Criminology* (Oxford: Clarendon Press, 1994).

GENDERS, E. and PLAYER, E., *Grendon: A Study of a Therapeutic Prison* (Oxford: Oxford University Press, 1995).

GENDREAU, P. and ROSS, R., 'Revivication of Rehabilitation: Evidence from the 1980s', *Justice Quarterly* (1987), vol 4, no 3, 349–407.

GIDDENS, A., *The Constitution of Society* (Oxford: Polity Press, 1984).

—— *The Consequences of Modernity* (Oxford: Polity Press, 1990).

GILENS, M., *Why Americans Hate Welfare* (Chicago: The University of Chicago Press, 1999).

GILLING, D., 'Crime Prevention Discourses and the Multi-Agency Approach', *International Journal of the Sociology of Law* (1993), vol 21, 145–57.

—— *Crime Prevention: Theory, Policy and Politics* (London: UCL Press, 1997).

GIRLING, E., LOADER, I. and SPARKS, J. R., *Crime and Social Order in Middle England* (London: Routledge, 2000).

GITLIN, T., *The Sixties: Years of Hope, Days of Rage* (New York: Bantam Books, 1987).

—— *The Twilight of Common Dreams: Why America is Wracked by Culture Wars* (New York: Metropolitan Books, 1995).

GLAZER, N., 'Towards a Self-Service Society', *Public Interest* (1987), no 70, 66–90.

—— *The Limits of Social Policy* (Cambridge, MA: Harvard University Press, 1988).

GOFFMAN, E., *Asylums* (Harmondsworth: Penguin Books, 1968).

—— *The Presentation of Self in Everyday Life* (Harmondsworth: Penguin Books, 1969).

GOLDSTEIN, H., 'Improving policing: A problem-oriented approach', *Crime and Delinquency* (1979), vol 25, 236–58.

—— *Problem-Oriented Policing* (New York: McGraw Hill, 1990).

GOLDSTEIN, J. (ed), *Foucault and the Writing of History* (Oxford: Blackwell, 1994).

GOLDTHORPE J., LOCKWOOD, D., BECHHOFER, F., and PLATT, J., *The Affluent Worker in the Class Structure* (London: Cambridge University Press, 1969).

GOODE, E.,'Round up the Usual Suspects: Crime, Deviance, and the Limits of Contructionism', *The American Sociologist* (1994), vol 25, 90–104.

GOODIN, R. E. and LE GRAND, J. (eds), *Not Only the Poor: The Middle Classes and the Welfare State* (London: Allen Unwin, 1987).

GORDON, D., *The Justice Juggernaut: Fighting Street Crime, Controlling Citizens* (New Brunswick, NJ: Rutgers University Press, 1991).

GOTTFREDSON, M. and HIRSCHI, T., *A General Theory of Crime* (Stanford: Stanford University Press, 1990).

GRABOWSKY, P. N., 'Law Enforcement and the Citizen: Non-Governmental Participants in Crime Prevention and Control', *Policing and Society* (1992), vol 2, 249–71.

GREENBERG, D. and HUMPRIES, D.,'The Co-Optation of Fixed Sentencing Reform', *Crime and Delinquency* (1980), vol 26, 205–25.

GRIFFIN, T. (ed.), *Social Trends* (London: HMSO, 1991).

GUNN, J., MADEN, A., and SWINTON, M., *Mentally Disordered Prisoners* (London: Institute of Psychiatry, 1991).

GURR, T. R., 'Historical Trends in Violent Crime: Europe and the United States', in T. Gurr (ed), *Violence in America, Vol 1, The History of Crime* (Beverly Hills CA: Sage, 1989).

HACKER, A., *Two Nations: Black and White, Separate, Hostile, Unequal* (New York: Ballantine Books, 1992).

HALE, C., 'Fear of Crime: a Review of the Literature', *International Review of Victimology* (1996), vol 4, 79–150.

HALL, P., *Governing the Economy: The Politics of Satte Intervention in Britain and France* (Cambridge: Polity Press, 1986).

HALL, S., *The Hard Road to Renewal* (London: Verso, 1988).

——CRITCHER, C., JEFFERSON, T., CLARKE, J., and ROBERTS, B., *Policing the Crisis: Mugging, the State and Law and Order* (London: MacMillan, 1978).

HARCOURT, B., 'Reflecting on the Subject: A Critique of the Social Influence Conception of Deterrence, the Broken Windows Theory, and Order-Maintenance Policing New York Style', *Michigan Law Review*, vol 97, no 2, November 1998.

HARDING, R., 'Private Prisons' in M.Tonry (ed) *The Handbook of Crime and Punishment* (New York: Oxford University Press, 1998).

HART, H. L. A., 'Prolegemenon to the Principles of Punishment', in H. L. A. Hart, *Punishment and Responsibility* (Oxford: Oxford University Press, 1968).

HARVEY, D., *The Condition of Post-Modernity:An Inquiry into the Origins of Social Change* (Oxford: Basil Blackwell, 1989).

HAY, C., 'Mobilization Through Interpellation: James Bulger, Juvenile Crime and the Construction of a Moral Panic', *Social and Legal Studies* (1995), 4 (2).

HEAL, K., TARLING, R., and BURROWS, J. (eds), *Policing Today* (London: Home Office, 1985).

——and LAYCOCK, G., 'Principles, Issues and Further Action', in K. Heal and G. Laycock (eds), *Situational Crime Prevention: From Theory to Practice* (London: HMSO, 1986).

HEATH, J., *Eighteenth Century Penal Theory* (Oxford: Oxford University Press, 1963).

HEBENTON, B. and THOMAS, T., 'Sexual Offenders in the Community: Reflections on Problems of Law, Community and Risk Management in the U.S.A., England and Wales', *International Journal of the Sociology of Law* (1996), 24: 427–43.

Her Majesty's Prison Department, *Report of the Work of the Prison Department 1981* (London: HMSO, 1982).

Her Majesty's Prison Service, *Audit of Prison Resources* (London: HM Prison Service, 1996).

——*Framework Document* (London: HM Prison Service, 1999).

HERNANDEZ, D. and MYERS, D. E., 'Revolutions in Children's Lives', in A. Skolnick and J. Skolnick (eds), *Family in Transition*, 10th edn (New York: Longman, 1999).

HESS, L., 'Changing Familty Patterns in Western Europe', in M. Rutter and D. J. Smith (eds), *Psycho-Social Disorders in Young People* (London: Wiley, 1995), 104–93.

HEWITT, P., *About Time: The Revolution in Work and Family Life* (London: Institute of Public Policy Research, 1993).

HEYDEBRAND, W. and SERON, C., *Rationalizing Justice: The Political Economy of the Federal District Courts* (Albany, NY: SUNY Press, 1990).

HILL, M., *The Policy Process in the Modern State*, 3rd edn (London: Prentice Hall/Harvester Wheatsheaf, 1997).

HIMMELFARB, G., *The De-moralization of Society: From Victorian Virtues to Modern Values* (London: IEA Health and Welfare Unit, 1995).

——'Preface' to D. Anderson (ed), *This Will Hurt: The Restoration of Virtue and Civic Order* (London: Social Affairs Unit, 1995).

HINDELANG, M. J., GOTTFREDSON, M. R., and GAROFAO, J., *Victims of Personal Crime: An Empirical Foundation for a theory of Victimization* (Cambridge MA: Ballinger, 1978).

HIRSCHI, T., *Causes of Delinquency* (Berkele: University of California Press 1969).

HIRSCHMAN, A., *The Rhetoric of Reaction* (Cambridge, MA: Harvard University Press, 1991).

HIRST, P., 'The Genesis of the Social', *Power and Politics* (1980), 3: 67–84.

——*After Thatcher* (London: Collins, 1989).

HIRST, P., 'The Concept of Punishment', in R. A. Duff and D. Garland (eds), *A Reader on Punishment* (Oxford: Oxford University Press, 1994).

—— *Associative Democracy : New Forms of Economic and Social Governance* (Oxford: Polity Press, 1994).

—— 'Statism, Pluralism and Social Control', in D. Garland and J. R. Sparks (eds), *Criminology and Social Theory* (Oxford: Oxford University Press, 2000).

HOBBES, T., *Leviathan* (London: J. M. Dent, originally 1651).

HOBSBAWM, E., *Age of Extremes: The Short Twentieth Century* (London: Michael Joseph, 1994).

HOCHSCHILD, A. R., *The Time Bind: When Work Becomes Home and Home Becomes Work* (New York: Metropolitan Books, 1997).

HOGG, R. and BROWN, D., *Rethinking Law and Order* (Annandale, NSW: Pluto Press, 1998).

HOLMWOOD, J., 'The Americanization of British Social Policy' (on file with the author).

Home Office, *Prisons and Borstals: England and Wales* (London: Home Office, 1950).

—— *Penal Practice in a Changing Society* (London: HMSO, 1959).

—— *The War Against Crime* (London: HMSO, 1964).

—— *A Review of Criminal Justice Policy 1976* (London: HMSO, 1977).

—— *Report of the Committee of Inquiry into the UK Prisons Services (The May Report)* (Cmnd 7673) (London: HMSO, 1979).

—— and others, *Crime Prevention*, Circular 8/1984 (London: Home Office, 1984).

—— *Criminal Justice: A Working Paper* (London: Home Office, 1986).

—— Memo to the Chief Probation Officers of England and Wales, *Tackling Offending: An Action Plan* (17 August 1988).

—— *Punishment, Custody and the Community* (London: HMSO, 1988).

—— *Crime, Justice and Protecting the Public* (London: HMSO, 1990).

—— *A Practical Guide to Crime Prevention for Local Partnerships* (London: HMSO, 1993).

—— *Partners Against Crime*, Circular (London: Home Office Public Relations Branch, 1994).

—— *Criminal Statistics for England and Wales* (London: HMSO, 1996).

—— *Guidance on Statutory Crime and Disorder Partnerships* (1998).

—— *Digest 4: Information on the Criminal Justice System*, ed. G. C. Barclay and C. Travers (London: Home Office, 1999).

HOOD, R.,*Tolerance and the Tariff: Some Reflections on Fixing the Time Prisoners Serve in Custody* (London: NACRO, 1974).

—— and SHUTE, S., 'Protecting the Public: Automatic Life Sentences, Parole and High Risk Offenders', *Criminal Law Review*, November 1996, 788–800.

HOPE, T., book review, *British Journal of Criminology* (1997). vol 37, no 1, 151–3.

HOPKINS, J., 'Social Work Through the Looking Glass', in N. Parton (ed), *Social Theory, Social Change and Social Work* (London: Routledge, 1996).

HOUGH, M., *Anxiety About Crime: Findings From the 1994 British Crime Survey* (London: Home Office, 1995).

—— CLARKE, R., and MAYHEW, P., 'Introduction' to R. Clarke and P. Mayhew (eds), *Designing Out Crime* (London: HMSO, 1980).

—— and MOXON, D., 'Dealing With Offenders: Popular Opinion and the Views of Victims', in *The Howard Journal* (1985), vol 24, no 3, 160–75.

—— and ROBERTS, J., *Attitudes to Punishment: Findings from the British 1996 Crime Survey* (London: Home Office, 1998).

————'Sentencing Trends in Britain: Public Knowledge and Public Opinion', *Punishment & Society: The International Journal of Penology* (1999), 1 (1).

HOWARD, C., *The Hidden Welfare State: Tax Expenditures and Social Policy in the United States* (Princeton, NJ: Princeton University Press, 1997).

Howard League, *Whose Discretion? Fairness and Flexibility in the Penal System* (London: Howard League for Penal Reform, 1975).

HOWARD, M., Speech by the Rt. Hon. Michael Howard QC MP, the Home Secretary, to the 110th Conservative Party Conference, 6 October 1993 (London: Conservative Party Central Office).

HUDSON, J. and GALAWAY, B. (eds), *Restorative Justice: International Perspectives* (Monsey, NY: Willow Tree Pub, 1996).

HUSSEY, F. 'Just Deserts and Determinate Sentencing: Impact on the Rehabilitation Ideal', *The Prison Journal* (1980), vol LIX, no 2 (Autumn– Winter), 36–47.

HUTTON, W., *The State We're In* (London: Jonathan Cape, 1995).

IGNATIEFF, M., *A Just Measure of Pain* (London: MacMillan, 1978).

——'Citizenship and Moral Narcissism', *The Political Quarterly* (1988), vol 59.

JACKSON, K. T., *Crabgrass Frontier: The Suburbanization of the United States* (New York/Oxford: Oxford University Press, 1985).

JACOB, H., *The Frustration of Policy* (Boston: Little, Brown and Co, 1984).

JACOBS, J. B., *Stateville: The Penitentiary in Mass Society* (Chicago: University of Chicago Press, 1977).

——'The Prisoners' Rights Movement and its Impacts, 1960–1980', in N. Morris and M. Tonry (eds), *Crime and Justice: An Annual Review of Research* (Chicago: University of Chicago Press, 1980).

JACOBS, M. D., *Screwing the System and making it Work: Juvenile Justice in the No-Fault Society* (Chicago: University of Chicago Press, 1990).

JAMES, A. and RAINE, J., *The New Politics of Criminal Justice* (London: Longman, 1998).

JENCKS, C., *Rethinking Social Policy: Race, Poverty, and the Underclass* (Cambridge, MA: Harvard University Press, 1992).

—— *The Homeless* (Cambridge, MA and London: Harvard University Press, 1994).

—— and PETERSON, P. E. (eds), *The Urban Underclass* (Washingon DC: The Brookings Institute, 1991).

JENNINGS, A. F., 'More resounding silence', in *New Law Journal* (1999), vol 149, no 6899, 1180.

JOHNSON, D. B., *National Party Platforms, vol II 1960–1976* (Urbana: University of Illinois Press, 1978).

JOHNSTON, L., *The Rebirth of Private Policing* (London: Routledge, 1992).

JOHNSTONE, G. and BOTTOMLEY, K., 'Introduction: Labour's Crime Policy in Context', *Policy Studies* (1998), vol 19, no 3/4.

JONES, C., 'Auditing Criminal Justice', *British Journal of Criminology* (1993), vol 33, no 2, 187–202.

JONES, T. and NEWBURN, T., *Private Security and Public Policing* (Oxford: Clarendon Press, 1998).

————and SMITH, D. J., *Democracy and Policing* (London: Policy Studies Institute, 1997).

KAMINER, W., *It's All the Rage: Crime and Culture* (New York: Addison-Wesley, 1995).

KARP, D. R. (ed), *Community Justice: An Emerging Field* (New York: Rowman and Littlefield, 1998).

KARP, D. R. 'The Judicial and Judicious Use of Shame Penalties', *Crime and Delinquency* (1998), 44, 277–94.

KATZ, M. B., *The Undeserving Poor: From the War on Poverty to the War on Welfare* (New York: Pantheon, 1989).

—— *Improving Poor People* (Princeton, NJ: Princeton University Press, 1995).

KEAT, R. and ABERCROMBIE N. (eds), *Enterprise Culture* (London: Routledge, 1991).

KELLING, G. L., PATE, T., DIECKMAN, D., and BROWN, C. E., *The Kansas City Preventive Patrol Experiment* (Washington DC: Police Foundation, 1974).

—— and COLES, C. M., *Fixing Broken Windows* (New York: The Free Press, 1996).

KEMSHALL, H., 'Risk in Probation Practice: The Hazards and Dangers of Supervision', *Probation Journal*, vol 42, no 2 (June 1995), 67–71.

—— *Risk in Probation Practice* (Aldershot: Ashgate, 1998)

KENNEDY, D. J., 'Residential Associations as State Actors: Regulating the Impact of Gated Communities on Nonmembers', *Yale Law Journal* (1995), vol 105, 761–93.

KILBRANDON, LORD, *Children and Young Persons in Scotland* (The Kilbrandon Report) (Cmnd 2306) (Edinburgh: HMSO, 1964).

KING, R. D., 'The Rise and Fall of Supermax: An American Solution in Search of a Problem?', *Punishment & Society* (1999), vol 1, no 2.

—— and MCDERMOTT, K., *The State of Our Prisons* (Oxford, Oxford University Press, 1995).

KITTRIE, N. N., *The Right to be Different: Deviance and Enforced Therapy* (Baltimore and London: The Johns Hopkins Press, 1971).

KLEINIG, J., *Punishment and Desert* (The Hague: Martin Nijhoff, 1973).

KNEMEYER, F.-L., 'Polizei', *Economy and Society* (1980), 9:2, 172–96.

KOOIMAN, J., *Modern Governance: New Social-Governmental Interactions* (London: Sage, 1993).

KRAHN, H. and KENNEDY, L. W., 'Producing Personal Safety: The Effects of Crime Rates, Police Force Size, and Fear of Crime', *Criminology* (1985, vol 23, no 4, 697–710.

KURKI, L., *Incorporating Restorative and Community Justice Initiatives into American Sentencing and Corrections*, Research in Brief, No 3 (Washington DC: US Department of Justice, 1999).

—— 'Restorative and Community Justice in the United States', *Crime and Justice*, vol. 27 (2000).

Labour Party, *Crime: A Challenge To Us All* (The Longford Report) (London: Labour Party, 1964).

—— *Everyone's a Victim*, 28 March (London: Central Office, 1995).

LACEY, N., 'Government as Manager, Citizen as Consumer: The Case of the Criminal Justice Act of 1991', *The Modern Law Review* (1994) 57: 534–54.

LAFREE, G., *Losing Legitimacy: Street Crime and the Decline of Social Institutions in America* (Boulder, CO: Westview, 1998).

LANE, R., 'Urban Police and Crime in Nineteenth Century America', in *Crime and Justice: An Annual Review of Research*, vol 2 (1980).

—— *Murder in America* (Columbus, OH: Ohio State University Press, 1997).

LANGAN, P. A. and FARRINGTON, D. P, 'Crime and Justice in the United States and in England and Wales, 1981–96', *Bureau of Justice Statistics Executive Summary* (Washington DC: US Department of Justice, Bureau of Justice Statistics 1998).

LANGBEIN, J., *Torture and the Law of Proof* (Chicago: University of Chicago Press, 1976).

LASH, S. and URRY, J., *The End of Organised Capitalism* (Cambridge: Polity Press, 1987).

LAYCOCK, G. and HEAL, K., 'Crime prevention: The British Experience', in D. J. Evans and D. T. Herbert (eds), *The Geography of Crime* (London: Routledge, 1989), 315–30.

LEADBETTER, C., *The Self-Policing Society* (London: Demos, 1996).

LEARMONT, SIR J., *Review of Prison Service Security in England and Wales* (Cm 3020) (London: HMSO, 1995).

LEWIS, C. S., 'The Humanitarian Theory of Punishment', *Res Judicatae* (1953), vol 6.

LEWIS, D., *Hidden Agendas: Politics, Law and Disorder* (London: Hamish Hamilton, 1997).

LIEBMAN, J., FAGAN, J., and WEST, V., *A Broken System: Error Rates in Capital Cases, 1973–1995* (New York: The Justice Project, 2000).

LILLY, J. R. and KNEPPER, P., 'The Corrections-Commercial Complex', *Crime & Delinquency* (1993), vol 39, no 2, 150–66.

LIPTON, D., MARTINSON, R., and WILKS, J., *The Effectiveness of Correctional Treatment* (New York: Praeger, 1975).

LOCKWOOD, D. 'Social Integration and System Integration', repr. in Lockwood, *Solidarity and Schism* (Oxford: Oxford University Press, 1992).

LYNCH, J., 'Crime in International Perspective', in J. Q. Wilson and J. Petersilia (eds), *Crime* (San Francisco, CA: Institute of Contemporary Studies, 1995), 11–39.

McARA, L., 'The Politics of Penality: An Overview of the Development of Penal Policy in Scotland', in P. Duff and N. Hutton (eds), *Criminal Justice in Scotland* (Aldershot: Ashgate, 1999), 355–80.

McDONALD, R. (ed), *Youth, 'the Underclass' and Social Exclusion* (London: Routledge, 1997).

McGuire, J., 'Reducing Re-Offending: Research Findings and Guidelines for Practice', paper delivered at the Howard League Conference, London, 1994.

—— *What Works?: Reducing Reoffending* (New York: Wiley 1995).

McKELVEY, B., *American Prisons: A History of Good Intentions* (orig. publ. 1936, repr. Montclair, NJ: Patterson Smith, 1979).

McMULLAN, J. L., 'The Arresting Eye: Discourse, Surveillance and Disciplinary Administration in Early English Police Thinking', in *Social & Legal Studies* (1998), 7: 97–128.

MADRIZ, E., *Nothing Bad Happens to Good Girls: Fear of Crime in Women's Lives* (Berkeley, CA: University of California Press, 1997).

MAGNET, M., *The Dream and the Nightmare: The Sixties Legacy to the Underclass* (New York: Encounter Books, 1993).

MAGUIRE, K. and PASTORE, A., *Sourcebook of Criminal Justice Statistics 1998* (Washington DC: Bureau of Justice Statistics, 1999).

MAGUIRE, M., VAGG, J., and MORGAN, R. (eds), *Accountability and Prisons* (London: Tavistock, 1985).

MAGUIRE, M., 'The Needs and Rights of Victims', in M.Tonry (ed), *Crime and Justice: A Review of Research*, vol 14 (Chicago, University of Chicago Press, 1991), 363–433

MANNING, P. K., *Police Work: The Social Organization of Policing*, 2nd edn (Illinois: Waveland Press, Inc., 1997).

MARKIN, D., Review of Inga Clendinnen's 'Reading the Holocaust', in the *New York Times Book Review* (11 April 1999), 17.

MARSHALL, T. H., 'Citizenship and Social Class', in T. H. Marshall, *Sociology at the Crossroads* (London: Heinemann, 1963).

MARTINSON, R. L., 'What Works?—Questions and Answers About Prison Reform', *The Public Interest* (1974), vol 35, 22–54

—— 'New Findings, New Views: A Note of Caution Regarding sentencing Reform', *Hofstra Law Review* (1979), vol 7, 242–58.

MARX K. and ENGELS, F., *The Communist Manifesto* (New York: Verso, 1998, originally published in 1848).

MASSEY, D. S. and DENTON, N. A., *American Apartheid: Segregation and the Making of the Underclass* (Cambridge, MA: Harvard University Press, 1993).

MATHIESEN, T., *The Politics of Abolition* (London: Martin Robertson, 1974).

MATZA, D., *Delinquency and Drift* (Englewood Cliffs, NJ: Prentice Hall, 1964).

MAUER, M., *Americans Behind Bars: The International Use of Incarceration, 1995* (Washington, DC: The Sentencing Project, 1996).

—— *Race to Incarcerate* (New York: The New Press, 1999).

MAXFIELD, M., *Fear of Crime in England and Wales* (London: HMSO, 1984).

MAXFIELD, M., 'Lifestyle and Routine Activities Theories of Crime: Empirical Studies of Victimization, Delinquency and Offender Decision-Making', *Journal of Quantitative Criminology* (1987), vol 3, no 4, 275–82.

MEAD, L. M., *The New Politics of Poverty: The Nonworking Poor in America* (New York: Basic Books, 1992).

MERTON, R. K., 'Social Structure and Anomie', in R. K. Merton, *Social Theory and Social Structure*, rev. edn (New York: Free Press, 1968).

—— *Sociological Ambivalence and Other Essays* (New York: The Free Press, 1976).

MESSINGER, K., *The Crime of Punishment* (New York: Viking, 1968).

MEYROWITZ, J., *No Sense of Place* (New York and Oxford: Oxford University Press, 1985).

MILIBAND, R., 'A State of De-Subordination', *British Journal of Sociology* (1978), 29 (4): 399–409.

MILLER, M., 'Cells vs. Cops vs. Classrooms', in L. Friedman and G. Fisher (eds), *The Crime Conundrum* (Boulder, CO: Westview Press, 1997), 127–62.

MIRRLEES-BLACK, C., MAYHEW, P., and PERCY, A., *The 1996 British Crime Survey* (London: HMSO, 1996).

MITFORD, J., *Kind and Usual Punishment: The Prison Business* (New York: Random House, 1973).

MONKKONEN, E. H. (ed), *Crime and Justice in American History* (Westport, CN: Meckler, 1991).

—— 'History of Urban Police', in *Crime and Justice: A Review of Research* (1992), vol 15 (Chicago: University of Chicago Press, 1992).

MOORE, M. H., 'The Legitimation of Criminal Justice Policies and Practices', *Perspectives on Crime and Justice: 1996–97 Lecture Series* (Washington DC: National Institute of Justice, 1997).

—— 'Public Health and Criminal Justice Approaches to Prevention', in M. Tonry and D. P. Farrington (eds), *Building a Safer Society* (Chicago: University of Chicago Press 1995), 237–62.

MORRIS, H., 'Persons and Punishment', *The Monist* (1968), vol 52, 475–501.

MORRIS, L., *Dangerous Classes: The Underclass and Social Citizenship*) London: Routledge, 1994).

MORRIS, N., *The Future of Imprisonment* (Chicago: University of Chicago Press, 1974).

—— and BUCKLE, D.,'The Humanitarian Theory of Punishment: A Reply', *Res Judicatae*, vol 6 (1953), 231–7.

——and TONRY, T., *Between Prison and Probation* (New York: Oxford University Press, 1990).

MORRIS, T., 'Social Values and the Criminal Act', *The Nation*, 4 July 1959.

MORTIMER, E. and MAY, C., 'Electronic Monitoring of Curfew Orders the Second Year of the Trials', *Research Findings, No 66*, Home Office Research and Statistics Directorate (London: HMSO, 1998).

MOYNIHAN, D. P., *Maximum Feasible Misunderstanding* (New York: Free Press, 1969).

——'Defining Deviance Down', in *The American Scholar* (Autumn 1992).

——'Towards a New Intolerance' *The Public Interest*, no 112 (Winter 1993).

MUNCIE, J. and SPARKS, J. R. (eds), *Imprisonment: European Perspectives* (Hemel Hempstead: Harvester Wheatsheaf, 1991).

MURIE, A., 'Linking Housing Changes to Crime', in C. J. Finer and M. Nellis (eds), *Crime and Social Exclusion* (Oxford: Blackwell, 1998), 22–36.

MURPHY, J., 'Marxism and Retribution', *Philosophy and Public Affairs* (1973), vol 2, 217–43.

MURRAY, C., *The Emerging British Underclass* (London: The IEA Health and Welfare Unit, 1990).

——*Losing Ground: American Social Policy 1950–1980* (New York: Basic Books, 1984).

——*Underclass: The Crisis Deepens* (London: IEA Health and Welfare Unit in association with *The Sunday Times*, 1994).

National Congress on Penitentiary and Reformatory Discipline, 'A Statement of Principles', *Transactions of the National Congress on Penitentiary and Reformatory Discipline* (Albany: Weed, Parsons, 1871), 541–7.

National Advisory Commission on Criminal Justice Standards and Goals, *A National Strategy to Reduce Crime Final Report* (Washington DC: Government Printing Office, 1973).

NELKIN, D., 'Discipline and Punish: Some Notes on the Margin', *Howard Journal* (1989) 28/4, 245–54.

New York Times Editorial, 'Tough and Smart on Crime', *The New York Times*, 27 January 1994.

NEWBURN, T., *Permission and Regulation: Law and Morals in Postwar Britain* (London: Routledge, 1992).

NORRIE, A. and ADELMAN, S., ' "Consensual Authoritarianism" and Criminal Justice in Thatcher's Britain', *Journal of Law & Society* (1989), 16 (1): 112–28.

NOSSITER, J., 'Making Hard Times Harder', *New York Times*, 17 September 1994, section 1, page 1.

NUTTALL, C. and PEASE, K., 'Changes in the Use of Imprisonment in England and Wales 1950—1991', *Criminal Law Review* (1994), 316–23.

OESTREICH, G., *Neostoicism and the Early Modern State* (Cambridge: Cambridge University Press, 1982).

OFFE, C., *Contradictions of the Welfare State* (London: Hutchinson, 1984).

O'MALLEY, P., 'Risk, Power, and Crime Prevention', *Economy and Society* (1992), 21: 252–75.

——'Post-Keynesian Policing', *Economy and Society* (1996) 25(2):137–155.

——'Volatile and Contradictory Punishment', *Theoretical Criminology* (1999), 3(2) 175–96.

OPPENHEIM, C., *Poverty: The Facts* (London: Child Poverty Action Group, 1993).

PACK, J. R., 'BIDs, DIDs, SIDs, SADs: Private Governments in Urban America', *The Brookings Review* (Fall 1992), 18–21.

PALMER, T., 'Martinson Revisited', *Journal of Research in Crime and Delinquency* (1975), vol 12, 133–52.

PARTON, N., 'Social Work, Risk and "the Blaming System"', in N. Parton (ed), *Social Theory, Social Change and Social Work* (London: Routledge, 1996).

—— (ed), *Social Theory, Social Change and Social Work* (London: Routledge, 1996).

PASQUINO, P., 'Theatrum Politicum: The Genealogy of Capital—Police and the State of Prosperity' in G. Burchell, C. Gordon, and P. Miller (eds), *The Foucault Effect* (Hemel Hempstead: Harvester Wheatsheaf, 1991).

PATTEN, J., 'Crime: a Middle Class Disease?' *New Society* (13 May 1988).

PERKIN, H., *The Rise of Professional Society* (London: Routledge, 1989).

PETTINICO, G., 'Crime and Punishment; America Changes Its Mind', *The Public Perspective* (September/October 1994).

PIORE, M. and SABEL, C., *The Second Industrial Divide* (New York: Basic Books, 1984).

PHILIPS, D.,' "A New Engine of Power and Authority": The Institutionalization of Law-Enforcement in England 1780–1830', in V. A. C. Gatrell, B. Lehman, and G. Parker (eds), *Crime and the Law: The Social History of Crime in Western Europe Since 1500* (London: Europa Publications, Ltd, 1980).

PIERSON, C., *Beyond the Welfare State?* (Pennsylvania: The Pennsylvania State University Press, 1991).

PIERSON, P., *Dismantling the Welfare State?* (New York: Cambridge University Press, 1994).

PILLSBURY, S., 'Why Are We Ignored? The Peculiar Place of Experts in the Current Debate About Crime and Justice', *Criminal Law Bulletin* (July/ August 1995).

PISCIOTTA, A., 'A Retrospective Look at the Task Force Report on Juvenile Delinquency and Youth Crime', in J.A. Conley (ed), *The 1967 President's Crime Commission Report: Its Impact 25 Years Later* (Cincinatti: Anderson, 1994).

PLATT, T. and TAKAGI, P., 'Intellectuals for Law and Order; A Critique of the New "Realists"', *Crime and Social Justice*, 8 (Fall, Winter, 1977), 1–16.

POLSKY, A. J., *The Rise of the Therapeutic State* (Princeton, NJ: Princeton University Press, 1991).

POVEY, D. and COTTON, J., *Recorded Crime Statistics: England and Wales, October 1998 to September 1999* (London: Home Office, 18 January 2000).

POWER, M., *The Audit Explosion* (London: Demos, 1994).

PRATT, J., 'The Return of the Wheelbarrow Men', *British Journal of Criminology* (2000), vol 40, no 1, 127–45.

—— 'Emotive and Ostentatious Punishments', *Punishment & Society* (2000), vol 2(4), 416–38.

President's Commission on Law Enforcement and Administration, *The Challenge of Crime in a Free Society Report* (Washington DC: US Govt. Printing Office, 1967).

President's Task Force on Victims, *Final Report* (Washington, DC: US Government Printing Office, 1982).

PUTNAM, R., *Bowling Alone* (New York: Simon & Schuster, 2000).

PYLE, D., *Cutting the Costs of Crime: The Economics of Crime and Criminal Justice* (London: IEA, 1995).

QUIN, J., 'The Labour Government's New Approach to Criminal Justice', *Policy Studies* (December 1998), vol 19, no. 3/4.

RAAB, T. K., *The Struggle for Stability in Early Modern Europe* (New York: Oxford University Press, 1975).

RADZINOWICZ, L., *The History of the English Criminal Law and Its Administration*, vol 3 (London: Stevens, 1956).

—— *The Need for Criminology* (London: Heinemann, 1965).

—— 'Public Opinion and Crime', in *Medicine, Science and Law* (1961), vol 2, no 1, 24–32.

—— *The Cambridge Institute: Its Background and Scope* (London: HMSO, 1988).

—— *Adventures in Criminology* (London: Routledge, 1999).

—— and KING, J., *The Growth of Crime* (Harmondsworth: Penguin Books, 1979).

—— and HOOD, R., 'The American *Volte-Face* in Sentencing Thought and Practice' in C. Tapper (ed), *Crime, Proof & Punishment* (London: Butterworth, 1981).

—— —— *A History of the English Criminal Law and its Administration*, vol 5 (Oxford: Clarendon Press, 1990).

RAINE, J. and WILLSON, M., *Managing Criminal Justice* (London: Harvester Wheatsheaf, 1983).

RANULF, S., *Moral Indignation and Middle Class Psychology* (New York: Schoken, 1964).

RAWLS, J., *A Theory of Justice* (Oxford: Clarendon Press, 1962).

REES, H. and WILLIAMS, E. H., *Punishment, Custody and the Community* (London: LSE, 1989).

REES, J. R., *Mental Health and the Offender* (London: Clarke Hall Fellowship, 1947).

REICH, R., 'The Secession of the Successful', *The New York Times Magazine*, 29 January 1991.

REID, J. P., *Policing the Elephant: Crime, Punishment and Social Behavior on the Overland Trail* (San Marino, CA: Huntington Library, 1997).

REINER, R., *The Politics of the Police*, 2nd edn (Hemel Hempstead: Wheatsheaf, 1992).

—— 'Policing a Postmodern Society', in *The Modern Law Review* (1992), vol 55, 761–81.

—— and Cross, M., *Beyond Law and Order: Criminal Justice Policy and Politics into the 1990s* (London: MacMillan, 1991).

Reinventing Probation Council, *Broken Windows Probation: The Next Step in Fighting Crime* (New York: Manhattan Institute, 7 August 1999).

REITH, C., *British Police and the Democratic Ideal* (Oxford: Oxford University Press, 1943).

Research and Forecasts Inc., *America Afraid: How Fear of Crime Changes the Way We Live (The Figgie Reports)* (New York: NAL, 1983).

RIGER, S., GORDON, M. T., and LeBAILLY, R. K., 'Coping With Urban Crime: Women's Use of Precautionary Behaviors', *American Journal of Community Psychology* (1982) vol 10, no 4, 369–86.

RILEY, D. and MAYHEW, P., *Crime Prevention Publicity: An Assessment*, Home Office Research Study No 63 (London: Home Office, 1980).

RIVELAND, C., *Supermax Prisons: Overview and General Considerations* (Washington DC: US Deptartment of Justice, National Institute of Corrections, 1999).

—— 'Prison Management Trends, 1975–2025', in M. Tonry and J. Petersilia (eds), *Prisons* (Chicago: University of Chicago Press, 1999).

ROBERTS, J., 'Public Opinion, Crime and Criminal Justice', *Crime and Justice* (1992), vol 16, 99–180.

—— and STALANS, R., *Public Opinion, Crime and Criminal Justice* (Boulder, CO: Westview, 1997).

ROBINSON, J. and SMITH, G.,'The Effectiveness of Correctional Programs', *Crime and Delinquency* (January 1971), 67–80.

ROCK, P., 'The Present State of Criminology in Britain', in P. Rock (ed), *A History of British Criminology* (Oxford: Oxford University Press, 1988).

—— *Helping Victims of Crime: The Home Office and the Rise of Victim Support in England and Wales* (Oxford: Clarendon Press, 1990).

—— 'The Organization of a Home Office Initiative', *European Journal of Crime, Criminal Law and Criminal Justice* (1994), 2(2): 141–67.

—— (ed), *The History of Criminology* (Aldershot: Dartmouth, 1994).

Roper Reports Editors, 'The Big Picture: Crime Fears', *American Demographics* (July 1997).

ROSCH, J., 'Crime as an issue in American Politics', in E. S. Fairchild and V. J. Webb (eds), *The Politics of Crime and Criminal Justice* (New York: Sage, 1985).

ROSE, D., *In the Name of the Law: The Collapse of Criminal Justice* (London: Jonathan Cape, 1996).

ROSENBAUM, D. R., *Community Crime Prevention* (Beverly Hills, CA: Sage, 1986).

—— 'Community Crime Prevention: A Review and Synthesis of the Literature', *Justice Quarterly* (1988), vol 5, 323–95.

ROSENBLATT, R., 'Social Duties and the Problem of Rights in the American Welfare State', in D. Kairys (ed), *The Politics of Law*, rev. edn (New York: Pantheon Books, 1990), 90–114.

ROTHMAN, D., 'Prisons: The Failure Model', *The Nation*, 21 December 1974

—— *Conscience and Convenience: The Asylum and its Alternatives in Progressive America* (Boston: Little Brown and Co., 1980).

RUTHERFORD, A., *Criminal Justice and the Pursuit of Decency* (Oxford: Oxford University Press, 1993).

RUTTER, M. and SMITH, D. J. (eds), *Psychosocial Disorders in Young People* (London: John Wiley & Sons, 1995).

RYCROFT, C., *A Critical Dictionary of Psychoanalysis* (Harmondsworth: Penguin Books, 1968).

SACCO, V. H. and JOHNSON, H., *Patterns of Criminal Victimization in Canada.* (Canada: Minister of Supply and Services, 1990).

SAINT AUGUSTINE, *The City of God* (New York: Image Books, 1958).

SAMPSON, A., *Acts of Abuse: Sex Offenders and the Criminal Justice System* (London: Routledge, 1994).

SARAT, A. (ed), *The Killing State: Capital Punishment in Law, Politics and Culture* (New York: Oxford University Press, 1999).

SCHEINGOLD, S., *The Politics of Street Crime.* (Philadelphia: Temple University Press, 1991).

—— 'Politics, Public Policy, and Street Crime', *ANNALS, AAPSS*, May 1995.

—— 'Constructing the New Political Criminology: Power, Authority and the Post-Liberal State', in *Law and Social Inquiry* (forthcoming).

SHICHOR, D. and SECHREST, D. K. (eds), *Three Strikes and You're Out: Vengeance as Public Policy* (Thousand Oaks, CA: Sage, 1996).

SCHNEIDER, A. L. and SCHNEIDER, P. B., *Private and Public-Minded Citizen Responses to a Neighborhood-Based Crime Prevention Strategy* (Eugene, Ore.: Institute of Policy Analysis, 1977).

SCHOR, J. B., *The Overworked American* (New York: Basic Books, 1992).

Schrag, P., *Paradise Lost: California's Experience, America's Future* (California: University of California Press, 1998).

Scott, J. C., *Seeing Like a State* (New Haven, CN: Yale University Press, 1998).

Scottish Conservative Party, *Tomorrow Scotland: Better with the Conservatives* (Edinburgh: Scottish Conservative and Unionist Party Central Office, 1970).

Scottish Home Department, *The Scottish Borstal System* (Edinburgh: HMSO, 1947).

Scottish Home and Health Department, *Parole and Related Issues in Scotland: Report of the Review Committee* (The Kincraig Report) (Edinburgh: HMSO, 1989).

Scottish Office, *Preventing Crime Together in Scotland: A Strategy for the 90s* (Edinburgh: Scottish Office, 1992).

——*Preventing Crime Together in Scotland: A Guide to Good Practice in Business* (Edinburgh: Scottish Office, 1993).

Scottish Prison Service, *Opportunity and Responsibility: Developing New Approaches to the Management of the Long Term Prison System in Scotland.* (Edinburgh: Scottish Prison Service, 1990).

Seamon, T. M., 'Private Forces for Public Good', *Security Management*, September 1995, 92–7.

Sechrest, L., White, S. O., and Brown, E. D., *The Rehabilitation of Criminal Offenders: Problems and Prospects* (Washington DC: National Academy of Science, 1979).

Selsdon, A., *Wither the Welfare State* (London: The Institute of Economic Affairs, 1981).

Selznick, P., *The Moral Commonwealth* (Berkeley: University of California Press, 1992).

Sennett, R., *The Corrosion of Character: The Personal Consequences of Work in the New Capitalism* (New York: Norton, 1998).

Serrill, M. S., 'Determinate Sentencing: The History, the Theory, the Debate', *Corrections Magazine* (1977), vol 3: 3–13.

Shapiro, B., 'Victims & Vengeance: Why the Victims' Rights Amendment is a Bad Idea', *The Nation*, 10 February 1997.

——'Capital Offense', *The New York Sunday Times*, 26 March 2000.

Sharman, C., 'Writing on Wall for Graffiti with "Times Sq. Effect" Britain Could Soon Adopt a Smartness Habit from US Colin Sharman Reports', *The Daily Telegraph*, 23 February 1998, 31.

Sharpe, E. B., *The Sometime Connection: Public Opinion and Social Policy* (New York: State University of New York Press, 1999).

Shearing, C., 'The Relation Between Public and Private Policing', in M. Tonry and N. Morris (eds), *Modern Policing* (Chicago: University of Chicago Press, 1992), 399–434.

Sherman, L., 'Attacking Crime: Police and Crime Control', in M. Tonry and N. Morris (eds), *Modern Policing* Chicago: University of Chicago Press, 1992), 159–230.

Shichor, D. and Sechrest, D. K. (eds), *Three Strikes and You're Out: Vengeance As Public Policy* (Thousand Oaks, CA: Sage, 1996).

Short, J. F. and Nye, F. I., 'Extent of unrecorded delinquency: Some tentative conclusions', *Journal of Criminal Law, Criminology and Police Science* (1958), vol 49, 296–302.

Sibley, D., *Geographies of Exclusion* (London: Routledge, 1995).

Simon, J., *Poor Discipline: Parole and the Social Control of the Underclass, 1890–1990* (Chicago: University of Chicago Press, 1993).

SIMON, J. and FEELEY, M., 'True Crime: The New Penology and the Public Discourse on Crime', in T. Blomberg and S. Cohen (eds), *Punishment and Social Control* (New York: Aldine de Gruyter, 1995).

SINGER, S. I. , *Recriminalizing Delinquency* (New York: Cambridge University Press, 1996).

SKOGAN, W. G., 'The Changing Distribution of Big-City Crime: A Multi-City Time-Series Analysis', *Urban Affairs Quarterly* (1977), 13(1): 33–49.

—— 'Community Organizations and Crime', in M. Tonry and N. Morris (eds), *Crime and Justice: An Annual Review of Research* (Chicago: University of Chicago Press, 1988).

—— *Disorder and Decline* (New York: The Free Press, 1990).

—— and MAXFIELD, M., *Coping With Crime* (Beverly Hills, CA: Sage, 1981).

SMITH, D. J., 'Living Conditions in the Twentieth Century, in M. Rutter and D. J. Smith (eds), *Psychosocial Disorders in Young People: Time Trends and Their Causes* (London: Wiley, 1995).

—— 'Youth Crime and Conduct Disorders: Trends, Patterns and Causal Explanations', in M. Rutter and D. J. Smith, *Psycho-Social Disorders in Young People: Time Trends and Their Causes* (London: Wiley, 1995).

—— 'Less Crime Without More Punishment', *Edinburgh Law Review* (1999), vol 3, 294–316.

SNACKEN, S, Beyens, K., and Tubex, H., 'Changing Prison Populations in Western countries: Fate or Policy?' *European Journal of Crime, Criminal Law and Criminal Justice*, vol 3, no 1 (1995), 18–53.

SPARKS, J. R. (1992), *Television and the Drama of Crime* (Milton Keynes: Open University Press, 1992).

—— 'Risk and blame in criminal justice controversies', in M. Brown and J. Pratt (eds), *Dangerous Offenders: Criminal Justice and Social Order* (London: Routledge, 2000).

—— 'Penal austerity and social anxiety at the century's turn: governmental rationalities, legitimation deficits and populism in English penal politics in the 1990s', in L. Wacquant (ed), *From Social State to Penal State* (New York: Oxford University Press, forthcoming).

STANKO, E., *Everyday Violence: How Women and Men Experience Sexual and Physical Danger* (London: Pandora's Press, 1990).

STEINMETZ, G., *Regulating the Social: The Welfare State and Local Politics in Imperial Germany* (Princeon NJ: Princeton University Press, 1993).

Stewart Committee, *Keeping Offenders Out of Court: Further Alternatives to Prosecution* (Cmnd 8958) (Edinburgh: HMSO, 1983).

STITH, K. and CABRANES, J. A., *Fear of Judging: Sentencing Guidelines in the Federal Courts* (Chicago: University of Chicago Press, 1998).

STRANGE, S., *The Retreat of the State* (Cambridge: Cambridge University Press, 1996).

STRAW, J., Open letter to Penal Affairs Consortium, August 1997.

—— 'The Criminal Justice Crisis', *Criminal Justice Matters*, no 26 (Winter 96/97).

—— 'Crime and Old Labour's Punishment', *The Times*, 8 April 1998.

—— *Making Prisons Work*, The Prison Reform Trust Annual Lecture, December 1998.

SYKES, C., *A Nation of Victims* (New York: St. Martin's Press, 1992).

TAYLOR, D. G., SCHEPPELE, K., and STINCHCOMBE, A., 'Salience of Crime and Support for Harsher Criminal Sanctions', *Social Problems* (1979), vol 26, no 4, 413–24.

TAYLOR, I., 'Left Realist Criminology and the Free Market Experiment in Britain', J. Young and R. Matthews (eds), *Rethinking Criminology: The Realist Debate* (London: Sage, 1992).

—— 'Private Homes and Public Others', *British Journal of Criminology* (1995) vol 35, no 2, 263–85.

—— *Crime in Context: A Critical Criminology of Market Societies* (Oxford: Polity, 1999).

TAYLOR, L., LACEY, R., and BRACKEN, D., *In Whose Best Interests?* (London: Cobden Trust, 1980).

TAYLOR, R., *Forty Years of Crime and Criminal Justice Statistics, 1958 to 1997* (London: Home Office, 1998).

TERRILL, R. J., 'Margaret Thatcher's Law and Order Agenda', *American Journal of Comparative Law* (1989), vol 37, 429–56.

THERBORN, G., *Why Some Peoples Are More Unemployed Than Others* (London: Verso, 1986).

—— *European Modernity and Beyond* (London: Sage, 1995).

THOMPSON, J. B., *Ideology and Modern Culture* (Cambridge: Polity Press, 1990).

TILLY, C. (ed), *The Formation of National States in Western Europe* (Princeton, Princeton University Press, 1975).

TITTLE, C., *Control Balance: Towards a General Theory of Deviance* (Boulder CO: Westview Press, 1995).

TOLNEY, S. E. and Beck, E. M., *A Festival of Violence: An Analysis of Southern Lynchings, 1882–1930* (Urbana: University of Illinios Press, 1995).

TONRY, M., *Malign Neglect—Race, Crime, and Punishment in America* (New York: Oxford University Press, 1995).

—— *Sentencing Matters* (New York: Oxford University Press, 1996).

—— 'Rethinking Unthinkable Punishment Policies in America', *UCLA Law Review* (1999), vol 46, no 6, 1751–91.

—— and FARRINGTON, D. P. (eds), *Building a Safer Society* (Chicago: University of Chicago Press, 1995).

TUCK, M., 'Community and the Criminal Justice System', *Policy Studies* (1991), vol 12 (3): 22–37.

Twentieth Century Fund Task Force, *Fair and Certain Punishment* (New York: Wiley, 1976).

TYLER, T. R. and BOECKMANN, R. J., 'Three Strikes and You Are Out, But Why? The Psychology of Public Support for Punishing Rule Breakers', *Law and Society Review* (1997), vol 331, no 2.

United States Bureau of the Census, *Statistical Abstracts of the United States* (Washington, DC: US Government Printing Office, 1996).

United States Department of Justice Bureau of Justice Statistics, *Census of State and Federal Correctional Facilities, 1995* (Washington, DC: Department of Justice, Government Printing Office, 1996).

United States Department of Justice Federal Bureau of Investigation, *Crime in the United States: Uniform Crime Reports 1987* (Washington DC: Government Printing Office, 1988).

—— Federal Bureau of Investigation Uniform Crime Reports, *Crime in the United States 1995* (Washington, DC: US Government Printing Office, 1995).

—— *Criminal Victimization in the United States: 1973–1992 Trends* (Washington, DC: US Government Printing Office, 1994).

United States Department of Justice Federal Bureau of Investigation, *Sourcebook of Criminal Justice Statistics 1995* (Washington, DC: US Government Printing Office, 1996).

—— *Criminal Victimization* (Washington, DC: US Government Printing Office, 1996).

United States National Center for Educational Statistics, *Statistics in Brief* (Washington, DC: US Government Printing Office, 1996).

Vera Institute, *Felony Arrests: Their Prosecution and Disposition in New York City's Courts* (New York: Vera Institute, 1977).

Visiting Committee of the Correctional Association of New York, *Rehabilitation that Works: Improving and Expanding Shock Incarceration in New York State* (New York: Correctional Association of New York, April 1996),

Vold G. B. and Bernard, T., *Theoretical Criminology*, 2nd edn (New York: Oxford University Press, 1979).

VAN DIJK, J. J. M., 'Understanding Crime Rates: On the interactions between the rational choices of victims and offenders', *British Journal of Criminology* (1994), vol 34, no 2, 105–21.

VON HIRSCH, A., *Doing Justice: The Choice of Punishments—Report of the Committee for the Study of Incarceration* (New York: Hill and Wang, 1976).

—— 'Review of F. Allen's Decline of the Rehabilitative Ideal', *University of Pennsylvania Law Review* (1983), vol 131, 822–00.

—— *Past or Future Crimes? Deservedness or Dangerousness in the Sentencing of Criminals* (Manchester: Manchester University Press, 1985).

—— *Censure and Sanctions* (Oxford: Clarendon Press, 1993).

—— and ASHWORTH, A. (eds), *Principled Sentencing: Readings on Theory and Policy*, 2nd edn (Oxford: Hart Publishing, 1998).

—— GARLAND, D,. and WAKEFIELD, A. (eds), *The Ethics of Situational Crime Prevention* (Oxford: Hart Publishing, 2000).

WACQUANT, L., 'Pierre Bourdieu', in R. Stones (ed), *Key Sociological Thinkers.* (London: MacMillan 1990).

—— 'Deadly symbiosis: when ghetto and prison meet and merge', *Punishment & Society* (2001), vol 3, no 1.

WALKER, N., *Treatment and Justice in Penology and Psychiatry: The 1976 Sandoz Lecture* (Edinburgh: Edinburgh University, 1976).

—— 'Introduction', in Heal and Laycock (eds), *Situational Crime Prevention* (London: HMSO, 1986).

WALKER, S., *Taming the System: The Control of Discretion in Criminal Justice, 1950–1990* (New York: Oxford University Press, 1993).

—— *Popular Justice: A History of American Criminal Justice*, 2nd edn (New York: Oxford University Press, 1998).

WALLIS, E., 'A New Choreography: Breaking Away from the Elaborate Corporate Dance', in R. Burnett (ed), *The Probation Service: Responding to Change* (Oxford: Probation Studies Unit, Oxford University, 1997), 91–104

WARREN, R., ROSENTRAUB, M. S., and HARLOW, K. S., 'Co-production, Equity and the Distribution of Safety', *Urban Affairs Quarterly* (1984), vol 19, 447–64.

WECHSLER, H., 'Sentencing, corrections and the Model Penal Code', 109 *University of Pennsylvania Law Review* (1961), no 6, 465–93.

WEIR, M., ORLOFF, A. S., and SKOCPOL, T. (eds), *The Politics of Social Policy in the United States* (Princeton NJ: Princeton University Press, 1988).

WEST, C., *Race Matters* (New York: Vintage Books, 1994).

WESTERN, B. and BECKETT, K., 'How Unregulated is the US Labor Market? The Penal System as a Labor Market Institution', *American Journal of Sociology* (1999), 104, 1135–72.

WHITE, P., WOODBRIDGE, J., and FLACK, K., *Projections of Long Term Trends in the Prison Population to 2006* (London: Home Office, 2000).

WIENER, M., *Reconstructing the Criminal* (Cambridge: Cambridge University Press, 1990).

WILLIAMS, D. R., 'Women's Part-Time Employment', *Monthly Labor Review* (April 1995), 36–44.

WILSON, J. Q., *Thinking About Crime*, 2me edn (New York: Basic Books, 1983).

—— 'Crime and Public Policy', in J. Q. Wilson and J. Petersilia (eds), *Crime* (San Francisco: Institute for Contemporary Studies, 1995).

—— and HERRNSTEIN, R.J., *Crime and Human Nature* (New York: Simon & Schuster, 1986).

WILSON, W. J., *The Truly Disadvantaged* (Chicago: University of Chicago Press, 1987).

—— *When Work Disappears* (Chicago: University of Chicago Press, 1997).

WINDLESHAM, LORD, *Responses to Crime, Vol 2, Penal Policy in the Making* (Oxford: Clarendon Press, 1993).

—— *Responses to Crime, Vol 3, Legislating with the Tide* (Oxford: Clarendon Press, 1996).

—— *Politics, Punishment, and Populism* (New York: Oxford University Press, 1998).

WOLFE, A., *One Nation, After All* (New York: Viking, 1998).

WOOTTON, B., *Social Science and Social Pathology* (London: Allen & Unwin, 1959).

WOUTERS, C., 'Changing Patterns of Social Controls and Self Controls', *British Journal of Criminology* (1999), vol 39, no 3, 416–32.

WRONG, D., *The Problem of Order* (New York: Free Press, 1994).

YERGIN, D. and STANISLAW, J., *The Commanding Heights: The Battle Between Government and the Market Place* (New York: Simon & Schuster, 1998).

YOUNG, J., 'Working Class Criminology', in I. Taylor, P. Walton, and J. Young (eds), *Critical Criminology* (London: Routledge & Kegan Paul, 1975).

—— 'The Failure of Criminology: The Need for a Radical Realism', in R. Matthews and J. Young (eds), *Confronting Crime* (London: Sage, 1986).

—— *The Exclusive Society* (London: Sage, 1999).

YOUNG, P., *The Prison Cell : The Start of a Better Approach to Prison Management* (London: Adam Smith Institute, 1987).

YOUNG, P. J., *Punishment, Money and Legal Order*, unpublished Ph.D, thesis (Edinburgh: University of Edinburgh, 1987).

ZIMRING, F. E., 'Populism, Democratic Government, and the Decline of Expert Authority: Some Reflections on "Three Strikes" in California', *Pacific Law Journal* 28 (Fall 1996): 243–56.

—— 'The New Politics of Criminal Justice', in D. Garland (ed), *Mass Imprisonment in the USA* (London: Sage, 2001).

—— and HAWKINS, G., *Capital Punishment and the American Agenda* (New York: Cambridge University Press, 1986).

—— —— *Incapacitation* (New York: Oxford University Press, 1995).

—— —— *Crime is Not the Problem: Lethal Violence in America* (New York: Oxford University Press, 1997).

Index